**Latin American Studies Series**

Series Editors Michael C. Meyer John D. Martz Miguel León-Portilla

This inaugural volume in the Latin American Studies Series of the University of Nebraska Press presents eight essays that examine, from an interdisciplinary perspective, the precolonial, colonial, and early republican antecedents of contemporary Indian cultures in Yucatán, Chiapas, and Guatemala. Recurrent themes include the ways in which Spanish administrators and colonists organized and employed native labor; the demographic effects of conquest, disease, and colonization; the ways in which native communities responded to such interrelated practices as the *repartimiento de mercancías* and the *derrama* (which apparently played a larger role in this region than in central Mexico); the effects of the activities of the great missionary orders in the south; and the basic nature of Indian villages—whether they were closed, corporate structures, as long believed, or open, fluid, interrelated communities. Collectively, the essays represent a state-of-the-art assessment of research on southeastern Mesoamerica and suggest future trends.

University of Nebraska Press   Lincoln and London

Spaniards

and Indians

in Southeastern

Mesoamerica

Essays on the

History of

Ethnic Relations

Edited by Murdo J. MacLeod and Robert Wasserstrom

The paper in this book meets
the guidelines for
permanence and durability
of the Committee on
Production Guidelines for
Book Longevity of the
Council on Library Resources.

Library of Congress
Cataloging in Publication Data

Main entry under title:
Spaniards and Indians in
southeastern mesoamerica.

(Latin American studies series)

Bibliography: p.
Includes index.
Contents: Introduction – Indians
in colonial Yucatan /
by Nancy M. Farriss – Lowland
Maya political economy /
by David Freidel – [etc.]
1. Mayas – Government relations –
Addresses, essays, lectures.
2. Indians of Mexico – Government
relations – Addresses, essays,
lectures.   3. Indians of Central
America – Guatemala – Government
relations – Addresses, essays,
lectures.   4. Mexico –
Ethnic relations – Addresses,
essays, lectures.   5. Guatemala –
Ethnic relations – Addresses,
essays, lectures.
I. MacLeod, Murdo J.
II. Wasserstrom, Robert
III. Series.
F1435.3.P7S63   1983
972.81'01   82-23725
ISBN 0-8032-3082-6

Contents

Acknowledgments

The essays in this volume have their origins in a multi-disciplinary conference entitled "Indian Societies in Southern Mesoamerica: Colonial Origins and Post-Colonial Growth," which took place on October 12–17, 1980, at Endicott House, Dedham, Massachusetts. Support for the project in all its phases was most generously provided by the Tinker Foundation and the Wenner-Gren Foundation, and to a lesser degree by the Institute of Latin American and Iberian Studies at Columbia University. Our thanks are also due to Martin Diskin and Peter Smith at the Massachusetts Institute of Technology for making Endicott House available to us and for sponsoring the conference itself. Similar gratitude must be expressed to Arturo Warman, Eric Wolf, and especially Woodrow Borah for their able performance as commentators at the meeting and afterward. Additional suggestions for revision were offered by Leon G. Campbell and Benjamin Keen, and have for the most part been incorporated into the revised text. At the same time, we would like to acknowledge the valuable contribution of several participants who are not represented in the final volume: Luis Aboites, Marcelo Carmagnani, Martin Diskin, and Ronald Spores. And finally, we benefited greatly from the capable assistance of Marilyn Bradian, Julie Mayer-Orozco, and Georganne Chapin, who prepared the manuscript in its finished form.

Introduction

This volume brings together a group of historically-minded anthropologists and anthropologically-minded historians who, in their own individual ways, discuss a common theme: the genesis in precolonial, colonial, and early republican society of contemporary Indian cultures in Yucatan, Chiapas and Guatemala.

Some three years ago the editors of this volume undertook a review of ethnohistorical work on southeastern Mesoamerica, a review that included the writers in this volume and many others. They concluded that research on the region had reached a stage where a cohesive reappraisal, a pulling together of findings, would be not only interesting to scholars but also in some ways essential before further variety and advances were introduced. Clearly, southeastern Mesoamerica has emerged as distinctive, in many ways quite unlike the better-known structures and patterns of central Mexico.

Such cohesive reviews are inherently incomplete. Writers and scholars are idiosyncratic. Some are local, and hate to stray from their own familiar turf. Others are too quick to lay claim to large and poorly-mapped territories. As readers will soon perceive, this group of writers is no exception. Nevertheless, they all aim at synthesis, at a broader understanding of the processes going on in their regions as found in the corpus of research available to them. Each of them, too, has tried to open some doors to the future. What are the prospects? Where is research going? Where, given the many unknowns in southeastern Mesoamerica, should it be going?

A certain commonality of themes also emerged. Not all of the essayists covered or even mentioned every topic, but the reader will find that certain questions and structural features, some of them peculiar to this area, recur with frequency, often in different forms and guises. These persistent themes include the following: the ways in which Spanish administrators and colonists organized and employed native labor in the various regions of southeastern Mesoamerica; the demographic effects of conquest, disease, and colonization; the variety of ways in which native communities responded to such interrelated practices as the *repartimiento de mercancías* and the *derrama,* which seem to have played a larger and more significant role in this region than in central Mexico; the effects of missionary activities and the great missionary orders in the region, especially as such activities and groups affected what became such basic native institutions as *cofradías* and *cajas de communidad;* the basic nature of Indian village society—closed corporate structures, as has been believed for so long, or interrelated, fluid, open communities; the nature of political leadership in native communities and the persistence or decline of the noble class in response to outside pressure; the peculiar nature of, and the regional variations among, haciendas in these regions, and their relationships with native communities; and, finally, given the great differences and occasional complementarity of ecological and climatic zones, the extent to which such differences between highlands and lowlands influenced the development of divergent cultural, political, and economic institutions and practices. The picture that emerges from these nine very diverse articles is of variety within the region that concerns us, but also of a regional entity that is unique unto itself and quite different from dominant central Mexican models.

In her excellent essay on colonial Yucatan, for example, Nancy Farriss points out that most scholars have viewed Indians in Mesoamerica from essentially two perspectives—either as a vestige of the pre-Columbian past or as an object of colonial rule. The reasons for this choice are obvious: Indians remain the area's "chief exploitable resource," an apparently limitless source of clues about bygone civilizations or about the nature of Spanish domination. What is missing from this discussion, she suggests, is the sense of Indians as actors, as makers of their own history and shapers of regional society. Unlike traditional studies of acculturation (which she feels simply invite boredom), such a view of native history requires great flexibility of interpretation that carries us far away from central Mexican models. Arguing that European crops and commerce did not flourish in much of the southeast, she states that

What distinguished Yucatan within Mesoamerica, along with highland Chiapas . . . , was the combination of a dearth of natural resources with a relative abundance

Southeastern Mesoamerica, ca. 1540–1821

of human resources. And this explains Yucatan's peculiar type of backwardness: the long reliance on Indian tribute in various forms as the region's economic base.

Adapting themselves to these circumstances, Spanish authorities permitted local Mayas to maintain their accustomed forms of activity and patterns of production. As a result, she continues, native people were required "to make far less drastic adjustments in their own social arrangements, or even in their symbolic systems." But such facts, although they revise long-cherished concepts, still do not give us a very clear idea of how Indians functioned as initiators of their own action. And it is here that she provides a unique view of native society throughout the seventeenth and eighteenth centuries—a view that holds that community structure and organization underwent constant modification in ways that we are only now beginning to appreciate.

Indeed, as Grant Jones and David Freidel suggest, population movements, changing patterns of production, and shifting alliances played an extremely significant role in Yucatan both before the conquest and in areas where Spanish control remained relatively attenuated. According to Freidel, for example, by the late Postclassic, Maya society was cross-cut by a mosaic of productive relations, trade networks, and political allegiances that do not fit easily into established analytic categories. One critical problem that emerges from this state of affairs, he continues, involves the fallacy of "mistaking hypotheses for conclusions," of interpreting Postclassical Maya institutions in the light of such apparently analogous societies as European feudalism. By way of contrast, he argues that archaeological evidence from the preconquest period lends itself to a variety of interpretations, each of which possesses different implications for colonial history. Along similar lines, Jones contends that Indians from northern Yucatan moved southward into Belize and the Petén region during the seventeenth and eighteenth centuries not only to escape Spanish rule (an undertaking that in any case was doomed to failure) but also to develop their own "entrepreneurial agriculture and trading activities." As a result, they established a well-defined and well-defended buffer zone between Spanish civilization and the infamous Itzá frontier—a zone that was only breached around 1700 by British loggers. Even so, Jones believes, the existence of relatively autonomous Mayas in this area until the late colonial period had a significant effect on Indian life throughout the region, an effect that modern scholars have largely underestimated or ignored.

In contrast to these essays, those by Jan Rus and Robert Wasserstrom present a radically different interpretation of Indian society in highland Chiapas. Beginning around 1530 with the calculated elimination of native elites, Wasserstrom asserts that Spanish authorities engineered a highly profitable export economy based on the forced production of commodities like cacao, cochineal, and indigo. The cornerstone of this economy was the repartimiento de mercancías. In this undertaking, local officials were aided by the Dominican order, which enlisted their support in a campaign to exclude secular priests from the province. Although Dominican friars apparently did not themselves administer repartimientos, nonetheless they reorganized and reordered native communities to suit the requirements of enforced production—even at the expense of their own substantial enterprises. As a result, they were able to postpone almost to the end of colonial rule the day when their clerical rivals occupied Indian parishes. One peculiar consequence of this situation was that the number of Indians in Chiapas did not begin to grow appreciably until the late eighteenth century; as in Yucatan, community boundaries remained quite fluid as native men and women fled from one district to another or into the Lacandón jungle. And despite the fact that royal administrators in Guatemala and Spain granted frequent exemptions from tribute and other exactions, such communities did not assume their current shape until well after the repartimiento system was replaced during the nineteenth century by a network of commercial haciendas.

Naturally, economic changes of this magnitude produced a thoroughgoing transformation of Indian life at all levels. Between 1821 and 1880, according to Jan Rus, landowners in Chiapas jockeyed for control of the native labor force. Like their colonial forebears, they altered communal institutions and municipal boundaries to suit their convenience. And like their counterparts elsewhere in Mexico, they aligned themselves with liberal and conservative parties that themselves enlisted native people in a variety of political causes. Such was the case during the mid-1860s, when liberal officials in Chiapas, anxious to subvert the authority of their conservative rivals, encouraged highland Indians to withhold church taxes and to conduct their own religious affairs. The result of this intrigue, Rus suggests, was that Tzotzil people from several highland towns organized not only an independent set of fiestas and ceremonies but also an independent system of regional markets that quickly threatened the livelihoods of local creoles. Forgetting their political differences for the moment, liberals and conservatives closed ranks to combat what they later claimed was a full-fledged "caste war." In order to sustain this unlikely proposition, they executed a liberal agent from

Mexico City who had come to stir up anti-clerical sentiment and then proceeded to massacre three hundred Indian men, women, and children whom they found kneeling in the main square in Chamula. More important, however, Rus argues that anthropologists and historians alike have uncritically accepted a version of these events that was fabricated twenty years later by Vicente Pineda, leader of the conservative party. In so doing, they have propagated an antiquarian and conventional view of native society whose origins may be found in precisely those outmoded theories of racial superiority that modern scholarship should most directly call into question.

For Guatemala we are fortunate to have three studies that, although very different in emphasis and tone, cover the entire period from just before the conquest to the middle years of this century.

William Sherman's essay is very much a historian's account of what we know, what we do not know, and what we can never know about early colonial Guatemala. In general, Sherman, unlike Bartolomé de las Casas, believes that ill treatment of the Indians, at least near Santiago, was not as severe as in some other parts of the Spanish colonies, although he admits that conditions were certainly bad enough. This author, like all the others, has his own unique viewpoint as he looks at relationships between two races, emphasizing institutional and political history and the interplay of personalities and small groups. He puts individuals and individual decision-making squarely in the center of the historical stage, and feels that powerful individuals made decisive differences in historical processes. For example, Alonso López de Cerrato, on whom Sherman has written extensively elsewhere, defied creole elite society and did, according to the author, significantly improve the treatment of the Indians, so that in general the material situation of the natives improved gradually throughout the sixteenth century, and by 1600 Guatemala had become, Sherman says, "a more civilized society." These emphases reappear when Sherman charts a research course for the future. He calls for more biography and group biography so that colonial history does not become too depersonalized. Spanish society in Guatemala, and to some extent Indian society too, was articulated by kinship, clan, and regional networks. Nepotism, a powerful economic factor, grew out of these ties, and only by understanding the groups of major and minor officials and churchmen in these terms can we understand their treatment of, and interactions with, the Indian community.

MacLeod's essay, very different in emphasis, tries to isolate and examine the various social and economic factors that affected or brought pressure on Indian societies, thus causing Indian adaptation or reaction. Such matters as the tribute and other taxes, labor systems, regional variations, major economic activities and workplaces, demography, and land tenure are examined before MacLeod proceeds to a periodization of the two centuries. Neglect in the seventeenth century, together with such other factors as land availability and a depression in the Spanish economy, may have led to an improvement in Indian diet, work patterns, and village cohesion. Renewed pressure in the eighteenth century, as the Indian population revived, as land hunger increased, and as the Spanish economy began to grow and need more labor, probably led to a reversal of this trend. MacLeod concludes by calling for more studies of economic geography, demography, disease, food and diet, land tenure, and local history.

Robert Carmack's ethnohistorical essay ends this section. He divides his essay into two parts. Carmack examines the writing on Indian society in the nineteenth and early twentieth centuries, dividing such research into both chronological and topical categories and pointing out strengths and deficiencies in the research as he goes along. Liberal and Marxist historiographies are compared and contrasted, and studies of political, juridical, calendric, and religious structures receive special attention.

Carmack then moves to a case study and limits himself to his own work on the village of Santiago Momostenango. He is interested in "the dialectical relationship between material and cultural conditions," and sketches the history of this village, the outside influences on it, and the village's reaction to those influences during the national period and before. Recurrent waves of revolt, governmental violence and repression, cooptation and paternalism, commercialization and neglect, change the village and its structures.

Carmack concludes by asking anthropologists working on Guatemala to pay more attention to process and change, less to survivals and patterns. He finds that violence in Indian Guatemala, an endemic and powerful factor, has been ignored even by Marxist scholars, and that, in general, there is a tendency to move toward larger generalizations before the empirical evidence has been collected and sifted. Perhaps, he suggests, we need more case studies of historical change such as the one of Santiago Momostenango.

This group of essays should leave the reader with some very definite impressions. The notion of a static or slowly changing Indian society is surely gone. Wherever we look, Yucatan, Chiapas or Guatemala, we find process and movements, the decline and rise of populations, forced labor under a variety of guises, and, above all, endemic violence in social relations. All of which leads to a second theme. The existence of closed corporate Indian communities has its defenders in these pages, but others see large seasonal and permanent migrations, extensive trading patterns, rapid social transformations, and inter-ethnic violence as being so pervasive that a more fluid, cosmopolitan model is needed. To be sure, our essayists leave us with the impression of a region that is more "backward" than central Mexico. In spite of cochineal in Chiapas and cacao and then indigo in Guatemala, the area lacked and lacks a great unifying market product such as Mexican silver. As a result, Spaniards and capital were less attracted to the area than to central Mexico and, relatively speaking, there was less enculturation of Indian communities, which therefore remained more recognizably distinct.

What emerges is a history of a troubled region torn by strife, a region that even today—and Carmack's essay bears this out strongly—has never worked out a post-conquest synthesis, has never reached any kind of political or cultural consensus. Southeastern Mesoamerica faces a future very similar to its past, with conflict and violence as principal features in social and ethnic relations.

Spaniards and Indians in Southeastern Mesoamerica

Essays on the History of Ethnic Relations

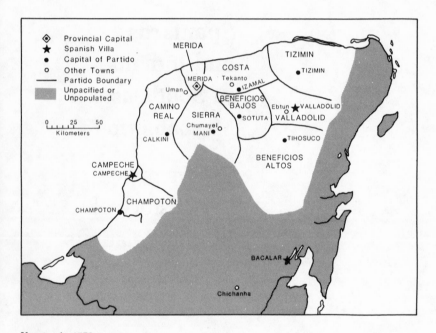

Yucatan in 1750

Nancy M. Farriss

Indians in Colonial Yucatan: Three Perspectives

The post-conquest history of the Indians of Mesoamerica can be approached from three points of view: the Indian as a vestige of the pre-Columbian past, as an object of colonial or neo-colonial rule, or as a subject in his own right. The third approach is the least common, and understandably so. History in the sense of a prelude to the past has passed the Indians by. They have played no active role in shaping its course and have no prospects of doing so in the future: since by definition Indians are powerless, anyone assuming an active role ceases to be an "Indian." By this measure of historical significance they rate above the Philippine Tasaday but well below the Yoruba of Nigeria or even the Burmese Shan, who have controlled a large part of the world's opium trade for the past century. Nor have the post-conquest Mayas or Zapotecs produced any magnificent works like their ancestors, works in a tradition that is now lost but that continues to beguile many moderns by its sophistication and its very remoteness.

The Mesoamerican Indians have some claim on our attention as descendents of one of the world's high civilizations, and there is a certain curiosity value in tracing how they got from there to here. But their history has value beyond a local, antiquarian interest. Mesoamerica provides some of the richest documentation available on the subject of culture contact. Anyone studying, say, the Roman conquests or the spread of Islam might well envy this material, and it could contribute much to a general understanding of the processes of acculturation.

To further that end, we will have to discard the term "acculturation" or at least define it more broadly. As it is most commonly understood in Mesoamerican studies, acculturation is too confining a concept. The conclusion of the analysis is already contained in the premise, which is that change will inevitably move in the direction of assimilation into the dominant culture, itself unaffected by the contact, and all one has to do is measure the rate.

A more neutral, open-ended definition would be more productive. We could regard culture contact as presenting a new configuration of options to both sides of the confrontation, defining the range of choices but without determining the particular ones that will be made. Simple acceptance and rejection of alien cultural elements are only two among many possible responses, and much more common may be the transformation of old forms into something that never existed in either of the original cultures. We need to broaden the search beyond the narrow limits of Hispanization and its obverse, pre-Columbian survivals, and look also for change in tangential directions, that is, change influenced but not necessarily guided by outside forces (Melanesian cargo cults come to mind as obvious examples). Unless we do so, we will miss much that was going on in Mesoamerican history and the opportunity for a dialogue with students of sociocultural change in other regions.[1]

The Colonial Indian as Vestige

Modern scholars, like the sixteenth-century colonists, have found the Maya Indians to be Yucatan's chief exploitable resource. Attracted primarily by the region's archaeological remains, the Carnegie Institution of Washington earlier in this century supported a blitzkrieg of ancillary research in linguistics, botany, ethnography, geography, meteorology, history, and ethnohistory.[2] This massive program and the further efforts it stimulated have produced an abundance of information on the colonial Indian that had no rival in Mesoamerica until the appearance of Charles Gibson's magisterial and singlehanded study of the valley of Mexico.[3] The quantity of data accessible to scholars, especially in the form of edited documents, remains unequaled in southern Mesoamerica, and the imbalance promises to continue, judging from the relative wealth of sources that remain unpublished.

Our understanding of colonial Maya history has not kept pace with this harvest of information. The lag is due in large measure to the predominance of a special sub-genre of ethnohistory that has flourished in Mesoamerican studies, particularly in Yucatan. I take ethnohistory to be anthropology with a time dimension or history informed by anthropological concepts. Ethnohistory in Yucatan has most often, with important exceptions that I shall note, functioned as a handmaiden to archaeology, defining its task as the culling from historical documents of information that will help illuminate the area's pre-Columbian past. In other words, the colonial Indian has been viewed as a vestige.

This emphasis is understandable. Scholars were first lured to Yucatan by its magnificent pre-Columbian ruins, products of a civilization that remains Yucatan's chief claim to uniqueness. Without the ancient Mayas, Yucatan would be simply another ex-colonial backwater, valuable as a source of case studies to compare this or that topic of broader concern but without intrinsic interest. It is for this reason, no doubt, that archaeology has been the prima donna of regional disciplines. It has set the framework of scholarly enquiry, posing the questions that ethnohistory, linguistics, botany, and others have sought answers to. These questions have become increasingly sophisticated of late, but they are not historical ones, or at least not colonial historical ones.

Ralph L. Roys is the pre-eminent practitioner of this genre. Colonial historiography in all its sub-fields is so indebted to Roys's monumental *ouevre* that it seems niggardly to point out any limitations. His *Political Geography of the Yucatan Maya,*[4] an encyclopedia of information painstakingly assembled from a wide variety of primary sources, is an indispensable tool for any study of colonial Maya demography, settlement patterns, and indeed almost any aspect of geopolitical organization. His translations and interpretations of documents written in Yucatan Maya have given other scholars direct glimpses into the colonial Maya world,[5] which they would otherwise have to view solely through Spanish eyes. Those who seek to read untranslated documents on their own, especially the more esoteric colonial Maya texts, must inevitably draw on Roys's vast knowledge of Maya philology.

In most of Roys's own work, as distinct from his collaborative efforts with historians, the colonial Mayas serve as a source for the pre-conquest history of the region rather than as subjects in themselves. The quantity of colonial material assembled is vast, but it must often be subjected to a further process of sifting and reorganizing within a different analytical framework before it will yield insights into the colonial Indian experience. A case in point is the *Indian Background to Colonial Yucatan,*[6] in which the mention of, say, early colonial trade in beeswax is embedded in a discussion of pre-Columbian apiculture. Another example, less known to colonialists, is Roys's "Conquest Sites and the Subsequent Destruction of Maya Architecture."[7] The title betrays its archaeological emphasis and has doubtless obscured the fact that the data primarily concern church construction, with much tangential but useful material on evangelization, labor demands, and parish administration.

The retrospective focus of much Yucatecan ethnohistory helps to account for its emphasis on regions—as well as topics—ordinarily regarded as peripheral if not wholly irrelevant to colonial history. The frontier zones in the Petén, Belize, and southern Campeche and on the Caribbean coast (present-day Quintana Roo), which were either conquered late in the colonial period or abandoned early, have served archaeologists' and ethnohistorians' purposes precisely because they have remained relatively undisturbed and "uncontaminated."[8] Yet the assumption of marginality carries risks, and the division of issues and information into discrete areas impoverishes the explanatory tool kit of all concerned. Colonialists could profitably include such topics as Maya cosmology, trade, and political culture in their interpretative schemas. Prehistorians should consider the possible effect, both direct and indirect, of colonial rule in assessing the reliability of post-conquest clues to pre-Columbian mysteries. For example, Eric Thompson's reconstruction of pre-Columbian ethnic boundaries in the central lowlands does not give sufficient weight to the large flow of colonial and Caste War refugees from the north.[9]

In contrast, I can cite several works that because of their concern with colonial change have contributed substantially to our understanding of the pre-Columbian as well as the colonial Mayas. These are the study by Scholes and Roys of the Maya Chontal of Acalán-Tixchel,[10] a well-nigh flawless model of an ethnohistorical monograph, and two shorter, more recent studies by Grant Jones.[11] The Acalán-Tixchel monograph illuminates many aspects of colonial Maya history. Here I will concentrate on one issue, with which Jones is also concerned: the link between trade and political organization among the Mayas. This is a subject of intense interest to archaeologists, who have already made Scholes and Roys's revelations about the role of the Putún traders a cornerstone of modern interpretations of Maya prehistory.[12] Jones's work on the unconquered Petén Itzá and their neighbors in the southern lowlands during the sixteenth and seventeenth centuries provides the most convincing evidence I have seen for the role of trade as a stimulus and support for—as distinct from a mere expression of—social stratification and political centralization among the pre-Columbian Mayas. Previous arguments have been based on long-distance trade in luxury goods, but Jones deals with regional integration through the medium-range exchange of perishable staples—a more plausible link, but one that the archaeological record would not preserve.

All three studies address chiefly what might be considered anthropological questions: the nature of Maya society before contact with Europeans. But they do so in a thoroughly historical way. They emphasize processes of change rather than static structures or a search for fossil remnants. They also take into account the larger colonial context in which post-conquest processes unfolded, on both sides of the frontier. The Spanish enter into the picture not merely as recorders of ethnographic material but also as influences on its content. Such an approach is more likely to yield reliable clues to the pre-Columbian past; it unquestionably yields more insights into the colonial history of the Mayas. In particular these studies indicate that we should give greater weight to the indirect consequences of Spanish actions.

The disintegration of pre-Columbian political organization is usually attributed to the imposition of Spanish rule. The Spanish sought to consolidate control over the newly conquered territories by breaking up imperial and provincial structures into smaller units and within them undermining the political power and wealth of the native elites. This explanation is fine as far as it goes, but it leaves out some effects of Spanish activity *before* actual conquest, effects that the Spanish neither planned nor recognized.

If trade and socio-political integration were mutually supportive within the Maya system, any disruption in one would weaken the other. Scholes and Roys have suggested a link between the depopulation of the Acalán region of southern Campeche and the decline of commerce, both of which processes began before Spanish occupation (effected without military resistance).[13] European disease played its part as everywhere in the New World, aided here by climate. Within the Maya region the most humid lowland areas also coincided with the most intensive trading networks, from Tabasco across the base of the Yucatan peninsula into Honduras and also to the east coast, a favorable environment for Old World microbes and parasites, but also areas particularly dependent on commerce. A third element, interdependent with both demography and trade, is political organization, which also must have been weakened when the underpinnings of local labor and external exchange were eroded.

None of these processes required the direct action or even presence of the Spanish in the affected area. Disease spread before them, and the conquests of neighboring groups and more distant trading partners severed the commercial links. Jones has helped to propel this idea from conjecture toward fact through his study of a later and better-documented process among the Petén Itzá. Gradual encirclement by the Spanish had already disrupted their trade networks and political alliances and led to the disintegration of the Itzá polity itself before their final conquest in 1697.[14]

Itzá trade links were not confined to other unconquered Mayas. By giving prominence to the exchange of goods and people across the fluctuating colonial frontiers, these studies demonstrate the importance of indirect Spanish influence on the borderlands.[15] They also make clear that the borderlands deserve more attention in the history of the pacified Mayas to the north.

The Colonial Indian as Object

If the colonial Mayas have often been studied in isolation from their colonial context, this is in part because that context until recently has been very nebulous. An odd complaint in a survey of literature on colonial Indians, but nevertheless a valid one for Yucatan, is that the Indians have been emphasized at the expense of the Spaniards and the interaction between the two.[16] The reverse is the case in most other parts of Latin America, where historians and their traditional concerns have prevailed. Historiographical density follows the pecking order within the colonial system, and in Mesoamerica Yucatan ranks far down on both scales: slightly above Tabasco and Chiapas, but below Guatemala and Oaxaca, and like all of them well below central Mexico.

Central Mexico's position within the imperial system as secondary metropolis, the dynamic economic core as well as the administrative seat of the viceroyalty, earns it priority in the historian's agenda. But suspicions, hardening into certainties, have arisen about the applicability of central Mexican models to the viceroyalty's poorer sisters. A comparative look at sociocultural change among colonial Indians must begin with a comparison of colonial regimes, since these provided the sets of constraints within which the social identity of the Indian—a colonial creation—was elaborated.

Colonial Economy

The Spanish colonial blueprint was fairly uniform throughout the New World. The "culture of conquest" that Foster presents is an assemblage of elements distilled from the diversity of Spanish regional forms.[17] Homogeneity is even more apparent at the more general level of goals, values, and institutions. The dominant principle behind the blueprint—the least dependent of the variables—seems to have been the search for wealth.

This conclusion is difficult to escape, regardless of the complexities and contradictions the colonial system manifested. The saving of Indian souls was a major value but remained functionally if not ideologically subordinate to economic gain, for, without that colonizing incentive, missionary activity could not be sustained.

Of the two universal systems that the conquest brought to America—Christianity and world trade—the latter took precedence. I would agree with Immanuel Wallerstein and André Gundar Frank, among others, that the central feature of European colonial rule, and by extension the significant feature of the colonial status of any subject group, was incorporation on subordinate terms into a global commercial system.[18] One may debate the precise effects of the incorporation without disputing its pivotal role in shaping the colonial regime and, in Latin America, the Indian experience within it. The major variations in that experience can be traced to differences in the pace and mode of incorporation, and these in turn depended on how local environments, both human and physical, modified the general colonial blueprint the Spanish brought with them.

Yucatan presents some notable and long-noted contrasts with highland Mesoamerica. A climate inhospitable to Europeans and their crops and, above all, a lack of exploitable resources condemned the region in colonial times to commercial isolation and poverty. But geography will not account entirely for the particular variety of colonial regime that developed in Yucatan. The Spanish empire contained many poor peripheral regions; indeed, the majority fall into that category. What distinguished Yucatan within Mesoamerica, along with highland Chiapas (despite the significant geographical contrasts), was the combination of a dearth of natural resources with a relative abundance of human resources. And this explains Yucatan's peculiar type of backwardness: the long reliance on Indian tribute in various forms as the region's economic base.[19]

A fundamental problem in analyzing colonial regimes lies in the definition of tribute, which logically should extend to all its structural equivalents. These include ecclesiastical tribute, *repartimientos,* the appropriation of community goods by church or state, and any other forced extraction of goods or services from the Indian economy.

The *encomienda* was a stable institution in Yucatan, lasting with but a few incorporations into the crown in the sixteenth century until its wholesale abolition in 1785.[20] Long before that, tribute in its narrowest sense had come to represent a minor proportion of local Spanish income. The Spanish population had grown and the Indian population had declined in the sixteenth and seventeenth centuries, and the crown had eaten into dwindling encomienda revenues with an increasing burden of taxes.[21] This decline did not, however, stimulate a corresponding shift to a market economy, for Spaniards (meaning both creoles and peninsulars) managed to expand the tribute system through a variety of strategems to bypass the strict laws regulating it.

There were the minor civil taxes, which went to support creole bureaucrats. These and the ecclesiastical taxes, which came to outweigh those imposed by the state, present no ambiguity. But other exactions, because they bear a superficial resemblance to trade, are less clear-cut. From early post-conquest times the Spaniards, *encomenderos* and non-encomenderos alike, engaged in a variety of "commercial" operations in the countryside, from which they derived a substantial portion of their income. They found it convenient to subsume all these exchanges under the heading of "tratos" or "grangerías" (business dealings) for the benefit of the crown and no doubt their own self-justification. But we should not obscure the difference between forced extraction and genuine commercial exchange, in which prices may be distorted by inequalities in power but the exchange itself is in some degree voluntary.

Only the loosest definition of trade—to the point of being meaningless—could include the repartimiento system, which rapidly became the principal device for extracting the colony's major export items (cotton cloth and beeswax) and thus the principal source of wealth. The forced sale of unwanted goods to Indians seems to have been a minor part of repartimiento operations in Yucatan. There, repartimiento usually referred to the forced advance of cash for the delivery of goods within a stipulated period.[22] As practiced by the provincial governors and their agents, these transactions were so unfavorable to the Indians—the recompense for their labor so far below current market prices and the size of the repartimiento often so excessive as to interfere with food production—that only the severest forms of physical coercion could induce the Indians to accept them.

Unofficial repartimientos, by which the rest of the colonial elite tapped the same source, seem to have offered somewhat better terms. But if Indian officials rarely complained about them, this is only because they were preferable to the official repartimientos in helping to meet the portion of the community's ordinary tribute assessments demanded in cash. The producers still had to be coerced by their own officials.

Some of the economic exchanges that were carried on between Indians and non-Indians can validly be considered trade. The latter controlled the distribution of the few non-indigenous items for which the Mayas developed a taste or had a use.[23] These were chiefly metal tools, gunpowder (in enormous quantities for fiesta fireworks), and *aguardiente* (cane liquor). They also supplied at least part of the salt and cacao consumed by the Mayas and, presumably, the luxury goods of European style that the native elites owned. By all accounts these items were genuinely desired and freely purchased by the Mayas. It is impossible to calculate the extent of this trade. A commonly-voiced frustration was the Mayas' imperviousness to the blandishments of a market economy. Whether through indifference or poverty or both, they bought little; once purchased, tools and trinkets were passed on through generations as treasured heirlooms. If the activities of peddlers and merchants in the countryside could be quantified, I suspect we would find that most were in the form of repartimientos or trade with other non-Indians.

Another form of exchange that needs scrutiny is the purchase of maize from the Indians to supplement tribute goods for the urban market. Indians continued to be the major suppliers even past the middle of the eighteenth century. Except for the Indian elites, who were able to produce surpluses and better able to negotiate reasonable terms, the bulk of the "trade" seems to have been a form of requisitioning, with some cash exchange but under coercion and at confiscatory prices. Further research may uncover more evidence of a free trade in maize and other staples. So far it looks more like tribute than trade.

Recent studies of Yucatan's colonial economy all agree, explicitly or implicitly, that the area lagged far behind central Mexico in the transition from a tribute to a market economy.[24] The implications of this lag for the Mayas are considerable: the difference between a parasite that merely fastens on and weakens the host and one that invades and destroys the organism, in this case a social organism. As long as the Spanish merely extracted from the Mayas their accustomed goods, such as maize and cotton cloth, which they produced in their accustomed way while retaining ownership of the means of production, the Mayas would have to make far less drastic adjustments in their own social arrangements, or even in their symbolic systems, which were so closely linked with their mode of agriculture, than as peones or wage-earners in Spanish-owned and Spanish-directed enterprises.

Consensus on Yucatan's economic history collapses when it comes to timing. A mixture between the two types of economy existed throughout the colonial period. But at what rate did Spanish production and commercial activity grow, and when did they replace tribute as the main source of supply for the local and export markets? The development of the hacienda is a key issue, and I have elsewhere stated how my own findings support Robert Patch's conclusions that the hacienda emerged from the small, labor-extensive cattle ranch considerably later than the late seventeenth-century date suggested by Marta Hunt.[25] Where we diverge is on pace and causation. Patch assigns primary importance to the growth of internal markets and thus sees a fairly gradual transition. I see a more abrupt leap in the 1780s, due to a concatenation of factors: rapid recovery from the century's most severe famine, which lasted from 1769 to 1794, the confiscation of Indian *cofradía* lands, and most especially a boom in the export trade due to the recent extension of free trade to Yucatan.[26] Different sources provide different perspectives. Exchequer records on tithes and external trade, which Patch did not consult, do reveal a leap, but one that may well have seemed less dramatic had I delved as deeply into *cabildo* and notarial records as he had done. Yucatan still lacks the equivalent of Murdo MacLeod's comprehensive treatment of the Central American economy, which traces local trends over a long period and places them within the wider imperial framework.[27]

In most of the empire's peripheral areas the absence of mining, and the other entrepreneurial activities it stimulated, made the hacienda the chief vehicle both for transforming the local economy and for integrating the Indians more fully into it. In Yucatan the landed estate developed in three stages, from early cattle estancias through the haciendas of the later colonial period, which combined ranching with the production of maize and other staple crops, to the sugar and—most characteristically—henequen plantations that had begun to dominate the local economy by the mid-nineteenth century.[28] Each transition intensified the competition for land between the Indian communities and the estates because of the accelerated rates of expansion and the changing patterns of land use that together marked the different stages.

The issue of land ownership arose late in colonial Yucatan. For one thing, the ranching phase coincided with a period of Indian population decline. For another, property boundaries were ill defined on paper and on the ground, so that Indian farmers and Spanish ranchers were able to share the same general stretches of bush. The conflicts that arose were conflicts over land use, between the owners of free-ranging cattle and the cultivators of unfenced, shifting *milpas*.[29]

How seriously Spanish ranching interfered with Indian food production is hard to tell. A comparison of human and livestock populations (the latter figures derived from estate inventories) in selected parishes over time would provide some measure of the competition for the same resource. But alongside the growth in numbers of people and cattle, a more serious threat developed in the shift to commercial agriculture. The introduction of large-scale crop production meant that the ranchers, as they became hacendados, needed more land. And they needed land over which they could claim exclusive rights rather than sharing its use with the Indian communities.

In his article comparing the growth of the landed estate in southern Mesoamerica and central Mexico, William Taylor has suggested that the Indian communities in the south were better able to resist hacienda expansion because of their greater internal cohesiveness: they presented a stronger, more united front.[30] The correlation between social cohesion and a strong land base could be considered a general rule for Indian communities, but on the basis of evidence from Yucatan I would suggest reversing the cause-and-effect relationship that Taylor has presented. The community remained strong so long as it controlled sufficient resources, not vice versa, and this it could do only so long as Spanish pressure was weak. Incentives to encroach on Indian land were unevenly distributed within Mesoamerica, and this applies to the particular regions as well. The main published source available for Yucatan is a collection of land titles belonging to the town of Ebtún in the eastern part of the peninsula,[31] where population densities were very low and the Spanish presence very thin—a particularly underdeveloped portion of an underdeveloped region. The preservation of these documents in an area distant from the centers of commercial agriculture is not exactly fortuitous, for one of the effects of hacienda growth was loss of the ancient land titles, one of the stratagems for expansion their expropriation.

The general lines of expansion have now been traced. They proceeded at first chiefly in a radius around the regional hub of Mérida and from there along three axes: east through the Costa region to the secondary center of Izamal; southeast into the fertile Puuc or Sierra region, which became the colony's breadbasket; and south along the Camino Real connecting the capital with the main port of Campeche.

What we need now is more details on the shifts in land tenure. How much land was acquired, where, when, and—most important—what part of the whole did it represent? Without some rough notion of proportions, isolated figures such as the number of haciendas in the jurisdiction of a particular parish lack much meaning, although the increase in their number is of some use. The difficulties in providing answers to these questions are enormous, and are familiar to any student of colonial Latin American agrarian history. In Yucatan, property boundaries may have been especially vague because of the practice of slash-and-burn agriculture and the relative abundance of land for so long. This apparent nonchalence eventually worked to the advantage of the hacendados, who could later, sometimes centuries after the original sale, claim lands that the Indians asserted had never been sold.

Only when the friction over land reached the point of stimulating boundary surveys and litigation over them can we hope to measure the amount of land actually (if not always legally) alienated. Only a small number of land disputes have survived in the public records. But many private estate titles have been preserved, and a systematic compilation of information from them and the late colonial notarial records would help to refine or revise the general conclusions that have been reached by more impressionistic means.

The fact of rapid hacienda growth in the late colonial period already stands on firm evidence. Further research can be expected to refine questions of chronology and causation so that the transition from a primitive tribute economy to commercial agriculture, leading eventually to the fully developed plantation system of the sugar and henequen eras, can be better understood.

Politics and Population

The backwardness of Yucatan's colonial regime extended beyond the economic sphere. The administrative structure and the system of political control over the conquered population were as primitive as the economy, and for much the same reasons. The region's poverty meant a lack of public revenues to support more than a rudimentary royal bureaucracy. This, together with the prolongation of the encomienda system and the relatively thin presence of Spaniards in the countryside (more of this later), helped to preserve a system of indirect rule over the Indians until well toward the end of the colonial period.[32]

Before the introduction of the intendancy system in 1786, each Indian community dealt directly with the provincial administration: the governor and his assistants, the officers of the Tribunal de Naturales (Indian court), and the Treasury officials lodged in Mérida and Campeche. The various agents that the governors managed to slip past the royal prohibition against the appointment of corregidores de indios in Yucatan were not perfect stand-ins. Their function was almost purely economic—to supervise the repartimientos, the recruitment and allocation of corvée labor, and the variety of other schemes for skimming off Indian surpluses that were devised.

Perhaps too sharp a contrast should not be drawn. Corregidores in other provinces, also regarding their offices primarily as business ventures, may have been equally inattentive to administrative matters. In Yucatan, local agents had no judicial authority. Nor had they any part in the collection of taxes, which were delivered directly by the Maya officials to the encomenderos, or to the Treasury in the case of crown pueblos.

Evidence on the political role of the encomenderos is equivocal. Once the crown separated Indian labor from the encomienda, it supposedly lost any element of jurisdiction and became a mere pension. It is not clear that encomenderos had more access to Indian labor than any other powerful Spaniard in the colony, access that had more to do with wealth, family ties, and other sources of influence with the provincial government than the status of encomendero. They were kept informed of local conditions by the Maya leaders and consulted by them, and they served as advocates when the piranha-like activities of other Spaniards threatened the welfare and tribute-producing abilities of their particular encomiendas. Clearly the title of *amo*, or lord, accorded them by the Indians was something more than an empty gesture toward the past. How much more would be useful to know. In any case, direct ties were greatly attenuated after the early post-conquest period. Encomienda grants became increasingly patchwork affairs of widely scattered towns and fractions of towns; with rare exceptions, encomenderos resided in the cities, and their mayordomos were attached to ranches or haciendas that might or might not lie in their owners' encomienda districts.

In the absence of a strong secular presence in the countryside, Yucatan retained the aspect of a mission territory long after the initial period of evangelization. The secular clergy made very slow inroads on the areas controlled by the Franciscans, who had monopolized the region and who were still holding on to more than a quarter of Indian parishes at independence, and these among the most populous. Whether secular or regular, the clergy continued to be the principal agents of Spanish control, the only ones on the ground with official responsibility for Indian behavior. Yet they were thinly scattered, and, as their numbers increased, their early zeal for social engineering decreased.

The local Indian leaders were left largely on their own, to deliver the goods and services the Spanish demanded and to keep order within their communities under the more or less watchful eye of the parish priest (when he was not absent attending to business affairs in Mérida or on his own hacienda).

Late eighteenth-century Bourbon administrative and fiscal reforms, designed to strengthen royal control over the colonies at all levels, placed serious checks on the de facto autonomy the Indian communities had enjoyed.[33] For the first time, royal officials with full judicial, fiscal, and administrative powers were residents in the hinterland, and the subdele- gates and their subordinates impinged directly on the authority of caciques and justicias: they heard appeals and overturned rulings; they enforced the orders and supervised the myriad projects that streamed from the newly energized provincial bureaucracy; and, as the severest blow of all, they took charge of local finances, collecting tribute and other taxes, managing the cajas de comunidad and forwarding the large sur- pluses that ensued to the Royal Treasury. Many of the abuses of the old regime were curtailed, but under that more slovenly rule the Mayas had at least retained much control over their own affairs.

To analyze the effect of a colonial regime purely in terms of adminis- trative structures would be misleading. Besides the representatives of church and state, the Indians were subject to the influence of a much larger group of informal agents of Spanish rule and culture. These were the Spaniards and the Hispanized Africans, mulattoes, and mestizos who traveled or resided outside the Spanish centers, all designated in colonial parlance as vecinos to distinguish them from the Indians.

To measure the thickness of Spanish and other vecino presence in Yucatan would appear to be a simple matter of numbers. How did the Indian and non-Indian populations compare in size and distribution during the course of the colonial period? The first problem is the numbers themselves. Characteristically for Yucatan, we have more information on the Indians than on vecinos, and not nearly enough on Indians at that. After central Mexico, Yucatan's demography must now be the most intensely studied of any area in the viceroyalty of New Spain.[34] The centerpiece of this literature is Cook and Borah's major study of popula- tion change from initial contact to 1960.[35] For the colonial period their chief interest, not surprisingly, is in charting the decline of the local Indian population and comparing it with central Mexico's "demographic catastrophe." Cristina García Bernal has taken issue on some particulars with their conclusions.[36] But all are in agreement on general outlines. Indisputably, the decline was less severe and proceeded at a much slower and more uneven pace, with a substantial recovery in the early seventeenth century interrupting the general downward trend. Where the two studies differ most significantly is in the shadowy period between this recovery and the clear upward curve of the latter part of the eighteenth century. García Bernal's revisions, which are based on much new and less equivocal evidence, also conform more closely with the general body of seventeenth-century sources I am familiar with.[37] All suggest a very sharp and sudden drop around the middle of the century (perhaps double the first post-conquest loss of 25 percent) that was already leveling off by the beginning of the eighteenth century, rather than a steady, gentle decline reaching a nadir shortly before the mid-1700s.[38]

The richness of these offerings merely whets the appetite for more, in particular for information on the shorter-term oscillations that are of so much interest. If we had no census figures between 1549 and 1794, we might assume that the Indian population had remained stable for over two centuries (ca. 240,000 in 1549 and 254,000 in 1794). Above all, these short-range, episodic variations would help to explain the relationship between demography, biology, and socio-cultural change.

Most pre-modern population curves would probably show many sharp dips. What we need to explain in colonial Yucatan, and the rest of Latin America, is the failure to recover and why the cumulative effect of high mortality followed different patterns over time in different places. Disease alone will not account for the population decline nor for the contrast between central Mexico and Yucatan. The effects of various kinds of stress on both mortality and recovery should be considered, although they are much harder to calculate.

Demography may be symptomatic of the colonial regime, reflecting the contrast between central Mexico and Yucatan, where conquest was less devastating in its immediate effects, though more protracted. I would say that, more than symptomatic, it is both a cause and an effect. The relative abundance of manpower (that is, the slower rate of population loss) and the primitive tribute economy helped to sustain each other. Spaniards had less stimulus to take charge of production directly; with less drastic disruptions in the traditional way of life, Indian society could reorganize after the trauma of conquest and resettlement (congregation) and begin to replenish itself.

Why, then, the precipitous decline in the middle of the seventeenth century that was not reversed until at least fifty years later? This crucial period remains shadowy, but with much unexploited documentation that would repay investigation. My own samplings suggest a disequilibrium in the tribute system (in its broadest sense), reaching a crisis in the 1660s, when an increasingly heavy burden of repartimientos and other exactions came on top of a series of epidemics and famines.[39] The increase in burdens may have been in part fortuitous in the shape of a particularly rapacious governor, whose *juicio de residencia* (judicial inquiry) fills a whole shelf in the Archivo General de Indias.[40] Perhaps the static tribute system simply reached a point where an ascending curve of Spanish demand (because of a gradual increase in Spanish population), without any basic technological or organizational innovations, bisected a descending curve of Indian resources. Disruptions in food production, lowered resistance to disease and famine, mass flight to zones of refuge, social disarray at community and family levels — all reinforced each other to sustain a prolonged deficit in the balance of birth and deaths.

As for the processes of stabilization and recovery, we need more precise information on their timing to supplement the biological explanations. No doubt increased immunity through natural selection played a major role, but both Spaniards and Indians pursued conscious policies of self-preservation also. The former eased their demands of repartimiento and other assessments, and the latter developed a new institution, the *cofradía*, to help cope with the twin evils of Spanish demands and crop shortages.[41]

The kinds of detailed information needed on mortality and fertility can only be derived from parish registers, which historians in many parts of Latin America have begun to mine. In Yucatan none has been preserved from the sixteenth century and only a small portion from the seventeenth. Still, a recent study of population change in the parish of Umán should lure followers as a taste of the insights an informed analysis of the extant records can yield.[42] The graphs of baptisms and burials (1690–1817) are alone a treat, providing the historian with the enviable task of matching the peaks and valleys, as well as the long-range trends, against the events and processes that other documents reveal. Of course, spatial variations need to be added to temporal ones to complete the picture, and these will be referred to later.

Information on the vecino population of Yucatan, to match against the studies of Indian demography, is disappointingly sparse. In fact, no full, reliable count exists prior to the late eighteenth century. Cook and Borah have made valiant efforts to overcome these deficiencies in the record and estimate the non-Indian population in 1639 at 5.5 percent of the total, increasing to 25–30 percent by the late eighteenth century.[43] There is no reason to doubt these figures. But the later figures do raise some serious questions about the relationship between quantitative and qualitative data.

The mass of colonial documentation of many varieties leaves one with the overwhelming impression that Yucatan was much more "Indian" than central Mexico.[44] The predominance of attention devoted to Indians in ecclesiastical and civil administration compared to central Mexico is one indicator. Another is that the Spanish in Yucatan not only harped repeatedly on how vastly outnumbered they were by Indians but also behaved accordingly. Cook and Borah themselves state that one of the major points of contrast between the two regions is Yucatan's proportionately lower Spanish and African migration, resulting in the genetic predominance of the Indian element.[45]

Yet by the 1780s non-Indians amounted to roughly equal proportions of the population in both Yucatan and central Mexico, and approximately double the ratio in Oaxaca.[46] There is a clear discrepancy between these figures, on the one hand, and the accumulation of impressions by and from the Spanish rulers on the other, a discrepancy that cannot be explained away by differences in spatial distribution. Spaniards and other vecinos remained heavily concentrated in urban centers in Yucatan. They retained this clustering tendency even when they filtered out into the countryside, so that many smaller towns, especially as distance from the capital increased, remained exclusively Indian. However, a similar pattern of urban concentration was characteristic of central Mexican vecinos too.

Both types of evidence may be both correct in their own terms and reconcilable if we enquire into what the numbers mean. We know that ethnic identities recorded in colonial censuses were merely legal categories based only in part on biological criteria, and these highly flexible ones. A mestizo could have almost any genetic mix between pure Spaniard and pure Indian, and in practice the boundaries marking off the supposedly pure groups were far from fixed. If the rate of Spanish and African migration to Yucatan was proportionately lower, then presumably the *castas* at least, and perhaps even the creole Spaniards, contained a larger Indian component there.

The genetic composition of vecino populations would be difficult to determine even from parish registers, given the rate of illegitimacy and therefore of unknown paternity. Culturally the boundary between Indians and the vast majority of those who were placed in non-Indian categories was certainly nebulous in the extreme. *Naborias*, who were simply Mayas who had become officially detached from the pueblos and usually resided in suburban barrios; indios hidalgos, descended from central Mexico auxiliaries who had taken part in the conquest and subsequently inter-married extensively with local Mayas; even the mestizos and pardos (any mixture of African with European and/or Indian) were indistinct in many ways from their Maya neighbors. As late as 1811 perhaps 80 percent of the castas, almost all of the indios hidalgos, and a large proportion of the suburban naborias were, like the official Indians, fulltime subsistence farmers practicing the same kind of shifting milpa agriculture,[47] by all indications sharing a similar kind of life, and speaking the same language—all monolingual in Yucatec Maya. Creoles were generally bilingual but, according to some peninsular critics, imperfectly so, since Maya was their first and preferred language.

I do not have the information to pursue cultural comparisons with central Mexico. Perhaps many of the vecinos there were also non-Indian in little more than name. What I suggest is that numbers need decoding before they can be translated into social realities. One cannot assume any direct correlation between numbers and cultural change, or, for that matter, between physical and cultural change.

Marta Hunt has accumulated a rich fund of data on the activities of Spaniards in the countryside and also of Hispanized castas—the mes-tizos and mulattoes integrated enough into the Spanish system to appear in the notarial records of Mérida.[48] Clearly the two groups did not operate in total isolation from each other, for Indians were also drawn into the urban orbit, temporarily on rotating labor drafts, or more permanently as naborias, just as vecinos came eventually to settle permanently in almost all the rural *cabeceras*.

The consequences of this contact are another question altogether. Leaving aside the issue of indirect influences on culture change (for example, the possible effects on kinship structure of innovations in laws of inheritance), much would depend on the nature of the contact, on what vecinos were doing in the countryside and Indians doing in or near the cities. It is my contention that a primitive tribute system stimulated less interaction and less consequential interaction than a more developed economy. The vecinos fanned out into the countryside, but mainly to collect and to requisition. Their contact with the Indians was fleeting, and was mediated through the Indian officials rather than the sustained, direct contact of an employer or patron. The labor draftees and the naborias performed in the cities the same unskilled domestic tasks they were accustomed to in the villages, to which many naborias returned.

One could say in general that the Indians and vecinos inhabited separate social worlds.[49] Some Indians were in but not of the city, just as vecinos who visited or settled in the countryside were in but not of the Indian communities. Yet there were some patterns of regular social interaction within the shared territories that deserve further investigation. We know there was some buying and selling of real estate and other commodities. There was also, despite a high rate of caste endogamy, some intermarriage, as well as concubinage and more ephemeral unions. Vecinos consulted Indian shamans, and Indian cofradías employed vecino cabinet makers. The colonial documents do not easily yield information on these and other unoffical forms of interaction, much less on how they affected perceptions and behavior on either side. Yet without it we will still have a very imperfect idea of the processes of Hispanization and Mayanization that were unfolding independently of the policies of church and state.

The Colonial Indian as Subject

The colonial Indian as a subject in his own right, rather than as a source of information about the pre-Columbian past or an object of colonial rule, has primarily been the province of ethnohistory in the broad sense that I defined earlier of combining questions and methods from both anthropology and history. There is no reason why history on its own, without an anthropological bent, should not deal with the effects of colonial rule on Indian sociocultural systems; it is simply that for the most part historians have found other topics to be of more compelling interest.

The literature on the post-conquest Indian in Mesoamerica has tended to focus on the Indian community as the unit of study. Kinship systems are elusive in the colonial documentation and simple to the point of nullity in modern times. And whatever larger polities existed at the time of conquest, ranging from empire to mini-state, they quickly disintegrated into smaller components. In Mesoamerica at least, the territorially-based community of a pueblo and its dependencies seems to have been an enduring feature of Indian social organization from pre-Columbian times to the present, with or without extended kinship ties that may have originally co-existed as a basis for social integration.

Micro-analysis of the community as an isolated unit carries the risk of obscuring wider ties, not only with the dominant colonial or national society but also with the rest of Indian society. In colonial Yucatan such ties existed and could on occasion support concerted action, but they were otherwise highly tenuous and unsystematic and increasingly unrelated to former political links. Yet, in other regions, especially highland Guatemala and Chiapas, distinctive ethnolinguistic boundaries have survived the post-conquest breakdown of formal structures. It has been suggested that these boundaries are supported by internal networks of economic exchange,[50] and it would be worth exploring further the correlation in Mesoamerica between the degree of ecological diversity, fostering regional integration, and the persistence of a strong, if largely informal, supra-community organization.

The community remains nonetheless the most obvious unit of analysis and has often been, too, the principal *subject* of analysis, as the key to Indian social organization both before and after the conquest. The standard model for the entire post-conquest period has long been Eric Wolf's "closed corporate community," which he sees as a response to conquest: the besieged Indians' withdrawal into tightly-knit communities to defend their culture and land from Spanish encroachment.[51] Recent studies of the colonial Indian in Yucatan have questioned the model's applicability to that region (see below). There the principal effect of colonial rule seems to have been the loosening of community ties. And if a corporate social structure (of pre-Columbian origin, by all accounts) survived, it did so despite considerable movement away from and between communities.

Population Movements

Three types of population movement, which I have called flight, drift, and dispersal,[52] seem to have been unusually prevalent in colonial Yucatan, especially the first of these. The characteristic Maya response to famine, epidemic, or any other crisis was to take off into the unpopulated bush. Many returned once the crisis had passed, but others made their way to the unpacified regions to the east and south.

Scholars have long been aware, as were the colonial authorities, that a substantial portion of the population losses recorded in colonial Yucatan were due to flight rather than mortality.[53] The existence of zones of refuge with organized groups of unconquered and apostate Mayas sharing the same language, and most of the same customs, affected social and political realities as well as demographic profiles on the other side of the frontier. We do not know how many Mayas became permanent refugees nor how far they had to be pushed before making this choice. But there were limits of tolerance, defined in part by the frontier's accessibility. And if the ease of escape subverted the colonial regime in Yucatan, challenging the absoluteless of Spanish rule, it also undermined the strength of social ties among the Mayas themselves.

Flight was no doubt primarily a form of protest against Spanish domination, although it must at the same time be seen against a background of pre-Columbian migrations—some of them, perhaps, also in reaction to foreign invasions. But the Mayas were also moving around in large numbers within the pacified areas. This movement, a seemingly aimless drift from one community to another, is easier to trace in the colonial records than it is to explain. It directly challenges the picture of "closed" Indian communities that needed to restrict access to limited resources and might therefore encourage out-migration to new areas or cities. The colonial Maya were moving into, as well as out of, long-established communities and during times of population increase as well as decrease.

The colonial Indians' refusal to stay put will come as no surprise to scholars familiar with the Andean area or other parts of Mesoamerica. The degree of their restlessness in Yucatan seems to have been uniquely high within Mesoamerica,[54] and it has only become apparent through a recent series of studies based on parish registers. Kevin Gosner was the first to note the large proportion of outsiders listed in the registers of Umán parish in the late eighteenth century; up to two-thirds of the marriage partners and their parents and sponsors were noted as *naturales* of other communities.[55] That these findings were not peculiar to the time and place is evident from a number of reports and censuses[56] and from an expanded study by David Robinson covering four parishes from the late seventeenth century to the early nineteenth.[57]

As with many such measurements of social phenomena, the censuses and parish registers present some knotty issues of interpretation. One of them is the meaning of *naturalidad*, which ordinarily refers to one's birthplace. However, some people in the Umán register were listed as naturales of one place baptized in another. I had suggested to Gosner that because of the persistence in Yucatan of the private encomienda, naturalidad might refer there to encomienda affiliation, which could be inherited regardless of one's own birthplace and domicile, and that therefore the records would represent an accumulation of migrations over generations.

Tracing naturalidad designations over several generations would of course resolve the issue with certainty. In the meantime, I find that the idea of inherited affiliation solves one small puzzle and raises a host of larger problems. For one thing, fathers and children do not always share the same naturalidad. For another, tribute collection would have been virtually impossible in view of the range and complexity of migratory patterns. There is evidence that Indian officials made some effort to track down defectors within a limited area, but these may have been simply the ones who had left some tax debt behind, and there was no attempt to cover the peninsula systematically. Finally, it was the clergy, not the civil authorities or encomenderos, who showed most concern over place of origin. They had no financial basis for the concern, and they continued to make note of it long after all encomiendas had been incorporated into the crown. The reason, according to one bishop, was canonical rather than fiscal and of particular relevance to marriage records. With so few patronymics among the Mayas, the bishop argued, the only way to identify and trace people who left their home parishes, and thus prevent bigamy, was to keep track of their place of birth and identify them by both surname and naturalidad.[58]

We may yet find some other basis for questioning the magnitude of the internal migrations the records seem to reveal for colonial Yucatan. Until then, we are faced with an exceedingly high rate, which varied over time and from place to place but might reach the level of one-third of the adult Indian population. These movements do not necessarily signify the disintegration of the corporate community. Community boundaries can be preserved even when permeable in both directions. But we need to know a lot more about the spatial and temporal patterns of migration before we can conclude with certainty how they reflected and affected colonial Maya social organization.

Such patterns are difficult to detect in the maze of crisscrossing tracks that cover the peninsula. A few regularities have been discovered, and I offer here a tentative model of internal migrations from my own expanded study of population movements,[59] a model that seeks to account both for the regularities and for the apparent lack of any overall coherence.

To understand these movements it is useful to break the process down into three separate choices: leaving home, not returning, and resettling elsewhere. Migrations were not always or even usually a steady trickle of people. They correlate with and were immediately caused by particular crises in which many people scattered from their home communities. The decision not to return had various motives, but land hunger can be eliminated from them, since people were as likely to move to densely populated parishes that also contained many Spanish estates as to areas where land was much more abundant. Escape from accumulated tax debts is a much more likely motive, supported by the finding that when people moved at all they usually moved to another district altogether.[60]

The reasons for choosing a specific new location are still the most elusive. David Robinson has opened a promising line of enquiry that should be pursued, the reconstruction of family ties among migrants. It may be that people followed family members, friends, or neighbors, as they have done the world over in migrating from their home towns. However, the slight degree of regularity noted in the records could as well be explained by the movement in one stage of one or two entire families. Either way, one seeks some larger pattern transcending particular towns, and some general attraction in the new locations besides distance from debt collectors or the presence of a kinsman. The most we can discern at the moment is certain tendencies. One of them is a movement toward Mérida, the provincial capital, which Marta Hunt sees as luring Indians to nearby pueblos and then to the suburban barrios.[61] Hunt was unaware of the considerable exodus out of the barrios and also of movements that "leapfrogged" the city.[62] Still, there was clearly a gradual build-up of population in the Mérida vicinity at the expense of other regions. The attraction was economic, but not so much in the sense of opportunity. Rather, the migrants sought security from the vicissitudes of village life that association with Spaniards could provide, some of the vicissitudes of course created by the Spaniards themselves. In the eighteenth century and possibly earlier, Spaniards were looked to for immediate and concrete relief. During famines Indians flocked to Mérida and the surrounding area, where grain supplies (requisitioned from the countryside as well as imported) were concentrated, to beg from private and public stores. The authorities sought to return the survivors to their villages, but many remained.

The search for security, temporary and long-term, could send people in the opposite direction too, away from population centers and in particular away from the Spanish. Outsiders were also evident in the remoter parishes, whose populations nevertheless failed to increase because they suffered a further drain across the nearby frontiers and out of the colonial censuses. Thus a very general two-way flow can be seen, the choice between them dictated by individual calculation of whether survival would be enhanced by greater proximity to or distance from the colonial masters who came increasingly to control the region's resources. Either choice, and indeed all the migrations, reflected a less than compelling attachment to particular communities.

The third type of population movement, dispersal from congregated or nuclear towns to dependent hamlets, I have discussed at length, mainly in terms of the centrifugal force exerted by the system of shifting agriculture prevalent in the region.[63] I have since added to the physical convenience of dispersed settlement the social advantages of physical distance from the pueblo, which brought greater freedom from social constraints and the burdens of community membership.

The move to Spanish-owned estates was part of the same process of dispersal and was impelled by much the same motives until its later stages. It is worth repeating that for most of the colonial period land was almost a free good. The estates offered no refuge for land-hungry Indians, nor for the most part any financial security. Only a very small part of the work force on the ranches and later the haciendas fell in the category of *criados*, the semi-skilled workers who were paid wages and whose taxes were the responsibility of the employer. They were often advanced credit, although I have seen no evidence that this constituted debt peonage.[64] The vast majority of estate residents were tenant farmers of the kind called *luneros*, who received no wages or advances and who were liable for their own tribute and taxes. It is the luneros' motives and status that need explanation.

Robert Patch has suggested that the haciendas offered some security from famine by advancing grain from their own stores during lean years.[65] Yet this became possible—and also more necessary—only after the estates had begun to produce food on a large scale. For much of its history what the Spanish estate offered the Indians was the same attractions that lured them to the hamlets: the same convenience of residing in small clusters close to their milpas rather than in the town centers and, paradoxically, the same type of independence, only in greater degree. The dispersed populations in both types of settlement (except for the criados) were by law members of the incorporated pueblos and subject to their jurisdictions. But luneros were more effectively shielded by the power of the hacendado from the authority of the clergy, pueblo officials, and anyone else who could claim their obedience and their labor. In effect the luneros transferred their residential labor tax, called "tequíos" in the pueblos, from pueblo to hacienda, gaining thereby a certain immunity from other community obligations. Traditionally, Monday (*lunes*) was the allotted day, hence the designation lunero. What the estanciero or hacendado gained was a resident labor force, which in the earlier years might exceed the labor needs of his estate but which could be useful for crop production on a small scale and for odd jobs, and which was unlikely to complain to the authorities about his cattle's invading their milpas.

Gradually the terms changed as the hacienda's labor demands increased with the shift to cash crops. But at the same time that the luneros' life became less attractive—more days of labor for the right to use hacienda land and more supervision from the mayordomos—the haciendas were engulfing community lands, and moving onto an hacienda and staying there were no longer matters of choice.

Maya Social Organization: The Fate of the Nobility

Discussions of movement away from and between communities touch only obliquely on what was happening within the communities, which after all remained the focal point of colonial Maya life. Migration and dispersal may have weakened the communities, but they did not destroy them. Migrants were incorporated into similar structures elsewhere. Ties with dispersed population were not totally severed until the haciendas were turned into quasi-communities themselves, acquiring in the hacienda churches the emblem of full social autonomy.

Without looking at post-conquest Indian society from the inside we can only guess at the effects of Spanish domination and its variations over time and space. I shall concentrate here on one topic that is particularly amenable to comparisons, the changing role and status of the native nobility. This topic has received much attention in the literature, partly because it is relatively well documented, but also because the fate of the nobility is such an important yardstick for the changes in indigenous social organization as a whole.

In this discussion I shall touch only tangentially on colonial Maya religion. The relationship between the body social and the supernatural was of intense interest to the colonial Mayas. No explanation of their social and ideational system makes much sense without reference to this central, pervasive concern, and a large part of my own lengthy study of the colonial Mayas deals in one way or another with the role of the sacred in society.[66] Even that treatment seems to me cramped and sketchy and will be expanded in a separate work. The subject is highly elusive, dependent largely on inference from recalcitrant primary sources. For that reason, I imagine, it has received so little attention. I can point to only a few published items on Yucatan.[67] The rest of Mesoamerica seems more barren still. There is some discussion of the institutional aspects of religion, the cofradías,[68] but little of either beliefs or rituals and that mostly confined, so far as I know, to Chiapas.[69] Rather than try to compress my

own treatment of this complex subject further, I will pass on to the nobility, with the caveat that their role and status, like everything else in Maya society, had strong links with religion.

Pre-Columbian Mesoamerica shared certain basic similarities in socio-political organization that were common to and in fact serve to define the areas of advanced civilization throughout Latin America—the areas sometimes referred to as "Nuclear America." Whether incorporated into the Aztec and Inca empires or still autonomous, all the polities were some form of territorial state ruled by hereditary lords, with a stratified social structure consisting of a nobility of various ranks, a mass of subordinate but more or less free commoners, and a group of slaves and/or serfs who were directly dependent on the nobility.

These same areas also now share the basic characteristics of a peasant society. As in all such societies, they may contain more economic and social differentiation than generally recognized, but it would be hard to argue for the existence of a hereditary nobility. The earlier and convenient supposition that the nobility were eliminated as a direct and immediate result of conquest has been demolished by the work of, among others, Charles Gibson, William Taylor, and Karen Spalding,[70] who have shown a more gradual and complex transformation during the colonial period. Although no one has carried the story past independence, the new social order appears to have been well established before then.

My question is whether the changes in native society outlined for central Mexico (including Oaxaca) and Peru hold true for Yucatan. The initial stages seem common enough. The larger hierarchical political structures were broken up into constituent units and the power of territorial rulers confined to their own local areas, a conscious Spanish policy that was also aided, as I have suggested earlier, by an erosion of economic ties. In Yucatan this meant that, regardless of the degree of centralized control that had existed in a particular province, which varied greatly, all the native lords were reduced to the level of batab, a local ruler with sovereignty over a single town, who had in some cases ruled independently and in others had been subordinate to provincial or sub-provincial lords.[71]

A concurrent program of congregation drew scattered subordinate villages into the principal towns, so that territorial stratification was compressed from both directions into a uniform level. Subordinate batabs continued to defer for a time to their former lords, the provincial halach uinic; some remnants of the old hierarchy persisted longer in the cabecera-visita relationship within the parishes. But each incorporated community had total autonomy in theory and, increasingly, in practice.[72]

Where Yucatan seems to depart from the standard Mesoamerican and Andean model is in the fortunes of the ruler and lesser nobility within the circumscribed limits of the single community. The model offers two diverging destinies, both of which entail the disappearance of the indigenous nobility *within* indigenous society. The fortunate few managed to preserve high status and wealth, transferring their traditional sources of wealth within native society into landed estates and commerce in the Spanish style. They not only competed successfully with Spanish entrepreneurs, they even emulated the Spanish in language, dress, and way of life, including absentee residence in the cities. Only their native titles distinguished them, titles they preserved by operating through the Spanish system.

These acknowledged hereditary caciques retained and developed their wealth but at the expense of local political power. They withdrew from Indian society while continuing to claim some of the material rewards of sovereignty. The understandable disaffection of their *macehual* "subjects," combined with their increasing identification with Spanish society, eventually completed the process of separation.[73]

The majority of the nobility remained within native society, either by choice or by necessity, and became gradually depressed into the mass of macehuales. They lost their political power to the rival structures of the elected municipal cabildo, created by the Spanish and used by macehuales with Spanish encouragement to challenge and replace the hereditary leaders.[74] In either case, by assimilation into Spanish society or into the common mass of Indians, the native nobility *qua* native nobility ceased to exist.

A somewhat different picture emerges from the records on Yucatan as presented in two recent studies of colonial Maya social organization: a detailed study of the community of Tekanto in the eighteenth century by Philip Thompson[75] and my own more comprehensive but inevitably more superficial regional survey from conquest to independence. The deviations are not startling but are significant enough to require some explanation. It is possible, of course, that much of the divergence is in interpretation, arising from different perspectives and different sources. Both studies on Yucatan take a more emic approach to the colonial Indian than has been common, relying more on the admittedly fragmentary native sources and seeking to discover what meaning the Indians gave to what the Spanish sources reveal. There is also the disciplinary leaning of the anthropologist, and crypto-anthropologist, in favor of continuity, which comes from an emphasis on structural-functional analysis as opposed to the historian's emphasis on change. Let me examine briefly some of the deviations that emerge from the two studies.

The first is that the cacique class, the descendents of the old territorial rulers, remained within native society. More accurately, they retreated back into it after an initial flirtation with assimilation. Roys and Scholes have given a detailed account of one protagonist's progress through this early, experimental stage in their Acalán-Tixchel monograph.[76] But Don Pablo Paxbolón was one among many Hispanized caciques who were able to use their local authority and their positions of confidence serving the Spanish to reinforce each other and to secure a high-ranking position for themselves in the new order.

Why their successors were unable to consolidate this position is not certain. I suspect that the obstacles were mainly economic, the area's retarded transition to a market economy. The primitive tribute system could not support two rival elites in the same style, and the Maya elite lost out to the Spanish in their traditional economic bases of long-distance trade and control over native labor, itself a shrinking resource. Unlike central Mexico and Peru, Yucatan offered little opportunity, and that too late, to parlay traditional sources of wealth into a new economic base of commercial agriculture combined with local trade. The native nobility was left to squeeze what it could from the native economy in unequal competition with the Spanish.

Within fifty years or so after conquest, the cacique class in Yucatan had disappeared from view. There is strong evidence, however, that they had disappeared only from Spanish view. They had retreated back into Maya society (some had never left). There they continued to enjoy privileged access to both wealth and political power, although on a greatly reduced scale.

There is one known exception, the Xiu family of Mani province. Roys used the Xiu papers, supplemented with material from central Mexico, for his earlier account of the cacique system in Yucatan. Not surprisingly, his account closely resembles the central Mexican model.[77] The Xius were, I think, an unusual and not wholly successful imitation of this model: removed from the local power structure, but without assimilation into Spanish society; gaining confirmation of hereditary titles, but titles that had no wealth attached to or supporting them. If other noble families did not bother to seek official acknowledgement of their rank, it was because their position within Maya society depended on recognition from their fellow Mayas and not from the Spanish.

What are the criteria for establishing the preservation or disappearance of a native nobility, or any nobility for that matter? First, there must be more structural and functional continuity. This may have been more pronounced throughout Mesoamerica than is commonly realized. In Yucatan, at any rate, social stratification persisted throughout the colonial period despite compression from above and below. This compression failed to erase the line dividing the masses from a privileged minority. The first group hovered around the line of bare subsistence and had no say in the conduct of community affairs. The second, though far from rich by the standards of the pre-Columbian lords or the new rulers (though not necessarily poorer than all Spaniards), monopolized what wealth was available within the colonial Indian economy and controlled through public office the lives and labor of the majority—ultimately subject, of course, to the authority of the Spanish overlords.[78]

The municipal cabildo and the rest of the local administrative apparatus introduced by the Spanish may have been designed to supplant the traditional system of government, but the replication of function, structure, and sometimes of nomenclature within the new system suggests that they did not succeed. Even the religious establishment, which would seem to have been appropriated in toto by the Christian clergy, contained strong links with the past. One link was the cofradía system by which the Maya leaders reconstituted their mediatory role between the community and the supernatural—in the guise of the corporate deity-saints. An even clearer link was the figure of the *maestro cantor*. This powerful personage, who served as the *cura*'s deputy and alter ego in all but the major sacraments, has been traced to the pre-Columbian *canbecah*, or teacher, an alternate title he retained in colonial Maya and Spanish documents.[79] My own reading is that the maestros also incorporated many of the attributes of the *ahkinob*, or chief priests, as these were gradually suppressed.

A colonial native elite with functions similar to those of the pre-Columbian ruling group could perhaps be found all over Mesoamerica and is not necessarily the same as a native nobility. To qualify, one must possess some formal distinction in rank correlating with the socioeconomic divisions and with the differential access to political office—and that distinction must be hereditary.

Ideally, we would trace the descendants of the pre-Columbian nobility and their political and economic fortunes down through the colonial period, but the records are too spotty for this. However, the many scattered pieces I have assembled, along with the large chunk that has survived from the town of Tekanto for the late seventeenth century to the nineteenth, point to the group's survival. For a start, there is evidence that the Mayas continued to distinguish between macehuales and *almehenob* (nobles) until at least the end of the colonial period.[80] There is also evidence for a correlation between the status of almehen on the one hand and wealth and political office on the other. Moreover, the title of almehen, which means one who can trace his ancestry through both the male and the female lines, continued to be hereditary in fact as well as theory. In other words, public office was linked in some way to lineage.

Yet public offices were supposed to be either appointive or elective under the administrative system created by the Spanish. The key to the discrepancy lies in the dynamics of local political power and the indigenous rules of succession that governed them. According to the rule of primogeniture the Spanish applied to the *cacizcagos*, colonial Maya politics appear to be a bit of a free-for-all. But then pre-Columbian politics might seem equally disorderly by the same narrow criterion, especially in the late Postclassic. Leaving aside the many illegitimate seizures of power by force and concentrating solely on the accepted rules of succession, we find that leaders were chosen (elected?) from among eligible lineages. The evidence for colonial times is consonant with the same principle. Only eligibility for office was hereditary, and actual accession to political power was determined by some consensus among the entire pool of eligibles. Thus a territorial lordship might fall to a brother or younger son, presumably chosen by agreement among the senior members of the patrilineage, but possibly also in consultation with the lesser nobles who filled the lower slots in the hierarchy.

In colonial times the formal procedure was election by the cabildo, which drew its members from the larger pool of eligibles, with a proforma confirmation from the provincial governor. This apparently hereditary elite continued to be divided into two tiers. The first was a restricted group of what could be called batab lineages, which provided candidates for the higher, life-time (or at least long-term) offices of batab, patron of the cofradía, maestro cantor, and scribe. The maestro had control over succession to the last two offices, which depended on the qualification of literacy imparted by the maestro. The second, larger group filled the lower ranks of the civil-religious hierarchy in a system of ascending rotation that Philip Thompson has linked to the ritual calendar of the Maya.[81]

The pattern is discernible, but what the fragmentary evidence will not tell is the extent of deviation from it. There are some well-documented shifts in family fortunes, as well as a few cryptic allusions to "upstarts," and no doubt some proportion of the many officials listed whose antecedents cannot be traced had none to boast of. Aristocracies have commonly experienced attrition and allowed a certain amount of replenishment from below to survive, and I do not know at exactly what point the boundary separating nobility from commoners can be said to disappear.

Whatever the degree of mobility within colonial Maya society—and all the movement should be viewed against the background of factional struggles and dynastic reshufflings that characterized the Postclassic—I find no evidence that the Spanish encouraged any attacks on the nobility's exclusive claims. The major ruling dynasties were merged into a larger category of batab lineages, and no doubt the local gentry experienced some shifts in personnel, if not some expansion. Nevertheless, the principle of hereditary access to political power was still preserved, with wealth—(itself partly dependent on inheritance), probity, and adroitness at political maneuvering all playing their part. Nor do I see why the Spanish authorities, if they did exercise more control over the choice of leaders than the records suggest, would try to impose candidates with dubious credentials or support populist challenges, in violation of their own hierarchical principles and their own interests, which rested on a well-ordered native society.

Nevertheless, the Indian nobility did eventually disappear as a distinct social group in Yucatan as in the rest of Mesoamerica. If the "when" and the "how" have yet to be established, this may be because the denouement was prolonged into the somewhat hazy post-independence period where scholars have not pursued it. One might find that noble descent lingered on as a mark of distinction within Maya society for some time. But a more useful way to chart post-conquest social change would be to look at the substance or meaning of rank. Seen as a vessel containing power and wealth, hereditary nobility would cease to exist when emptied of its contents, even if the vessel itself remained unshattered by parvenu challengers.

This occurred late in Yucatan by the established central Mexican chronology. The sixteenth-century conquest greatly reduced the nobility's power in Yucatan, but it left much for a second, less heralded assault beginning in the late eighteenth century. The modernizing policies of the

Bourbon reformers—pursued in more extreme form by republican Liberal regimes—though more subtle, were in their way as destructive as the original conquest.

I have mentioned some of the main features of this assault, which was a combined attack on the economic base of Indian communities and on the political power of their leaders. The last shreds of that power were removed with the post-independence abolition of the Indian communities, after a trial run under the short-lived 1812 Constitution of Cádiz.[82]

That loss might seem a welcome relief, since public office is supposed to have been a main vehicle for the impoverishment of the colonial Indian nobility. This was not, however, necessarily or even usually the case in Yucatan so long as the Indian officials had control over the public resources of the community—that is, so long as they possessed political power. The divorce between leadership and political power marks the chief distinction between Indian politics in colonial Yucatan and the modern civil-religious hierarchies, including the *cargo* system described for the Maya highlands, which is also supposed to impoverish its participants.[83]

Like participants in the cargo system, the Indian elites in colonial Yucatan, whether or not they can be defined as a nobility, performed elaborate and expensive ritual functions on behalf of their communities. In addition, they were held liable for the collective burden of tribute in its various forms. They sometimes suffered personal losses because of these sacred and secular responsibilities, especially in times of acute population decline. But they were not endemic losses. Until they were deprived of political power, the elites were able to mobilize macehual labor and other community resources to suport public ritual, to meet Spanish demands, and to maintain or replenish their own wealth. Some were simply more successful than others in corporate and private finance. The systematic impoverishment of the elites would more likely take place when expectations for their support of the religious cult continued while their capacity to draw on public resources was diminished—in other words, when they lost political power.

Conclusion

The work that has been done so far on colonial Yucatan underlines the need for caution in generalizing about all of Mesoamerica from central Mexican evidence. Yucatan was different by a variety of measures. Some of them may be revised from either side—or both sides—in the direction of convergence. The majority will stand.

Similar caution is needed in interpreting the differences. It is easy to see Yucatan as a simple case of arrested or delayed development, with quibbles confined to the extent of the lag behind central Mexico. The temptation is still to rely on a central Mexican model, merely transposing to a later date changes that were evident there in the sixteenth century. This is only one step removed from assuming that all of Mesoamerica was homogeneous.

The idea of identical but delayed processes is certainly risky in the economic sphere. The one aspect of dependency theory that all economists seem to agree on, however they may view the prospects for development, is that time-lag produces structural differences.[84]

If Latin America has been one of the peripheral regions within the world economy, Yucatan has been a periphery of a periphery, or of a secondary metropolis. It is no more likely to replicate the exact processes of change in central Mexico than central Mexico is likely to follow the same path as western Europe. Even now Yucatan has yet to reproduce the economic and social complexity of colonial Mexico. When the hacienda emerged it was never tied to a strong local market, and the hacienda was a relatively brief episode in Yucatan's transition from semi-autarchy to export monoculture.

The same might apply to the reshaping of Indian society under Spanish rule. We may be dealing with somewhat different processes instead of a simple time-lag. In comparing the results of evangelization in the former Aztec and Inca empires, it has been argued that because of a delay between the military and spiritual conquests in the Andes, conversion was more superficial there than in Mexico, producing less of an amalgam than a veneer of Christianity over a pagan base. I suspect that the pagan base itself underwent considerable change.

I suggest that in Mesoamerica we consider another alternative to Hispanization besides conservation of old ways. A less abrupt and drastic break with the past would allow the Indians time to develop their own adaptations to Spanish pressures, somewhat analagous to what has been

called "strategic acculturation": making some changes in order to preserve essentials. We would thus expect culture change to occur everywhere, even among those groups that seem most conservative, most
"untouched." Change would be universal, but according to the speed and
thoroughness of colonization it would proceed to a greater or lesser
degree along Indian lines.

Notes

1. I am indebted mainly to Sidney W. Mintz and Richard S. Price, *An Anthropological Approach to the Afro-American Past: A Caribbean Perspective*
(Philadelphia, 1976), for suggesting this approach to acculturation studies. It is,
however, implicit in many other studies, for example, Peter Worsley, *The Trumpet
Shall Sound* (London, 1957), and J. D. Y. Peel, *Aladura: A Religious Movement
among the Yoruba* (London, 1968).

2. The Carnegie Institution sponsored an entire generation of scholars, most
notably in history and ethnohistory: Eleanor Adams, Robert Chamberlain, Ralph
Roys, J. Ignacio Rubio Mañé, France Scholes, and Eric Thompson.

3. Charles Gibson, *The Aztecs under Spanish Rule* (Stanford, 1964).

4. Ralph L. Roys, *Political Geography of the Yucatan Maya* (Washington, 1957).

5. Among the major documents that Roys edited and translated are *The Book of
Chilam Balam of Chumayel* (Washington, D.C., 1933), *Ritual of the Bacabs* (Norman, Oklahoma, 1965), and *The Titles of Ebtún* (Washington, D.C., 1939).

6. Ralph L. Roys, *The Indian Background to Colonial Yucatan* (Washington, D.C.,
1943). A more recent treatment of the subject is his "Lowland Maya Native Society
at Spanish Contact," in *Handbook of Middle American Indians*, vol. 3, *Archaeology of Southern Mesoamerica. Part 2* (Austin, 1965), pp. 659–78.

7. Ralph L. Roys, "Conquest Sites and the Subsequent Destruction of Maya
Architecture in the Interior of Northern Yucatan," *Contributions to American
Anthropology and History* 11. Carnegie Institution Publications 596 (Washington,
D.C., 1952), pp. 129–82.

8. For some recent examples on the Petén, see Nicholas Hellmuth, "Some Notes
on the Ytza, Quejache, Verapaz Chol, and Toquegua Maya," mimeograph (New
Haven, 1971), and various contributions to the debate over the location of Tayasal,
by Rubén E. Reina in *Expeditions* 9 (1966), Ian Graham in a personal communication, Arlen F. Chase in *American Antiquity* (1976), and Grant D. Jones, Don S. Rice,
and Prudence M. Rice in *American Antiquity* (1981).

9. J. E. S. Thompson, "A Proposal for Constituting a Maya Subgroup, Cultural and
Linguistic, in the Peten and Adjacent Regions," in Grant D. Jones, ed., *Anthropology and History in Yucatan* (Austin, 1977), pp. 3–42.

10. France V. Scholes and Ralph L. Roys, *The Maya Chontal Indians of Acalán-
Tixchel* (Washington, D.C., 1948).

11. Grant D. Jones, "Southern Lowland Maya Political Organization: A Model of Change from Protohistoric through Colonial Times," *Actes du XLIIe Congrès International des Américanistes. Paris. 1976*, vol. 8 (1979), pp. 83–94; and "Agriculture and Trade in the Colonial Period Central Maya Lowlands," in Kent V. Flannery, ed., *Maya Subsistence* (New York, 1982).

12. Beginning with J. E. S. Thompson's seminal piece, "Putún (Chontal Maya) Expansion in Yucatan and the Pasión Drainage," in *Maya History and Religion* (Norman, Oklahoma, 1970), pp. 3–47.

13. Scholes and Roys, *Maya Chontal*, pp. 164–167.

14. Jones, "Southern Lowland," pp. 12–13.

15. Robert S. Chamberlain, *The Conquest and Colonization of Yucatan, 1517–1550* (Washington, D.C., 1948).

16. Aside from the general regional histories, such as Juan Francisco Molina Solís, *Historia de Yucatán durante la dominación española* (4 vols., Mérida, 1904–12), which are primarily political in focus, there is the long introduction by France V. Scholes and Eleanor B. Adams to their collection of documents, *Don Diego de Quijada, Alcalde Mayor de Yucatán, 1561–1565* (2 vols., Mexico City, 1938), and numerous items published over the years by J. Ignacio Rubio Mañé in the *Boletín del Archivo General de la Nación* (Mexico City).

17. George M. Foster, *Culture and Conquest* (New York, 1961), especially chapters 2 and 3.

18. Immanuel Wallerstein, "The Rise and Future of the World Capitalist System," *Comparative Studies in Society and History* 19 (1974): 387–415; André Gundar Frank, *Capitalism and Underdevelopment in Latin America* (2nd ed., New York, 1969).

19. Most of the topics raised in this essay are developed at length in my forthcoming study of the Yucatan Mayas, "Colonial Maya Society: The Collective Purchase of Survival." On the colonial economic regime, see chapter 1.

20. On the encomienda in Yucatan, see two complementary studies by Manuela Cristina García Bernal, *Yucatán: Población y encomienda bajo los Austrias* (Seville, 1978), and *La sociedad de Yucatán, 1700–1750* (Seville, 1972).

21. García Bernal, *Yucatán*, pp. 282–97, 399–420.

22. On the operation of the repartimiento system in Yucatan, see García Bernal, *Sociedad*, pp. 126–33.

23. Marta Espejo-Ponce Hunt, "Colonial Yucatan: Town and Region in the Seventeenth Century," Ph.D. dissertation, University of California, Los Angeles, 1974, deals with many of the activities of non-Indians and has an especially useful section on peddlers in the countryside (pp. 513–36).

24. Nancy M. Farriss, "Propiedades territoriales en Yucatán en la época colonial," *Historia Mexicana* 30 (1980): 153–208; García Bernal, *Sociedad* and *Yucatán*; Hunt, "Colonial Yucatan," and "Processes of the Development of Yucatan, 1600–1700," in Ida Altman and James Lockhart, eds., *Provinces of Early Mexico* (Los Angeles, 1976), pp. 32–62; and Robert W. Patch, "La formación de estancias y

haciendas en Yucatán durante la colonia," *Boletín de la Escuela de Ciencias Antropológicas de la Universidad de Yucatán* 19 (1976): 21–61, and an expanded treatment in "A Colonial Regime: Maya and Spaniard in Yucatan," Ph.D. dissertation, Princeton University, 1979, both of which emphasize the eighteenth century.

25. Hunt, "Colonial Yucatan," p. 589, and "Processes," pp. 51, 54–57; Patch, "Formación," p. 21; Farriss, "Propiedades," pp. 156–63, 193–205.

26. Late colonial economic, as well as social and political, changes are discussed in Farriss, "Colonial Maya," chapter 12.

27. Murdo J. MacLeod, *Spanish Central America* (Berkeley, 1973).

28. Howard F. Cline, "The Henequen Episode in Yucatan," *Inter-American Economic Affairs* 2:1 (1948): 30–51, and "The Sugar Episode in Yucatan, 1825–1850," *Inter-American Economic Affairs*, 1:4 (1948): 79–100; and Moisés González Navarro, *Raza y tierra* (Mexico City, 1972).

29. The issue of land ownership versus land use is discussed in Farriss, "Propiedades," pp. 178–82, 196–97, and "Colonial Maya," chapter 9.

30. William B. Taylor, "Landed Society in New Spain," *Hispanic American Historical Review* 54 (1974): 408–9.

31. Roys, *Titles of Ebtún*.

32. Farriss, "Colonial Maya," chapter 3, discusses the role of royal officials, encomenderos, and parish clergy in the administration of Indian pueblos. See also Hunt, "Colonial Yucatan," pp. 476–88.

33. Farriss, "Colonial Maya," chapter 12.

34. In addition to the works cited below, see Ralph L. Roys, France V. Scholes, and Eleanor B. Adams, eds., "Report and Census of the Indians of Cozumel, 1570," *Contributions to American History and Anthropology* 6, Carnegie Institution Publication 523 (Washington, D.C., 1940), pp. 1–30, and "Census and Inspection of the Town of Pencuyut," *Ethnohistory* 6 (1959): 195–225; J.E.S. Thompson, "The Maya Central Area at the Spanish Conquest and Later: A Problem in Demography," in *Maya History and Religion*, pp. 48–83; Frederick Lange, "Una reevaluación de la población del norte de Yucatán en el tiempo del contacto español, 1528," *América Indígena* 31 (1971): 117–39; Francisco de Solano y Pérez-Lila, "La población indígena de Yucatán durante la primera mitad del siglo 17," *Anuario de Estudios Americanos* 28 (1971): 165–200. Patch, "Colonial Regime," chapter 6, also contains a considerable amount of demographic material for the late eighteenth and early nineteenth centuries.

35. Sherburne F. Cook and Woodrow Borah, *Essays in Population History: Mexico and the Caribbean* (3 vols., Berkeley, 1971–1978), II, 1–179.

36. García Bernal, *Yucatán*, pp. 7–166, deals entirely with population through the seventeenth century.

37. García Bernal, *Yucatán*, pp. 126–43.

38. Cook and Borah, *Essays*, II, 112–14.

39. See Farriss, "Colonial Maya," chapter 2, on Indian responses (including demographic) to the colonial regime.

40. "Residencia de don Rodrigo Flores de Aldana, 1670–1680" (including a separate "causa criminal"), Archivo General de Indias, Escribanía de Cámara, legajos 315-A to 317-C. See also Manuela Cristina García Bernal, "La visita de Fray Luis de Cifuentes, obispo de Yucatán," *Anuario de Estudios Americanos* 29 (1972); 229–60.

41. On the development of cofradías, see Farriss, "Propiedades," pp.164–85, and "Colonial Maya," chapter 9.

42. David J. Robinson and Carolyn G. McGovern, "Population Change in the Yucatan, 1700–1820," paper presented at the Association of American Geographers, Philadelphia, 1979.

43. Cook and Borah, *Essays*, II, 83 (1639), 84, 93.

44. An impression first gained during research on my *Crown and Clergy in Colonial Mexico* (London, 1968), which covered the audiencia districts of Mexico and Guadalajara.

45. Cook and Borah, *Essays*, II, 178–79.

46. Cook and Borah, *Essays*, II, 214.

47. Archivo del Estado de Yucatán, Censos y padrones 1, expedientes 3–11, censuses for the partidos of Tizimín, Camino Real Alto, Valladolid, Beneficios Bajos, Sierra Baja and Sierra Alta, Costa Alta and Costa Baja, Champotón, and Bolonchencavich, 1811.

48. Hunt, "Colonial Yucatan," pp. 513–36.

49. See Farris, "Colonial Maya," chapter 3, for a discussion of caste boundaries and cultural exchanges.

50. Michael Morris, "Ethno-Linguistic Systems in the Southern Maya Area," M. A. thesis, University of Pennsylvania, 1973. Kevin Gosner is investigating inter-community links in the Chiapas highlands (see his "Tzeltal Revolt of 1712," paper presented at the International Congress of Americanists, Vancouver, 1979) but finds no evidence for an underlying market system (personal communication).

51. Eric R. Wolf, "Closed Corporate Peasant Communities in Meso-America and Central Java," *Southwestern Journal of Anthropology* 13 (1957): 1–8.

52. Nancy M. Farriss, "Nucleation versus Dispersal: Population Movements in Colonial Yucatan," *Hispanic American Historical Review* 58 (1978): 204.

53. Molina Solís, *Historia de Yucatán*, especially volume 2, refers frequently to these losses through flight. See also Cook and Borah, *Essays*, II, 114–20, 178.

54. Robinson and McGovern, "Population Change," pp. 5–7.

55. Kevin Gosner, "Umán Parish: Open, Corporate Communities in Eighteenth-Century Yucatan," paper presented at the Association of American Geographers, Philadelphia, 1979.

56. See, for example, the parish *matrículas* of 1688 in Archivo General de Indias, Contaduría 920, many of which listed people from elsewhere separately; and the Franciscan matrículas of 1721, in Archivo General de Indias, Mexico 1039.

57. David J. Robinson, "Indian Migration in Eighteenth-Century Yucatan," paper presented at the International Congress of Americanists, Vancouver, 1979.

58. Archivo del Arzobispado (Mérida) Oficios y decretos 3, Bishop Francisco Pina y Mazo to Audiencia de México, 22 November 1786.

59. Farriss, "Colonial Maya," chapter 7.

60. Robinson, "Indian Migration," p. 11.

61. Hunt, "Colonial Yucatan," pp. 225–27, 237.

62. Robinson, "Indian Migration," pp. 18–20.

63. Farriss, "Nucleation versus dispersal."

64. Patch, "Formación de estancias," pp. 47–49, makes a stronger case for colonial peonage than I would but as a still very undeveloped system compared to the post-independence period.

65. Patch, "Formación de estancias," p. 46.

66. Farriss, "Colonial Maya," but most especially in chapters 10 and 11.

67. Donald E. Thompson, "Maya Paganism and Christianity," in Margaret A. L. Harrison and Robert Wauchope, eds., Naturism and Syncretism, Middle American Research Publication 19 (New Orleans, 1960), pp. 5–36, is a thoughtful treatment based on published sources. See also France V. Scholes and Ralph L. Roys, "Fray Diego de Landa and the Problem of Idolatry in Yucatan," in Cooperation in Research, Carnegie Institution Publication 501 (Washington, D.C., 1938), pp. 585–620; and Arthur G. Miller and Nancy M. Farriss, "Religious Syncretism in Colonial Yucatan: The Archaeological and Ethnohistorical Evidence from Tancah, Quintana Roo," in Norman Hammond, ed., Maya Archaeology and Ethnohistory (Austin, 1979), pp. 223–40. I refer to studies and not to the many published documents that deal with colonial Maya religion.

68. Gibson, Aztecs, chapter 5; Ernesto de la Torre Villar, "Algunos aspectos de las cofradías y la propiedad territorial en Michoacán," Jahrbuch für Geschichte von Staat, Wirtschaft und Gesellschaft Lateinamerikas 4 (1967): 410–39.

69. A notable exception is Richard E. Greenleaf, Zumárraga and the Mexican Inquisition, 1536–1543 (Washington, D.C., 1962). MacLeod, Spanish Central America, p. 328, mentions some religious practices in the Maya highlands in general. For Chiapas, see Kevin Gosner, "Soldiers of the Virgin: An Ethnohistorical Analysis of the Tzeltal Revolt of 1712 in Highland Chiapas," Ph.D. dissertation, University of Pennsylvania, 1984, chapter 5.

70. Gibson, Aztecs, especially pp. 65–76, 155–93, and "The Aztec Aristocracy in Colonial Mexico," Comparative Studies in Society and History 2 (1959–60): 169–96; William B. Taylor, Landlord and Peasant in Colonial Oaxaca (Stanford, 1972), chapter 2. On Peru, see Karen Spalding, "Indian Rural Society in Colonial Peru," Ph.D. dissertation, University of California, Berkeley, 1967, chapters 5 and 6; "Social Climbers: Changing Patterns of Mobility among the Indians of Colonial Peru," Hispanic American Historical Review 50 (1970): 645–64; and "Kurakas and Commerce: A Chapter in the Evolution of Andean Civilization," Hispanic American Historical Review 53 (1973): 581–99.

71. Information on lowland Maya political organization at the time of contact is

scattered in many primary sources; much of it has been assembled by Ralph Roys in his *Indian Background,* chapter 9, and *Political Geography.*

72. Farris, "Colonial Maya," chapter 5.

73. See, especially, Gibson, *Aztecs,* pp. 156, 163–64, and Taylor, *Landlord,* pp. 35–36.

74. In addition to the sources cited in note 70, see MacLeod, *Spanish Central America,* pp. 135–42, for a discussion of the vicissitudes of the cacique class in Guatemala.

75. Philip C. Thompson, "Tekanto in the Eighteenth Century," Ph.D. dissertation, Tulane University, 1978.

76. Roys and Scholes, *Maya Chontal,* pp. 175–291.

77. Roys, *Indian Background,* pp. 129–71.

78. On economic differentiation and the prerogatives of office-holding, see Philip Thompson, "Tekanto," pp. 183–92, 332–45, 366–69; and Farriss, "Colonial Maya," chapters 6 and 8.

79. Anne C. Collins, "The *Maestros Cantores* in Yucatan," in Grant D. Jones, ed., *History and Anthropology in Yucatan* (Austin, 1977), pp. 233–47.

80. Philip Thompson, "Tekanto," pp. 222–23; and Roys, *Titles of Ebtún,* passim.

81. Philip Thompson, "Tekanto," pp. 229–323. See also Michael D. Coe, "A Model of Ancient Community Structure in the Maya Lowlands," *Southwestern Journal of Anthropology* 21 (1965): 96–114, on uayeb rites among the pre-Columbian Maya; and Farriss, "Colonial Maya," chapter 11, on the political dimensions of fiestas.

82. Farriss, "Colonial Maya," chapter 12. See also J. Ignacio Rubio Mañé, *Los sanjuanistas de Yucatán* (Mexico City, 1971).

83. This older view has been challenged by, for example, Frank Cancian, *Economics and Prestige in a Maya Community* (Stanford, 1965). Barbara Price, "The Burden of the Cargo: Ethnographic Models and Archaeological Inference," in Norman Hammond, ed., *Mesoamerican Archaeology* (London, 1974), pp. 445–65, has pointed out the missing element of political power in challenging the usefulness of ethnographic analogy for pre-conquest explanations.

84. See, among the more optimistic pundits, W. W. Rostow, *The Stages of Economic Growth* (Cambridge, Mass., 1960).

David Freidel

Lowland Maya Political Economy: Historical and Archaeological Perspectives in Light of Intensive Agriculture

Introduction

Archaeology ends and history begins on the Yucatan peninsula with the arrival of the Spanish. The Conquest stands as a boundary marker for the dominions of historiography and archaeological analysis of material remains. Like all boundaries, this one is subject to some questioning. Mayanist archaeologists and historians alike have generally championed the reality of a continuum bridging the pre-Columbian and Christian eras.[1] Indeed, much archaelogical interpretation in the areas rests on the validity of "specific historical analogy".[2] Yet students of these related disciplines have maintained, until quite recently, a respectful distance from an area in which they might have engaged in serious collaboration: the Contact, or epi-historical, period of the sixteenth century.[3] A critical examination of archaeological data in light of coeval texts (and vice versa) is still in its infancy. Until historians and archaeologists meet at the boundary, judgments concerning the state of affairs at Contact and the dynamics of acculturation that ensued might best be regarded as hypotheses not yet corroborated by independent data.

The problem of mistaking hypotheses for conclusions in the Contact period has ramifications both forward and backward in time. If one looks backward, the major ramification is the application of imperfect analogy. As the examples outlined in this paper indicate, analogical models based on tests alone are inherently vulnerable. First, even in those cases in which early observations refer to specific incidents, practices, or material ambience, sifting the significant from the incidental facts must be guided by a self-limiting historiographic conception of general context in the absence of archaeological information. Second, the violent confrontation of alien worlds dictated an initial unconscious selection by observers for the central, fascinating, and overt, and a blindness to the dispersed, banal, and covert. And third, the realities of continuity and disjunction are only selectively displayed in early colonial texts, since these routinely sub-stantiate political, economic, or ideological positions taken by the writers. The objective here is to persuade scholars on both sides of the boundary that an inter-disciplinary approach is not only feasible but is a potential source of stimulating insight into the Maya past. What follows constitutes a series of particular cases wherein the interplay of texts and archaeologi-cal remains has shaped perspectives on critical features of ancient Maya life.

Maya Agriculture

"There were large gardens and orchards in the towns, and in the country maize, squash, and beans were raised by so-called *milpa* farming, which is the well known slash-and-burn method."[4] Such general statements on the art of agriculture at the outset of the sixteenth century made by eminent historians have long provided the foundation for an archaeologi-cal view that the ancient Mayas, unique among archaic civilizations, relied almost exclusively on extensive agricultural techniques. For years archaeologists chafed against the improbability that such a system could have supported a complex society and a highly productive economy.[5] Many specialists reached the conclusion that the Mayas were a not-quite-civilized peculiarity in the annals of human history.[6] Ultimately the historical analogy and the following impasse were circumvented and a case was proposed on strictly archaeological grounds for the existence of intensive agriculture among the lowland Mayas.[7] The history of ancient Maya agriculture is still in the process of revolutionary revision,[8] in which an enthusiastic new consensus has formed around the notion that the Mayas not only practiced intensive irrigation and drained field agricul-ture but outdid their contemporaries in Mesoamerica in this regard. Although the empirical data lag somewhat behind, recent research suggests that elaborate intensive systems were in operation by the Late Preclassic period,[9] and even the most conservative estimates, based on ground surveys and aerial photographs, indicate that these systems in-volved thousands of hectares.[10]

Ironically, in the rush to rewrite Classic and Preclassic Maya develop-ments Mayanist have virtually neglected the implications of their discov-ery for the later periods on which their perception was once based. In fact, the implications could be most profound and discomforting for archaeologists committed to the "specific historical" approach.[11] If the statements by Roys and other historians are taken at face value, then we are dealing with a disjunction at the roots of Maya life of massive proportions. In the last analysis, such a disjunction is not a matter of conjecture but of fact. Otherwise, the problem of swidden agriculture never would have arisen in the first place. The real issue is when did the disjunction occur and under what circumstances?

There is a possibility that sheet erosion on high ground brought about by short fallow swidden agriculture during the Classic period (300–900 A.D.) adversely affected raised-field agriculture in the Petén lowlands of Guatemala[12] and that this turn of events contributed to the Maya collapse. Such reasoning is highly speculative given the state of the data, but current research does suggest that intensive agriculture was practiced in these low-lying areas.[13] Even so, this kind of catastrophe would have had little effect on the flanking riverine environments. Hence there is no reason to suppose that intensive practices ceased to be used in the river basins at the time of the Classic collapse. Moreover, other kinds of intensive agriculture, involving stone terraces and field demarcation with stone walls, were practiced by the ancient Mayas.[14] These techniques are not tied to the rivers or the lowlands. In brief, although the Classic collapse might explain the cessation of intensive agriculture in some areas, it does not account for the disjunction evident in the later colonial period.

Turning to the later Postclassic period, the data on the persistence of intensive techniques are scanty but suggestive. The area around El Tigre, thought to be ancient Izancanec,[15] is surrounded by raised fields.[16] Although Izancanac was a major community at the time of the Conquest, archaeologists have yet to confirm a Postclassic or post-Conquest association of raised-field agriculture with occupied settlement. In contrast, by using archaeological information, field-wall networks can be definitely assigned to the Late Postclassic and Contact periods on Cozumel island and the east coast of the peninsula.[17] On Cozumel, the network of rectilinear plots formed by field walls pervades the entire island, both within and between communities, and is in clear association with Late Postclassic buildings. The manner in which such fields were employed remains an enigma. Nonetheless, there is reason to believe that intensive agricultural techniques were employed within them because the individual plots average roughly a tenth the size of modern swidden milpas (i.e., ten *mecates* or .1 hectares). Identical field-wall networks have been reported from the Classic period site of Chunchicmil on the northwest coast of the Yucatan,[18] indicating a continuity in practices from Classic times. Terraces are also found on Cozumel in the context of Postclassic communities. Thus there is reason to believe that continuing research in the Maya lowlands will confirm the persistence of intensive agriculture right up to the time of the Conquest.

It would seem that if intensive agricultural techniques were still in use when the Spanish arrived, they would have commented on them. There are, in fact, some incidental descriptions that might pertain to raised-field agriculture. For example, at the battle of Cintla outside Potonchán, Cortés's army was lured into an area where the natives enjoyed a distinct advantage: "The meeting place of the two armies was cultivated land, cut by many ditches and deep streams, difficult to cross, among which our men became confused and disorganized . . . the foot [soldiers] went to the right, crossing ditches at every step."[19] Cintla, of course, is the Nahuatl term for corn. There are many more vague allusions to milpas bordering swamps and lakes in Cortés's fifth letter.[20] Regarding field walls, it is worth noting that while Cortés's army sloshed around in the ditches of Cintla the natives held the bordering high ground: "Our men did some mischief among the Indians . . . but even so could not force them to retreat, because the enemy took cover behind trees and fences."[21]

The Motul dictionary has *Ticin Cot,* a term that means field or houselot wall.[22] Houselot walls are described by Las Casas in a town that is supposed to be on Cozumel[23] but is probably Chanpotón.[24] Technically and in principle, houselot walls and field walls are essentially the same, so it is reasonable to suppose that people using the one would know about the other. Finally, Helmuth[25] has recently reported on very rich archival sources for the Cholti-Lacandón, making a case for intensive cultivation based on repeated assertions that milpa plots were cultivated for twenty years or more.

The germane textual data are scanty and far from conclusive, but if they are taken together with the archaeologically-documented existence of the wall systems on the east coast of Quintana Roo in the Contact period and similar houselot walls at Mayapán,[26] there is some reason to believe that the Mayas gave up intensive agricultural techniques and concentrated on swidden agriculture (which no doubt has always been an option) during the Contact period. Helmuth[27] addresses this issue squarely and suggests that the combined effects of the Spanish "scorched-earth" warfare and the reduction of the population resulted in both a simplification of the agricultural repertoire and the switch to extensive techniques. Helmuth[28] further reasons that the Spanish demand for storable, measureable staple foodstuffs also encouraged agricultural simplification and the imposition of the corn, beans, and squash triad on the Mayas.

The forced removal of people from their lands and their subsequent concentration in new locations indeed might have discouraged the re-creation of labor-intensive ridged field systems. Such an argument might hold for the Acalán who were driven out of Izancanac and forced to live again in Tixchel near the coast beginning in 1557.[29] But if we presume that the Spanish were not stupid and that they recognized not only the great subsistence potential but the manifest commercial potential of the cotton fields and cacao groves of Acalán, we must consider why they were willing to pay so high a price to have these people in a more convenient location. Perhaps the destruction of the groves and fields of Acalán was a matter of local political expediency, for Grant Jones[30] has noted that the apostate Mayas maintained a clandestine long-distance trade network in luxury agricultural commodities long after the Conquest. It would have been virtually impossible for the conquerors to inhibit the siphoning off of goods onto this network in the swamps of the region, to the detriment of Spanish order.

Such a scenario must remain in the realm of sheer speculation until Izancanac and Tixchel have been archaeologically investigated with these problems in mind. But through such work it should be possible to establish whether or not in fact the Contact-period people of Acalán practiced raised field agriculture; whether or not they returned to swid-den when forced to move to Tixchel; and whether or not this move was accompanied by agricultural simplification. Roys[31] believes Tixchel can be identified with the modern hacienda of Tichel. The site of Izancanac is likewise identifiable.[32] The work is worth doing because the historical stakes are high. It seems quite clear that the existence of chinampa-like fields in the swamps of Tabasco was never officially recognized or known in the courts of Spain. If the above scenario were empirically corrobo-rated, it might constitute a local political cover-up of staggering pro-portions, with profound ramifications for the later agricultural history of the region.

Similar scenarios might be constructed to account for the abandonment of the elaborate network of tiny fields on the east coast of the peninsula. Indeed, in this case it remains uncertain what kinds of intensification were involved. Some new answers might result from further archival research with this problem in mind, but the questions can also be ad-dressed archaeologically in the context of sixteenth- and early seventeenth-century communities of the region. An ideal setting for joint archaeological and historical research would be the site of Ecab, El Gran Cairo of the Spaniards, on the northern east coast. If the monumental scale of the church is any guide,[33] Ecab was an important center of early Spanish occupation. In the later colonial period the community was abandoned and has never been reoccupied. Here the timing of disjunction and the circumstances under which it occurred might be investigated.

Political Economy and Social Hierarchy

Mayanists working with evidence of landscape modification and agricultural intensification in the context of the Classic-period settlements have recognized that these data allow and require consideration of sociopolitical control of agricultural production.[34] The diverse ways of parceling land now known for the Classic Mayas and the increasingly wide-spread evidence for such careful definition have encouraged some students of the region to infer that control of agricultural production was the preeminent feature of Classic Maya political economy and social structure.[35] This general position has been eloquently reified by R.E.W. Adams and W. Smith[36] into a feudal model for Classic Maya society that draws analogical inspiration from historically-documented feudal political systems in the Old World.

The feudal model signals not only the welcome re-introduction[37] of the mode of production into interpretations of ancient Maya life but also the initiation of what should prove to be an intellectually useful dialectic. For the feudal model relegates trade and exchange to a distinctly secondary role in Classic Maya politics, whereas a number of Mayanists have argued that control of the distribution of raw materials and finished products was politically crucial in the context of a horizontally and vertically integrated regional economy.[38]

To date, proponents of the feudal model have concentrated their attention on the earlier periods of Maya prehistory, for, as Gordon Willey has recently stated, "I am inclined to favour the feudal model for the Preclassic and Classic Periods; but in the Terminal Classic and Postclassic profound changes were underway throughout Mesoamerica as a whole and in the Maya Lowlands, and interregional trade was a significant element in these changes."[39]

Yet it is quite clear that the empirical evidence for intensive agriculture is the mainstay of the position,[40] and, as I have argued above, there is reason to believe intensive agriculture continued to be practiced by the

Postclassic and Contact-period Mayas. In light of this probable continuity, I feel justified in exploring the utility of the feudal model in explaining Maya political and social organization in these later periods.

One of the inherent problems encountered when comparing complex societies, as in the case of Old World feudal societies compared with the Prehistoric and Protohistoric Mayas, is that these diversified and hetero-geneous systems can be made to yield one-to-one correlations of almost any kind if other factors are ignored. In an attempt to avoid this problem, I shall examine the general characteristics of such feudal systems given by Adams and Smith[41] and address them in an equally general fashion. On the whole, these criteria are derived from Coulborn's[42] discussion of feudalism as a general social type.

Adams and Smith[43] suggest that in feudal systems "Political authority and power are diffused among chiefs who are vested with limited pro-prietary rights in their authority, usually under a suzerain." Moreover, they suggest that "legal and political relationships center around complex systems of 'horizontal' family connections and 'vertical' personal obliga-tions."[44] Power was indeed diffused among the rulers of the warring and bickering provinces at the time of the Conquest. Adams and Smith[45] make note of this state of affairs and the evidence of a graded distribution of settlement size accompanying it. In this manner they imply that the feudal model should fit the Postclassic as well as the Classic Maya situation. They go on[46] to contrast this settlement pattern with that found in the contemporary states of highland Mexico, which had a primate-capital form of settlement pattern.

Unfortunately this line of reasoning does not hold for the better part of the Postclassic era in the Maya lowlands. Only some seventy years before the Spanish Conquest the Mayas of Yucatan were organized into the Mayapán Confederacy.[47] The city of Mayapán was unquestionably a primate capital during some two hundred years of the Late Postclassic period. No known Late Postclassic settlement elsewhere on the peninsula begins to approach its size or density. Prior to Mayapán, the city of Chichén Itzá held a similar primate position in the settlement patterns of the Early Postclassic period. If primate settlement patterns generally reflect state-level and bureaucratic governance, as suggested by Adams and Smith[48] and others,[49] then the Postclassic Mayas must be seriously considered in this light.

Below the Postclassic capital of Mayapán, it is fair to say that the settlement hierarchy approaches a gradient.[50] But does this pattern reflect the diffusion of power, or does it signify the coordination of power through the hierarchy? Adams and Smith[51] suggest that the evident replication of architectural forms involved in governance at descending levels of Classic Maya settlement size registers the simple scaling-down of the same kind of political organization at descending levels of power in a system of vertical personal obligations between chiefs. In the first place, architectural replication of this kind has been used elsewhere to document the existence of bureaucratic state organizations.[52] Second, the organization of public, political facilities varies significantly from level to level in Late Postclassic Maya settlements. Third, such facilities do not focus on or reify the personal power of rulers (as in the courts of feudal Europe) in higher-order Late Postclassic Maya settlements.

At Mayapán, it is clear that the principle of confederate government (*multepal*) overrides material focus on individual rulers (*halach uinicob*). The center at Mayapán[53] does not comprise an imperial residence or court, but rather consists of a set of colonnaded halls (possibly public buildings of constituent provinces)[54] surrounding the shared cult temple of Kukulcán.[55] The most elaborate residences, those that may have housed rulers or their representatives, are scattered throughout the city.[56]

The textual data on the city of Mayapán are relatively abundant by Lowland Maya standards.[57] Nevertheless, it is difficult to get any clear picture of the internal workings of government in the city because the accounts are painted in highly personal terms befitting the noble ancestry of the informants.[58] Although the head of the Cocom family appears to have played the role of suzerain, his powers and superiority seem to have been quite limited and dependent on the good will of his nominal vassals. Indeed, he was called "vax halach uinic," the green or central head-chief, a mere qualifier added to the normal term applied to leaders of other states in the confederacy. In brief, there is no reason to believe that there was ever such an office as king or suzerain at Mayapán: the Cocom's power rested on his personal sources of wealth and labor plus a coalition of supportive leaders from other states within the confederacy. His faction was opposed by one led by the Tutul Xiu, whose family controlled the office of head priest to Kulkulcán (Ah Kin Mai). Despite the vision of personal power politics left to us by the descendants of these families, it seems clear that policy at the top level in Mayapán was created through discussion, dispute, and consensus among halach uinicob who considered themselves equals rather than through divine fiat from a single office. This historical reconstruction is commensurate with the settlement pattern data.

What were the central functions of Mayapán in the confederacy? What kind of policy was enacted at the capital and what were the institutional means for carrying out policy? These are questions for which the texts and the archaeological record supply only potential leads, not answers. Tozzer has observed: "In fact it may have been a kind of District of Columbia."[59] That is, Mayapán seems to have functioned as a "disembedded capital"[60] spatially distant from such major productive resources as fertile land, flint-bearing mountains, or salt beds. The texts[61] give the distinct impression that its prime function was the creation of coordinated policy for member states, that is, the regulation of interstate relations. Archaeological research[62] confirms that the functions were primarily administrative and that there is no evidence of concentrated warehousing or production of goods within the city. The roughly twelve thousand citizens of the capital[63] were evidently supported by tribute,[64] but there is no archaeological evidence of a central facility handling collection and reallocation of such necessities.

If the prime function of Mayapán was the enactment and execution of policy, then it follows logically that the bulk of the population there was involved either directly in administration or in the material support of administrators. As there is no separate cluster of modest dwellings associated with the center, the archaeological evidence would support the notion that most of these people were attached to provincial noble residences as retainers and servants.

But if the provincial states were maintaining both a contingent in the capital and a government in the provinces, then clearly the halach uinicob were required to delegate important official responsibilites to others. There is textual support for the identification of such duties with defined and named offices, with formal bureaucratic organizations. The chief functionary in the capital, and chief liaison between the provincial government and the representative court at Mayapán, is described as follows:

Each one then established in these houses his mayordomo, who bore for his badge of office a short and thick stick, and they called him caluac. He kept account with the towns and with those who ruled them; and to them was sent notice of what was needed in the house of their lord, much as birds, maize, honey, salt, fish, game, cloth and other things.[65]

While the caluac administered in the capital, individual towns of the provinces were administered by batabob, of whom more will be said shortly. The point is that the provincial courts in the capital were not administered directly by the nobles, nor were their activities those of informal family organizations. They had named offices that were replicated in each provincial delegation. The fact that only major bureaucrats are mentioned in the texts should not delude us into thinking that they lacked numerous minor officials to carry out daily business.

Moreover, there must have been institutional means, and associated personnel, cross-cutting and integrating the provincial courts at the capital to allow central policy to emerge and to reinforce its execution. One central bureaucracy was the priesthood. It is clear in the textual data that the priesthood was: 1) hierarchically organized; 2) centralized at Mayapán; 3) influential in provincial government by means of "college"-trained recruits in the courts of batabob; and 4) influential in capital government by way of the head priests and those attached to representative courts in the capital.[66] The central and transcendent nature of religion in politics is materially expressed in the central placement of the temple of Kukulcán in the "government square" at Mayapán.

Although the priesthood may have functioned to coordinate and sanction policy at the "federal" level, there is reason to believe that the government maintained a standing army of foreign mercenaries to enforce it. The *canul*, or "protectors,"[67] were evidently soldiers brought in from Tabasco; and although they figure priminently in the events leading to the downfall of the city as henchmen of the Cocom, their original function was evidently attached to the city government as such.[68] It is certainly rational to see an army of foreign mercenaries acting on behalf of central government, since they would have no inherent loyalties to any particular provincial state.

As to the kinds of policy enacted at Mayapán, this is best deduced from the nature of endemic disputes between the provinces following the city's collapse: conflict over territorial borders, conflict over access to precious resources such as salt beds, and conflict over trade routes and markets.[69] The essential function of government was evidently the settlement of such disputes in an orderly fashion.

Sketchy as our picture of Mayapán's government must remain, the indications are that it was not a king's court but a complicated mosaic of provincial bureaucracies coordinated through central ones. But although it would be misleading to reduce such complexity to the patron-client politics of the feudal model,[70] it would be just as misleading to reduce Maya politics to the machinations of faceless bureaucrats. The leaders of provinces and coalitions no doubt played a critical role, as leaders do in any government, and this role is expressed in the location of official residence in the public domain.

The elite residences scattered throughout Mayapán, for example, are undoubtedly the homes of ruling noble families or their representatives. Many of these architectural groups also contain colonnades of the kind that can be identified as public administrative buildings.[71] These, then, are residential courts of the kind prescribed in the feudal model,[72] but it should be pointed out that such personalized political arenas are in fact characteristic of most complex societies (e.g., the White House) and not just those dominated by patron-client relationships. The personal courts in the public domain must be placed in the larger context of other facilities of government before the structure of power can be elucidated.

The principle of multepal, or confederate government, is materially expressed at second-order Late Postclassic centers, but not in the same fashion nor necessarily to the same extent as at Mayapán. Two such centers are sufficiently well documented to allow qualitative comparison to Mayapán: San Gervasio on the island of Cozumel[73] and Tulum on the east coast.[74] San Gervasio, the Late Postclassic capital of Cozumel, has a disembedded government district at a remove from the traditional residential areas of the community.[75] In this fashion, it parallels the capital of the confederacy. The government district consists of a central public quadrangle housing colonnades and temples. Surrounding this quadrangle in a ritually significant manner are four elite residences: to the north, south, east, and west. All but the western residence complex are materially connected to the center by stone causeways. The ideally quadrupartite organization for the circulation of ritual and political responsibility in Contact-period Maya communities has been discussed by Coe.[76] Here as at Mayapán the spatial separation of the elite residences from the public government plaza suggests confederate government. In contrast to Mayapán, however, San Gervasio materially expresses the idealized and ritually-sanctioned relationship between the constituent sociopolitical factions. That the scaling-down of government facilities should be accompanied by an increasingly formal and structured spatial arrangement makes some sense. In the smaller arena, the interests and actions of individual rulers would not be buffered by bureaucratic organizations of the size and complexity of those in Mayapán. A more formal protocol defined by a clearer statement of multepal in space would mitigate against a dissolution of politics into personal confrontation and encourage political action to focus on the shared public center.

It should be stressed that the elite residences at San Gervasio are definitely "official" homes. This is expressed not only in the spatial relationships between them but also in their internal design.[77] Each elite residence compound contains a highly standardized Mayapán-style tandem dwelling and a Mayapán-style oratory. Three of these buildings are so similar in dimensions and plan that they give the distinct impression that their primary function was to express alliance with the capital of Mayapán (indeed, the local favored dwelling plan is single-roomed). The inhabitants of these dwellings, then, were not just representatives of local constituencies. They were also functionaries in the government of the confederacy. It is this kind of formal replication of facilities at descending levels of settlement hierarchy that might indicate the coordination rather than the diffusion of power.

Several pertinent observations can be gleaned from Contact-period documents concerning the organization of provincial governments. In the first place, Oviedo y Valdés[78] states that there was a halach uinic on Cozumel. Again, as in the case of Mayapán, there is no material expression of a single suzerain in the capital at San Gervasio. Moreover, Roys[79] notes references to several batabob on the island, in some instances two living in the same town with different names and lineages. There are other reasons to suspect that the position of batab (town magistrate, mayor, or provincial governor) was an official one, neither strictly hereditary nor strictly personal vassalage to a halach uinic. A sort of "civil service" exam is described in the famous interrogation of the chiefs in the *Chilam Balam of Chumayel.*[80] This "exam" was evidently designed to establish the noble birth of the batab and to weed out commoner upstarts who had insinuated themselves into this level of officialdom. The text includes a lengthy description of the horrible punishment meted out to such impostors, which suggests that fraud was not exceptional. The existence of the "exam" indicates two things: the position of batab was an official one, with recruitment defined by class or caste rather than personal vassalage, and, like bureaucratic positions the world over, it could be bought. Roys[81] notes that the Cocom family of Mayapán "owned 23 good pueblos," presumably second- and third-order settlements governed by batabob. I have already noted that routine affairs involving the provinces were handled by a caluac, or steward. The number of batabob in this case, and the "exam," reinforce the identification of this term with an office of government rather than with a vague position within a personalized network of power.

The settlement pattern of the fortress of Tulum on the mainland coast south of Cozumel is in stark contrast to that found in San Gervasio. This contrast hints that the range in political organization at the provincial level was no less during the confederacy than after it.[82] Like San Gervasio, Tulum shows clear formal ties with Mayapán, but these are expressed in different ways. Most obviously, Tulum shared with Mayapán an enclosing wall. Within the wall there are a number of "palace" buildings and shrines. These "palaces" are well within the normal range of variation for provincial government facilities at Mayapán, but are quite different from the three Mayapán-style compounds described above for San Gervasio. The "palace" represents a conflation of the three primary facilities of the elite residence compound: the tandem-plan dwelling, the shrine or oratory, and the colonnade.[83] The conflation of evident function for these facilities interjects an unavoidable note of ambiguity into any analysis: has the "home" of the political leader absorbed the more public colonnade, signifying a more clearly personal control, or has the "home" been pushed farther out into the public domain, signifying an increased detachment of office from family?

The fourth elite residence compound at San Gervasio contains a typical Tulum-style palace,[84] and, given the contrast between this formal plan and the others at San Gervasio, this arrangement likely reflects political alliance between Tulum and Cozumel at a level distinct from their alliance with Mayapán. In this case, it can be stated empirically that the "home" absorbed the colonnade;[85] and the direction of change was toward increased power of the leader at the expense of other political figures whose arena was the colonnade. At the same time, the more public nature of the leader's dwelling would diminish the kinship quality of his role and enhance the official quality.

Why all this fuss about "palaces"? Because the community at Tulum is quite clearly dominated by an especially large and elaborate one. Given the formal similarities between this preeminent compound and smaller "palaces" at Tulum and elsewhere, it seems reasonable to me to identify this as the court and official residence of a halach uinic. Here at last is the "king's court" prescribed by the feudal model—not the typical or even most common organization, but a definite factor in the range of Late Postclassic political institutions.

But if Tulum was dominated by a halach uinic, I doubt that the principle of multepal was entirely suppressed. In the first place, the secondary "palaces" rival the primary one in size if not elaborateness. Second, these buildings do not focus spatially on the main "palace" the way that the settlement of Mayapán focuses on the government "square" or the way that the elite residences focus on the public quadrangle at San Gervasio. Instead, the buildings at Tulum are lined up on streets in a rectilinear grid pattern unique in pre-Columbian Yucatan. In brief, formal plan and spatial arrangement suggest that the secondary "palaces" constituted separate and distinct loci for political activity.

Tertiary settlements in the Late Postclassic hierarchy are more numerous than higher-level settlements, but the range of variability in organization is poorly documented outside the east coast of Quintana Roo. On Cozumel, the centers of tertiary sites routinely contain both dwellings and public buildings, replicating in general pattern the provincial governments at Mayapán, but not the capital of the island. This arrangement would seem to bolster the notion of feudal-style patron-client relationships at this lowest level of government.[86] But, ironically, on the mainland—where we might reasonably expect such a pattern, given the organization of Tulum—the documented tertiary centers show no such intimate spatial association with the homes of rulers. Instead, they take on the appearance of shrine groups,[87] clusters of small masonry temples and pyramids. No doubt there is much more variability, and colonnades have been reported[88] in the context of "temple assemblages" typical at Mayapán.[89] In brief, the elite-residence administrative center as found on Cozumel has yet to be reported on the mainland. Was the better part of the coast ruled out of Tulum, with no local homes for the leaders? If so, political organization on the coast and on Cozumel were fundamentally different.

One final point on the nature of political relationships as such: textual data indicate that they were constrained by formal law in addition to personal influence and sanction. At the highest level, it was seemingly a violation of confederacy law by the ruling Cocom family that precipitated the revolt in the provinces and the revolution in the city that culminated in the sudden abandonment of Mayapán. Conflicting reports surround this tumultuous event, but essentially the Cocom family allegedly attempted to sell people of its villages into slavery in the lucrative markets of the Laguna de los Términos area.[90] The rules relating to bondage are explicitly given by Landa,[91] and these do not include mere residence in a farming village. In the end, the majority of ruling families rallied behind the opposition in Mayapán and overthrew the Cocom. Although central government was strained beyond repair, confederacy law prevailed.

Evidence for law and professional adjudication can be found elsewhere in historical documents. One of the reported functions of the batab was to judge lawsuits in which litigants were represented by officials acting as lawyers.[92] If the case were sufficiently difficult, it would be referred to the halach uinic. Market places in Yucatan[93] had judges in courts to resolve disputes. In short, there is reason to believe that both the confederacy and the states following it were governed in the name of public law, constraining the policy of the most despotic and powerful of rulers.[94] In part, the use made by the Mayas of the Spanish legal system following the conquest may be due to established tradition on the peninsula.

So far, I have tried to point to archaeological and historical evidence that indicates a complex legal and official dimension to power relationships in Late Postclassic Yucatan. It is now time to turn to the economic underpinning of such power. As one of their criteria for the feudal model, Adams and Smith[95] suggest that such systems have "distribution of authority, status and economic wealth . . . based upon the ownership of land regularly cultivated by people other than the owners." The documentary sources do not yield a clear picture of the status of land tenure at the time of the conquest.[96] On the one hand, there are various accounts of communal ownership,[97] but, on the other, Roys cites sources[98] to the effect that the nobility had special prerogatives with regard to land. Noble rulers did own private estates worked by slaves.[99] However, it does not seem likely that these estates constituted their sole means of support, given the lengthy discussions of tribute in historical texts. Free farmers clearly made up the bulk of the population. Undoubtedly such individuals paid tribute to their lords, but I can find no allusions to tribute as rent. Another factor to consider here is the subclass of wealthy commoners that appears to have formed an integral feature of the governmental system in the town council (ah-cuch-cabob).[100] How did these commoners get wealthy if they did not own land or command a large share of its products?

One way to reconcile the statements on ownership by commoners and nobles is to make the Maya distinction between property in land and property by its products. I can envision a system in which land within townships was technically owned by the town government. Given the principle of multepal, it would be most accurate to consider this public rather than private ownership. Such ownership would give governments the right to intervene in disputes over land and reallocate lands as necessary. Such a system would provide a powerful means of political control. At the same time, the products of the land would belong to the farmer working the land.

There are textual data which support this notion of land and property. Firstly, Chi clearly notes that the common farmers were not serfs: "As for these vassals, there were no towns expressly assigned (to them to live in) . . . with others, and they were considered to have license . . . were free to marry and dwell (wherever they wished. The reason for this was that they might) multiply, (that if they restrained them) they could not fail (to decrease in number)."[101] And Landa states: "And the greatest number were cultivators and men who apply themselves to harvesting maize and other grains, which they keep in fine underground places and granaries, so as to be able to sell (their crops) at the proper time."[102] Tozzer cites Oviedo and other sources documenting the fact that markets were used to sell produce as well as other products.

The field wall network on Cozumel seems to fit this kind of scheme.[103] The rectangular pattern covers most of the island, maintaining an orientation to the primary north-south axis of the island and breaking only in areas of rough terrain. There are no noticeable breaks between communities. The grid continues right through communities, with the exception of the capital at San Gervasio. Thus, the network is island-wide and island-oriented. There is nothing to suggest private ownership in this careful definition of the landscape except one phenomenon: directly within communities the wall network becomes distorted. It is possible that the lots immediately around dwellings were considered "improved" lands, falling into that special category of lands (e.g., cacao trees in hollows) that could be owned outright and inherited. Indeed, such distortion as occurs seems to correlate with the sub-division of lots accompanying the building of additional dwellings.

In terms of agricultural land, a hierarchically-organized system of allocation with ultimate ownership in the hands of the island's central government would best account for the observed pattern. It might be technically correct to say that the halah uinic of Cozumel, as the ultimate political authority, owned the island. But given the regularity of the grid it seems unlikely that such ownership entailed the right of alienation and sale. Moreover, given the Maya conception that improvements, including agricultural products, belong to the improver,[104] it does not necessarily follow that the halach uinic owned the products of the land. It does not even follow that he was solely responsible for its allocation.

· Some features of the tribute system provide support for this conception of land tenure. Tribute was apparently paid only to the highest political authority. In the case of a province ruled by a halach uinic, the batabob did not receive tribute but rather had a corn field cultivated for them by their town.[105] In addition, however, "in his capacity of magistrate . . . he received certain gifts from petitioners and litigants according to their capacity to pay."[106] Tribute was evidently a matter of political and perhaps military dominance. For although halach uinicob appear to have exacted light tribute, some towns in the Cupul area that dominated neighboring towns exacted heavy tribute in the form of cacao and beads of red shell and greenstone.[107] There is nothing in this situation to suggest the accumulation of rent by local lords who subsequently paid tribute to suzerains above them.

Where the feudal analogy most clearly fails in the context of Late Postclassic Maya life is in the status of trade: "Trade frequently exists in feudal societies, in large part to support the elite classes with status goods and with highly valued food items, but generally cannot be considered the prime element of economic life, even for the elite."[108]

Contrary to this expectation, there is substantial and comprehensive evidence in both the texts and the archaeological record that trade was an integral and important feature of Late Postclassic Maya economy.[109] High-volume trade in salt, cacao, cotton, and slaves was accompanied by trade in a wide variety of other products among Honduras, the Yucatan, and Mexico. Trade within the peninsula was likewise active and substantial. The importance of such trade in maintaining the area's political structure is attested by the intimate involvement of the nobility in these activities. We know, for example, that the ruler of Acalán, Fulano Paxbolón, considered himself and his ancestors to be primarily traders.[110] The son of the Cocom ruler at Mayapán was on a trading mission when his father was murdered.[111] Indeed, the murder itself must be viewed as the outcome of an ill-fated trading venture. Trade was no mere pastime for the maintenance of social relationships. It was a major activity in which the elite participated and from which it no doubt derived a major part of its income. But trade also penetrated to the lower strata of society as well, for we read of trading guilds and itinerant merchants carrying out their business in established marketplaces.[112]

If, on the one hand, the elite monopolized long- and medium-distance trade in certain critical resources, either commonly produced on the peninsula or commonly desired, and if, on the other, the products of the land and of labor belonged to the producer, then a major source of economic control by the elite over the sustaining populations would have focused on the markets. By supplying their populations with desirable products in the markets, the elite could maintain loyalty without direct recourse to sanction or coercion. At the same time, by controlling supply and demand the elite could reap the bulk of the profit. No doubt this is a simplistic vision of a much more complicated economy. Nevertheless, it seems highly unlikely that the elite would have participated in trade with such enthusiasm if it had not benefited them greatly. The downward penetration of such trade into the lower levels of society is archaeologically demonstrable.

It is noteworthy that such regions as the east coast of Quintana Roo and the Acalán territory where Late Postclassic intensive agriculture is either demonstrable or predictable were also areas heavily involved in commerce. The assumption that local production exceeded subsistence requirements and was siphoned off into trade is not only commonsensical but is overtly discussed in the documentary literature.[113] Adams and Smith[114] consider the identification of intensive agriculture in the Maya lowlands to be a major building block in the feudal model; but in the late Postclassic period it seemingly points not to autarchy or a manorial political-economic system but to expanding commercial enterprise.[115]

Conclusions

The recognition of intensive agriculture in the Maya lowlands requires fundamental reformulation of our understanding of pre-Columbian political economics in this area. This conceptual revolution has implications for our understanding of post-Conquest acculturation as well, for there is good reason to believe that the Mayas were still practicing intensive agriculture at the time of Contact. These are problems that would greatly benefit from a joint historical and archaeological approach.

Clearly, man-land relationships will be a central factor in future models of Maya political economics. The feudal model provides a usefully simplistic ideal, a sort of qualitative null hypothesis against which we can measure actual complexity in the past as we currently understand it. When the feudal model is compared to Late Postclassic and Contact-period information, certain important deviations from the ideal become apparent. First, although personalized power relationships were undeniably important, they were embedded in impersonal institutional structures. Second, the economic ramifications of land as property among the Mayas deviated from the feudal ideal in the form of a significant distinction between ownership of the means of production and ownership of products. Finally, there is clear evidence that the Maya economy was vertically and horizontally integrated through complex distribution systems. The prime institutions in this economy were the marketplace and the pilgrimage-fair.[116] Political control of the mode of distribution was also an important feature of government and elite power.

The extent to which these deviations hold for the Maya Classic and Preclassic periods must be investigated in light of the archaeological record for these periods and of conceptions of continuity and disjunction between the Classic and Postclassic periods. I have suggested that intensive agriculture provides one continuous condition; Leventhal[117] has recently discussed continuity in domestic religious practices. Disjunction, however, is an undeniable feature of the Classic-Postclassic transition, and the utility of the ideal feudal model in dealing with the Classic Maya must be resolved in light of future research and analysis.

I suspect, however, that on-going consideration will yield deviations of similar magnitude if not of the same kind. The material evidence of trade in the Classic and Preclassic periods is as strong as, if not stronger than, that found in Late Postclassic contexts. There is also a clear absence of centralized and edified storage facilities of the sort that should be found in a manorial system or autarchy. The distribution of raw materials and finished products cannot be ignored in light of the archaeological evidence of its importance. The pursuit of realistic models of Classic and Preclassic Maya political economy should be guided toward an understanding of the interplay of production and distribution systems.

Notes

1. J. E. S. Thompson, *The Rise and Fall of Maya Civilization*, (Norman, Oklahoma, 1966), R. L. Roys, *The Indian Background of Colonial Yucatan* (Norman, Oklahoma, 1972), and F. Scholes and R. L. Roys, *The Maya Chontal Indians of Acalán-Tixchel*, Carnegie Institution Publication 560 (Washington, D.C., 1948).

2. G. R. Willey, "Mesoamerican Art and Iconography," in *The Iconography of Middle American Sculpture* (New York, 1973), pp. 153–62.

3. A. P. Andrews, "Historical Archaeology in Yucatan: A Preliminary Framework," in *Historical Archaeology* 15, in press.

4. R. L. Roys, *The Political Geography of the Yucatan Maya*, Carnegie Institution Publication 613 (Washington, D.C., 1957), p. 4.

5. O. G. Ricketson and E. B. Ricketson, *Uaxactún, Guatemala, Group E, 1926–1931*, Carnegie Institution Publication 477 (Washington, D.C., 1937), p. 12.

6. W. T. Sanders and B. J. Price, *Mesoamerica: The Evolution of a Civilization* (New York, 1968).

7. A. H. Seimens and D. E. Puleston, "Ridged Fields and Associated Features in Southern Campeche," *American Antiquity* 37 (1972): 228–39.

8. P. D. Harrison and B. L. Turner II, eds., *Pre-Hispanic Maya Agriculture* (Albuquerque, 1978).

9. D. A. Freidel and V. Scarborough, "Subsistence, Trade and the Coastal Maya," in K. V. Flannery, ed., *Maya Subsistence* (New York, 1982).

10. R. E. W. Adams and W. D. Smith, "Feudal Models for Maya Civilization," in

W.Ashmore,*Lowland Maya Settlement Patterns* (Albuquerque, 1981), pp.335–49.

11. E.S.Deevy et al., "Maya Urbanism: Impact on a Tropical Karst Environment," *Science* 206 (1979): 298–306.

12. P. D. Harrison, "The Rise of the Bajos and the Fall of the Maya," in N. Hammond, ed., *Social Process in Maya Prehistory* (New York, 1977) pp.469–508.

13. R. E. W. Adams, W. E. Brown, Jr., and T. Patrick Culbert, "Radar Mapping, Archaeology, and Ancient Maya Land Use," *Science* 213 (1981): 1457–63.

14. B. L. Turner, "Prehistoric Intensive Agriculture in the Mayan Lowlands," *Science* 185 (1974): 118–24; R.E.W.Adams, "Río Bec Archaeology and the Rise of Maya Civilization," in R. E. W. Adams, ed., *The Origins of Maya Civilization* (Albuquerque, 1977), pp. 77–99; J. A. Sabloff and D. A. Freidel, "A Model of a Pre-Columbian Trading Center," in J. A. Sabloff and C. C. Lamberg-Karlovsky, eds., *Ancient Civilization and Trade* (Albuquerque, 1975), pp. 369–408.

15. Scholes and Roys, *Maya Chontal,* map 3.

16. Seimens and Puleston, "Ridged Fields."

17. J. A. Sabloff et al. "Trade and Power in Postclassic Yucatan: Initial Observations," in N. Hammond, ed., *Mesoamerican Archaeology: New Approaches* (London, 1974), pp.397–416; Sabloff and Freidel, "A Model of a Pre-Columbian Trading Center"; D. A. Feidel, "Late Postclassic Settlement Patterns on Cozumel Island," Ph.D. dissertation (Harvard, 1976).

18. D.T.Vlchek et al., "Contemporary Farming and Ancient Maya Settlements," in P. D. Harrison and B. L. Turner, eds., *Pre-Hispanic Maya Agriculture,* pp. 185–223.

19. L. B. Simpson, trans. and ed., *Cortés: The Life of the Conqueror* (Berkeley, 1966), p. 46.

20. A. R. Pagden, trans. and ed., *Hernan Cortés: Letters from Mexico* (New York, 1971), pp. 356, 362, 374.

21. Simpson, *Cortés,* p. 46.

22. R. Wauchope, *Modern Maya Houses,* Carnegie Institution Publication 502 (Washington, D.C., 1938).

23. H.R.Wagner, trans. and ed., *The Discovery of New Spain in 1518 by Juan de Grijalva* (Pasadena, California, 1942).

24. Freidel, "Late Postclassic Settlement Patterns."

25. N.Helmuth, "Cholti-Lacandón (Chiapas) and Petén-Ytzá Agriculture," in N. Hammond, ed., *Social Process.*

26. A. L. Smith, "Residential and Associated Structures at Mayapán," in H. E. D. Pollock, R. L. Roys, and T. Proskouriakoff, eds., *Mayapán, Yucatan, Mexico,* Carnegie Institution Publication 619 (Washington, D.C., 1962), p. 208.

27. Helmuth, "Cholti-Lacandón."

28. Helmuth, "Cholti-Lacandón," pp. 436, 444.

29. Scholes and Roys, *Maya Chontal.*

30. G. D. Jones, "Agriculture and Trade in the Colonial Period Central Maya Lowlands," in K. V. Flannery, ed., *Maya Subsistence* (New York, 1982).

31. Scholes and Roys, *Maya Chontal*, p. 170.

32. W. T. Sanders, "Cultural Ecology of the Maya Lowlands," part 2, *Estudios de Cultura Maya* 3 (1963): 203–41.

33. A. P. Andrews, personal communication, 1980.

34. Turner, "Prehistoric Intensive Agriculture"; Adams, "Río Bec Archaeology"; P. Harrison, "Rise of the Bajos," in N. Hammond, ed., *Social Process;* Harrison and Turner, eds., *Pre-Hispanic Maya Agriculture.*

35. Adams and Smith, "Feudal Models"; R. M. Leventhal, "Household Groups and Classic Maya Religion," in E. Z. Vogt and R. M. Leventhal, eds., *Prehistoric Settlement Patterns* (New York, 1980); G. R. Willey, "Towards an Holistic view of Ancient Maya Civilization," *Man* (N.S.) 15:249–66.

36. Adams and Smith, "Feudal Models."

37. W. T. Sanders, "Cultural Ecology of the Lowland Maya," parts 1 and 2, *Estudios de Cultura Maya* 2 and 3 (1962–63).

38. W. L. Rathje, "The Origin and Development of Lowland Classic Maya Civilization," *American Antiquity* 36 (1971): 275–85; W. L. Rathje, "Classic Maya Development and Denouement," in T. Patrick Culbert, *The Classic Maya Collapse* (Albuquerque, 1973), pp. 405–54; D. A. Phillips and W. L. Rathje, "Streets Ahead: Exchanges Values and the Rise of the Classic Maya," in N. Hammond, ed., *Social Process*, pp. 103–12; T. P. Culbert, "Maya Development and Prehistory" in N. Hammond, ed., *Social Process*, pp. 510–30; D. A. Freidel, "Culture Areas and Interaction Spheres," *American Antiquity* 44:1 (1979): 36–56; D. A. Freidel, "Maritime Adaptation and the Rise of Maya," in B. Stark and B. Voorhies, eds., *Prehistoric Coastal Adaptations* (New York, 1978), pp. 239–65.

39. G. R. Willey, "Towards a Holistic View of Ancient Maya Civilization," *Man* 15 (1980): 249–66.

40. Adams and Smith, "Feudal Models," p. 347.

41. Ibid., pp. 336–37.

42. R. Coulborn, ed., *Feudalism in History* (Princeton, 1956).

43. Adams and Smith, "Feudal Models," p. 336.

44. Ibid., p. 337.

45. Ibid., p. 338.

46. Ibid., p. 339.

47. Pollock et al., *Mayapán.*

48. Adams and Smith, "Feudal Models," p. 338.

49. H. T. Wright and G. A. Johnson, "Population, Exchange and Early State Formation," *American Anthropologist* 77 (1975): 267–89; W. H. Isbell and K. J. Schreiber, "Was Hauri a State?", *American Antiquity* 43:3 (1978) 372–89.

50. E. W. Andrews IV, "Archaeology and Prehistory in the Northern Maya Lowlands: An Introduction," in R. Wauchope and G. R. Willey, eds., *Handbook of Middle American Indians*, vol. 2 (Austin, 1965); W. T. Sanders, *Prehistoric Ceramics and Settlement Patterns in Quintana Roo, Mexico*, Carnegie Institution Publication

606, Contribution 60 (Washington, D.C., 1960); Freidel, "Late Postclassic Settlement Patterns."

51. Adams and Smith, "Feudal Models," p. 343.

52. Wright and Johnson, "Population," and Isbell and Schreiber, "Hauri."

53. Pollock et al., *Mayapán*.

54. Roys in *Mayapán*, p. 65.

55. Proskouriakoff in *Mayapán*.

56. Smith in *Mayapán*.

57. Roys in *Mayapán*.

58. Gaspar Antonio Chi in *Mayapán*, p. 48; and possibly Nanchi Cocom in ibid., p. 57.

59. A. M. Tozzer, *Landa's Relación de las Cosas de Yucatan, a Translation*, Papers of the Peabody Museum 18 (Cambridge, Mass., 1941), p. 35.

60. R. E. Blanton, *Monte Albán, Settlement Patterns at the Ancient Zapotec Capital* (New York, 1978).

61. Roys in *Mayapán*.

62. Pollock et al. in *Mayapán*.

63. Smith in *Mayapán*.

64. Tozzer, *Landa*, p. 35.

65. Roys in *Mayapán*, p. 57.

66. Roys in *Mayapán*, pp. 57–58.

67. Roys, *Political Geography*, (1957), pp. 11–12; Tozzer, *Landa*, p. 39.

68. R. L. Roys, *The Book of Chilam Balam of Chumayel* (Norman, Oklahoma, 1967), p. 69.

69. Roys, *Political Geography*; Scholes and Roys, *Maya Chontal*.

70. Adams and Smith, "Feudal Models," p. 337.

71. Smith in *Mayapán*, figure 6.

72. Adams and Smith, "Feudal Models," p. 347.

73. D. A. Gregory, "San Gervasio," in J. A. Sabloff and W. L. Rathje, eds., *Changing Pre-Columbian Commercial Systems: The 1972–1973 Seasons at Cozumel, Mexico*, Monographs of the Peabody Museum No. 3 (Cambridge, 1975), pp. 88–106; Freidel "Late Postclassic Settlement Patterns."

74. S. K. Lothrop, *Tulum: An Archaeological Study of the East Coast of Yucatan*, Carnegie Institution Publication 335 (Washington, D.C., 1924), and Sanders, *Prehistoric Ceramics and Settlement Patterns*.

75. Freidel, "Late Postclassic Settlement Patterns," pp. 324–36.

76. M. Coe, "A Model of Ancient Community Structure in the Maya Lowlands," *Southwestern Journal of Anthropology* 21:2 (1965): 97–114.

77. Gregory, "San Gervasio," figure 15.

78. Roys, *Political Geography*, p. 156.

79. Ibid.

80. Roys, *Chilam Balam*, pp. 88–89 and Appendix E.

81. Roys in *Mayapán*, p. 61.

82. Roys, *Political Geography*, for post-Mayapán diversity.

83. Lothrop, *Tulum*, p. 25.

84. Freidel, "Late Postclassic Settlement Patterns," p. 332.

85. Ibid., p. 331.

86. Sabloff et al., "Trade and Power," p. 406.

87. E. W. Andrews IV, and A. P. Andrews, *A Preliminary Study of the Ruins of Xcaret, Quintana Roo, Mexico*, Middle American Research Institute Publication 40 (New Orleans, 1975).

88. Lothrop, *Tulum*, p. 161.

89. Proskouriakoff in *Mayapán*, p. 91.

90. Roys in *Mayapán*.

91. Tozzer, *Landa*, p. 298.

92. Roys, *Chilam Balam*, p. 190.

93. Roys, *Political Geography*, p. 152.

94. Roys, *Chilam Balam*, p. 191.

95. Adams and Smith, "Feudal Models," p. 336.

96. R. L. Roys, *Indian Background of Colonial Yucatan*, Carnegie Institution Publication 548 (Washington, D.C. 1943), p. 36.

97. Gaspar Antonio Chi in Tozzer, *Landa*.

98. Roys, *Indian Background*, p. 37.

99. Ibid., p. 34.

100. Roys, *Political Geography*, p. 7.

101. Roys in *Mayapán*, p. 65.

102. Tozzer, *Landa*, p. 96.

103. Freidel, "Late Postclassic Settlement Patterns."

104. Roys, *Indian Background*, p. 37.

105. Ibid., pp. 62–63.

106. Ibid., p. 62.

107. Ibid., p. 63.

108. Adams and Smith, "Feudal Models," p. 337.

109. Scholes and Roys, *Chontal Maya*; Roys, *Indian Background*; Roys, *Political Geography*; J. E. S. Thompson, *Maya History and Religion* (Norman, Oklahoma, 1970); Tozzer, *Landa*.

110. Scholes and Roys, *Maya Chontal*, p. 81.

111. Roys in *Mayapán*, p. 59.

112. R. L. Roys, *The Title of Ebtun*, Carnegie Institution Publication 505 (Washington, D.C., 1939).

113. Scholes and Roys, *Maya Chontal*, p. 59.

114. Adams and Smith, "Feudal Models," p. 347.

115. Freidel and Scarborough, "Subsistence, Trade and the Coastal Maya."

116. D. A. Freidel, "The Political Economics of Residential Dispersion," in W. Ashmore, ed., *Lowland Maya Settlement Patterns* (Albuquerque, 1981), pp. 371–82.

117. R. M. Leventhal, "Household Groups and Classic Maya Religion," in Vogt and Leventhal, eds., *Prehistoric Settlement Patterns.*

Grant D. Jones

The Last Maya
Frontiers of
Colonial Yucatan

Throughout the Spanish colonial period the southern portion of the Maya lowlands was well beyond effective, continuous centralized control. Present-day Belize, the Guatemalan Petén, and most of present-day Campeche and Quintana Roo, though in some cases subjected to brief flurries of conquest activity, remained beyond the mainstream of colonial society. These regions constituted a vast frontier hinterland beyond the more densely populated, more fully administered regions of northern Yucatan and eastern Guatemala. It is therefore not surprising that the peoples of this frontier region are poorly known to students of colonial-period Maya society. There has been only one intensive, focused study of a colonial-period Maya group in the southern lowlands,[1] and the few other writings attempt to do little more than to outline the potential for future study.[2]

Nevertheless, one now senses an increasing concern among archaeologists, historians, and ethnohistorians for combining forces in the intensive study of protohistoric- and historic-period society in the Maya frontier zones.[3] Two primary factors, among others, may be responsible for this renewed interest. First, there is an increasing awareness that the dynamics of colonial society in the more fully administered regions—northern Yucatan in particular—were deeply affected by the continued existence of a relatively "free" frontier zone beyond their borders. Second, it is increasingly apparent that the internal dynamics of the frontier zones were far more coherent, structured, and extensive in scale than had been previously imagined. The frontier zone comprised far more than a few scattered pagan settlements beyond the pale of civilization. It was, in fact, a critical element in the total colonial society, a force that played a central role in the affairs of Yucatan from the level of the *ranchería*, or hamlet, to the very seats of colonial government.

This discussion focuses on a limited region of the vast southern "Chan

Maya" frontier.[4] This area, the Belize missions subregion, played a major role, I shall argue, in the survival of independent Maya frontier polities in the neighboring Petén region of Guatemala. This role must be understood, furthermore, in light of both Maya and Spanish postures toward the continued survival of an unconquered frontier. I first review the question of "region" in Belize and adjacent areas, concluding that for future purposes it is most realistic to eschew considerations of indigenous cultural variation and be content, rather, with a region identified in terms of Spanish colonial experience. I then review the history of colonial activity in the Belize missions subregion and attempt to account for the remarkable rise of rebellious activity throughout the region beginning in the 1630s. The archaeological study of historically known settlements is briefly considered. Finally, I draw together the results of this discussion in a summary of our present knowledge about the wider significance of the Belize missions subregion for the colonial-period Maya lowlands as a whole.

The Question of Region

One of the central problems in the study of colonial-period populations is that of regionality. This, of course, is an issue that concerns anthropological study at all levels, whether the methods of study are archaeological, ethnohistorical, or ethnographic. However, the approaches used to identify regions must differ considerably depending on the nature of the data at hand. There is an understandable emphasis in archaeological study to focus on the site as the unit of analysis, given the costs in time and funding of pursuing a broadly-based survey and sample strategy. This is especially the case when the population under consideration is relatively scattered and where the sites are not easily distinguishable on the basis of identified architectural and ceramic features.

Our documentary knowledge of the historical period is based on evidence of social interaction, often involving multi-community units and geographically-dispersed settlements. Ethnohistorical study can therefore offer a delineation of such zones of interaction that could well serve to focus archaeological discovery in a more fruitful manner. Historical research tends by the nature of the data to be regional rather than site-oriented. I believe that this is a special advantage in that it frees our investigations from the bias of locality. Societies, after all, are organized in terms of spatial processes, not as temporal sequences at individual sites.

How, then, may we best attack the problem of regionality in central and northern Belize? Since this is hardly the first attempt to clarify the regional problem, I first consider the views of earlier writers.

The most significant early attempt to delineate the region in question was that of Ralph L. Roys.[5] Roys spent much of his career in mapping the "political geography" of Yucatan at the time of the conquest, concluding that the peninsula had been divided into sixteen "native states" or provinces of varying degrees of political coherency and centralization. All of these except Chanputún were Yucatec-speaking, and their boundaries were to be considered as political rather than ethnic markers. Roys's boundaries have largely withstood the test of time, although it is by no means clear that a single set of criteria may be applied to define the political or cultural identity of each of the sixteen provinces. This is especially clear in the case of the Chetumal province, the southernmost of Roys's regions.

Roys's Chetumal province (map 1), which extends from Lake Bacalar to the south end of the New River Lagoon, appears to be an arbitrary designation. It serves simply to distinguish one area, presumed to be administered by the hierarchy of the conquest-period town of Chetumal, from the better-established Uaymil province extending from Bacalar northward. Actually, however, there is no firm evidence that the vast region south of the mouth of the New River was actually part of a polity that included the town of Chetumal. Our present information concerning the region south of that town is no earlier than 1582, long after the town's abandonment and the colonial conquest of the region in the 1540s. Actually, there is more empirical justification for establishing provinces of Cebach and Chanes in the center of the peninsula than there is for the province of Chetumal; these, however, are omitted by Roys.

More recently the late Sir Eric Thompson contributed a major statement on regionality in the central Maya lowlands, suggesting that the Yucatec-speaking "Petén Maya, the Mopán Maya, the Cehach, the Chinamita, and the Yucatec-speaking Lacandón should be constituted a subgroup, related rather closely to the Yucatec Mayas but attached with considerably looser bonds to the Putún and Chol-speaking groups to their west, south, and southeast."[6] Thompson referred to this vast territory (map 2) as the Chan Maya Region, distinguishing it from the Yucatec region north of a line drawn from Río Bec to Lake Bacalar. His use of empirical evidence makes it clear that he regarded the region as culturally distinguishable throughout the colonial period, even into the Caste War period of the nineteenth century. Further, he took the controversial stance that ancestors of the Chan Mayas, speakers of variants of Yucatec, might well have

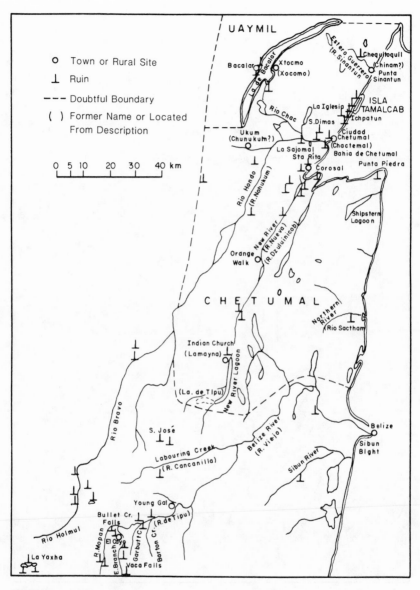

The Province of Chetumal

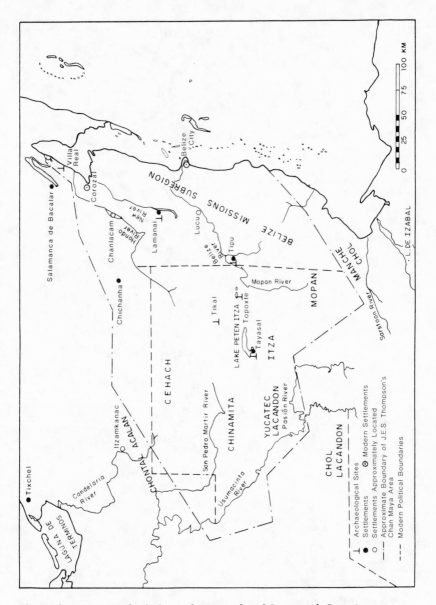

The Southern Maya Lowlands during the Sixteenth and Seventeenth Centuries

occupied the same region during Classic times.[7] Looking to our own area, Thompson suggested that all of the Mayas of central Belize were in colonial times cultural brethren. He dubbed these the Mayas of Tipu, after the important town of that name on the upper Belize River and in recognition of the fact that in colonial times Tipu was a general designation for the central and western Belize region. Though not openly including the New River settlements in the Tipu category, he pointed out that in the seventeenth century they were closely allied with the Belize River settlements. Unlike Roys, he did not relegate any of these settlements to an imagined Chetumal province; he pointed out that the Putún-influenced town of Chetumal probably had control over a local "Chan" peasantry, but suggested no wider political sphere.[8]

At the present time we know nothing about the Belize Mayas south of Chetumal at the time of early Spanish contact; we may never know anything concrete about the region at that time from documentary sources. Roys's efforts to establish a Chetumal province necessarily fails on such grounds. Thompson's Tipu Mayas designation reflects the reality of a later date (1582 and later) for our knowledge of the area, and there is actually a strong basis for assuming that the town of Tipu was in later years a dominant political center as far north as New River Lagoon. The widespread Maya rebellion of the 1630s, extending from Tipu north to Bacalar, indicates an alliance under Tipu influence, although this is clearest for the Belize River valley.

The picture is complicated by the large number of northern Yucatec Maya migrants entering the Belize area throughout the colonial period. The possibility of a pre-Spanish origin for a seventeenth-century political reality is clouded, as in the case of Thompson's Tipu Maya argument, by the strong influence of the southward movement of Mayas from northern Yucatan. Although such migrations may have been a continuation of pre-conquest trends, it is also possible that a political alliance of the seventeenth century represents less a pre-Spanish ethnic reality than a secondary effect of the conquest of northern Yucatan. If the ethnic boundary is pushed as far forward as the nineteenth century, as Thompson[9] attempted to do, all resemblance to the early contact period is probably lost; massive migrations from northern Yucatan during the Caste War completely masked any remnants of the earlier Maya populations of Belize.

Given such empirical difficulties, we might ask, pragmatically, whether after the Spanish conquest this "region" maintained any sort of functional unity with the colonial system at large. Since we cannot at

present know anything of substance about the ethnic or political autonomy of the indigenous population, we can profitably turn to the role of the
region in the wider affairs of the colonial society. It was the colonial
society that in fact created the "necessity" of rebellion, apostasy, alliance,
migration, and even occasional acts of cooperation with church and civil
authorities. Since it is from these acts that we know a little about the
inhabitants, we should allow our regions to reflect historical reality.

That historical reality is clearly rooted in political and economic geography. Central and northern Belize is striking for its river systems, which
form a major drainage system for the eastern Petén and the northern Maya
Mountains. At least during pre-contact times these major river systems—the Belize River, the New River, and the Río Hondo—were almost
certainly of agricultural importance, providing an environment far
superior to that of the Petén and northern Yucatan for the production of
such crops as cacao, cotton, and perhaps even fish.[10] I shall suggest later
that during the colonial period such riverine agricultural activities continued to be important and that cacao produced along these rivers was
destined for a northern Yucatecan market. The rivers, however, in addition to providing an environment for crop production and an avenue for
trade, provided for over a half century an essential arterial system for the
Spanish in their efforts to reach the pagan and refugee Mayas of interior
Belize, and beyond them the Itzás and other inhabitants of the central
Petén lakes. It is not an exaggeration to state that those groups who could
control the waterways both before and after the initial conquest were in a
position to influence all interregional affairs between the central Petén
and northern Yucatan, including questions of interregional exchange and
the ultimate determination of wider political alliances. The anticolonial
rebellion of this region beginning in the 1630s is eloquent testimony to
that fact.

Although a similar argument could be made for the strategic location of
Putún Acalán peoples along the Usumacinta-Candelaria drainage system
to the west of the Petén lakes region, Spanish control over an absolutely
critical portion of that region was exercised forcefully and positively at an
early date.[11] On the other hand, Spanish control over the Belize rivers was
never firmly established: once lost after the mission rebellions of the
1630s, Spanish control over the area was never regained. It was actually
the British who ultimately pressed their logging operations far upstream
in the eighteenth and early nineteenth centuries and thus effectively
destroyed Maya control over the entire region.

The contrast between early Spanish-Maya interaction in the Putún

Acalán and Belize areas is an illustrative one. The Usumacinta and Candelaria rivers were populated from the gulf coast to points far upstream by Chontal-speaking Putún peoples. The important Putún Acalán town of the Itzamkanac was transferred by the Spanish to the Campeche coast during the 1550s. The Putún of this region were not fully pacified until some time later,[12] but by and large the former rulers of Itzamkanac enabled the Spanish to gain effective control over the northern Putún region, actually going so far as to aid in military expeditions against Maya fugitives from northern Yucatan who had settled in the Cehach area.[13] Although a Putún nobility may also have controlled the town of Chetumal at the time of the contact, they would appear to have been a minority of the population of that region, in contrast to their demographic dominance to the west of Thompson's Chan Maya region. After their crushing defeat at the hands of the Pachecos during the 1540s, the area from Chetumal south into Belize was left in the hands of peoples of Yucatec affiliation who, like the Cehach to their northwest, were sympathetic to fugitive migrants from northern Yucatan. In short, the bloody conquest of the Chetumal-Bacalar region left central and northern Belize in control of pagan Mayas who welcomed their northern apostate brethen with open arms, whereas the waterways of the Putún region fell into Spanish hands due to the cooperation of an essentially foreign people.

As long as the Lake Petén Mayas—the Itzás and their neighbors—remained hostile to any threat of Spanish domination (and they did remain so until their conquest in 1697), the Belize Mayas were in an advantageous but shaky position to control military and spiritual access by the Spanish to one of two principal points of entry to the Petén from northern Yucatan. Until the rebellion of the 1630s the Belize Mayas appear to have attempted to balance their relations with the potentially hostile but nevertheless allied Itzás on their west with the allowance of limited missionary activities by a potentially even stronger Spanish presence on their north. The Belize Mayas were thus frontier peoples of the classic sort, balancing the weight of their commitments among stronger peoples on their borders. Their advantage in this game, of course, was the ease with which they could control a system of rivers that prevented the movement of large armies far upstream. Given the remoteness of the central Petén from the mouths of the great rivers on the west of that region, in addition to the absence of a north-south road from Yucatan to the central Petén until the eve of the 1697 Itzá conquest, the Belize Mayas' control over their own river system was in fact a key element in the late date of that conquest of the last independent lowland Maya polity.

Another factor in the weakness of Spanish activity in this area was the dominating influence of refugees from northern Yucatan, who probably began to enter the region in colonial times as early as the 1540s. Although the question of pre-conquest politics in unclear, it is likely that the inhabitants of central and northern Belize, as well as the better-documented central Petén lakes region, had long-standing trade and political relationships with northern Yucatan. The rapid acceptance of large numbers of migrants from the north into this region may suggest the reinforcement of such earlier ties against a new common enemy. Had the region remained cut off from northern contacts, the indigenous people would have been deprived of sources of intelligence and material exchange and of a wider base of support from people with deeper experience in the colonial system. As it was, however, by the early seventeenth century, people of northern Yucatan origin dominated any indigenous population both politically and economically.

The Belize Missions Subregion

This designation emphasizes the colonial reality of this Maya frontier. It reflects the fact that the most effective and widely-imposed Spanish institution in central and northern Belize was the *visita* mission and that in this area there was unity in the Maya response to the wider colonial situation. Although we know that there were many Mayas who did not reside in the missions, it was nevertheless the missions that defined the Spanish presence in the area and thus defined the behavior that the Mayas expressed toward the wider society. In order to understand this process, we must turn to a review of colonial activity in the region and to Maya responses to that activity.

Colonial Activity in the Belize Missions Subregion

Two early events in the central Maya lowlands deeply affected the later history of the Belize missions subregion. The first of these was Hernán Cortés's *entrada* through the Petén by way of Tayasal, the Itzá capital, in 1525. The second was the fifteen years of conquest activity (1531–1545) in the Bacalar-Chetumal region that led to the establishment of Salamanca de Bacalar and the later missionization of the hinterland south of that town.

Cortés's 1525 entrada through Putún, Cehach, Itzá, Mopán, and Manché Chol territory provided the Spanish conquerors with their earliest view of the immensity of territory and vastness and variety of population of the interior Maya lowlands.[14] A close reading of Cortés's itinerary indicates that the political and economic heart of much of this territory was Tayasal itself, located on the present-day island of Flores in Lake Petén[15] and ruled by one of a series of "kings" named Can Ek. The Can Ek of that time controlled a large trade network between the Manché Chol region through Mopán territory all the way north to Lake Petén. Tayasal apparently owned or controlled cacao plantations all the way to the Maya Mountains. It is possible that, to the south, trade in cacao was linked to the Acalán trading outpost at Nito on Lake Izabal. Given Tayasal's control over this economic sphere, it is difficult to imagine that political controls of some form were not also extended through much of this territory.[16]

For the next 172 years the Spanish made a concerted but gradual attempt to weaken Itzá influence throughout the region. From the north, the conquest of Putún Acalán was followed by intensive mission activities in the Cehach area immediately to the north of Itzá territory.[17] From the south, the reduction of Verapaz was followed in the 1570s by missionization activities in the Manché Chol and Mopán regions; these activities continued throughout the next century.[18] Finally, from the north and east, the pacification and missionization of Belize by the late sixteenth century was followed by intense efforts to seek the conversion of the Itzá and their submission to Spanish colonial rule. By the late seventeenth century these efforts had led, however, to only a partial encirclement of the central Petén lakes region, for after 1636 the Belize missions subregion remained relatively independent of Spanish control. The final conquest of the Itzás in 1697 may well have been the final small step in the gradual Spanish destruction of much of the Itzá political and economic control over their formerly vast territory[19]; the Belize missions subregion ultimately drew out this long process as a result of their growing alliance in the seventeenth century with the Itzá polity.

Cortés's 1525 entrada was thus the precipitating event that led to Spanish preoccupation with the conquest of the Petén lakes region through increasing efforts to control that region's adjacent and partially-dependent territories. The direct events that led to the establishment of the Belize missions, however, were closer to home. These events concern the conquest of the Chetumal-Bacalar region, one of the most brutal episodes of the conquest of Yucatan, summarized by Chamberlain.[20]

At the time of Spanish contact, the town of Chetumal was an important agricultural and trading center controlled by a Putún elite from the territory of Acalán.[21] The coastal town was certainly located either near the present-day Corozal town or north of the Río Hondo at the archaeological site known as Villa Real.[22] Chetumal seems to have controlled a relatively narrow area on either side of the Río Hondo and was bounded immediately on the north by the province of Uaymil, with its major town of Bakhalal on Lake Bacalar, and on the south by a poorly known region that later became the Belize missions subregion. It is evident that the Chol-speaking Putún at Chetumal were a ruling minority who had imposed tribute on the indigenous Yucatec population[23] and that the town was a relatively autonomous island in a great sea of Yucatec speakers. Chetumal was first contacted in 1528 by Francisco de Montejo, but it was not until 1531 that Alonso D'Avila made a major attempt to reduce that town and the towns of the neighboring Uaymil province. D'Avila found Chetumal deserted, its population having retreated up the coast of Chequitaquil. He found the town of Villa Real at the site of Chetumal but soon discovered that the initially friendly Uaymil towns to the north were in revolt. He and his troops attempted to suppress the widespread rebellion but were eventually forced to retreat to Villa Real and later to abandon the area in ignominious retreat to Honduras.

In 1544, Gaspar Pacheco, with his son Melchor and nephew Alonso, began their infamous final conquest of Uaymil and Chetumal.[24] Gaspar sickened and returned to Merida, leaving Melchor in command. Their methods were those of total destruction. Chamberlain, otherwise sympathetic to most Spanish activities, observed:

This type of opposition [Maya destruction of their own crops as a defensive measure] drove the Spanish captains, Melchor and Alonso Pacheco, to exasperation, and they deliberately resorted to wanton acts of cruelty of a kind of which the Montejos and their other principal captains were seldom, if ever, guilty. Maya, both male and female, were killed in numbers with the garrote, or were thrown into the lakes to drown with weights attached to them. Savage dogs of war, although used not for the first time in Yucatan, tore many defenseless natives to pieces. It is said that the Pachecos cut off the hands, ears, and noses of many Indians.[25]

Gaspar Pacheco then founded in 1544 the town of Salamanca de Bacalar, assigning the towns of the now burned-over territory in encomienda to the twenty citizens of the new town.

The immediately subsequent events in the Bacalar region have not been studied, nor have the already identified documents pertaining to the Pacheco conquest itself been analyzed in detail.[26] Chamberlain noted that war and famine had left the region "to a large degree depopulated" and that many of the survivors retreated to more remote regions, including that of the Itzás in the central Petén.[27] We may be certain, I believe, that among the zones sought for refuge was that of northern and central Belize, which had been spared the wrath of the Pacheco campaign and which was on the fringes of Itzá control.

López de Cogolludo claimed that Salamanca de Bacalar was founded in order to discourage pirate attacks and to put a stop to the flight of Maya fugitives from northern Yucatan to the "Itzá gentiles."[28] However, because the Mayas could pass unnoticed through the forests, the presence of the town, he recognized, had little effect.

In late 1546 all of eastern Yucatan, from the Sotuta-Cupul region in the north to the Bacalar region in the south, broke out in rebellion. The territorial scope of this rebellion suggests some degree of internal organization in the wider Maya community, or at least an effective system of communication throughout the territory. The rebellion could, in fact, have been sparked by the violence and cruelty of the Pacheco conquest. The rebellion in the south was centered at the island fortified town of Chanlacam (Chanlacao), a town that also participated in the 1630s rebellion in the Bacalar-Belize missions area.[29] Roys concluded that Chanlacam must have been on one of the small lagoons between Lake Bacalar and the Río Hondo,[30] but Scholes and Thompson made the intriguing suggestion that the town may have been on Albion Island, above Douglas in the Río Hondo.[31] If their surmise is correct, this location would suggest that the Maya leadership of the Bacalar region retreated southward after the Pacheco conquest. During the rebellion of the 1630s, the center of resistence had moved even further southward to the town or region of Tipu on the upper Belize River.

Chanlacam submitted peacefully in the face of certain defeat by the Spanish, and we find that town among a list of twenty-four secular missions administered by the curato of Bacalar in the year 1582.[32] Also appearing on this list is Lamanai and several other missions known to be in Belize, including Tipu. In that year we are informed that the Bacalar missions were small and barely exposed to the influences of a priest.[33] Of the twenty-two visita pueblos under the cura of Bacalar, nine were quite certainly south of the Río Hondo, in the present territory of Belize. The rest were for the most part along the Ichmul-Bacalar and Chunhuhub-Bacalar roads and on the coast of Chetumal Bay north of the Río Hondo.

The twenty-two visitas comprised a total of about two hundred and fifty tribute-payers, suggesting a total Christian Maya population in 1582 of

some one thousand souls (assuming a factor of 4.0).[34] The average population of the visita settlements would thus have been only about forty-five persons. It is also stated that each of the pueblos had only four to six *vecinos* or household heads,[35] suggesting a conversion factor of vecinos of about nine; this would conform to the large multi-dwelling households reported in later years for the Itzás. By implication, however, we may assume that there were many more Mayas not living at the mission settlements. These visitas were considered remote; their location near large forests encouraged the inhabitants to flee in order to escape tribute and *doctrina*. Once separated from the mission, so the complaint went, they returned to their "rites and idolatries."[36] The new bishop of Yucatan, Gregorio de Montalvo, rejected, however, the usual solution to such problems, i.e., to bring the scattered population into a single central town. This would be difficult, he pointed out, because they would then have to abandon their cacao orchards and because, besides, they would die of "pure sadness, being such unhappy people."[37] He noted, though, that "in the time of their infidelity" the area had been more heavily populated.

The low population of the missions is difficult to interpret. The bishop's observation of significant population decline since the conquest must certainly be correct. However, his view of the situation was complicated by the presence of an unknown body of pagan Mayas in the forests, beyond the missions, by the constant southward trickle of fugitives from the north to remote areas of the province, and probably by a loss of some population to the Itzá region of the central Petén. Thirty-six years later, in 1618, Tipu was estimated to have a hundred vecinos.[38] On the basis of the vecino factor of nine, Tipu itself in 1618 would have had a population of about nine hundred persons. I suspect that this probable rise in population at Tipu was due mainly to increasing migrations from northern Yucatan,[39] as suggested also in the demographic history of Pencuyut, a town near Tekax.[40] It may have been due as well, however, to a gradual movement from the settlements of the outlands to a town of increasing economic and political importance; Tipu's experience in population growth may not have been duplicated at other mission settlements.

It is interesting to note that census figures for the district of Bacalar from 1609 through the eighteenth century remain virtually unchanged at about a thousand inhabitants, despite an average 39.3 percent drop in population in Yucatan as a whole between 1639 and 1736.[41] One can only assume that the constant figure of approximately a thousand was convenient guesswork in a territory whose actual population was totally unknown. It is a virtual certainty that the actual 1582 population was much in excess of a thousand and that by the mid-seventeenth century it had grown very considerably. The seventeenth-century drop in population elsewhere in northern Yucatan must be partly explained in terms of migration; the Belize missions subregion was surely the recipient of a large portion of those migrants.

The Belize missions do not enter even a faint limelight until 1618, when the Franciscans Bartolomé de Fuensalida and Juan de Orbita journeyed to Tipu via Bacalar and the New River missions with the intention of evangelizing the Itzás on Lake Petén. Scholes and Thompson discussed this journey in some detail, including their effort to locate the Maya missions and other settlements they passed along the way.[42] I shall refer the reader to the details of this discussion and summarize only certain aspects of their entrada.[43]

The padres, leaving Bacalar, traveled down the Río Hondo, skirted the shores of Corozal Bay, and entered the New River or Dzuluinicob. They saw three towns along the river before reaching New River Lagoon, where they found Lamanai. From the south end of the lagoon they traveled across Ramgoat Creek and Pine Ridge to Labouring Creek, then called the Cancanilla. Eventually they arrived overland at the Belize River, at a point that I calculate to be near the modern settlement of Ontario, some twelve leagues from the south end of New River Lagoon (further upstream from the site selected by Scholes and Thompson).[44] At that point they found the non-mission settlement of Lucu, still twelve leagues downstream from Tipu. In three hard days of upstream travel on that river they arrived at Tipu, now known to be at the location of Negroman on the eastern or Macal branch of the Belize River (see below).

In 1618 Tipu, the last Christian settlement before the territory of the Itzás, was a cosmopolitan town with its own frontier colonial history. Its population, as suggested above, may have been about nine hundred souls. It possessed a church and priest's quarters, both adjacent to the house of one of the town's principal women, Isabel Pech. This woman's husband, Luis Mazún, had been executed some time earlier because he had been found practicing idolatry.[45] Another of the town's leading inhabitants, Francisco Cumux, was "the descendant of a lord of the island of Cozumel, he who received D. Fernando Cortéz when he passed on his way to the conquest of New Spain. And the account says that he demonstrated clearly his nobility and good blood in the courtesy and affability with which he treated the religious, even though he was an Indian."[46] Whether

Cumux had moved to Tipu from Cozumel, or was born at Tipu itself, is not clarified. In either case a strong suggestion of preexisting relations between those two regions may be drawn. A third individual, the *maestro de capilla* (choirmaster), had fled to the region from Hecelchakan, a town between Mérida and Campeche. Although he was supposed to have escaped to Tipu because of charges of idolatry, he had become an economic success at his new home: "he was a great worker and was very rich with many fine cacao orchards, he alone by his hand had planted 8,000 cacao trees."[47]

Tipu's ties with northern Yucatan were thus well established. Tipuans were responsible for the payment of tribute, dutifully collected on the spot by the Bacalar *alcalde* who accompanied the priests.[48] This act, noted Scholes and Thompson, was "doubtless something which did not contribute to the joy of the Tipu Maya at being reincorporated in the Spanish polity."[49]

Fuensalida and Orbita's visit to Tayasal, the Itzá capital, was marred by Orbita's impetuous destruction of an Itzá idol. A few days later they left, chased in canoes by angry armed Itzás who warned them never to come again."[50] Fuensalida later returned to Mérida, leaving Orbita to tend the flock at Tipu. On his return to Tipu in 1619 Fuensalida learned that Orbita had been suffering a less than enthusiastic reception. They shortly discovered widespread "idolatry" in the community, involving most of the inhabitants. Isabel Pech, the late cacique's widow, was found with quantities of idols and the garments of Maya priests in a hiding-place adjoining her house. Even after being whipped by the priests she insisted that they had been left there by her husband and that they came from the Itzás. Further investigation turned up "a great multitude of idols, so many that the padre Fuensalida says that they cannot be counted."[51] These, I believe, may also have come from the Itzás. The idols were broken and thrown into the river. When the secular priest from Bacalar arrived with the alcalde of that town, more serious punishment followed, with stern warnings that punishment by death would befall future offenders.

Later that year Fuensalida and Orbita visited Can Ek at Tayasal again. This time their welcome was short-lived, and they were forced to leave, barely escaping with their lives. When they left Tipu, Fuensalida later wrote, the people of that town only feigned their desire that the priests should later return; he presumed that they actually hoped to be left alone "to live as they wished."[52]

Three years later, in 1623, Fr. Diego Delgado slipped away from a military party headed for Tayasal from the north, under Francisco de

Mirones, in the hope of forestalling an armed invasion of Tayasal. He reached Tipu and was provided with eighty men to accompany his small party to Tayasal, where he hoped to treat peacefully with the Itzás. Received hospitably at first, the visitors, Spaniards and Tipuans alike, were captured and killed, their hearts offered as a sacrifice to the religious improprieties committed by Fuensalida and Orbita.[53] Mirones and his entire force were in turn massacred at Sacalúm (perhaps near Chichanha to the north) on Candlemas Day, 1624.

The activities of Fuensalida and Orbita at Tayasal, the harsh treatment of the "idolaters" at Tipu, and the murder of the Tipuans with Delgado at Tayasal were major initiatory factors that led to sentiments of dissent throughout the Belize missions. In about 1636 an uprising broke out among the Mayas of Bacalar "and all its jurisdiction." Both the native population and those who had fled to the area from northern Yucatan began to desert their towns, moving south toward the "forests of Tipu . . . which are the closest to the Itzá gentiles."[54] By 1639, López de Cogolludo wrote, "they denied all obedience to God and king, and apostasizing miserably from our holy Catholic faith, they returned to the vomit of the idolatries and abominations of their forebears, abusing the images and burning the temples consecrated to the Divine Majesty; and later [burning] their towns, they fled to the hidden forests."[55] The effect of this uprising was to seal off the Belize missions from even the relatively slack Spanish control to which they had previously been subjected. Fuensalida and other Franciscans were later commissioned to attempt to reconvert the region, and in 1641 they traveled up the New River toward their dstination of Tipu. Stopping first at Lamanai, they found the houses and church burned; the Indians, allied and confederated with those of Tipu, had moved from the other part of the lake to the region to the north. Those from Tipu had placed spies among these so that they might be advised if they saw Spaniards pass by, or people sent against them by the governor or by those of Belize.[56] I doubt that the Spanish had good evidence for a conspiracy theory of such proportions, although it is likely that Tipu was in fact the center of the rebellious leadership. The Franciscans were not allowed to reach Tipu, which was reported to be the headquarters of this rebellion. At Hubelna, somewhere along the Belize (Tipu) River, they barely escaped with their lives to Bacalar.[57] It is interesting that on this occasion they were still blamed for Orbita's destruction of the Itzá idol Tzimin-Chac; in fact, it was said that some Itzás were among the group of attackers at Hubelna.

Although any reconstruction of the internal political events that might have led to the 1630s rebellion and the expulsion of the Franciscans in 1641 must involve a degree of speculation, a picture of the probable scenario is beginning to emerge. It will be recalled that the leaders of Tipu had cooperated with efforts by Fuensalida and Orbita in 1618–19 and by Delgado in 1633 to visit the Itzás. The massacre of some eighty Tipuans at Tayasal in the latter entrada certainly conveyed a clear message from Can Ek to the people of Tipu. The presence of idols reputed to be from the Itzá at Tipu in 1619 would suggest an earlier pattern of anti-Spanish encouragement from Tayasal. The 1641 presence of Itzás at Hubelna, centrally located in the Belize mission subregion, five years after the outbreak of widespread rebellion would seem to provide even further support for the central role of the Itzá polity in that uprising. Although in 1618 relations between Tayasal and Tipu seem to have been peaceful, there is no evidence that there was a formal alliance at that date between the two centers. The dominating presence of the Franciscans and secular authorities in the region, however, appears to have been the stimulus that led to the forging of such an alliance. I suspect that the actual political leadership of Tipu was replaced soon after 1623 by individuals more sympathetic to a long-term commitment to the independence of Tayasal and to an anti-Spanish policy throughout the Belize mission subregion. Such a commitment was probably the inspiration of the 1630s rebellion and of the continuing hostility of the region thereafter. In 1695–96, on the eve of the conquest of Tayasal, relations between Tayasal and Tipu were intimate: even the noble families of the two centers were intermarried.[58]

I believe, therefore, that the 1630s rebellion represented strong Itzá influence, both political and religious, in the Belize missions subregion. If this conclusion is correct, it would explain why the final Itzá conquest was pursued directly south from Mérida along a new road built to Lake Petén, rather than through the Belize missions subregion, which had earlier been the principal route to the Itzás. To have taken the latter route after 1636 would have been to add another twenty-five leagues or so through hostile Itzá-allied territory (much of it in the former Belize missions subregion), whereas the new road led through previously pacified Cahach area directly to the western end of Lake Petén. In short, in accepting a degree of Itzá domination over their lives and territory, the Mayas of the Belize missions subregion ensured their isolation from Spanish military, economic, and spiritual control.

The Belize missions region apparently continued to be isolated from direct colonial intervention until 1654, when one Captain Francisco Pérez made the first of four journeys into the area in order to quell signs of resurgent Maya hostility near Bacalar.[59] During late 1653 or early 1654 Mayas not far south of Bacalar had burned and abandoned their villages, apparently fleeing toward the general area of Tipu. On his third journey in 1655 Pérez reached as far as the settlement of Chunukúm on the Belize River, downstream from Tipu, Lucu, and Zaczuuz, the chief towns of the Tipu region. At Chunukúm he summoned the inhabitants of the other towns and prepared a listing of the 442 individuals who were congregated at the town.[60] Pérez never ventured further upstream toward Tipu but was content with the Mayas' promise that they would build a church at Chunukúm before his next visit. Scholes and Thompson interpret this superficially friendly gesture to indicate that the inhabitants of Tipu actually thus hoped "to keep priest and government official from poking around Tipu, where some highly unchristian practices might have come to light."[61]

Among the names appearing on the Tipu list are those of thirty *indios del monte,* or unpacified Indians. Clearly a non-Yucatan group, their names have several unusual characteristics: "all are double-barreled names; all lack baptismal names; nearly all names of women carry the female prefix *ix,* and one of the four names of the men has the masculine prefix *ah;* finally, and most important of all, half of the group has a Maya day name which, in every case, precedes the other name."[62] Scholes and Thompson consider that the heathen indios del monte may have belonged to a people known as Muzul, who may have occupied a stretch of country between the middle Belize valley to the Sittee River. In fact, they suggest,

perhaps it is not too implausible to see Tipu and the other villages of the upper Belize valley as having been part of the Muzul group before their culture was disrupted first by Spanish crown and church and later by Maya refugees from the north. Conceivably, the parents or grandparents of the indios del monte were, indeed, born near Tipu but, resisting settlement in the town, had fled further into the forest.[63]

If this were actually the case—and we are not in a position to confirm on the basis of present data—we would have excellent indication of the complexity of Maya ethnic identity in the Belize missions subregion during the colonial period. By the early seventeenth century it is possible that Yucatecan migrants had effectively taken over the region politically, economically, and demographically. Having also moved in large numbers into the central Petén, they may have affected the political organization of that district as well. For these reasons it must be emphasized once again that the colonial-period populations of these regions must be understood as elements in the larger colonial setting, not simply as survivals of a pre-contact situation.

Subsequent known information pertaining to the Belize missions subregion is limited to the period during which Martín de Ursua y Arismendi's conquest of the Lake Petén region was carried out. Tipu is the only Belize town mentioned during this period. The Tipu towns were visited in 1695 by the alcalde of Bacalar, who took twenty newly-baptized Tipuans with him to Mérida to offer obedience to the governor. Can Ek meanwhile sent an independent delegation of Lake Petén Mayas to Mérida to discuss possible terms of submission.[64] It is during this period of obvious cooperative spirit between Tayasal and Tipu that we learn that the families of nobility among the Itzás and the Tipuans were in alliance through marriage ties.[65] These ties were strained during the period of the conquest, and those Mayas associated with Tipu were generally more cooperative with the Spanish than were those associated with Tayasal. References to Tipu during and immediately after the 1697 conquest are infrequent.[66]

Tipu and the other Belize missions subregion settlements faded into obscurity during the eighteenth century, a period that remains poorly known.[67] However, early in the nineteenth century there is a substantial record of attacks by interior Maya groups against British logging operations along the interior rivers.[68] It is reasonable to assume that these early nineteenth-century Mayas were partially descended from earlier inhabitants of the region.

The Location of Settlements

Lamanai was the first Belize visita mission to be archaeologically identified. López de Cogolludo made it clear that Lamanai was on New River Lagoon; no other mission site appears to have been located on that lake, although non-visita settlements were found on its shores.[69] The presence of a ruined Spanish church on the site and an adjacent Christian burying ground has fully confirmed the discovery of the Lamanai Mission.[70] However, the actual mission-period community of Lamanai remains to be fully identified.

Following Scholes and Thompson's hypothesis that Tipu was located in the Negroman-Macaw Bank area along the Macal River (eastern branch of the Belize River), Robert R. Kautz and I initiated excavations at Negroman during the summer of 1980. A Postclassic site had been identified at

Negroman in 1978, and the 1980 and 1981 excavations (including a chapel and associated Christian burials) produced evidence that confirm that the site is actually the ruins of Tipu. The results of these and successive seasons will be published elsewhere.[71] Should the identification prove to be correct, the site will provide a rare opportunity to examine at a nearly undisturbed site the effect of colonial transformations on a lowland Maya town of prehispanic origins.

The location of other colonial-period sites in Belize has barely progressed past the map-plotting stage. Scholes and Thompson[72] and Thompson[73] reviewed the known historical sources carefully and produced a map with tentative locations for eleven colonial-period sites (including six visitas—Chinam, Uatibal, Mayapán, Holpatín, Chanlacúm, Chetumal—and "certain" locations for three other sites, including the visita site of Lamanai.[74] The two other "location certain" sites, Holzuuz and Colmotz, though certainly known to have been located on the south end of the New River Lagoon,[75] have not been identified archaeologically. Given the relative certainty of their general location, reconaissance of the southern lake shore should certainly be carried out. Neither community was a mission site, and neither was associated with a major preconquest site.

Unfortunately, the evidence for the exact location of other colonial sites in Belize is poor. My own reading of the evidence is in several cases at odds with that of Scholes and Thompson, but until better documentary evidence on site location is discovered, relatively little may be accomplished in the archaeological identification of such settlements.

The identified settlements of the colonial period in Belize are virtually all known to be located along the shores of rivers or on the western and southern shore of New River Lagoon. Whether or not this picture is a result of the limited knowledge of the Spanish, who, traveling only by river, never saw the interior settlements, cannot now be ascertained. I am inclined, however, to conclude that the bulk of the colonial-period Mayas in central and northern Belize did live along the rivers and lake shores, principally for the ease of transportation of people and trade goods. This appears to have been the pattern for much of the Postclassic period in the Petén as well. During the latter half of the nineteenth century Yucatecan migrants in the eastern Petén and in western Belize, mostly refugees from the Caste War, settled almost entirely along the shores of small rivers and creeks.[76]

Our limited information on the rebellious period in the Belize missions subregion—1636 to 1697—suggests that highly-dispersed inter-village alliances under the political leadership of the town of Tipu were well developed. There are also indications that population mobility throughout the area was great, as it had been in northern Yucatan[77] and as it was in the nineteenth century in Belize.[78] However, the significant difference in the case of the Belize missions subregion was a pattern of intensive river valley agriculture that stimulated the more permanent settlement of those valleys and, to a lesser extent, the shores of large lakes. I suspect that colonial-period settlements in the Belize–eastern Petén river valleys— like those of the Classic and Postclassic periods[79]—were strung out along major waterways. Locations were chosen for their suitability for orchard crops, especially cacao, and for their accessibility by canoe transport. Such factors were not important in later years, as the more nearly "solar" pattern of settlement distribution during the late nineteenth century reflected the practice of shifting cultivation as the major agricultural activity and a general avoidance (with only a few exceptions) of locations on major river routes.

The Belize Missions Subregion in Interregional Perspective

One of the weaknesses of Thompson's concept of a contact-period Chan Maya region[80] is the ahistorical perspective that served to define that region. Neither the region as a whole nor the subregions that we can reconstruct from historical documents, such as the Belize missions subregion, should be understood primarily as cultural survivals, for the southern Maya lowlands were markedly affected by a variety of historical processes that had begun some time before contact and that continued in varying forms throughout the colonial period. These processes included the migration of northern Yucatec Mayas to the central Petén at least as early as the mid-fifteenth century; the development of an elite group of these immigrants at the head of a stratified political order in the central lakes region of the Petén; significant depopulation and dislocation of the entire region after Spanish contact due to warfare and disease; the renewed migration of many thousands of Mayas from northern Yucatan to the southern frontier throughout the sixteenth and seventeenth centuries; the establishment of visita missions in many parts of the southern frontier; and the reestablishment of Maya control over the Belize missions between 1636 and 1697, forcing the delay of the final conquest of the central Petén region.[81] Although the Belize missions subregion played a major role in the protracted attempt by the Spanish to control the Chan Maya region, the importance of that role must be understood in terms of the historical transformations of that role taken as a whole.

To the immediate west of the Belize mission subregion were the various groups of the central lakes subregion, dominated by the so-called Itzás at the town of Tayasal on Lake Petén Itzá.[82] At the time of contact the Itzá rulers engaged in exchange, notably in the importation of cacao, with groups at least as far south as the Sarstoon River. It is likely that Petén trade contacts with northern Yucatan, probably in such items as cotton cloth, forest products, and salt, were also well developed.[83] Such northern contacts accompanied and reinforced the intense interregional movement of peoples between the southern Maya lowlands and northern Yucatan during the colonial period, especially through the Belize missions subregion. However, Spanish missionization and reduction activities on the northern (Cehach territory) and southern (Mopán territory) fringes of Itzá control gradually led to the weakening of the pre-contact Itzá exchange system. These activities had the effect of slowly strangling the exchange basis of the Itzá economy, and the death of that economy and the polity that it supported would surely have occurred much earlier had it not been for the cooperation and successful resistance of the Belize missions subregion.

At the time of contact the Putún Acalán of the lower Candelaria River maintained a powerful role in the exchange of goods between northern Yucatan, the Tabasco lowlands, the central Petén, the Chetumal area, and various points as far south as the cacao-producing region of eastern Guatemala.[84] Thompson, in an influential and controversial article, attempted to relate the activities of the contact-period Putún Acalán to evidence for various politically expansionary trading peoples active in the lowlands from Late Classic through Postclassic times.[85] However, Spanish authorities forcibly removed most of the Acalán population from their homeland around Itzamkanac to the coastal area around Tixchel, south of Campeche, beginning in 1571. The most influential of all Maya exchange systems linking the southern and northern Maya lowlands was thus severely weakened, and by the beginning of the seventeenth century only a few relatively wealthy Acalán merchant traders still survived.

The net effect of the combined decline of the trading networks that linked the central lake subregion of the Petén and the Putún Acalán with points as far south as the Bay of Honduras and eastern Guatemala and with northern Yucatan was to stimulate, beginning in the late sixteenth century, the development of entrepreneurial agricultural and trading activities in the Belize missions subregion. The northern Yucatec Mayas who moved to the Tipu area sought more than refuge from persecution and exploitation, as it was apparent by the early seventeenth century that export-level cacao production was already established as an important cash crop. The documentation of this trend is quite explicit.

It is well known that at the time of contact, cacao was grown in the river valleys of eastern Honduras and Guatemala. It was also produced in the Chetumal region,[86] an area at that time under the control of the same Petén traders who carried that crop and other luxury items from points south along the east coast to northern Yucatan and along the western side of the Petén to Tabasco and Campeche. That trade was disrupted by the Spanish conquest, leaving northern Yucatan, where cacao was grown on a smaller scale, without a steady supply of that crop. It would appear, however, that cacao continued to be produced during the late sixteenth century around the south end of Lake Bacalar, possibly along Chac Creek. At that time cacao was purchased by merchants from Mani who carried it overland to Northern Yucatan.[87]

It was noted earlier that in 1582 the bishop of Yucatan despaired of reducing the scattered missions of central and northern Belize because of the inhabitants' resistance to abandoning their cacao orchards.[88] In later years we find that the crop continued to dominate the riverine settlements of the Belize missions subregion. At Lucu on the Belize River, Fuensalida and Orbita found in 1618 "much achiote, which is the best that is known in all New Spain; very good fat cacao that produces a deep color and is by itself a good flavor; vanillas that they call *cizbiques*, very good and fragrant for chocolate [beverage]."[89]

Once settled in Tipu, Fuensalida and Orbita were offered "much kindness and charity," being provided "for their sustenance even more than necessary, for as they raised much cacao they were rich and wealthy."[90] As mentioned earlier, they learned that the maestro de capilla who had moved to Tipu from Hecelchakan, north of Campeche, was a wealthy man as a result of having planted an extensive cacao orchard. Food crops were also grown at Tipu, as the priests learned when the more than twenty "indios principales" (native nobles) who accompanied them on their first abortive journey to Lake Petén refused to continue the trip before returning home to harvest their crops.[91]

In 1641, when Fuensalida and his party attempted to recontact the then rebellious leaders of Tipu, they found a cacao orchard at Chantome on the Belize River. Further upstream at Zaczuuz they camped in a cacao orchard belonging to the cacique of that settlement. There they were visited by emissaries from Tipu who "brought a little cacao and vanillas, and some tablets of chocolate, as they were accustomed to bring some small gift when they came to visit a person whom they knew should be respected."[92]

From these examples we may reasonably conclude that cacao, and perhaps other specialized crops such as vanilla and possibly achiote, were grown throughout the Belize valley during the seventeenth century. Since cacao grew well in the Chetumal-Bacalar region, it may be supposed that it was also produced by the settlements on New River Lagoon, on the New River, and on the Río Hondo. It is most likely that the producers of cacao were migrants from northern Yucatan, who by the early seventeenth century probably well outnumbered the indigenous population. If the Hecelchakan choirmaster at Tipu was typical, these settlers were entrepreneurs seeking good lands for the production of a crop known to have a secure and ready market in these Yucatan homelands.

On the basis of still inadequate evidence I have suggested elsewhere[93] that Belize cacao was exchanged for iron tools, primarily axes, machetes, and knives, available in northern Yucatan. Such items were in demand in the central Petén as well as in Belize, and the central lakes subregion apparently paid for manufactured items imported through the Belize missions subregion with their own woven cotton cloth. If this model is correct, it provides strong support for the argument that the rapid growth of the Belize missions subregion during the late sixteenth and seventeenth centuries was due primarily to the continuing demand for elite items such as cacao in northern Yucatan and, to a lesser extent, in the central Petén, and for utility items such as manufactured iron tools. However, it must be stressed that economic factors alone were not able to maintain balanced political ties between Belize and the central lakes, for the Tipu area held the dominant values in any economic exchange system. As was argued earlier, the critical long-term factor in the maintenance of such a balance was the buffer role of the Tipu area planter/ merchants between the Itzás and their neighbors on the one hand and the continuing threats of Spanish intrusion on the other.

It is remarkable that this buffer region was not challenged directly by the Spanish following the 1636 rebellion. However, the conquest of the Itzás in 1697 was pursued without regard to the Belize mission subregion, which remained outside Spanish control for the rest of the colonial period. The eventual conquest of the Tipu area was achieved not by the Spanish but by British loggers during the eighteenth and early nineteenth centuries. The Mayas of Tipu gradually faded from sight as they faced alone the little-known conquest of the last British mainland frontier in the Western Hemisphere.

Notes

1. France V. Scholes and Ralph L. Roys, *The Maya Chontal Indians of Acalan-Tixchel: A Contribution to the History and Ethnography of the Yucatan Peninsula* (Washington, D.C., 1948).

2. Nicholas M. Hellmuth, "Progreso y notas sobre la investigación etnohistórica de las tierras bajas mayas de los siglos XVI a XIX," *América Indígena* 32 (1972): 179–244; Grant D. Jones, "Agriculture and Trade in the Colonial Period Southern Maya Lowlands," in Kent V. Flannery, ed., *Maya Subsistence* (New York, 1982); J. Eric S. Thompson, "A Proposal for Constituting a Maya Subgroup, Cultural and Linguistic, in the Peten and Adjacent Regions," in Grant D. Jones, ed., *Anthropology and History in Yucatan* (Austin, 1977), pp. 3–42.

3. Anthony P. Andrews, "Historical Archaeology in Yucatan: A Preliminary Framework," *Historical Archaeology* 15 (1981): 1–18; E. W. Andrews IV and Anthony P. Andrews, *A Preliminary Study of the Ruins of Xcaret, Quintana Roo, Mexico* (New Orleans, 1975); Antonio Benavides C. and Antonio P. Andrews, *Ecab: Poblado y provincia del siglo XVI en Yucatán* (Mexico City, 1979); Grant D. Jones, Don S. Rice, and Prudence M. Rice, "The Location of Tayasal: A Reconsideration in Light of Peten Maya Ethnohistory and Archaeology," *American Antiquity* 46 (1981): 530–47; Arthur G. Miller and Nancy M. Farriss, "Religious Syncretism in Colonial Yucatan: The Archaeological Ethnohistorical Evidence from Tancah, Quintana Roo," in Norman Hammond and Gordon R. Willey, eds., *Maya Archaeology and Ethnohistory* (Austin, 1979).

4. Thomspon, "A Proposal."

5. Ralph L. Roys, *The Political Geography of the Yucatan Maya* (Washington, D.C., 1957). This delineation is also followed by Peter Gerhard in *The Southeast Frontier of New Spain* (Princeton, 1979), pp. 67–69.

6. Thompson, "A Proposal," p. 3.

7. Ibid., p. 39.

8. Ibid., p. 11.

9. Ibid., p. 37.

10. Bruce H. Dahlin, "Cropping Cash in the Protoclassic: A Cultural Impact Statement," in Hammond and Willey, eds., *Maya Archaeology*, pp. 21–37.

11. Scholes and Roys, *The Maya Chontal*.

12. Ibid., p. 173.

13. Ibid., p. 335.

14. Hernán Cortés, *Cartas de relación*, ninth ed. (Mexico City, 1976).

15. Jones, Rice, and Rice, "The Location of Tayasal."

16. Grant D. Jones, "Southern Lowland Maya Political Organization: A Model of

Change from Protohistoric through Colonial Times," *Actes de XLIIIᵉ Congrès International des Américanistes, Congrès de Centenaire, Paris, 2–9 September 1976*, vol. 8 (Paris, 1979), pp. 83–94.

17. Scholes and Roys, *The Maya Chontal.*

18. Juan de Villagutierre Soto-Mayor, *Historia de la conquista de la provincia de el Itzá, reducción y progresos de la de el Lacandón*, vol. 9 (Guatemala, 1933; orig. 1701); Francisco Ximénez, *Historia de la provincia de San Vicente de Chiapa y Guatemala de la Orden de Predicadores* (Guatemala, 1929–31); Ethel-Jane W. Bunting, "From Cahabon to Bacalar in 1677," *Maya Society Quarterly* 1 (1932): 112–19; Arden R. King, *Coban and the Verapaz: History and Cultural Process in Northern Guatemala* (New Orleans, 1974).

19. Jones, "Southern Lowland Maya."

20. Robert S. Chamberlain, *The Conquest and Colonization of Yucatan, 1517–1550* (Washington, D.C., 1948), pp. 100–127, 232–36.

21. Scholes and Roys, *The Maya Chontal*, pp. 83, 321, 385.

22. Alberto Escalona Ramos, "Algunas construcciones de tipo colonial en Quintana Roo," *Anales del Instituto de Investigaciones Estéticas* 3 (1943): 17–40; and Alberto Escalona Ramos, "Algunas ruinas prehispánicas en Quintana Roo," *Boletín de la Sociedad Mexicana de Geografía y Estadística* 61 (1946): 513–628.

23. Scholes and Roys, *The Maya Chontal*, p. 385.

24. Chamberlain, *The Conquest*, pp. 232–36.

25. Ibid., p. 234.

26. Cited in ibid., pp. 231–36.

27. Ibid., p. 236.

28. Diego López de Cogolludo, *Historia de Yucatán* (Madrid, 1957), bk. 4, chap. 16.

29. López de Cogolludo, *Historia de Yucatán*, bk. 5, chap. 3–4; Chamberlain, *The Conquest*, p. 248; France V. Scholes and J. Eric S. Thomspon, "The Francisco Pérez probanza of 1654–1656 and the matrícula of Tipu (Belize)," in Grant D. Jones, ed., *Anthropology and History*, pp. 43–68; Roys, *Political Geography*, p. 162.

30. Roys, *Political Geography*, p. 162.

31. Scholes and Thompson, "Francisco Pérez," p. 47.

32. France V. Scholes et al., eds., *Documentos para la historia de Yucatán*. I. *1550–1561*; II. *La iglesia en Yucatán, 1560–1610*; III. *Discurso sobre la constitucíon de las provincias de Yucatán y Campeche* (Mérida, 1936–38). This information can be found in vol. II, p. 63.

33. Scholes et al., *Documentos*, vol. II, p. 81.

34. See Sherburne F. Cook and Woodrow Borah, "The Population of Yucatan, 1517–1960," in Cook and Borah, eds., *Essays in Population History: Mexico and the Caribbean*, vol. 2 (Berkeley, 1974), pp. 1–170. For this reference, see p. 63.

35. Scholes et al., *Documentos*, vol. II, pp. 81, 117.

36. Ibid., p. 81.

37. Ibid.

38. López de Cogolludo, *Historia de Yucatán*, bk. 9, chap. 6.

39. Nancy M. Farriss, "Nucleation vs. Dispersal: the Dynamics of Population Movement in Colonial Yucatan," *Hispanic American Historical Review* 58 (1978): pp. 187–216.

40. James W. Ryder, "Internal Migration in Yucatan: Interpretation of Historical Demography and Current Patterns," in Grant D. Jones, ed., *Anthropology and History*, pp. 191–321.

41. Cook and Borah, "Population," pp. 110–12.

42. Scholes and Thompson, "Francisco Pérez," pp. 43–49.

43. Reported by López de Cogolludo, *Historia de Yucatán*, bk. 9, chap. 4–13.

44. Scholes and Thompson, "Francisco Pérez," p. 45.

45. López de Cogolludo, *Historia de Yucatán*, bk. 9, chap. 6.

46. Ibid., chap. 7.

47. Ibid., chap. 7.

48. Ibid., chap. 7.

49. Scholes and Thomspon, "Francisco Pérez," pp. 48–49.

50. López de Cogolludo, *Historia de Yucatán*, bk. 9, chaps. 10–11.

51. Ibid., chap. 12.

52. Ibid., chap. 13.

53. Ibid., bk. 10, chaps. 2–3.

54. Ibid., bk. 11, chap. 12.

55. Ibid., chap. 12.

56. Ibid., chap. 13.

57. Ibid., chap. 14.

58. See discussion in Scholes and Thompson, "Francisco Pérez," p. 57.

59. Ibid., pp. 51–56.

60. Ibid., pp. 58–64.

61. Ibid., pp. 55–56.

62. Ibid., p. 65.

63. Ibid., pp. 67–68.

64. Villagutierre Soto-Mayor, *Historia*, bk. 5, chap. 12; bk. 6, chap. 3.

65. Scholes and Thompson, "Francisco Pérez," p. 57.

66. Villagutierre Soto-Mayor, *Historia*, bk. 8, chap. 18.

67. Lawrence H. Feldman has recently reported the existence of extensive eighteenth-century Spanish documentation for Belize in "Belize and Its Neighbors: Spanish Colonial Records of the Audiencia of Guatemala, a Preliminary Report" (unpublished manuscript, 1981, Columbia, Missouri).

68. O. Nigel Bolland, *The Formation of a Colonial Society: Belize, from Conquest to Crown Colony* (Baltimore, 1977), pp. 17–23; O. Nigel Bolland, "The Maya and the Colonization of Belize in the Nineteenth Century," in Jones, ed., *Anthropology and History*, pp. 69–99; Thompson, "A Proposal," pp. 9–10.

69. López de Cogolludo, *Historia de Yucatán*, bk. 9, chap. 6.

70. David M. Pendergast, "The Church in the Jungle; the ROM's First Season at

Lamanai," *Rotunda* 8 (1975): 32–40; David M. Pendergast, "Royal Ontario Museum Excavation: Finds at Lamanai, Belize," *Archaeology* 30 (1977): 139–41; David M. Pendergast, "Lamanai, Belize: Summary of Excavation Results, 1974–1980," *Journal of Field Archaeology* 8 (1981): 29–53.

71. Preliminary reports of this work are found in: Grant D. Jones and Robert R. Kautz, "Archaeology and Ethnohistory on a Spanish Colonial Frontier: The Macal-Tipu Project in Western Belize," XVII Mesa Redonda de la Sociedad Mexicana de Antropología, San Cristóbal de las Casas, Chiapas, 1981; and Jones and Kautz, "Native Elites on the Colonial Frontiers of Yucatan: A Model for Continuing Research," 80th Annual Meeting of the Mexican Anthropological Association, Los Angeles, 1981.

72. Scholes and Thompson, "Francisco Pérez."

73. J. Eric S. Thompson, *The Maya of Belize: Historical Chapters Since Columbus* (Belize [1972]).

74. Scholes and Thomspon, "Francisco Pérez," map 2-1.

75. López de Cogolludo, *Historia de Yucatán*, bk. 11, chap. 3; Scholes and Thompson, "Francisco Pérez," p. 45.

76. Grant D. Jones, "Levels of Settlement Alliance among the San Pedro Maya of Western Belize and Eastern Peten, 1857–1936," in Jones, ed., *Anthropology and History*, pp. 139–89 (see especially pp. 141–43).

77. Farriss, "Nucleation vs. Dispersal."

78. Jones, "Levels of Settlement Alliance."

79. Gordon R. Willey et al., *Prehistoric Maya Settlements in the Belize Valley* (Cambridge, 1965); Dahlin, "Cropping Cash," p. 32.

80. Thompson, "A Proposal."

81. Jones, "Agriculture and Trade."

82. Jones, Rice, and Rice, "The Location of Tayasal."

83. Cortés, *Cartas*, pp. 243–45. On the Maya salt trade, see Anthony P. Andrews, "Salt-Making, Merchants and Markets: The Role of a Critical Resource in the Development of Maya Civilization," (Ph.D. dissertation, University of Mexico, 1980).

84. Scholes and Roys, *The Maya Chontal.*

85. J. Eric S. Thompson, *Maya History and Religion* (Norman, 1970), pp. 3–47.

86. Gonzalo Fernández de Oviedo y Valdez, *Historia general y natural de las Indias*, vol. 4 (Madrid, 1959), bk. 32, chap. 6.

87. Ralph L. Roys, *The Indian Background of Colonial Yucatán* (Washington, D.C., 1943), p. 52; Roys, *Political Geography*, p. 164.

88. Scholes et al., *Documentos*, II, 81.

89. López de Cogolludo, *Historia de Yucatán*, bk. 9, chap. 6.

90. Ibid., chap. 7.

91. Ibid., chap. 8.

92. Ibid., bk. 11, chap. 3.

93. Grant D. Jones, "Agriculture and Trade."

Robert Wasserstrom

Spaniards and Indians in Colonial Chiapas, 1528–1790

Introduction

Among students of Latin America, the undiminished vitality of sizable Indian communities today in areas like highland Chiapas has provoked a lively debate about the relationship between ethnicity and social class. Such communities have failed to become part of class society, it is often said, because they retain those customs and traditions that arose under colonialism, because in some sense they remain encapsulated to this day within the feudal social order. A few experts even claim that Indian customs have themselves become the primary agent of economic and political exploitation in rural areas.[1] According to this view, native people have accepted more or less passively a culture that was foisted on them by Spanish missionaries and administrators, a culture that emphasized ethnic differences at the expense of class solidarity.[2] In contrast to these ideas, contemporary records indicate that such people did not simply resign themselves to the fate that colonial authorities designed for them. Of primary importance, native protests and rebellions, messianic movements and religious heresies occurred in Chiapas with astonishing regularity throughout the centuries before independence. By focusing on these events, then, and particularly on the motives that moved their participants to action, we may formulate a more coherent view of colonial society—a view that also helps us to understand the question of ethnicity among Indians today.

For a variety of reasons, Chiapas would seem to lend itself ideally to such an exercise. First, the central highlands, inhabited at present by nearly 500,000 Tzeltal, Tzotzil, and Chol (Maya) people, have provided much of the anthropological evidence on which modern debates about ethnicity in Latin America are based. For nearly three generations, scholars have celebrated the apparently limitless resilience of native social and religious institutions—institutions that have survived major changes in the country's economic and political structure.[3] Second, almost twenty years have elapsed since historians became interested in the area, particularly in the so-called Tzeltal uprising of 1712.[4] Like its counterpart in Peru, the Túpac Amaru rebellion (1780), this movement eventually included men and women from a wide range of ethnic groups and culminated in the establishment of a native monarchy. And as in Peru almost seventy years later, Spanish repression was so ferocious and violent that even today oral tradition preserves only the faintest and most distorted memory of these events. Despite such similarities, however, and despite the fact that anthropologists have persisted in regarding the highlands as a laboratory for studying pre-conquest Maya culture *in vitro*, virtually no serious historical research has been conducted that might shed some light on the day-to-day existence of Spaniards and Indians in the region. Nor do we possess a clear idea of how the province was governed, how its economy functioned, how native communities were organized and exploited.[5] Isolated from both Guatemala and Mexico City, it has been largely ignored by historians of Central America and New Spain alike.[6] In the rest of this essay, therefore, I shall present some preliminary information on such topics and suggest a few lines of comparison with other areas.

Spanish Settlement in Central Chiapas, 1528–1790

Unlike New Spain, Chiapas did not enter a period of economic depression after 1580, at least not in the usual sense. Sustained at the first by *encomiendas* and regional trade, Spanish settlers in Ciudad Real (who in 1555 numbered about 50) increased to more than 250 by 1620.[7] Unfortunately, the native population did not fare so well: decimated by wave after wave of pestilence, it declined from around 114,400 in 1570 to 74,990 a century later.[8] As a result, Indian towns maintained a bleak and attenuated existence or were abandoned altogether.[9] In Zinacantan, for example, a community that before the conquest had dominated local commerce, only a handful of individuals survived those first decades of colonial rule.[10] Faced with a serious decline in native tribute, most *encomenderos* found themselves increasingly unable to make ends meet.[11] In fact, as the English-born monk Thomas Gage noted, by 1620 such people lived in extremely modest, indeed often penurious circumstances. "It is a common thing among them," he wrote, "to come out to the street-door of their homes to see and be seen, and . . . to say: "Ah, señor; qué linda perdiz he comido hoy!" . . . whereas they pick out of their teeth nothing but a black husk of a dry *frijol.*"[12] In order to bolster their sagging fortunes, then, as early as 1530 enterprising *vecinos* began to produce sugar and cattle on *fincas* in the fertile Grijalva river valley.[13] A few years later, between 1590 and 1600, their descendents received permission from the crown to raise horses, mules, and wheat on land taken from native communities in the altiplano.[14] Even so, according to the *ayuntamiento* of Ciudad Real, such measures failed to stem the tide of Spanish emigration to other provinces. By 1684, they declared, Chiapas had lost over half of its non-Indian inhabitants.[15] And within another fifty years this number had declined to its lowest point since the conquest: of the forty-nine families that remained, only thirty-five resided in the city; the rest eked out a marginal livelihood on their isolated estates.

Like private *hacendados*, religious orders in Chiapas quite early took up cattle raising and sugar planting to counteract the effects of declining native populations and public revenues. Beginning with modest gifts of royal lands (*realengas*) and *tierras baldías*, they soon established sugar plantations in the Grijalva and Ocosingo valleys. Unlike secular landowners, ecclesiastical corporations—convents, monasteries, and other pious works—enjoyed ready access to liquid capital, capital they acquired from private donors and Indian *cofradías*. In this way, for example, the Dominicans, who in 1572 possessed "not one handsbredth of land throughout the province," had sixty years later founded three prosperous sugar mills and a dozen or more cattle ranches.[16] Even so, the church possessed more uncommitted revenues than it could profitably invest in such ventures. Selecting their clients carefully, religious corporations loaned money to the better sort of hacendados and urban vecinos in Chiapa and Ciudad Real. By the end of the colonial period, these institutions had acquired a significant interest in virtually every important agricultural enterprise and property within the province.[17]

Among ecclesiastical landowners, the Dominicans distinguished themselves both for their resourcefulness and their greed. Unlike their *confrères* in Oaxaca, these mendicants preferred to obtain their properties not through private donations, but rather by direct purchase or by royal concessions. As in Oaxaca, however, their early interest in landowning gave them a strategic advantage over later arrivals in the area. By 1620, for example, the convent in Comitán had already established its famous haciendas de la Frailesca, ten profitable cattle ranches in the upper Grijalva valley. A few years later, this monastery founded a sugar mill near

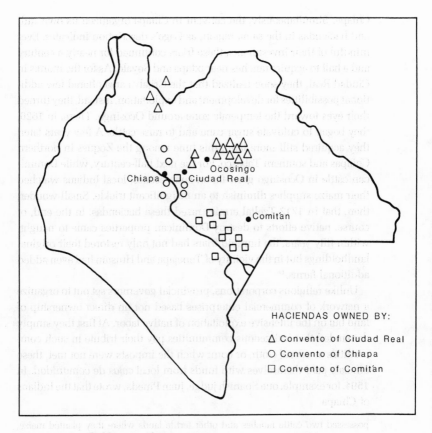

Chiapa Ciudad Real
Ocosingo

Comitán

HACIENDAS OWNED BY:

△ Convento of Ciudad Real
○ Convento of Chiapa
□ Convento of Comitán

Dominican Landholdings in Chiapas, 1778

Chiapa. Simultaneously, the convent in Chiapa organized its own mill and haciendas in the same region, as Gage's description indicates. Ever mindful of their investments, these friars continued for nearly a century and a half to acquire ranches near Ixtapa and Soyaló. As for the monks in Ciudad Real, they soon realized that the Grijalva area offered few additional possibilities for development and exploitation. Instead, they turned their eyes toward the temperate zone around Ocosingo. There, in 1626, they began to cultivate sugar cane and to raise cattle. A few years later, they acquired still more land, this time among the Zoques in northern Chiapas and southern Tabasco. For the next half-century, while Dominican cattle in Ocosingo grew fat on such estates, local Indians watched their maize supplies diminish to an insignificant trickle. Small wonder, then, that in 1712 Tzeltal armies razed these haciendas. In the end, of course, native efforts to destroy Dominican properties came to naught: within fifty years, the intrepid friars had not only restored their original landholdings but in the vicinity of Tenejapa and Huistán had even added additional farms.[18]

Unlike religious corporations, provincial governors set out to organize a network of commercial enterprises based not on direct ownership of land but on the intensive exploitation of native labor. At first they simply demanded that indigenous communities pay their tribute in such commodities as cacao, cloth, or corn; when the imposts were not met, these officials paid themselves with funds from local *cajas de comunidad*. In 1594, for example, one Spanish judge, Juan Pineda, wrote that the Indians of Chiapa

possessed two cattle ranches and other fertile lands where they planted maize, beans, peppers, cotton, and dye plants. In the town reside many artisans, such as carpenters, tailors, blacksmiths, shoemakers, sandalmakers, and other craftsmen. The vecinos of this settlement also manufactured white cotton cloth called *toldillo*, which they used to pay their tribute. The administration of the Sacraments and other religious offices was in the hands of Dominican friars, and these monks also managed the town's caja de comunidad.[19]

But in the following years, income from tribute alone plummeted, from 80,000 pesos annually in 1636 to 11,000 in 1663. Finally, by 1734, the *alcalde mayor* was moved to complain that "one of the main reasons for the reduction in tributaries is the lack of a regular count of the Indians . . . Because diseases like measles, smallpox, and similar contagions are frequent in these villages, it is not uncommon for them to lose many people, and particularly the very young."[20] As a result, he con-

Table 1: Amount Paid for Alcaldía Mayor of Chiapas, 1683–1738

Year	Amount
1683	4,000 pesos (and loan of 200 pesos)
1685	5,000 pesos
1711	6,000 pesos (and 6,000 pesos at end of term)
1722	200 ducados
1738	8,000 pesos

Sources: "Real cédula a favor de Don Martín de Urdáñiz, 1683," López Sánchez, *Apuntes Históricos*, p. 677; "Real cédula a favor de Don Manuel de Maisterra y Atocha, 1685," in ibid., p.679; "Real cédula a favor de Don Pedro Gutiérrez de Mier y Terán, 1711," in ibid., pp.695–96; "Título de alcalde mayor de Chiapa concedido a don Juan Buatista Garracín Ponce de Leon . . . , 1738," in ibid., p. 795.

tinued, in towns such as Huitiupán, Oxchuc, and Huistán those few men and women who survived were required to pay the crown as much as seven pesos a year. And despite their constant petitions for redress and relief, in times of scarcity such people endured not only famine but the undiminished rapacity of provincial officials who sold them corn and beans at inflated prices. Indeed, it was precisely such unequal commerce that precipitated the 1712 rebellion.[21]

Interestingly, after the uprising such arrangements underwent significant modification—though they did not culminate, as Henri Favre has claimed, in a relaxation of Spanish authority.[22] As the native population began to recover, local alcaldes mayores became increasingly jealous of their right to control Indian trade. Faced with the possibility of producing augmented quantities of cacao, cotton, cochineal, and other products, they readily paid the crown higher fees for the right to hold office in Chiapas. Consider the letter Bishop Jacinto de Olivera y Pardo wrote in 1716 to the king. "Your Grace has asked me to report on the corn, beans and chile which the Indians of this province pay in tribute," he began,

and which the alcaldes mayores purchase by means of third parties at prices that prevailed four or six years ago. . . . I understand that for many years now in the month of February a public auction is held in which corn and other products paid by the Indians are offered to the highest bidder, and that these products are bought by third parties for the alcalde mayor without competition . . . because the vecinos are reluctant to arouse his ire. . . . [23]

So single-mindedly did such officials pursue their own enrichment, in fact, that they even insisted on supplying meat to the public market in Ciudad Real—an office the local *cabildo* had previously auctioned off among its own members. Naturally, Spanish vecinos protested against such measures—first to provincial authorities, later to the *audiencia* itself. By way of response, Gabriel de Laguna, who became alcalde mayor in 1732, refused to certify the election of municipal counselors and thereby in effect suspended the city's *ayuntamiento*.[24] Freed from the interference of this body, Laguna and his successors proceeded to amass considerable fortunes, which included money embezzled directly from the royal treasury or municipal funds.[25] And until 1781, despite repeated instructions to the contrary, they refused to reconvene the city council.[26]

Let us now consider in more detail how these alcaldes mayores managed their affairs. Having overcome organized resistance to their authority, provincial governors nonetheless selected their deputies from among the better class of local vecinos, that is, from among those men who possessed the experience and skill to administer complex *repartimientos*. In so doing, they neatly divided the area's hacendados and merchants into two hostile factions: on the one hand, a few prominent merchants abandoned independent enterprise and shared in the spoils of royal office; on the other, the majority of traders and landowners found themselves compelled to fill minor roles as suppliers and agents. In 1760, for example, one governor, Joaquín Fernández Prieto, named an important vecino, Pedro Tomás de Murga, to the post of deputy. A few years earlier, Murga—who held the rank of colonel in the provincial militia and had served as senior counselor in the cabildo—had been active in the fight against Laguna and his successor, Juan Bautista Garracín.[27] Now, however, he dutifully took up the task of administering Prieto's far-flung enterprises; indeed, in 1767, when Prieto was subjected to a judicial inquiry, Murga filed a financial statement (largely perjured) in which he attempted to exonerate his former patron of any wrongdoing.[28] Ironically, it is from this document that we may gain a valuable, albeit incomplete, idea of how the repartimiento system functioned at mid-century.

Rather than correct such abuses, however, royal authorities in Guatemala, anxious to enhance public revenues (and to enrich themselves in the bargain), chose instead to turn a blind eye or even to encourage them. In 1768, for example, they divided central Chiapas into two separate

Table 2: Profits Earned by the Alcalde Mayor
of Ciudad Real on Repartimientos, 1760–1765

Activity	Profit (in pesos)
Spinning 500,000 lbs. of raw cotton into 100,000 lbs. of thread (in central Tzotzil and Tzeltal region)	27,500
Forced production of 100,000 lbs. of cochineal (Zoque region)	16,000
Forced production of 150,000 lbs. of cacao (Zoque region)	10,000
Forced production of 12,000 bunches of tobacco (northern Tzotzil region)	3,750
Others (largely involuntary sales of trade goods to native communities)	13,475
Total	70,725

Source: Boletín del Archivo General del Gobierno de Guatemala (2, no. 4, 1937): 476–78.

N. B. This information is taken from testimony given by the alcalde's personal assistant, who claimed that Indian producers were paid in all cases to transport their goods to Ciudad Real or Chiapa. Because such labor was generally uncompensated, however, we may estimate that the alcalde's profits approached 100,000 pesos.

alcaldías, a measure that effectively doubled the exactions to which native people were subjected. Pursuing this mandate, the new alcalde mayor of Tuxtla, Juan de Oliver, wasted little time in reorganizing the cacao trade. On assuming office, he appointed a deputy in Ixtacomitán, Salvador Esponda, who utilized both forced sales and public whippings to stimulate commercial production. Traveling from one town to another, Esponda and his mayordomos compelled native people to abandon altogether their small plots of corn and beans in order to plant cacao. For their part, members of the audiencia willingly overlooked such excesses—at least until a particularly devastating plague of locusts threatened to destroy agriculture in the province entirely. In June 1770, these insects made their appearances in Zoque fields; by August, according to one local priest, maize and beans had become so scarce that virtually none of his parishioners could afford them. But the true origins of this dreadful situation, he continued, could be traced less to capricious nature than to Oliver and his unprincipled minions. "A legion of devils in the guise of deputies," he wrote, "has sprung up upon this earth, a sect of exacting Herodians who by unscrupulous means lay waste to, sack, destroy and annihilate the province. . . . To establish their violent monopoly, they have set a thousand traps . . . so that buyers must purchase cacao from them by whatever means, and sellers must sell it to them."[29]

Within a few months, similar complaints were voiced in other quarters. In January 1771, Bartolomé Guitiérrez, treasurer of the cathedral in Ciudad Real, wrote to the audiencia that "civic duty obliges me to mention the notorious epidemic of hunger that was experienced in the city and throughout the province last year and that assuredly will occur again in the present one, despite a copious harvest, because many private individuals have withheld their fruits with the intention of selling them at more than one ear of corn per *medio real.*"[30] Furthermore, these officials were told that native people themselves often engaged in speculation. "If Your Lordship will send a special judge," wrote one parish priest to Bishop Juan Manuel García de Vargas y Rivera in a letter Gutiérrez forwarded to the audiencia, "I will show him the fields that have been planted in this town [Oxchuc] so that the Indians may be compelled to sell their produce in the city. Merely offering to purchase it is useless, because they have told me and other Spaniards that they have none, and will only sell it to Indians in other towns at a price of 18 pesos per *fanega.*"[31] By way of response, the royal *fiscal* ordered Chiapas's governors to require all vecinos of Ciudad Real, Tuxtla, and Comitán to sell their stores "at moderate prices that, taking into consideration the current conditions of scarcity, nonetheless afford them a modest and equitable profit."[32] Those *ladinos* who refused to comply with such orders, or who insisted on cheating in other ways, were to forfeit their merchandise. As for rural communities, the audiencia asked Bishop García de Vargas to ascertain how much corn, beans, and chile were currently available for commercial use—although it cautioned him not to "allow the Indians to perish in order to provision the city." For his part, convinced that native sloth and indifference, rather than excessive repartimientos and poverty, had prompted indigenous families to reduce their plantings, García in turn commanded his priests to undertake an inspection of native fields in the company of local *justicias* so that they might "stimulate the Indians to plant larger *milpas* . . . and take measures to extinguish or contain the plague of locusts."

The results of this exercise, which continued throughout February and March, 1771, provided a desolate and startling view that gave royal authorities great cause for alarm. In contrast to the curate of Oxchuc, most highland priests did not uncover great stores of hidden grain in their districts. On the contrary, what they found in almost every case was a condition of endemic starvation. "These towns are in such a state," wrote the *cura* of Ocosingo, "that most of the inhabitants have abandoned their houses, taking refuge in the hills and living on roots or dispersing themselves among other towns. And although they have planted the corn they call *sijumal* [sweet corn], the Lord our God has punished us with a lack of spring rains and an abundance of sun, for which reasons the corn has dried up or become stunted."[33] Similar accounts were forthcoming from virtually every town along the lower slopes of the altiplano. In Chilón, the local priest found only one man, a ladino named Lorenzo de Vera, who possessed a small surplus of corn—a surplus he was very reluctant to sell. As for preventive measures, this cura continued, only Divine Providence could overcome the plague, "which becomes stronger every hour, wasting the strength of the miserable Indians who remain in their fields day and night to protect their crops, contracting incurable fevers from the fatigue and exposure to which they are subjected. In this way, most of the people of Yajalón, Petalcingo, Tila, Tumbala, and Chilón have perished, a fact that makes it impossible to collect the locust eggs or larvae."[34] Such discouraging opinions were shared by the priest in Tila, whose parishioners "declare that they do not possess sufficient corn even to sustain themselves. . . . And I assure you that the pueblos in my parish are in such a miserable state that many of the Indians have abandoned their homes and fled to the forests in search of wild roots and others have gone to the province of Tabasco."[35]

Faced with a crisis of such proportions, royal authorities were forced to take bold and dramatic action. In 1754, men and women from Tumbala, afflicted by an earlier outbreak of pests, had already established a series of settlements in the Lacandón jungle.[36] Although they continued to pay tribute and serve municipal office in the highlands, they remained largely beyond the control of provincial governors in Ciudad Real. In order to prevent other Indians from joining these refugees, on October 31, 1771, the audiencia relieved native pueblos in Chiapas of most of their obligations; in a few cases, they cancelled tribute payments altogether.[37] Even so, highland communities recovered slowly from the devastation that both natural disaster and human avarice had wrought. On November 27, 1773, for example, royal judges in Guatemala were informed that these towns "have been successfully restored because of the good harvests they have enjoyed except for the district of Tzeltales and Guardianías consisting of twenty-five pueblos that have not experienced the same good fortune ... given the continuous waves of locusts that afflict them."[38] Then, too, there was the question of ecclesiastical imposts: between 1737 and 1750, church revenues had stagnated at around 10,500 pesos a year; in the following years, this figure declined to about 8,000 pesos, that is, to the amount received a century earlier.[39] In order to offset such losses, of course, local bishops had customarily undertaken annual visitas and collected those derechos to which they were entitled. But when García de Vargas announced that he intended to conduct such a visit, Juan de Oliver, governor of Tuxtla, protested to the audiencia. Episcopal extravagance, he claimed, not legitimate enterprise or unkind nature, had brought the province to the edge of ruin.[40] As competition for native revenues grew, therefore, with the church placing greater demands on men and women already exhausted by burdensome repartimientos, the stage was set for a major confrontation between the province's civil and religious authorities.

In order to understand these events, it is necessary to consider briefly how the church itself had become divided during the previous century. As early as 1584, Bishop Pedro de Feria, fearful that the Council of the Indies might secularize New World doctrinas, persuaded regular clergymen in Chiapas to relinquish two minor parishes.[41] As for the other native towns, these remained by and large under Dominican control. By 1656, however, resentment against the friars had become so widespread among other clerics that the local bishop, Mauro de Tovar, attempted to install secular clérigos in several vacant benefices.[42] Predictably, Dominican superiors responded to this challenge by appealing to the audiencia in Guatemala. Asserting that they alone possessed the experience and linguistic training to administer Indian curatos, within a few months they had recovered their lost towns. Undaunted, a succession of bishops and their retainers pressed for secularization, and indeed in 1680 they obtained a cédula that permitted them to serve in seven important native towns.[43] By this time, too, such measures had gained considerable urgency: not only had native tithes declined, but the first graduates of Chiapas's new seminary, founded in 1678, were preparing for ordination. Despite such facts, however, the Dominicans refused to retire to their monasteries. By mobilizing their allies in Spain, they obtained a second cédula, one that allowed the audiencia—always a bastion of support for the mendicants—to postpone definitive action.[44] And in the kind of compromise that made consistent administration all but impossible in the American colonies, in 1682 the Consejo directed subordinate authorities to replace aging friars with qualified secular priests.[45]

What these disputes reveal is that for many years Dominican friars and provincial governors had developed a modus vivendi that—although it never involved them in common enterprises—nonetheless had coalesced into an overt political alliance. The orgins of this alliance are difficult to establish; in any case, I would suggest, it was undoubtedly reaffirmed in 1678 when the audiencia dispatched a special judge, José Descals, to investigate accusations of official misconduct in Ciudad Real.[46] Ironically, these accusations had been made by a Dominican bishop, Francisco Núñez de la Vega, and had embroiled him in a round of intrigues with the alcalde mayor. After issuing a set of regulations to rectify this situation, Descals turned his attention to the question of church revenues and particularly to the large number of fiestas the local friars celebrated in native parishes.[47] Infuriated at what he considered to be Descal's treachery, Núñez quickly maneuvered to force the judge out of Chiapas and then filed a complaint against him with the Inquisition in Guatemala. Moreover, Núñez drafted a body of diocesan regulations that questioned the authority of all royal officers in such affairs. Nor surprisingly, this controversial document, which clearly violated the *real patronato*, was soon suppressed. And although the Inquisition eventually vacated Descal's ordenances, thereafter the friars sought to resolve their differences with provincial governors in private.

In fact, this state of affairs might have prevailed until independence had not the arrival in 1774 of a new and particularly ambitious alcalde mayor, Cristóbal Ortíz de Avilés, followed the next year by a bishop of strong will and equal dedication, Francisco Polanco, precipitated a major political crisis throughout the region. Determined to expand his own revenues from cacao and cotton, Ortíz quickly developed a system of repartimientos so onerous and exacting that most native pueblos, which had barely recovered from the plagues of 1770–71, were thrown into a state of chaos. "This illicit commerce," wrote Polanco in one of his numerous complaints to the crown,

is the immediate and visible cause of the destruction of the pueblos, who are not accorded the rights of other human beings. . . . He buys cotton at a small price and sells it to them at a profit of 200 percent. I will not even discuss here the question of weights, the problem of shortweighting them. The importance of these operations must not be underestimated, because he regularly gives out cotton to the Indians that is yellow and of poor quality, and expects them to return it to him white and well-spun, having sold what they got from him at a lesser price and bought better stock at their own expense.[48]

In much the same vein, by 1776 Ortiz had confiscated most of the *cajas de comunidad,* with which he financed his own enterprises.[49] Deprived of these resources, Indian communities found themselves unable to provide fees to their priests. Faced once again with the likelihood of starvation and imprisonment, therefore, many local people simply abandoned their towns for the relative safety of peonage on lowland fincas. In the end, Polanco realized, forced production threatened to undermine the very basis of parish organization and ecclesiastical administration in central Chiapas.[50]

By 1776, then, it had become clear that the church might survive and prosper only if provincial governors were compelled to relinquish their control over native commerce: even Dominican *doctrineros* complained that highland repartimientos severely undermined their incomes. To this end, Polanco began to court the principal vecinos of Ciudad Real, who for nearly thirty years had watched helplessly as local alcaldes and their deputies enriched themselves at public expense. On behalf of these vecinos, he initiated a cascade of petitions that in 1780 and 1781 forced the audiencia to reinstate the city's ayuntamiento.[51] In fact, acting under orders directly from the Consejo, colonial authorities took the unusual step of charging the bishop himself with this task.[52] At the same time, in order to assure the sympathy of municipal functionaries, and also to improve the state of ecclesiastical revenues, Polanco utilized a device his predecessors had introduced into the province, the auction of tithes.[53] Whereas in 1775 no single bidder had come forth to bid on the collection of tithes, after 1778 these pledges regularly exceeded 5,000 pesos. By means of such devices, Polanco and his subordinates created a network of merchants and hacendados whose personal fortunes became inextricably linked with those of the church. But perhaps his most dramatic accomplishment involved a lawsuit that the alcalde mayor initiated in 1778 against the vicar of Chamula. Responding to the accusation that priestly advice, not repartimientos, had driven people in that beleaguered parish to desperation, Polanco prepared a lengthy set of documents on the subject of forced labor throughout the highlands. And despite the fact that

Chamula's *justicias* filed a detailed affidavit in favor of the governor (who had treated them less harshly than their own curate), the audiencia enjoined civil authorities from engaging in commerce of this sort altogether.[54]

Of course, it would be naive to assume that provincial governors automatically obeyed such orders, or that they did not continue to organize repartimientos wherever they were able to do so. On the contrary, in 1784 the *cabildo eclesiástico* complained that the alcalde mayor had "distributed among the Indians money or goods for [cacao] at its old price [of ten pesos per arroba] without taking into consideration the paucity of the harvest or notifying the growers that they might sell their product to private merchants. . . . He then sold it himself in [Guatemala] at 75 pesos per *arroba*."[55] Despite such incidents, however, it is nonetheless true that the repartimiento system, indeed the entire structure of forced production and commerce in the province, was clearly giving way to a more complex set of social relations. Stimulated by the smuggling boom that had revitalized economic life elsewhere in Central America, local merchants and hacendados expanded their enterprises in the Grijalva basin. Between 1780 and 1820, for example, three new plantations were founded in San Bartolomé; a few miles to the southeast, around Comitán, no fewer than twenty cattle ranches came into existence.[56] Moreover, such properties provided much greater returns to their owners than they had in the past: in 1819, mules sold for twice the price that they had brought fifty years earlier; horses had increased 50 percent in value, cattle 33 percent.[57] For their part, secular priests, whom by 1778 Polanco had installed in many native parishes, played an important role in this process: unfettered by membership in monastic orders, they freely extracted both cash and labor from highland communities and invested these in other ventures. In effect, then, the replacement of provincial alcaldes by a more honorable group of officials in 1790 merely ratified in administrative form what had already become an established economic fact. Thenceforth, the central altiplano was tranformed into a reservoir of unused Indian labor, a reservoir that might be tapped during moments of expansion and dammed at moments of contraction. Throughout the nineteenth century, the question of who controlled this flow and how it was regulated came to occupy a central position in the area's political life.

Native Life and the 1712 Rebellion

Although documentary sources on Spanish settlement in Chiapas abound, information about native people is much less abundant and much more unreliable. Most of what we know about Indian communities must be inferred from reports that were composed for other purposes or that deliberately set out to misrepresent the facts. Obviously, such sources pose special problems for the unwary researcher and require especial caution. In his attempt to reconstruct pre-conquest nagualism (spiritism) and religious practices, for example, Edward Calnek has cited lengthy passages from Núñez de la Vega's *Constituciones diocesanas*, which themselves became a model for later descriptions of native ritual. Unfortunately, as Eugenio Maurer has recently pointed out, these passages bear little resemblance to modern Tzotzil and Tzeltal customs—though they do present a fairly accurate catalogue of seventeenth-century European superstitions about witchcraft.[58] Nor should this fact surprise us: accusations of heterodoxy and paganism served to bolster Dominican claims to their native parishes. Only by arguing that Indians had not yet fully accepted Christ's message (or that they were always on the verge of rejecting it) could the friars justify their continued activities as interim curates. Hence the origins of a very tenacious, indeed almost indestructible kind of Black Legend: indigenous people feigned conversion to the new faith, it was said, in order to deceive their pastors and to practice their old religion in secret. By way of contrast, contemporary evidence suggests that Indians converted sincerely and with great devotion: after all, they were told, only their false gods kept them from enjoying the rights accorded to other Castilian subjects. Then, too, by 1580 native nobles, who might have preserved the ancient beliefs and organized resistance to Spanish domination, had either been assassinated or disinherited.[59] Thereafter, new forms of governance, coupled with indigenous varieties of Christianity, provided the idiom in which these people organized their world and simultaneously expressed their radical disaffection with the colonial order.

How did Indians react to the steady and unabated deterioration of their material circumstances that characterized Spanish rule in Chiapas? Given their position in colonial society, the future itself promised little relief: each year, fewer children were born to replace those men and women who had died. Each year, too, there were more monks and priests to support, more festivals to celebrate. If God had survived so much sinfulness, so many excesses in His name, then surely He listened to Indian prayers with a special ear. One day, they knew, perhaps tomorrow, perhaps in a century's time, He would answer their lamentations, He would inflict His terrible justice upon that band of merry monks and centurion-like governors—at once so mindful and so heedless of their Roman heritage—who week by week grew fat on the toil of red men. In preparation for that fateful day, they cleansed their souls, they danced "in His sight," and in the sight of His emissaries, the saints. They sang, they rejoiced. In the dark hours of early dawn, they called upon their ancestors, Indian saints whose great sufferings Christ had surely rewarded with eternal life. In the privacy of their houses, in the seclusion of the forests, on mountaintops, they offered their aguardiente and candles—sacramental wine and wafer—to Our Lord, while in village churches Spanish priests defiled these holy sacraments at the altar. "If you only knew how Christ suffers when you celebrate unworthily," wrote Bravo de la Serna to his priests in a rare moment of vision, "and the ways in which you crucify Him, how you would weep with pain and sorrow for your mis-deeds! . . . For more priests will be damned at the altar than ever common rogues and highwaymen were hung on the gallows."[60]

But of course most priests did not weep with contrition, nor did they leave off their parasitic and profligate exploitation of Indian labor. On the contrary, they became increasingly alarmed at native ceremony and ritual, which, they claimed, was inspired by superstitions and charms. In that vein, the same Bravo de la Serna, in his pastoral regulations of 1677, ordered parish priests to "attend the dances that Indians cele-brate . . . such as the dance of Bobat, when they jump and shiver as if from the cold, but at midday, and around their fires, through which they pass without the slightest injury."[61] Such observances, he continued, were prohibited. Equally reprehensible, he declared, was the custom of "re-moving [effigies] from churches to private houses, in order to continue their festivals with the profanation of food, drink, dances, and other operations, which are the effective causes of greater evils."[62] Finally, ten years later, Núñez de la Vega expressed his horror that "a painting of the nahual Tzihuitzin or Poxlom" had been discovered inside the church in Oxchuc. In order to remedy this situation, he not only conducted a public auto da fé there but also repeated and reaffirmed these prohibitions.[63]

Naturally, ecclesiastical attacks on native "superstition" were not lim-ited to autos da fé and other demonstrations of civic piety. By 1670, the insouciance with which local clerics had treated their pastoral responsi-bilities had created far greater doctrinal problems, problems that called for direct and decisive action on the part of church authorities. Not content to celebrate their strange and distasteful rituals in the shadow of Spanish liturgical practices, Chiapa's natives had carried such activities into village churches and public ceremonial life.[64] In response, therefore, Bravo de la Serna initiated a full-scale campaign to deprive indigenous ministers of their offices and functions, a campaign that Núñez de la Vega continued until his own death in 1710. "It is hereby ordered," Bravo wrote, "that no priest may permit Flags and Pennants to be unfurled as the Host and Chalice are raised, both because those who hold such Flags irreverently turn their backs upon the Divine Sacrament, and cover them-selves, and because of the disturbance they cause, diverting attention from the Sovereign Mystery."[65] In similar fashion, he declared, church ornaments and banners were not to be employed by "private persons or even legitimate officials of inferior grade, since no distinction is made regarding the position or rank of His Majesty's officers." And finally, he added, "out of reverence for the Divine Mysteries," only "consecrated priests, lords or nobles of Castile, Presidents and Judges and Governors, and alcaldes mayores" might remain seated in church during mass. However corrupt and unworthy these officials might be, he seemed to say, however many of them might one day be "condemned at the altar" like common thieves on the gallows, Indian vassals must respect and revere them—even as they revered the sacraments themselves.

Behind these regulations we vaguely perceive the outlines of an indige-nous religious experience that sought both to understand and to tran-scend the tragedy of colonialism. Out of the spiritual disorder that sixteenth-century evangelization had inflicted on Indian communities, native alcaldes and regidores, mayordomos and alféreces, labored to create an orderly and coherent ceremonial life of their own. Individual salvation, far too precarious an idea in those years of early death and sudden flight, remained in their minds strictly a Spanish notion. Among Indians, men and women might attain salvation only if their villages outlived individual members, if their descendents lit candles for them and wept over their graves on the Day of the Dead. As for their souls, these became absorbed into that collective soul commonly called "our ances-tors." To the memory of these righteous forebears—who, as Christ had promised, would one day rise again and live for a thousand years—to their memory and to the village saints, native men and women addressed their prayers and their lamentations. For had not the fathers told them that the souls of good Christians live forever at God's right hand? Inspired by the ideal of communal solidarity, then, they surrounded their pueblos with shrines and crosses. Beyond these limits, they seemed to say, lies a hostile world, a world of ladinos and untamed beasts, of human savagery and unbridled nature. Inside, they declared, our ancestors watch and wait, ready to speak on our behalf when the Day of Judgment arrives. And periodically, as if to reaffirm their faith, native mayordomos and alféreces carried their saints, flags flying, trumpets sounding, to the far corners of this animate landscape—there to recall the past and to contemplate their future deliverance.

Then one day, after almost two centuries of Spanish domination, they decided to wait no longer. In 1712, a young Tzeltal girl—who later called herself María de la Candelaria and claimed to be inspired by the Holy Virgin—told her followers in the highland town of Cancuc that both God and king had died. The time had come, she declared for *naturales* in the province to rise up against their Spanish overlords, to avenge their past sufferings and reestablish true religion. Within a week, word had spread to native pueblos as far away as Zinacantan, Simojovel, and San Bartolomé. According to the alcalde mayor of Tabasco, for example, a band of Indians "showing signs of rebelliousness" arrived three days later in the Chol town of Tila to take possession of the community's religious ornaments. Then, he continued, these men, who appeared to be acting as public heralds, stated their message: "It was God's will that [the Virgin] should come only for His native children to free them from the Spaniards and the ministers of the Church, and that the Angels would plant and tend their milpas, and that the sun and the moon had given signs that the King of Spain was dead, and that they must choose another."[66]

In order to understand these events, which took place between early August and mid-December 1712, when the revolt was crushed by Spanish troops from Guatemala and Tabasco, we must consider carefully the transformations that native society had undergone. Surely the greed and rapaciousness of Spanish authorities, as important as such elements may have been, had not by themselves brought highland Indians to the brink of despair. Nor can it be said, as Herbert Klein maintains, that such "rude exploitation" coincided with "a temporary relaxation of provincial government control."[67] Not diminished but unbearable authority—corrupt, self-serving and ultimately lawless—was what prompted Indians to rebel. Then, too, like most indigenous uprisings in America, the 1712 movement did not represent an isolated case of seditiousness or discontent. On the contrary, it was preceded by similar events elsewhere in the region. In 1660, native people in Tehuantepec revolted against the provincial authorities of Oaxaca; within a few weeks, Indians throughout that jurisdiction had risen in arms.[68] Thirty-three years later, in Tuxtla, Zoque people, disgusted by the onerous repartimientos to which they had been subjected, killed Chiapa's alcalde mayor, Manuel de Maisterra, in the public plaza.[69] Similarly, in 1722, ten years after the Cancuc uprising, still other Zoques (in Ocozocuautla) forced their overzealous parish priest to flee for his life.[70] And finally, in 1761, Yucatecan Indians attempted once again to end Spanish rule in southern Mexico.

Even in the central highlands, Spanish authorities had received ample warnings that something more serious and deadly than a grain riot was afoot. Miracles abounded, and prophets who proclaimed the end of the world appeared on the very outskirts of Ciudad Real. In March 1711, for example, Fr. José Monroy interrogated a young girl in Santa Marta (a Tzotzil pueblo in the parish of Chamula) who told him that, "arriving one day at my milpa, I found on a fallen branch this Lady who, calling to me, asked if I had a father and a mother, and when I answered no, she told me that she was a poor woman named Mary, who had come down from Heaven to give aid to the Indians, and she ordered me to inform my *justicias* that they should build her a chapel at the entrance to the town."[71] Like other priests of that region, Fr. Monroy had become alarmed at the growing signs of restiveness that had appeared three years earlier among highland Indians. Perhaps, too, he felt uncomfortable about the increasingly strident tone that his colleagues introduced into their sermons and the increasing disrespect that native people showed for their pastors. Several years later, he recalled that one day in 1708, "about two o'clock in the afternoon, some Indians from the town of Santo Domingo Zinacantan arrived . . . and told me that, on the road to that town, inside a tree trunk one could make out a statue of the Holy Virgin that, having descended from Heaven, emitted beams of light, giving them to believe that She had come to offer Her favor and aid."[72] On being questioned by Bishop Núñez de la Vega, this hermit (who proved to be a mestizo from New Spain) explained simply that he was "a poor sinner whom they will not allow to love God." Judging him to be insane, the bishop locked him away in the Franciscan monastery in Ciudad Real.

For two years, the matter was forgotten. Then, in 1710, church officials discovered this man again in Zinacantan, where he had built a chapel. By that time, word of the hermit's activities had reached native people as far away as Totolapa. In order to visit him, these men and women, like other Indians throughout the area, ceased to attend mass in their parish churches. After burning his chapel, therefore, Alvarez de Toledo banished him permanently from Chiapas. All to no avail: within a few months, the Virgin had reappeared in Santa Marta, where for half a year indigenous authorities hid her effigy from prying clerical eyes. And no sooner had Monroy confiscated this statue than he learned of still another and more impressive miracle: "The inhabitants of San Pedro Chenal-hó . . . arrived to give notice that several days before they had constructed a chapel for Señor San Sebastián in their town because his image had sweated on two occasions . . . and that one Sunday they had seen beams of light coming from the Image of San Pedro and from his face, and that the next Sunday the same thing had occurred again."[73]

Despite Monroy's sang-froid, however, native people refused to be calmed. In June 1712, a group of Indians from the Tzeltal town of Cancuc informed Alvarez that a miraculous cross, descended from Heaven, had appeared in their pueblo. To celebrate this event, Cancuc's civil authorities had constructed a chapel there, a chapel to which Indians from surrounding communities daily brought offerings and gifts. The town's pastor, Fr. Simón de Lara, immediately went to investigate. To his horror, he found that such a chapel had indeed been built—not, as had been suspected, to honor the cross, but rather to house the image of yet another Virgin. Like the effigy in Santa Marta, he learned, this image had been discovered in the forest by a young Indian girl. His horror was increased when he learned that this girl, surrounded by a group of mayordomos and religious officials, remained continuously in the Virgin's company and interpreted aloud her otherwise silent will. Infuriated by such sacrilege and nonsense, de Lara arrested the town's alcaldes and regidores, whom he sent to Ciudad Real. After replacing them with Indians in whom he trusted, he attempted to destroy the chapel—an act that almost cost him his life. To make matters worse, at that moment the regidores whom he had jailed returned to Cancuc, where they declared "that they alone were true friars and that only those whom they elected were alcaldes. . . . [They ordered] that the chapel, which was the work of their hands, be maintained, that other pueblos be called to defend it, and that the Indians count not their trials, for soon they would be relieved of all toil."[74]

In July 1712, when Alvarez de Toledo notified indigenous ayuntamientos of his impending visit, native people had already rejected the spiritual authority of Spanish clerics and had taken steps to free themselves from ecclesiastical domination. Although Alvarez did not create this situation, he undoubtedly provided the catalyst—the spark that ignited the powder, as one important Dominican official later wrote—that brought highland Indians to the point of open rebellion. Responding to his letter, the Virgin summoned native justicias from throughout the highlands to

Cancuc (now renamed Ciudad Real), where, She proclaimed, they were to celebrate a grand festival in her honor:

I the Virgin who have descended to this Sinful World call upon you in the name of Our Lady of the Rosary and command you to come to this town of Cancuc and bring with you all the silver of your churches and the ornaments and bells, together with the communal funds and drums and all the books of the cofradías, because now neither God nor King exist; and for this reason you must come immediately, for if you do not you will be punished for not coming when I and God called you.[75]

The Spanish God, she declared, that leering caricature of Our Lord, draped in episcopal finery—that God had died. In His place, a true Redeemer had appeared, an Indian king of kings who had come to reward native people for their sufferings and trials. And finally, she proclaimed, Indians must arm themselves, they must rise up against the "Jews in Ciudad Real" who even at that moment were preparing to kill her and reestablish once again their unholy rule over Christendom.

On August 10, five days after Alvarez departed from the city to begin his visit, civil and religious officials representing nearly twenty-five Tzeltal, Tzotzil, and Chol towns gathered in Cancuc to venerate the Virgin. Under the leadership of a Tzotzil prophet, Sebastián Gómez, they and their townsmen were divided into military divisions and placed under the command of native captains. These *capitanes generales*, who in previous years had frequently served as assistants and mayordomos to parish priests, seem especially to have despised the Dominican Order, for Gómez instructed indigenous alcaldes "that no one was to give food to the Fathers, under pain of death, an order that was punctually fulfilled."[76] Within a few days, Indian leaders took even more militant steps. First they attacked the Spanish settlement in Chilón and killed all the town's adult non-Indian men. Spanish women and children were taken to Cancuc, where they were called "Indians" and compelled to serve native authorities as domestics. A short time later, indigenous armies stormed Ocosingo, where they destroyed the Dominican haciendas and sugar mill. Thereafter they proceeded systematically to capture whatever hapless friars fell into their grasp. By late November, they had wrought havoc on the church in central Chiapas.

One naturally wonders about the form of worship these men and women preferred instead of Spanish religion. And in pursuing this question, we must examine in detail the attitudes and activities of Sebastián Gómez. Arriving in Cancuc in July 1712 from Chenalhó (where he led the unsuccessful movement to build a new chapel for San Sebastián),

Gómez proceeded to organize an indigenous church that, he hoped, would replace the church of the Jews: "He brought a small image of San Pedro wrapped in cloth which he placed in the chapel, and said that his saint had chosen him to be his Vicar, and had granted him the power to ordain and appoint other Vicars and Priests who would minister to the towns."[77] One month later, following the execution of Spanish clergymen, Gómez summoned Indian fiscales from seventeen Tzeltal towns to appear in Cancuc. After ascertaining which among them could read and write, he ordained several of them into the new priesthood:

The method of ordination was to compel each Fiscal to remain on his knees for twenty-four hours with a candle in his hand repeating the Rosary, and then in view of the whole town Don Sebastían de la Gloria [as he called himself] sprinkled him with water which, they claimed, had been blessed. . . . Having been ordained and assigned to their parishes, they began to exercise their office like very correct pastors, preaching, confessing, and administering [the sacraments].[78]

At first, Gómez seemed content to dispense with the elaborate hierarchies that characterized the Spanish church. In establishing a system of authority, he appointed one of his priests, Gerónimo Saraes, to the office of Vicar general—a common enough post in colonial dioceses. At the same time, Saraes and another native priest, Lucas Pérez, became secretaries to the Virgin. And in the true spirit of Christ, who, as we recall, washed His apostles' feet, Gómez named to the "See of Sibacá" an old man who "had spent his life making tortillas for the Fathers."[79] Soon, however, he expanded this primitive hierarchy until it had assumed alarming (and familiar) proportions. Thus Saraes, too, was granted an episcopal throne, and two Indian friars—both of whom enjoyed the title of *predicador general*—became vicars general. Little by little, divine justice became obscured behind a battery of new prelates and patriarchs.

Meanwhile Gómez turned his attention to the difficulties and problems of civil administration, for in his vision of a theocratic state he regarded Chiapas's *república de indios* as a New Spain, a second empire in which Indians had become Spaniards and Spaniards had become Indians.[80] But if God and king were dead, if native people no longer owed their obedience and loyalty to the audiencia in Guatemala, who would rule the republic in San Pedro's name and in the name of his earthly vicar? Within Indian pueblos, of course, native cabildos—appointed by the movement's leaders—continued to govern in local matters. But such elementary and primitive forms of government, he felt, were ill-suited to an Indian empire, especially an empire that was at war. In order to rectify these problems, as Ximénez tells us, "in order to dispense justice to those who required it, and to reward those who merited it, [they decided] that they would found an audencia and that this should be in Huitiupán. With this in mind they styled the town Guatemala with its President and Judges."[81] And finally, Gómez and other leaders promised at least one military commander, Juan García, that if the rebellion succeeded he would be crowned king of Cancuc.[82]

To be sure, Gómez's state was not universally admired. There were many Indians who refused to accept these measures, who even lost their lives in defense of the colonial order. The fiscal of Tenango, for example, Nicolás Pérez, who remained loyal to Fr. de Lara, was whipped to death in front of the chapel in Cancuc. Similarly, the inhabitants of Simojovel and Palenque chose to abandon their homes and hide in the mountains rather than join the rebellion.[83] In the same fashion, Indian pueblos along the periphery of highland Chiapas (San Bartolomé, Amatenango, Aguacatenango, Teopisca, and Comitán) and Zoque towns to the northeast of Ciudad Real refused to support the Virgin. More important, however, Gómez's empire-building, his careful imitation of Spanish administrative and ecclesiastical forms, soon provoked disenchantment even among many Indians who had at first followed the movement with enthusiasm. In particular, they demanded an end to tribute, to tithes, and, above all, to the Order of Saint Dominic. Instead, as one witness wrote, Gómez reprimanded them sharply:

Because there have been complaints among the subjects to the effect that [the Virgin's] word has not been fulfilled with respect to the abolition of tribute, of the Order of Santo Domingo, of the king, and of the rule of the Jews, let it be known that Señor Don Pedro told his chosen emissary Señor Don Sebastián Gómez de la Gloria that he could not preserve the world without earthly bondsmen. Our Father Señor San Pedro has offered himself as our bondsman before God and thus, according to the heavenly word that is not of the earth, there must be in each town a priest who will serve as bondsman before God by means of the Mass, because without them, as the world is filled with sin, the world will end, and for this reason the Masses that these Fathers celebrate will calm God's anger.[84]

In the end, it may well have been this theocratic bent that brought the Cancuc rebellion to a quick end. To be sure, Spanish authorities possessed sufficient military power to vanquish the Virgin's poorly-armed and ill-disciplined legions. But colonial forces had been taken by surprise, had found themselves unprepared to defend Spanish settlers. During those weeks when Ciudad Real's meager militia, entrenched in Huistán, stalled for time, Indians in Zinacantan and Chamula, sympathetic to the Virgin, enjoyed ample opportunity to attack and subdue the city. Why did they not do so? Certainly their love of Spanish bishops and governors was no more intense than that of other Indians elsewhere in the highlands. On the contrary, because of their talents as porters and their proximity to Ciudad Real, Zinacantecos had suffered even more acutely than many Indians at the hands of colonial authorities. Did they then fear the punishment these officials would surely inflict on them? Apparently not, for they prepared and organized themselves to march against the city. No, their reluctance to pursue this venture does not appear to have been inspired by fear or timorousness. Instead, they allowed themselves to be dissuaded by Fr. Monroy, who, we must presume, convinced them that the Virgin was in reality a fraud. And in the days that followed, such key towns as Chenalhó and Chalchihuitán also defected from Her cause. Why, they seem to have asked, should we exchange one earthly kingdom for another?

Indeed, Gómez himself, it would seem, anticipated such opposition. In his order to disgruntled tributaries, he declared that, even in the New Age, Indians would continue to sin and would therefore require the services of their priesthood. Otherwise, he wrote, the world would end. This vision of the Day of Judgment, however well it served his purposes, must in the end have inspired little enthusiasm among men and women who yearned for justice and for an end to exploitation. On the contrary, it undoubtedly offended them, for it violated that sense of community, that sense of promise that since the days of Bishop Bartolomé de Las Casas, the famous defender of the Indians, had become the cornerstone of their spiritual and political lives. The feelings of discontent and expectation that swept Chiapas between 1708 and 1712 had reflected a desire to realize those old ideals in modern form, to transform the multitude of isolated pueblos into a single native community founded on faith, equality, and divine law. For this reason, according to Klein, the movement's leaders declared at one point that their Spanish captives must marry Indians. From such a union, they proclaimed, there would spring a new race—neither Spanish nor Indian—that would truly merit salvation. And despite the movement's failure, these feelings continued to stir native imaginations, to hang in the air like incense—while colonial authorities, jubilant at their victory over the forces of darkness, took up the unfinished business of capricious law and systematic graft.

Given these motives, it is not difficult to understand the church's response to this cry for moral regeneration. As might be expected, the rebellion only confirmed those opinions, common among clerics of the day, that held that Indians suffered from a special variety of original sin. "The points upon which our sermons concentrated," wrote Ximénez, who preached to the subdued defenders of Cancuc, "were, first, the hardness of their hearts, because in two hundred years of instruction God's law had not taken hold in their hearts . . . ; second, how much better they lived under the rule of the King of Spain than in pagan times under Moctezuma . . . ; fourth, their origins, descended from the Jews whom God had punished for their idolatry and who later came to these lands by unknown routes."[85]

Moved by such convictions, Spanish priests intensified their efforts to suppress native religiosity and ritual. In his Tzotzil catechism, for example, F. Hidalgo took great pains to impress on his listeners that their own earthly travails—however great and painful these might be—paled to insignificance beside the agonies that Christ had suffered on their behalf. "Your price is a great one," Hidalgo wrote, "and for this reason He suffered terribly while here on earth."[86] Furthermore, in order to assure that Indians heard and understood this message, the number of priests and parishes doubled, then tripled. By 1780, most of these priests had installed themselves in their *curatos*, where they hoped they might maintain a closer and more vigilant watch over native religious life.

At this point, it is perhaps of interest to compare and contrast our view of the 1712 rebellion with that presented by Herbert Klein. Like other scholars, Klein has claimed that in large measure local "civil-religious hierarchies," composed primarily of older and wealthier Indians, organized and led the movement.[87] And yet, as we have seen, Gómez and his confederates did not allow local councils of this sort to assume more than a minor role in the uprising. Instead, they took great pains to organize civil and religious institutions, unknown in Indian pueblos, in unequivocal and direct copy of Spanish models. Kings, vicars general, bishops, predicadores generales, military governors—these were the men on whom they conferred political and spiritual powers. Like their non-Indian counterparts, these officials, who commanded the obedience of local cabildos, ruled within well-defined jurisdictions and territories. And, in contrast to Klein's belief, many of these officials, being quite young, had played only minor roles in municipal government before the rebellion: Juan García, capitán general and king-designate of Cancuc, had served previously as the town's chief constable and as servant to Fr. de Lara. Similarly, native fiscales like Lucas Pérez and Gerónimo Saraes, who became bishops and secretaries to the Virgin, were neither particularly aged nor particularly wealthy.[88] In fact, during the colonial period it is unlikely that civil-religious hierarchies or other such institutions emerged at any point in native communities. After all, these communities tended to be both small and highly fluid; as Kevin Gosner has recently shown, nearly half of the area's Indians married outside their own pueblos. Moreover, from the very beginning, indigenous cabildos were dominated not by hereditary nobles (who had all but disappeared) or by wealthy *macehuales*. Instead, royal governors preferred to appoint those men whose personal fortunes might be confiscated in lieu of unpaid tribute. With much of the same ends in mind, after 1570 Dominican friars had organized a series of cofradías that required all Indian men (and many women) to sponsor important religious festivals.[89] In 1793, for example, Zinacantan possessed five such brotherhoods, each headed by four mayordomos and endowed with a capital of around 100 pesos, which the members were required to borrow at 5 percent annual interest. Using this income, they paid their parish priest 185 pesos for fifty-eight masses celebrated in their behalf.[90] In theory, cofradía affairs were managed by two (or sometimes four) mayordomos elected each year from among the cofrades. In practice, however, such men were appointed by their parish priests, who presided over cofradía meetings and kept the books. And although the number of functions of these cofradías varied slightly from one town to another, until the mid-nineteenth century they nonetheless provided the common organizational pattern on which native social life throughout the highlands was structured.[91]

Conclusions

Unlike the Indians of Oaxaca who, according to William Taylor, "were still self-sufficient farmers on the eve of . . . independence," indigenous people in central Chiapas had long before abandoned their traditional economic and agricultural occupations.[92] Here and there, individual families or family groups managed to eke out a living from their small milpas. Indeed, throughout the highlands, land was not a major cause of concern in the seventeenth and eighteenth centuries among Indians. Only in a few highland valleys did they find themselves deprived of their ancestral patrimonies. In contrast, taxes, tribute, and the system of repartimientos to which these gave rise brought about profound transformations in Indian communities. By means of such devices, provincial governors organized and mobilized a vast native labor force, a labor force that produced cacao, cochineal, sugar, and cotton cloth. Even as late as 1819, thirty years after such repartimientos had been abolished, native people in

Chiapas still paid an exorbitant amount of tribute in comparison with Indians in New Spain.[93] In the absence of serious competition from private landowners, Chiapas's alcaldes mayores created a highly sophisticated network of plantations, markets, and manufacturers. And, incredibly, they devised this network without purchasing either a single vara of land or beast of burden. Both land and animals remained in Indian hands: they formed the capital that each year native people themselves husbanded and regenerated.

Contrary, perhaps, to our expectations, the wholesale reform of civil government in Chiapas after 1790 did not in general permit highland Indians to return to subsistence farming. Instead, large-scale smuggling in Central America created new demands for the region's hides, dyes, and other products. In order to augment their production, local landowners expanded their existing plantations and, in the area near Ciudad Real, founded new ones. Freed from the restraints that jealous alcaldes mayores had imposed on them, they nonetheless required more labor. As a result, they began to recruit Tzotzil and Tzeltal Indians from the southern highlands to work their properties as peons and tenant farmers. Because tribute requirements remained extremely high, many of these farmers acceded to their new fate with resignation. Others (primarily Zinacantecos) accepted merchandise on consignment from merchants in Ciudad Real. Using their wits and their mules, these Indians traveled as far afield as Oaxaca and Tabasco in search of customers for their wares. In both cases, such arrangements persisted and indeed predominated among native people until the end of the nineteenth century.

How did indigenous communities react to their new and ever-changing position in colonial society? First, as MacLeod has written, by creating barrier institutions they attempted to protect themselves as best they could from the depredations of Spanish governors and prelates. Among these institutions, colonial ayuntamientos and cofradías functioned primarily to assuage and pacify rapacious ladino authorities. But these ayuntamientos alone—controlled and regulated by Spaniards—could not effectively reconstruct an indigenous way of life. As we might expect, this most urgent task fell to native fiscales and religious officials, men and women who had kept faith with the militant and combative Christianity of an earlier age. Despite clerical efforts to substitute a banal and self-demeaning religiosity in place of Christ's promise of eternal life, these native officials integrated Christian teaching into the very soul of Indian identity. For if native people, uniquely among the area's inhabitants, had been elected to suffer at the hands of the mighty, they reasoned, would they not also be chosen to live forever in God's sight? And if they alone would rise and rejoice on the Day of Judgment, as they firmly believed, then surely their race inhabited that true Church, that community at whose head, as earlier friars had told them, stood the Redeemer Himself. And so, with these ideas in mind, they joyfully and willingly developed their own amalgam of doctrine and liturgy. Far better to honor Him on the hilltops than to obey those corrupt and unworthy men who celebrated in village churches.

It was this combination of sentiments—at once worldly and messianic—that by 1700 permeated native life in Chiapas. And as native communities in general began to recover and grow after 1720, so also did the notion of communal solidarity, often in the form of collective ritual, acquire new significance and urgency. By means of such ritual, indigenous people kept alive that spirit of resistence, that insistence on their collective distinctiveness and dignity, that mitigated the daily outrages of colonial life. For it must be remembered that colonial society brought Spaniards and Indians together not simply as distinct ethnic groups but as members of antagonistic social classes—that ethnic relations quickly became a pretense for perpetuating inequities and injustices of a much more familiar sort. Then, too, the options of emigration and transculturation, of *mestizaje*, which many chose to pursue, remained open to Indians in most parts of Mexico and Central America. But in Chiapas, at least, a significant number of these men and women chose instead to modify their beliefs and customs and traditions in every way possible so as to avoid the one fate they evidently feared most: the loss of their right to be naturales. After all, as Stéfano Varese has so eloquently argued, ethnic diversity did not emerge with the appearance of class society, much less with the advent of colonialism.[94] Under these circumstances, native people quite reasonably rejected transculturation as a solution to those problems of inequality and exploitation that plaued them: why, they asked, should we forsake what little we have salvaged to enter the lowest levels of ladino society? And to this question—a question that remains as perplexing to modern scholars as it was to colonial churchmen—we might add, how would such a sacrifice today alter the economic and political relations on which society in Mexico is currently based?

Notes

Abbreviations

AHE   Archivo Histórico del Estado, Tuxtla Gutiérrez, Chiapas
AGCh   Archivo General de Chiapas, Tuxtla Gutiérrez, Chiapas (successor
           of AHE)
AGGG   Archivo General del Gobierno de Guatemala, Guatemala City
AHDSC   Archivo Histórico Diocesano de San Cristóbal, San Cristóbal,
           Chiapas (unclassified ecclesiastical documents)

1. See Ricardo Pozas, *Los indios en las clases sociales de México* (Mexico City, 1971); Gonzalo Aguirre Beltrán, *Regiones de refugio* (Mexico City, 1967); Mercedes Olivera, "The Barrios of San Andrés Cholula," in Hugo Nutini et al., *Essays on Mexican Kinship* (Pittsburgh, 1976).

2. Such views have recently been expressed by Judith Friedlander, "The Secularization of the Civil-Religious Hierarchy: An Example from Post-Revolutionary Mexico," unpublished manuscript (1978). See also her book, *Being Indian in Hueyapan* (New York, 1976).

3. Ricardo Pozas, *Chamula, un pueblo indio de los altos de Chiapas* (Mexico City, 1957); E.Z. Vogt, *Los zinacantecos* (Mexico City, 1966); Rodolfo Stavenhagen, *Las clases sociales en las sociedades agrarias* (Mexico City, 1969); George Collier, *Fields of the Tzotzil* (Austin, 1975).

4. Herbert S. Klein, "Rebeliones de las communidades campesinas: La república tzeltal de 1712," in Norman A. McQuown and Julian Pitt-Rivers, eds., *Ensayos antropológicos* (Mexico City, 1970), pp. 149–70. Using early colonial documents, Edward E. Calnek has attempted to reconstruct the general outlines of pre-conquest Indian society (see Edward E. Calnek, "Highland Chiapas before the Spanish Conquest," Ph.D. dissertation, University of Chicago, 1962). More recently, Kevin Gosner has begun to reexamine the events of 1712. See his paper entitled "The Tzeltal Revolt of 1712: A Brief Overview," presented at the XLIII International Congress of Americanists, Vancouver, British Columbia, August 1979. Finally, a number of local historians have written on the subject of colonial society; by and large, their accounts adhere closely to descriptions provided by contemporary Dominican chroniclers. See Manuel B. Trens, *Historia de Chiapas* (Mexico City, 1942); Carlos Cáceres López, *Historia general del estado de Chiapas* (Mexico City, 1958). A useful compendium of documents from the Archivo General de Indias has been assembled by Hermilio López Sánchez; see his *Apuntes históricos de San Cristóbal de Las Casas, Chiapas, México* (Mexico City, 1960).

5. I have tried to touch on these matters in a number of articles. See Robert Wasserstrom, "El desarrollo de la economía regional en Chiapas," *Problemas del Desarrollo* 76 (1976); 83–104; "Land and Labour in Central Chiapas: A Regional Analysis," *Development and Change* 8 (1977); 441–64; "Population Growth and

Economic Development in Chiapas, 1524–1975," *Human Ecology* 6 (1978); 127–43; also, "White Fathers and Red Souls: Indian-Ladino Relations in Highland Chiapas, 1528–1973," Ph.D. dissertation, Harvard University, 1977.

6. Historians of these regions who have touched on Chiapas include William L. Sherman, *Forced Native Labor in Sixteenth-Century Central America* (Lincoln, 1979); Murdo J. MacLeod, *Spanish Central America. A Socioeconomic History, 1520–1720* (Berkeley and Los Angeles, 1973); Peter Gerhard, *The Southeast Frontier of New Spain* (Princeton, 1979). In general, MacLeod's interpretation of events in western Guatemala provides an excellent point of departure for discussions of colonial society in Chiapas.

7. Sherman, *Forced Native Labor*, pp. 357–58.

8. Gerhard, *Southeast Frontier*, p. 159; MacLeod, *Spanish Central America*, pp. 98–100.

9. Edward Calnek, "Los pueblos indígenas de los altos de Chiapas," in McQuown and Pitt-Rivers, eds. *Ensayos;* Antonio de Remesal, *Historia general de las indias occidentales, y particular de la gobernación de Chiapa y Guatemala* (Guatemala City, 1932), passim; Francisco Ximénez, *Historia de la provincia de San Vicente de Chiapa y Guatemala* (Guatemala City, 1929).

10. Remesal, *Historia general*, II, 76–79.

11. Gerhard, *Southeast Frontier*, p. 152, "In 1611," writes Gerhard, "there were just fifty-eight encomenderos, of whom six received an annual tribute income of about 2,500 pesos each, one-third received approximately 1,000 pesos, and the others had annuities of less than 500 pesos. In 1637 the tribute of five pueblos that had originally been assigned to one person was divided among nine holders. Those who could not qualify as encomenderos were often assigned pensions paid from the tributes of crown or privately held pueblos. Perhaps because there were so many aspirants to this income among the local Spaniards, relatively few encomiendas in Chiapa were granted to European absentee holders. . . . However, in 1630 the cabildo of Ciudad Real complained that more than half of the privately controlled tributaries were held by wealthy merchants and others in Guatemala City." See also AGGG, Serie Chiapas, "Tasación y encomienda del pueblos de San Bartolomé, 1656," A3.16.3905.290; "Vacante de la encomienda que fue del capitán don Juan de Cárdenas y Mazariegos, 1666," A3.16.3910.290; "Cuenta general del ramo de tributos de la provincia de Chiapa, 1679," A3.16.3914.290.

12. Thomas Gage, *The English-American* (Guatemala City, 1946), pp. 158–59.

13. Francisco Orozco y Jiménez, *Colección de documentos inéditos relativos a la iglesia de Chiapas* (San Cristóbal, 1905), I, 8; J. Eric S. Thompson, *Thomas Gage's Travels in the New World* (Norman, 1958), pp. 138–59. By the turn of the century, such *fincas* had spilled out of the central depression and onto the semi-arid plains that stretched westward toward Oaxaca. At the same time, near the Tabasco border, several residents of Ciudad Real had organized large plantations in which they combined cattle husbandry with the production of cacao. See Orozco y Jiménez, *Colección*, II, 212–29.

14. AGGG, Serie Chiapas: "Título de dos caballerías de tierra situadas en términos del pueblos de Chamula, jurisdicción de Chiapas, 22 de mayo de 1591," A1.57.45888.157; "Título de dos caballerías de tierra en los llanos de Huixtán en el arroyo de Cisintiq, a favor de Carlos de Estrada, vecino de Ciudad Real de Chiapa, 23 de abril de 1592," A1.57.4588.207; "Título de dos caballerías de tierra en términos de Zinacantan y Chamula en el paraje nombrado los Corrales a favor de Diego de Meza, vecino de Ciudad Real de Chiapa, 5 de junio 1592," A1.57.4588.210; "Título de una caballería de tierra y de un ejido de agua en términos del pueblo de Chamula a favor de Pedro de Solórzano, vecino de Ciudad Real, 27 de julio de 1592," A1.57.4588.214; "Título de un sitio de estancia para ganado mayor en términos del pueblo de Zinacantan a favor del indígena Christóbal Arias, 27 de mayo de 1599," A1.57.4588.270. In total, twenty-two such documents are listed in the *juzgado de tierras*.

15. "Acta del cabildo de Ciudad Real, 26 de marzo de 1684," in Hermilio López Sánchez, *Apuntes históricos de San Cristóbal Las Casas, Chiapas, México* (Mexico City, 1960), II, 677–78. This useful compendium, which includes documents transcribed in the Archivo General de Indias, Seville, unfortunately does not indicate the legajos and folios consulted by the author. See also, AGGG, Serie Chiapas: "Información sobre la necesidad de instruir un curato en el pueblo de las Chiapas de Indios, 1682," A1.4.686.69; "Nómina de todos los vecinos españoles del obispado de Chiapa, 1735," A1.52.185.13.

16. Thompson, *Thomas Gage's Travels*, pp. 146–48.

17. For a more extensive discussion of these matters, see Wasserstrom, "White Fathers," pp. 95–101.

18. Juan Manuel García de Vargas y Riveira, "Relación de los pueblos que comprehende el obispado de Chiapa, 1774," Madrid, Biblioteca del Palacio, Ms. 2840 (Misc. de Ayala XXCI), folio 282. Typescript available in Biblioteca "Fray Bartolomé de las Casas," San Cristóbal, Chiapas.

19. Juan de Pineda, "Descripción de la provincia de Guatemala, año 1594," in *Relaciones histórico-geográficas de América Central* vol. 3, Colección de Libros y Documentos Referentes a la Historia de América (Madrid, 1908).

20. AGGG, Serie Chiapas: "Informa el alcalde mayor de Chiapa que además de la extinción de varios pueblos la baja de tributos se debe a que no han sido empadronados los indígenas, 1734," A3.16.4635.359; and "Autos en que consta de la despoblación de varios pueblos de la provincia de Chiapa, 1734," A1.1.3.1.

21. Trens, *Historia de Chiapas*, p. 146; López Sánchez, *Apuntes Históricos*, II, 679. A few years earlier, in 1693, Zoque people in Tuxtla, infuriated by a similar set of circumstances, had killed the province's governor, Manuel de Maisterra. See "Carta del Sor. Obispo al Presidente Don Fernando López Vecino y Orbaneja," AGCh, *Boletín* 2 (1953): 37–51.

22. Henri Favre, *Changement et continuité chez les Mayas du Mexique* (Paris, 1971), p. 43.

23. "El obispo de Chiapa informa a V. M. sobre los remates de maíz, frijol y chile

que tributan los naturales de aquellas provincias y dice juzga conveniente se observe el estilo que se ha tenido en ellos con las calidades que expresa, 1716," in López Sánchez, *Apuntes históricos,* pp. 699–701. In fact, it was by means of such devices that in 1709 a previous alcalde mayor, Martín Gonzáles de Vergara, had monopolized the local trade in cochineal.

24. AHDSC, "Autos sobre secularización en Chiapas, 1735." Interestingly, a few years later, one alcalde mayor, Francisco de Elías y Saldívar, occupied the cabildo with his followers to prevent municipal counselors from auctioning off the right to supply meat to Ciudad Real, Chiapa, and San Bartolomé. In the ensuing melée, one regidor received a pistol wound and a servant of the alcalde mayor was stabbed to death. See "Zafarrancho en el cabildo de Ciudad Real entre el alcalde mayor y los capitulares, 1751," AGCh, *Boletín* 4 (1955); 69–112. For a description of Elías's position within Guatemalan society, consult "Título de alcalde mayor de Chiapa a favor de don Francisco de Elías Saldívar para cuando cumpla don Juan B. de Garracín Ponce de León, 1747," in López Sánchez, *Apuntes históricos,* p. 796.

25. In 1738, for example, the post was occupied by Antonio Zuazua y Múgica, who was subsequently imprisoned for defrauding the crown of 152,000 pesos. See AGGG, "El ex-alcalde mayor de Ciudad Real, don Antonio de Zuazua, sigue autos contra los justicias de San Lucas por el incendio de dho pueblo en que perdió varias pacas de algodón, 1744," A1.15.341.22; AGGG, "Autos seguidos contra el ex-alcalde mayor, Antonio de Zuazua, por esconder bienes de su magestad, 1742," A1.15.342.22; AGGG, "Juicio de tercería interpuesto por el prior del hospital de Ciudad Real en el juicio de embargo que se sigue al Pbro. José Linares, fiador del alcalde mayor Antonio de Zuazua, 1743," A1.15.345.22; AGGG, "Embargo de los bienes del ex-alcalde mayor Antonio Zuazua, 1742," A1.15.344.22; "Informe del obispo de Ciudad Real al virrey de Nueva España, 1744," in López Sánchez, *Apuntes históricos,* p.790. Zuazua was followed by Juan Bautista Garracín Ponce de León, who according to one historian was "examined and upon being vindicated returned to Spain. But after his death it was learned that he owed 30,000 pesos of tribute collected in Chiapas and by royal order his bondsmen forfeited the property they had pledged in his behalf." See López Sánchez, *Apuntes históricos,* p. 795.

26. López Sánchez, *Apuntes históricos,* pp. 829–34; AHDSC, "Expediente sobre restablecer el cabildo o ayuntamiento de Ciudad Real, 1781."

27. López Sánchez, *Apuntes históricos,* p. 810.

28. AGGG, *Boletín* 2 (1937): 474–79.

29. Letter from Fr. Eugenio Saldívar to the Dominican Provincial, August 23, 1770, AGCh, *Boletín* 4 (1955): 126–27.

30. Letter from Don Bartolomé Gutiérrez to the President of the Audiencia, January 14, 1771, AGCh, *Boletín* 4 (1955): 113–14.

31. AHDSC, "Cordillera a los padres curas para que animen a sus feligreses a que fomenten sus sementeras, 1771," and "Carta de Don Fray Manuel García de Vargas y contestaciones, 1771."

32. Ibid.

33. Ibid.

34. Ibid.

35. Ibid.

36. "Fundación del pueblo Sabaná de Tulijá, año 1816," AGCh, *Boletín* 6 (1956): 103.

37. López Sánchez, *Apuntes históricos,* p. 813.

38. Ibid.

39. Ibid., p. 815; AHDSC, "Una representación hecha por el cabildo al rey de España sobre la necesidad de esta santa iglesia agregando cinco curatos, 1759."

40. AHDSC, "Sobre si los indios deben pagar los derechos de visita del sor. obispo, 1770"; AGGG, Serie Chiapas, "Providencia del superior govierno prohibiendo a los curas del obispado de Chiapa el sistema de derramas y otras contribuciones so pretexto de visitas, 1771."

41. For more discussion of these events, see Wasserstrom, "White Fathers," pp. 71–73.

42. Trens, *Historia de Chiapas,* pp. 123–34; AGGG, Serie Chiapas, "Información recabada a solicitud del fiscal de la audiencia acerca de la manera en que los frailes dominicos administran las doctrinas de los tzendales, 1642," A1.11.12.707.72; AGGG, Serie Chiapas, "El obispo de Chiapa, Fr. Mauro de Tobar, sobre que el R. P. Provincial del Convento de Santo Domingo no ha cumplido con lo ordenado por cédula de 1603 sobre servicio de curatos por religiosos, 1656," A1.11.12.708.72; AHDSC, "Sobre administración eclesiástica en la provincia de Chiapa, 1665."

43. Ximénez, *Historia de la provincia,* II, 454; AHDSC, "Autos sobre secularización, 1735"; AGGG, Serie Chiapas, "El Dr. Fr. Mauro Bravo de la Serna Manrique, obispo de Chiapa, expone que el vicario general, Fr. Sebastián Mejía de la Orden de Predicadores no cumple con sus deberes," A1.11.13.710.72; AGGG, Serie Chiapas, "El provincial de la provincia de San Vicente de Chiapa y Guatemala protesta por el Venerable Deán y Cabildo Eclesiástico de Ciudad Real sedevacante nombró un clérigo para el servicio de cura de almas en el pueblo de Chiapa de los Indios, 1707, A1.11.13.712.72; AGGG, Serie Chiapas, "Certificación en que consta que los PP. dominicos que sirven en las doctrinas de Totolapa, San Lucas, el Barrio de Mexicanos, Cerrillo y Cuctitali han desempeñado cumplidamente, 1705," A1.11.160.13.

44. AGGG, Serie Chiapas, "Autos sobre la secularización de las docrinas servidas por regulares en la jurisdicción del obispado de Chiapa, 1733," A1.11.52.890.115. For a more extensive discussion, see Robert Wasserstrom, "Life and Society in Colonial Chiapas, 1528–1790," paper presented at the XLIII International Congress of Americanists, Vancouver, British Columbia, August 1979.

45. Wasserstrom, "Life and Society."

46. López Sánchez, *Apuntes históricos,* pp. 683–84.

47. Trens, *Historia de Chiapas,* p. 138.

48. AHDSC, "Carta del Sr. Polanco al rey, 1779" (Asuntos Secretos).

49. AHDSC, "Carta del alcalde mayor al presidente, 1778."

50. AHDSC, "Carta del Sr. Polanco al rey, 1779"; El cura de Chamula se queja del

alcalde mayor, también el de Teopisca, 1779"; "Informe del R. P. Fr. Tomás Luis Roca, cura de Zinacantan, 1779."

51. AHDSC, "Expediente sobre restablecer el cabildo o ayuntamiento de Ciudad Real, 1781."

52. López Sánchez, *Apuntes históricos*, p. 837.

53. AHDSC, "Remate de diezmos, 1774–1785."

54. AHDSC, "Instancia de los indios de Chamula . . . sobre que su cura . . . los grava con dros. y contribuciones excesivas, 1779"; AHDSC, "Fallo de la Real Audiencia, 1779."

55. "Pleito entre el alcalde mayor de Ciudad Real y el vicario de Chamula, 1785," AGCh, *Boletín* 6 (1956): 75–100.

56. AGGG, Serie Chiapas, "Padrones de los tributarios, 1816–1819," A3.16.3.4168.308.

57. Sociedad Económica de Ciudad Real, "Informe rendido . . . , 1819," AGCh, *Boletín* 6 (1956): 17.

58. Calnek, "Highland Chiapas," pp. 49–71; Eugenio Maurer, "Les Tseltales, des paiens superficellement christianisés ou des Indiens fondamentalement chrétiens," Thèse pour le Doctorat en 3ème Cycle, Ecole des Hautes Etudes en Sciences Sociales, Paris, 1978.

59. For more discussion, see Wasserstrom, "White Fathers," chapter 2.

60. Marcos Bravo de la Serna y Manrique, *Carta pastoral*, Guatemala, 1679, pp. 47–48 (typescript in the Biblioteca "Fray Bartolomé de Las Cassas," San Cristóbal).

61. Marcos Bravo de la Serna, p. 34.

62. Ibid., p. 33.

63. Trens, *Historia de Chiapas*, p. 181.

64. Naturally, such practices were condemned by Dominican authorities as idolatrous and pagan. It is ironic that many modern scholars accept these views, which hold that Indians in Chiapas had never truly understood or accepted Christianity and that they continued to practice their old rites whenever they could. In fact, native conversions appear to have been quite genuine, whereas allegations to the contrary almost invariably served to justify the misbehavior of the pastors. See Ximénez, *Historia de la provincia*, III, 261.

65. Marcos Bravo de la Serna, p. 34.

66. López Sánchez, *Apuntes históricos*, p. 714.

67. Klein, "Rebeliones," p. 153.

68. López Sánchez, *Apuntes históricos*, p. 704.

69. AGCh, *Boletín* 2 (1955): 25–52.

70. Ibid., pp. 53–66.

71. Ximénez, *Historia de la provincia*, III, 266.

72. Ibid., p. 263.

73. Ibid., p. 268.

74. Ibid., p. 270.

75. Ibid., p. 271. Cofradías were religious brotherhoods that collected funds to

pay for communal religious celebrations. By the mid-sixteenth century, they also permitted local priests to engage in a sort of ecclesiastical repartimiento. For a more complete discussion of this phenomenon, see my "Population Growth and Economic Development," and also my "Religious Service in Zinacantan, 1793–1975," unpublished manuscript, 1978.

76. Ximénez, Historia de la Provincia, III, 280.

77. López Sánchez, Apuntes históricos, p.720; Ximénez, Historia de la provincia, III, 281.

78. Ximénez, Historia de la provincia, III, 281–82.

79. Ibid., p. 284.

80. Ibid., p. 287.

81. Ibid., p. 287.

82. López Sánchez, Apuntes históricos, p. 716.

83. Francisco Orozco y Jiménez, Colección de documentos inéditos, II (1911), 152.

84. Ximénez, Historia de la provincia, III, 282–83.

85. Ibid., pp. 333–34.

86. P. Manuel Hidalgo, Libro en que se trata de la lengua tzotzil (Paris, 1735) (Bibliothèque Nationale, Département des Manuscripts, Ms. Mexicain 412, R27.747).

87. Klein, "Rebeliones," pp. 151–52.

88. See Gosner, "Tzeltal Revolt of 1712."

89. A more extended description of these cofradías may be found in Wasserstrom, "White Fathers," chapter 2, and in Jan Rus and Robert Wasserstrom, "Civil-Religious Hierarchies in Central Chiapas: A Critical Perspective," American Ethnologist 7 (1980): 466–78.

90. Rus and Wasserstrom, "Civil-Religious Hierarchies."

91. AHDSC, "Autos fechos en la secularización de curatos vacantes que poseían los regulares de Nuestro Padre Santo Domingo proveidos en clérigos interinos, 1771."

92. William Taylor, Landlord and Peasant in Colonial Oaxaca (Stanford, 1972).

93. Compare with Enrique Semo, Historia del capitalismo en México (Mexico City, 1973), p. 88.

94. Stefano Varese, "El estado y lo múltiple," unpublished manuscript, 1978.

Jan Rus

Whose Caste War?
Indians, Ladinos,
and the Chiapas
"Caste War" of 1869

Between 1868 and 1870, the people of Chamula and several related Tzotzil-speaking communities of the Chiapas highlands rose in a savage and cruel war of extermination against their "ladino" neighbors. Mobilized by an unscrupulous leader who fooled them into believing he could talk to a set of crude clay "saints," they first withdrew to the forest, where they built a temple to their new religion. Here the leader, in order to increase his power, had a young boy crucified on Good Friday, 1868, as an Indian "Christ."

Conscientious ladino authorities, horrified by such barbarity, strove for more than a year to make the Indians see the error of their ways and return to civilization. Unfortunately, all of their efforts were finally in vain: joined by a mysterious ladino outcast who trained them in military maneuvers, the Indian hordes swept out of the mountains in June 1869, pillaging and slaughtering all not of their own race. Their first victims were the very priests and school-teachers who had gone among them to enlighten them. In short order, they also massacred the families of small ladino farmers who had dared to take up vacant lands on the borders of their territories. Finally, they attacked the nearby capital of San Cristóbal itself, retreating only when driven back by ladino reinforcements spontaneously rallied from throughout the state. Although soundly beaten in every subsequent engagement, such were their fanaticism and cunning that it was still to be almost a year before the state militia was able to run the last of their renegade bands to earth.

Introduction

This version of the "Caste War of 1869," essentially that handed down to us by nineteenth-century ladino journalists and historians,[1] is still invoked today in the highlands of Chiapas to prove the precariousness of civilization's hold on the Indians and to demonstrate the danger of allowing even the slightest autonomous activity in their communities. Although anthropologists and others have worked it over in recent years,[2] often with the stated purpose of telling the Indians' side of the story, none seems to have questioned either its specific details or the overall impression it creates that the energy for the "Caste War" was drawn entirely from the Indians' own peculiar religious transformation of their hatred for ladinos.

What makes this unfortunate is that almost none of the story appears to be true.

Originally, the purpose of this paper was to review the history of Indian-ladino relations in the decades leading up to the "Caste War" in an attempt to develop a more satisfying picture, perhaps even an explanation, of the Indians' behavior. What it hoped to establish was that the Chamulas did indeed have objective reasons to rebel and that the "Caste War," far from being a sudden explosion, was actually the culmination of years of unrest. It also hoped to show that it was not sufficient to attribute the rebellion simply to religious hysteria—that calling it a "revitalization movement" not only obscured the fact that a vigorous tradition of native Christianity existed before and after 1869, but begged all of the interesting questions about why the Indians should have risen at this particular moment in this particular way.

What in fact emerged from this review, however, was something quite different. As it now stands, what took place in Chiapas in the late 1860s was not a "caste war" at all, at least not to the Indians. Instead, the provocation and violence were almost entirely on the side of the ladinos; the Indians, far from having been the perpetrators of massacres, were the victims!

Obviously, such a sharp reversal of the "traditional" history calls for substantiation. In attempting to provide it, the present paper departs from earlier treatments in two ways. First, given what seem to be misrepresentations in the classic sources—many of them written long after the facts—it attempts to build strictly from primary materials: diaries, official reports, and the recently discovered correspondence of the parish priests in the "rebel" communities. Second, and more important, it attempts to locate the "Caste War" in an overall history of Chiapas's development from independence in the 1820s through the first establishment of a national Mexican state in the late 1860s.

Seen in this larger context, the attacks on the Indians in 1869–70 appear to have been little more than the final act of a drama that began when Chiapas's ladinos began competing among themselves for control of the state's land and labor following independence. Through the decades, this competition led both to increasingly bitter confrontations within ladino society itself and to the progressive impoverishment of the state's Indians—a fact on which the liberal, lowland-based ladino faction attempted to capitalize in the mid-1860s by turning the Indians against its conservative rivals and their allies in the church. Realizing only afterward that the Indians' receptivity to this politicization jeopardized their own control of them as much as the conservatives', the liberals then joined the conservatives in the punitive expeditions that came to be known as the "Caste War."

Unfortunately, the Indians have been victimized twice by these events: once by the violence itself, and a second time by the myth that they, not the ladinos, were to blame. In a final section, then, the paper will attempt to trace the course of this myth during the last century, looking both at the interests it has served and the elaborations and distortions it has collected as it has gone along. Perhaps in this way it can restore some balance to discussions of the nature and possibilities of Chiapas's native societies, both of which have long been skewed by the memory of the "Caste War."

The Competition for Chiapas, 1821–1855

To Chiapas's ladino elite, the end of the colony in 1821 marked the beginning of a protracted, and increasingly violent, struggle for local power. Although stable political parties did not form until much later, two broad class and regional tendencies were apparent from the beginning: on one side the "conservatives" of San Cristóbal and the highlands; on the other, the "liberals" of Tuxtla, Chiapa, and the lowlands.[3]

San Cristóbal was the traditional capital of Chiapas and the seat of its diocese. Its elite were civil and religious bureaucrats and the owners of large estates: men who lived on the rents and taxes of the large surrounding Indian population. Following independence, such people saw themselves as the natural heirs of the power and privilege that had belonged to the colonial church and crown. Accordingly, they campaigned for a government of continuity after 1821—a centralized, paternalistic regime that would not only preserve the status quo but deliver it into their hands.

The lowlands, on the other hand, were already by the 1820s becoming host to a vigorous commerical agriculture. Their natural leaders were ranchers and merchants: men who, as they became successful, became

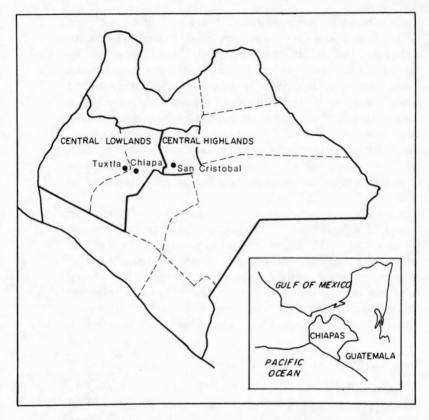

Departments of the Central Highlands and Central Lowlands of Chiapas

Source: *Carta General del Estado de Chiapas,* 1858

Table 1: Chiapas Population by Region, 1819

Region	Ladinos	Indians	Share of Total Indians
Central Highlands	5,677	56,389	54%
Central Lowlands	4,706	7,312	7%
Other	12,315	40,461	39%

Source: "Informe rendido por la Sociedad Económica de Ciudad Real sobre las ventajas y desventajas obtenidas con . . . el sistema de intendencias," 1819, in *Documentos históricos del estado de Chiapas*, Tuxtla, 1956.

hungry for more land and, especially, more Indian laborers. Under the centralist government favored by San Cristóbal, however, access to such resources would be controlled by a self-interested administration of highlanders. Hoping, then, for the local autonomy that would at least permit them to reorganize and develop their own region, such men opted after 1821 for a liberal, federal form of government.

Conflict between these two factions, whatever the appearances, was never so much over ideals or future models of society as over division of the spoils left by the colony. Chief of these was land — particularly, at first, Indian land. This was followed closely by labor and, what was essentially the same thing, tax revenues. Office-holding being the one proven route to a share of these, opportunities for "public service" were avidly sought by ambitious men on both sides — so avidly, in fact, that the continual pronunciamientos and revolts gave Chiapas more than twenty-five governors before 1850.[4] Meanwhile, through all of this instability, the one constant was a steady decline in the position of the Indians.

Of greatest consequence to native peoples was the loss of their lands. At the close of the colonial period, a great deal of Chiapas's territory was tied up in *terrenos baldíos*, or "vacant lands" — vast expanses that had been held in trust by the crown as a buffer around the Indian communities. Although these lands were technically part of the Indian townships, the Indians themselves were legally excluded from them, being limited instead to the *ejidos* laid out around their churches. However, they were also off limits to ladinos. Arguing after independence that to leave such an immense resource unexploited would unnecessarily retard the state's

development, successive governments between 1826 and 1844, liberal
and conservative alike, progressively simplified the process by which
private citizens could "denounce," or claim, them. As a result, by 1850
virtually all the state's Indian communities had been stripped of their
"excess" lands.[5]

The effects of this land-grab cannot be overemphasized. Lowland
communities, invaded during the 1830s and 40s by aggressive farmers
who actually intended to use their lands, found themselves driven out of
their townships altogether during this period. Their communal ties broken, many melted into the deculturated lower classes of nearby ladino
towns and "assimilated." In the highlands, on the other hand, where
denser populations, less fertile soils, and a more torpid economic tradition prevented the kind of development that would have dissolved communities, the land-grabbers instead folded whole townships—always
with the exception of a small central ejido—into great feudal estates. Of
the twenty-five intact Tzotzil and Tzeltal townships that existed at independence, all suffered this fate to one degree or another.[6] Such, for
example, was the case of Chamula.

Although attempts had been made to expropriate its terrenos baldíos as
early as the 1830s, it was not until 1846 that the Larraínzar family
succeeded in "denouncing" the three-quarters of Chamula's land—476
caballerías (47,600 acres) out of a total of 636—not protected by its ejido.
This tract, together with those in two adjacent townships expropriated at
the same time, formed the estate of "Nuevo Edén," containing a total of
some 874 caballerías.[7] Although it had not been strictly legal for
Chamulas to be living in these lands before their denunciation, population pressures had in fact forced many to take up residence there as early
as the mid-eighteenth century.[8] Faced after denunciation with the choice
of moving off or remaining as serfs, most of these clandestine settlers
stayed, becoming laborers on sugar and tobacco plantings belonging to
the Larraínzars in lower elevations. It can be calculated that by the early
1850s a minimum of 740 families were in this situation, each adult male of
whom furnished three days of labor per month to keep his plot—a total of
26,640 man-days of unpaid labor a year for lands where their ancestors
had lived without fee for generations.[9]

Although certainly one of the more spectacular depredations of its
kind, "Nuevo Edén" was hardly unique. On the contrary, highland
ladinos of more modest means and ambition also took advantage of the
new laws, with the result that by 1850 practically every township in the

region had acquired a permanent settlement of ladino "farmers" and "merchants." Through land denunciations, usurious loan practices, and sales of alcohol and over-priced commodities, such "homesteaders" were able in the barely twenty-five years from 1826 to the 1850s to transform more than a quarter of Chiapas's Indians from "free" villagers into permanently—and legally—obligated peons and laborers.[10]

This, in turn, partially accounts for the fate of native labor after independence: much of it simply went to those who got the land. The question, however, is more complicated than that. Although direct competition for land between liberals and conservatives was muted, at least at first, by the fact that there were terrenos baldíos in both highlands and lowlands, competition for control of native labor and taxes was not so easily dampened. On the one hand, the overwhelming majority of Indian workers lived in the highlands; on the other, the expansion of commercial agriculture in the lowlands made that region the one with the greater demand for laborers. Unfortunately, highland conservatives were loath to turn over control of "their" Indians to meet this demand, with the result that competition for Indian labor early became one of the great sources of interregional conflict.

In the years immediately after independence, Chiapas's conservative government had granted day-to-day control of Indian affairs throughout the state to the church. Through its parish priests it was thus empowered, as it had been under the colony, to register vital statistics, provide census (and thus tax) rolls, oversee the collection of native taxes, and defend the Indians' persons and property. In exchange, the government agreed to permit the church to collect its traditional emoluments, authorizing the use of civil force if necessary.[11]

The problem with this arrangement, from the liberals' point of view, was that it virtually cut them off from access to highland workers. First, it made the highland clergy, ever protective of its own interest in stationary, paying parishioners, gatekeepers of Indian labor.[12] Second, in a state where the head tax frequently accounted for more than 90 percent of the government's revenues, and where a disproportionate share of the heads belonged to highland Indians, it gave that same clergy a virtual veto over the state budget.[13] Accordingly, when the liberals came to power in 1830 one of their first acts was to secularize administration of the Indians, naming officials to handle all civil affairs in the native communities.[14]

For a decade and a half, that was where matters remained. In 1844, however, the conservatives' last major alteration of the state's agrarian laws—the one that permitted them to denounce even those terrenos baldíos already occupied by permanent Indian settlers—suddenly threatened the liberals' access to labor all over again. With denunciation of lands like those of Chamula, highland conservatives suddenly acquired almost exclusive control of the labor of entire communities. In response, liberal governments of the late 1840s, in an effort to "liberate" the Indian workers they needed, outlawed serfdom and even tried retroactively to enlarge the Indians' ejidos and force the return of lands to fill them.[15] Unfortunately, such efforts had little effect: before they could be enforced, Mexico was overtaken by yet another political crisis and the conservatives regained control of the state government.

While ladinos thus maneuvered among themselves for a better grip on the state's land and labor, the effect of the changes of these first decades on the Indians was little short of devastating. The condition of Chamula by the early 1850s is again perhaps typical of the highland Tzotzils and Tzeltals in general: by 1855, the community was providing the equivalent of twenty thousand man-days of labor a year to the government as its head tax.[16] At the same time, the value of the taxes, provisions, and personal service it rendered annually to its priests and their superiors—all of which continued to be required by law—came to another seventeen thousand man-days, a figure that does not even include the cost of the actual religious celebrations themselves.[17] Add to these exactions the labor on "Nuevo Edén" and the stipend the community was forced to pay both its secretary and schoolteacher, and the men of Chamula, numbering at most three thousand in the mid-1850s, were providing almost a month of labor per man per year to their various overlords, an almost intolerable burden for a people already on the lower edge of subsistence.[18]

In spite of the harshness of this regimen, however, the Indians of the central highlands seem to have been remarkably restrained and orderly in their protests during this period. Surviving records of the years 1840–59 tell of communities occasionally refusing to pay their priests what were considered unfair charges (eleven cases); of native leaders disputing the authority of secretaries and other petty officials (two cases); and of community members disagreeing with ladino settlers over land boundaries and wages (four cases).[19] What is perhaps most interesting about these cases, however, is that they are known at all only because they were eventually resolved by the superior civil and ecclesiastical authorities to whom the Indians themselves appealed. Essentially the Indians continued to respect—or at least obey—the laws and procedures to which they had been subject under the colony even while ladinos trampled them in their headlong race to enrich themselves.

Indeed, given their relative positions, it is ironic that the insecure, unstable element of Chiapas society during the first thirty years after independence was not the Indian one but the ladino. In addition to political factionalism, ladinos were also tortured by the conviction that a race war with the Indians was both imminent and inevitable, a fear that seems to have become particularly pronounced from the mid-1840s on—not coincidentally the period of greatest escalation in exploitation. Thus, for instance, a leitmotif of the bishop's letters to the parish priests in the 1840s became his questioning about the Indians' physical and moral condition, their particular vices, and, especially, the degree of their acceptance of the status quo.[20] Thus again the widespread panic that ensued in 1848 when news of the Caste War of Yucatan was quickly followed by rumors that Tzeltal Indians from several municipios were meeting in secret, perhaps to plan a caste war right in Chiapas. Although no ladino was attacked, even verbally, in this 1848 "uprising," such was the hysteria that fifty Indian "ringleaders" were arrested and sent to San Cristóbal, and many settlers fled their new lands to return permanently to civilization.[21]

Breakdown and Civil War, 1855–1864

By the mid-1850s, fear of the Indians, so prominent just a few years before, was being pushed aside as ladinos became ever more preoccupied with developments in their own society. The political and economic squabbles of the 1830s and 40s had by this time hardened into bitter regional factionalism. Conservatives, in retaliation for what they considered unreasonable attacks on their interests in the serfdom and ejido laws of the late 1840s, had tried in the early 1850s to wreck the agricultural economy of the lowlands by prohibiting the export of cattle and threatening to rescind titles to former terrenos baldíos.[22] Lowlanders, in turn, having no recourse locally, were driven by such measures to identify ever more closely with the national liberal opposition, adopting even its anticlericalism as it became clear in the middle of the decade that San Cristóbal's ecclesiastical hierarchy had thrown itself behind the conservatives.[23] The result was a dizzying escalation of hostility between highlands and lowlands, liberals and conservatives. Any resolution short of war seemed increasingly unlikely.

The explosion finally came with the national liberals' overthrow of the government in Mexico City in 1855. In an effort to break once and for all the "colonial institutions" they blamed for Mexico's distress, the resulting liberal government embarked almost immediately on a series of reforms designed to submit them to "popular," "democratic" rule. Foremost of their targets was the church, and within months they had not only undermined the authority of religious courts but nationalized church lands and abolished the civil enforcement of religious taxes. Ecclesiastics, of course, condemned these measures, and national conservatives, thus provided with the excuse they needed, pronounced against the government. The resulting War of Reform raged in central Mexico through 1860, finally ending with the liberals' re-entry into Mexico City in January 1861.[24] Even then the fighting did not end. Die-hard conservatives, unwilling to accept the liberals' triumph, now looked outside of Mexico for aid to continue their resistance. They soon found it in England, Spain, and France, which, using unpaid debts as an excuse, invaded Mexico on the conservatives' behalf in late 1861. Although England and Spain soon withdrew, the French remained until mid-1867, trying, in league with Mexican conservatives, to impose a European, Catholic monarchy.[25]

Events in Chiapas during this period closely paralleled those in central Mexico, the principal distinction being that Chiapas's wars were fought not by national armies, but entirely by bands representing the state's own sharply-defined regional factions. Thus, for instance, the War of Reform in the state began with the adherence in July 1856 of one Juan Ortega to the anti-Reform pronouncements that had emanated from central Mexico a few months earlier. In a matter of weeks, other highland dissidents had joined him, and by the fall of 1856 they were carrying on a running guerrilla war with the state's constitutional liberal authorities. Indeed, so hostile did they make the atmosphere in the highlands that in October the liberals withdrew from the region, taking the state capital to Chiapa until its safety in San Cristóbal could be guaranteed. Ortega's revolt continued until late 1860, when, with the defeat of the national conservative forces, further resistence became pointless. Peace re-established, the state capital was returned to the highlands in February 1861.[26]

The record of this first war's effect on the Tzotzils is fragmentary and contradictory. On the one hand, they seem to have welcomed the liberals' rise in 1855 because many of the leading conservative politicians— among them the owners of "Nuevo Edén"—sold their lands back to the native communities (the only ones who would buy them) and fled the state.[27] On the other, led by their priests, they also apparently provided bearers and supplies to the conservative rebels during those periods when they were operating in their territories.[28] Wherever their sympathies actually lay, however—and the fact is they had little reason to favor either side—the war itself seems to have benefited the Indians: no head tax was collected from 1856 to 1861; commerce was interrupted, thus relieving them of the burdens of long-distance cargo-bearing and mule-skinning; and religious taxes, although they were paid through 1858, were suspended after mid-1858 because many of the priests who had collaborated most actively with the conservatives fled when the balance in the highlands began to tip in favor of the liberals.[29] As a result, the years 1856–61 were probably among the Indians' best since 1821.

Unfortunately, such relatively good times were not to last. With the resumption of liberal control over the highlands in 1861, the "benign neglect" of the late 1850s suddenly came to an end. New secretaries were appointed, and through them the liberals set out to rebuild the state treasury by reviving the head tax. However, in 1862, before this effort could bear fruit, the need for troops to send against the French came to overshadow all other concerns. Chiapas was ordered by the federal government to provide and maintain a battalion of a thousand men in the central Mexican campaigns, and conscription for this purpose fell especially hard on the poor. Chamula, for instance, was required to supply a hundred soldiers—a demand that caused the pueblo to be virtually deserted during the first half of 1862 as families fled into the forest to avoid the draft.[30] Eventually, of course, the government would get its soldiers anyway, but no one was about to "volunteer" by making himself conspicuous.

Meanwhile, highland conservatives, alarmed by the liberals' inroads into "their" Indians, and encouraged by news of interventionist triumphs in central Mexico to try to counteract them, began trying to re-establish themselves in the native communities in mid-1862. The reception of the priests who were their emissaries was, however, at best wary. On the one hand, the Indians recognized their control of native religion, and thus their indispensability as religious practitioners. On the other, they also knew that the return of the priests meant the resumption of religious taxes—taxes their liberal secretaries had been assuring them for a year were no longer legal. Something of the resulting ambivalence comes through in the July 1862 report of Chamula's new priest, Manuel María Suárez, on his first interview with the community's leaders: "I exhorted them to comply with their ancient obligations and duties to the Church, to which they replied that it was only a shortage of grain that had prevented them from doing so in recent years, but that, their harvest completed, they will again begin to pay."[31] In fact, this supposed "shortage of grain" was probably an evasion: during the same period, the Indians of other communities, prompted by their secretaries, refused outright to pay the church. In Cancuc, for instance, officials informed their new priest in early 1863 that not only were they not obliged to pay him but that neither did they intend to give him anything to eat unless he could buy it![32] In Chamula, however, such flat rejection was apparently still not possible in 1862. Indeed, parish records for 1860–63 indicate that all religious taxes due in those years were eventually–though retroactively—paid.[33]

This retroactive payment is probably explained by the sudden reversal of liberal-conservative fortunes in the highlands in late 1862 and early 1863. During the second half of 1862, liberal setbacks in the war against the French led Chiapas's conservatives to feel ever more confident in their efforts to regain control of at least their own region. Local liberals, on the other hand, their mastery of the situation fading, again withdrew their capital to the lowlands, this time to Tuxtla, on January 1, 1863. For a few months, competition between the two parties for control of the Indians was closely contested, but then, in April, Ortega again pronounced, and within a month attacked and took San Cristóbal. Although soon driven out on this first attempt, he returned in August at the head of a force of six hundred men and this time succeeded in investing the city. In spite of a bombardment that, in the process of defeating the small liberal garrison, destroyed the city hall and much of the center, he and his troops were enthusiastically received by the church and the local elite, all of whom quickly pledged loyalty to the "Intervention" and new "Mexican Empire."[34]

Through the fall of 1863, Ortega and his allies organized the highlands and raised an army to subdue those parts of the state that chose to remain "in a state of rebellion" against the empire. Finally, in late October, leading a force of some twelve hundred men—two hundred of them Chamulas "recruited" by their parish priest—the imperialistas set off to attack Chiapa.[35] Despite superior numbers and the element of surprise, however, they were beaten back by the local liberal militia, suffering grievous—mostly Indian—casualties in the process. Within ten more weeks, liberal forces had besieged San Cristóbal, and after an eleven-day fight that left the center of the city in ruins, the Ortegistas were driven back into the hills.[36]

If anything, the material demands placed on the Indians by the brief imperial government were even harder than had been those of the liberal regime of 1861–62. Whereas the liberals had asked contributions and then levies of men, the conservatives took not only soldiers—and more of them than the liberals—but also forced labor crews, for the building of extensive fortifications in San Cristóbal.[37] In addition, the Indians were also forced to pay religious taxes, the priests making free use of imperial forces to support their authority.[38]

Even harder on the Indians than the material exactions to which they were subject between 1861 and 1864 were the conflicting political pressures. As much as each party wanted for itself the Indians' numbers and taxes, it seems to have wanted at least as much to deny those resources to its opponents. This explains the efforts of secretaries and priests alike to turn the Indians against their opposites. Not surprisingly, however, these efforts were profoundly traumatic for the Indian communities themselves. Whereas traditionally such communities had maintained strong chains of command firmly attuned to the dominant ladino authorities, now they were being forced to choose among competing authorities, none of whom could offer much certainty even of their own tenure. As a result, no matter what choice the Indians made, the other side was bound to disapprove and, perhaps, retaliate. This explains the caution of Chamula's officials when, with a liberal secretary still in the community, they demurred at the priest's first requests for payment in 1862. It also explains their eventual contributions to both sides, each during its respective period of dominance.

Under such contradictory pressures, it should not be surprising that discipline within communities, sustained even through the most exploitive days of the 1840s and early 50s, was beginning to break down. In Chamula, for example, there were disturbances in September 1862 and again in January 1863—"half the community turning against the other half," with twenty-three killed in a single day during the first.[39] Given the ladinos' hypersensitivity to inter-ethnic violence just a few years before, however, what was even more striking was that now, through their own efforts to politicize the native communities, they themselves were unraveling the social controls that had formerly made such violence almost unthinkable. On September 22, 1863, for instance, in the midst of his efforts to mobilize Chamula for the empire, the parish priest was briefly threatened by disgruntled community members who actually killed three of his Indian companions. Far from reflecting on his own activities, however—on the implications of preparing Chamula soldiers for a war against the liberal state government—he thought only of avenging himself on his assailants: "Although I miraculously escaped with my life, I beg the ecclesiastical government for permission to testify against the perpetrators before the imperical authorities, advising you in advance that Señor Ortega has promised me they will be shot. I thus ask dispensation so as to incur no irregularity for this effusion of blood.[40"]

Politicization of the Indians, 1864–1867

With the final defeat and expulsion of Ortega in early 1864, the liberals were for the first time undisputed masters of Chiapas. San Cristóbal, its army dispersed, its public buildings destroyed, and many of its leaders in exile in Guatemala and central Mexico, was not only beaten politically but ruined economically as well. Gone were most of its prewar sources of income: serfs, church estates, and possession of the state capital. In decline, as more and more Indians came to understand the meaning of the recent wars and reforms, was income from religious taxes. As a result, commerce in the city also suffered, and many merchants and artisans, unable to make a living in the highlands, migrated to the lowlands and coast between 1864 and 1870.[41]

Unfortunately, the conservatives' loss was not entirely the liberals' gain. For one thing, the war with the French continued in central Mexico for three more years—years during which, the national economy being disrupted, there was almost no demand for Chiapas's agricultural exports. This, in turn, retarded the lowlanders' efforts to assert control of the highland labor force that should have been their "prize" for winning the wars: having no markets for their products, they had little incentive to organize migrant workers to produce them.[42]

There being no other outlet for liberal energies after Ortega's defeat, the lowlanders soon took to quarreling among themselves for control of the state's government and armies. Finally, in December 1864, with a complete breakdown of public order a real threat, Porfirio Díaz, commander of the liberal forces in central Mexico, declared that a state of war existed in Chiapas and appointed Pantaleón Domínguez its military governor.[43] Domínguez belonged to no local faction: his following consisted entirely of members of the Chiapas battalion he had commanded against the French in 1862. Instead of placing him above petty squabbles, however, this status seems to have made him a special target for the wrath of local liberals, many of whom now united to denounce his "usurpation" of the state's "democratic traditions"! As a result, between 1864 and 1867 he had to contend not only with conservative guerrillas in outlying districts but with two pronunciamientos by fellow liberals and the indignity of a brief arrest at the hands of mutinous subordinates. In spite of these trials, however, when the imperialists were finally driven from Mexico in 1867 Domínguez succeeded in having himself chosen Chiapas's constitutional governor.[44]

Among the few things on which liberals could agree during the first part of Domínguez's tenure was the necessity of punishing San Cristóbal and the conservatives for their "treason" of 1863–64. Many, for example, thought that the ex-imperialistas, already deprived of their rights to vote and hold office, should also be forced to pay reparations for the costs of the war.[45] Given San Cristóbal's impoverishment, however, and the lowland-ers' own lack of unity, such payments were never collected. Instead, Domínguez settled on more bureaucratic, passive means of revenge: public expenditures in the highlands were virtually suspended, lowland-ers were appointed to all civil offices, and efforts were made to block access to arms and ammunition. As for replacing the church and conser-vatives as gatekeepers of Indian labor, here the government's distraction was perhaps most obvious, its measures most half-hearted. Some efforts were made through the secretaries to inform the Indians of their new rights under the reforms and to discourage them from paying religious taxes.[46] In addition, the head tax, already in abeyance since mid-1862, was suspended, ostensibly as an offering for the Indians' loyalty, although in fact there were no officials in the highlands capable of collecting it.[47]

Considering the relative leniency of these measures (lenient when compared to what the more radical lowlanders would have liked to demand), it is perhaps ironic that the national government's attempts after mid-1867 to heal the nation's wounds and reconcile former enemies should actually have had the opposite effect in Chiapas, aggravating liberal-conservative antagonisms rather than soothing them. First, in the late summer of 1867 the national government decreed that former im-perialistas were to be amnestied. Their civil rights restored, they would thus be eligible to participate fully in the elections planned for later in the fall.[48] Then, in November, it was announced that all state capitals dis-placed by the war should be returned to their original elites.[49] Taken together, what these "conciliatory gestures" meant in the case of Chiapas was that just as normal economic activity was about to resume, just as the lowlands were again going to need highland labor, the highlanders were to be restored to full control over that labor.

Domínguez's reaction was swift. In an attempt to "obey without com-plying," he moved the capital not to San Cristóbal but "part way"—from Tuxtla to Chiapa—vowing that there it would stay "until funds permitted the organization of sufficient forces to give it security" in the highlands.[50]

At the same time, to make sure the church and conservatives would never again threaten that security or block access to highland labor, he embarked on an all-out campaign to break their hold on the Indians.

To some extent, the persuasion of the secretaries between 1864 and 1867 had already begun to loosen this hold: reports from various communities during this period indicate that the movement against paying church taxes was slowly but steadily gaining momentum. Beginning in late 1867, however, liberal attacks were aimed not just at the church's financial arrangements in its Indian parishes but at its very grip on native religion itself. The assault began with the reiteration of earlier guarantees of religious tolerance and immunity from the forced collection of religious payments. Then, in November, a decree was issued abolishing the offices of mayordomo and alférez—religious *cargos* that were at once the pinnacle of native religious participation and the means by which parish priests collected funds from their Indian congregations.[51] Acting through the secretaries, the government went so far as to encourage the Indians to abandon the churches altogether if necessary to avoid such service—to practice Catholicism without the priests and their temples![52]

The success of these initiatives seems to have taken even the liberals by surprise. For more than three centuries Indian religious observance—the core of native communal life—had been controlled by a non-Indian clergy. By the mid-1860s, however, the conduct of this clergy, as of ladinos generally, had become so exploitive, so destructive, that given the chance to free themselves of any part of it the Indians leapt to take it. From throughout the highlands letters flooded into the ecclesiastical government from late 1867 through early 1869 telling of communities spurning the priests' services and worshipping on their own. If any priest dared complain, or even question the new laws, the communities, backed by their secretaries, immediately carried the case to the liberal government in Chiapa and had him reprimanded. Such repudiation of the clergy was reported from Zinacantan, Oxchuc, Huistán, Tenejapa, Chalchiguitán, Pantelhó, Chenalhó, Mitontic, and Chamula during this period—this in addition to Cancuc, which had made a similar choice several years earlier.[53]

The course of native religion after these breaks varied from community to community, apparently depending as much on the character of the priests as on the nature of the communities themselves. In Oxchuc and Huistán, for instance, where the priest was weak, community members continued to frequent their parish churches, simply ignoring the impotent father's nagging requests for money.[54] In Tenejapa, where the

Table 2: Episcopal Income from Indian Parishes,
1862–69 (Excluding the Vicarate of Chamula)

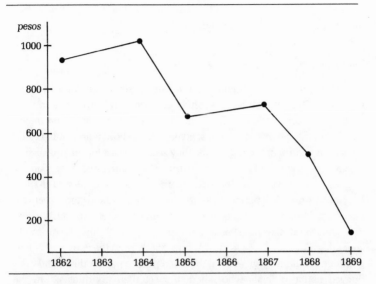

Source: "Estado general y comparativo . . . de los ingresos . . . 1° de Enero de 1862 a
31 de Diciembre de 1869, Yglesia Catedral de San Cristóbal de Las Casas, Dic. 14 de
1873" (Archivo Histórico Diocesano, San Cristóbal)

priest—Manuel Suárez, late of Chamula—was more interested in his
own standard of living than in religion, parishioners also continued to
worship in the church, while the priest occupied himself with com-
plaining to his superiors about his declining income and requesting permission to make it up by peddling the church's ornaments, in particular a
"chalice of very ancient manufacture that nobody will miss because it is
kept in a locked chest anyway."[55] In Zinacantan, on the other hand, where
the priest was more conscientious, the Indians partially withdrew from
the church, celebrating many of their services away from the pueblo
rather than face constant scoldings. Meetings at the shrine in the hamlet of
Atz'am, for example, became important during this period.[56] Finally, in
Chamula and its annexes (Mitontic, Chenalhó, San Andrés, Magdalenas,
Santa Marta, and Chalchiguitán), the vicar and his assistants, rather than
accept the new conditions of the mid-1860s and moderate their demands,
had actually tried between 1865 and 1868 to reimpose the taxes and
controls of the early 1850s. In response, many of the Indians under their

charge, when given the chance, withdrew from their churches and pueblos altogether, establishing an independent religious and marketing center of their own. It was this withdrawal, and ladino reactions to it, that finally led to the violence of 1869.

The Separatist Movement, 1867–1869

Against the trend in the highlands as a whole, religious income from the vicarate of Chamula actually rose after 1865, for a while even rivaling that of the pre-reform period. In part, this was due to the piety—and uncertainty—of the Indians themselves: given doubts about who would finally emerge in control of the highlands, they seem, at least for the time being, to have been willing to accept a return to the status quo ante. Equally important, however, was the rigor of their new vicar after mid-1865, Miguel Martínez. In a period when the rest of the highland clergy seems to have been in retreat, Martínez was almost uniquely zealous in his efforts to restore the Indian parishes to their former profitability. According to later allegations, he extracted funds improperly from the native cofradías, withheld religious services from those too poor to pay for them, and even flogged native officials who failed to meet their tax quotas.[57] In the uncertain period from 1865 through 1867 such excesses were apparently possible; after the anticlerical decrees of late 1867 they most certainly were not.

The first sign of unrest came in late 1867 with news that people from a large area of the townships of Chamula, Mitontic, and Chenalhó had begun gathering to venerate a set of magical "talking stones" discovered near the hamlet of Tzajalhemel by a Chamula woman, Agustina Gómez Checheb.[58] So important had this phenomenon become by the end of the year that Pedro Díaz Cuzcat, a fiscal from Chamula, journeyed to Tzajalhemel to investigate. After a brief inspection, he announced that he too, like Checheb, could "talk" to the stones, and almost as quickly declared that they represented the saints and had asked that a shrine be built for them on the place of their appearances. By the end of January 1868, the crowds at Tzajalhemel had become larger than ever, attracted now not only by the stones but by the regular sermons of their priest, Cuzcat.[59]

It is significant that Cuzcat was a fiscal. According to an 1855 document describing Chamula's religious structure for future priests, the fiscales were the principal brokers between the church and the local community: in addition to acting as translators for the priests, they also kept all parish records, taught catechism to the young, and even led religious services

Table 3: Episcopal Income from the Vicarate of Chamula, 1862–69

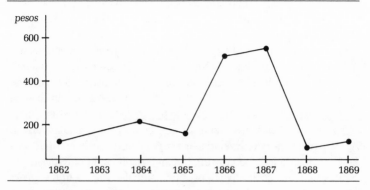

Source: "Cuentas parroquiales, vicaría de Chamula"
(Archivo Histórico Diocesano, San Cristóbal)

themselves in the priests' absence.[60] For this they were paid a small
stipend, and often served for a decade or more at a time.[61] They were, in
fact, the closest thing to a native clergy. Not only, then, did Cuzcat
undoubtedly know of the government's decrees with respect to Indians
and the church when he set out for Tzajalhemel, but he also had the
religious authority necessary to attract others to the new cult he intended
to found.

So quickly did worship at the shrine grow after Cuzcat's arrival that, by
mid-February 1868, Father Martínez himself was forced to visit Tzajalhemel to try to put a stop to it. What he found there was a small native
house, a box-altar with candles and incense burning on it, and a small clay
"saint" that worshippers tried at first to hide from him. Perhaps mindful
of the government's decrees, his reaction on this first occasion was
relatively mild: after lecturing those present about the perils of idolatry, he
ordered them to disperse and, apparently convinced they would, returned forthwith to Chamula.[62]

In fact, however, the next two months proved to be one of the new
religion's periods of fastest growth. Having been mistreated by ladinos of
all parties, especially during the preceding civil wars, many Indians
seemed to find in the isolated shrine a kind of sanctuary, a place where
they could not only pray in peace but could meet and trade with their
neighbors without fear of ladino interference. By March, Indians from

throughout the vicarate of Chamula and from such nearby Tzeltal communities as Tenejapa had begun to attend regularly, making Tzajalhemel
not only an important religious center but one of the highlands' busiest
marketing centers as well.[63]

All of this, of course, had profound effects on the ladinos. As attendance
at Tzajalhemel increased, religious income and commerce in the surrounding ladino towns necessarily decreased. To the lowlanders, this was
a great triumph. Since their reason for attacking the church in the first
place had been to strike at the power of he highland conservatives, these
economic side-effects were an unexpected bonus. To the highlanders, on
the other hand, the new developments appeared in a much more ominous
light. If it continued, the growing Indian boycott could only mean one
thing: utter ruin. Their anxiety became particularly acute in the weeks
following Easter (April 12), 1868, when for the first time in memory
Indians were almost completely absent from the ceremonies—and
businesses—of San Cristóbal.[64] Crying that the long-feared "caste war"
was finally upon them, the city's ladinos organized themselves into
self-defense companies and sent out urgent pleas for aid to the rest of the
highlands.[65]

Finally, on May 3—the Día de Santa Cruz, another important Indian
celebration that San Cristóbal passed without native commerce—the new
conservative *jefe político* of the highlands struck. Accompanied by a force
of twenty-five men, he raided Tzajalhemel, seized Checheb and the
"saints," and ordered the Indians to go home. Much to the highlanders'
consternation, however, the liberal state government—seeing in this raid
proof that its anti-conservative policies were working—promptly ordered Checheb released and the Indians' freedom of worship respected. In
attacking the separatists directly, the conservatives had inadvertently
strengthened them.[66]

Their hands thus tied politically, the highlanders tried a new tack. On
May 27 they sent a commission of three priests to reason with the Indians,
to try to talk them back into paying religion. Finding the masses gathered
at Tzajalhemel "sincere" in their beliefs—that is, still Catholic—but
nevertheless "deluded," the members of this commission blessed a cross
for them to worship and warned them in the direst terms of the dangers of
praying before unconsecrated (that is, "unfranchised") images. Convinced that their superior theology had won the day, they returned
triumphant to San Cristóbal that same afternoon.[67]

Whether due to this commission's persuasiveness or something else,
activity at the shrine did in fact decline during the next two months, a

normal crowd attending the fiesta of Chamula's patron saint, San Juan, on June 24. In August, however, before the feast of Santa Rosa, Tzajalhemel became busier than ever. Emboldened by the continued, tacit support of the state government, the Indians enlarged their temple, purchased a bell and trumpets, chose sacristans and acolytes to care for the building and altar, and named a mayordomo of Santa Rosa to organize the festivities.[68] Indeed, they showed every intention of making ceremonies in Tzajal-hemel as full of pomp and satisfaction as those in the traditional pueblos themselves.

After Santa Rosa, life in Tzajalhemel settled into a routine closely modeled on that of the older pueblos in other ways as well. By this time, Cuzcat had begun to assume more and more of the duties of the parish priests with whom he had formerly had such close contact. On Sundays, he donned a robe and preached at dawn and vespers—services announced by the sacristans with a touch of the bell. On other days, there were petitions to hear, sacraments to dispense, and always the cult of the saints to tend.[69] In addition, there were small daily markets to supervise, and larger, regional gatherings on Sundays and feast days. Although imitation may be the sincerest form of flattery highland ladinos were far from pleased. Aside from the few alcohol sellers and itinerant peddlers who had begun to frequent the new pueblo, Tzajalhemel remained for most anathema.[70]

Finally, on December 2, 1868, they could stand it no longer: concerned more with their own economic survival than with legal niceties, San Cristóbal's leaders dispatched a force of fifty men to put an end to the separatist movement once and for all. Although the Indians tried briefly to resist this invasion and defend their shrine, the ladinos fired into their midst and easily set them to flight. Checheb and several others were arrested, the images and implements were impounded, and the shrine itself was stripped of its decorations. Although Cuzcat escaped, he too was captured as he passed through Ixtapa on his way to beg the state government for relief. He was sent on to Chiapa in irons, and it was to be almost two months before he could prove his innocence of any wrongdoing—at which point the governor, instead of releasing him unconditionally, merely returned him to San Cristóbal, where he was promptly re-arrested by the conservatives on February 8, 1869.[71]

The "Caste War," 1869–70

In order to understand what happened next, it becomes necessary to review developments in ladino society itself during late 1868 and early 1869. In the highlands, on the one hand, the local economy, already weak at the end of 1867, had if anything declined even further during 1868. Although the Indian boycotts and accompanying strife had hurt the region economically, they also seem to have shaken it out of the political lethargy that had afflicted it since 1864. The decisive suppression of the Tzajalhemel movement was one sign of this change; another was the founding, in early 1869, of a weekly newspaper, *La Brújula,* to press the case for restoring San Cristóbal to its former political and economic position. Through its pages, the city's leading ex-imperialists now demanded not only return of the state capital but arms and munitions for a highland militia and public funds to repair buildings damanged and destroyed in 1863–64. Undaunted by their own history of pronunciamientos and insurgence, they also indulged in the most extravagant polemics about the state government's "disrespect" of federal law and authority in denying them these things.[72]

In the lowlands, on the other hand, the situation was just the reverse: economically the region had begun to recover during 1868, but politically it was more divided than at any time since the mid-1860s. According to many, the government had taxed the region unfairly (perhaps because it was the only one capable of paying) and yet had failed to provide such basic services as repair of the roads and ports now needed for continued economic growth. Even more damning, it had failed to extend positive control over the Indian communities of the highlands, and with the revival of lowland agriculture the "negative control" represented by Indian separatism now threatened lowland interests almost as much as highland ones.[73]

Realizing that unless he could consolidate his power quickly he would soon lose it, Domínguez set out in late 1868 to quiet the complaints of the state's two dominant regions while at the same time tightening his grip on its administrative apparatus. He began in December by quietly acceding to the suppression of the Tzajalhemel movement. Then, in early 1869, he announced his intention to begin enforcing the state tax code, particularly the head tax, counting on it not only to provide the funds for needed public services but also to win the support of local officials throughout the state who were to be granted 8 percent of what they collected in commissions. The new taxes were to be paid quarterly, the first installment coming due May 30—and, to make them more compelling, the collectors were authorized to jail indefinitely the ayuntamiento of any township that failed to cooperate.[74]

Unfortunately, Domínguez, his attention fixed on ladino society, does not seem to have given much thought to the effect his decrees might have on the Indians. From December 1868 through mid-April 1869 there had been no activity in Tzajalhemel, and apparently he assumed that the Chamulas and their neighbors would continue to accept meekly whatever new conditions were imposed on them. The assumption, however, was wrong—tragically so. When the new secretaries and schoolteachers began detaining people in their pueblos in April and early May to charge them the first quarter's head tax, the Indians, led this time by dissident members of their own ayuntamientos, simply returned to their refuge in the forest. Again commerce with non-Indians fell off, again church attendance declined, again ladinos throughout the vicarate of Chamula complained to the regional authorities in San Cristóbal.[75]

Events moved rapidly toward a showdown. By mid-May, feeling in San Cristóbal was running strongly in favor of another raid—one that promised to be even more violent, more of a "lesson," than that of the preceding December. Before such an attack could take place, however, Ignacio Fernández de Galindo, a liberal teacher from Central Mexico who had lived in San Cristóbal since early 1868, and who on several occasions had defended the Indians' rights in public debates, slipped out of the city on May 26 with his wife and a student, Benigno Trejo, to warn the Indians of their danger.[76]

What happened next is largely a matter of conjecture. Those who would see the separation of 1869 as a simple continuation of that of 1868—and both as the result of a conspiracy betwen Galindo and Cuzcat—claim that Galindo convinced the Indians he was a divinely-ordained successor to Cuzcat and then organized them into an army to make war on his own race. According to his own later testimony, on the other hand, he merely informed the Indians of their rights and offered to help them turn aside raids on their villages—and that only with the intention of preventing bloodshed.[77]

Whichever of these explanations is the more correct, the one that was believed in San Cristóbal in 1869 was the former. Under its influence, the Indians' withdrawal was by early June being seen not as just another annoying boycott but as the concentration of forces for an all-out attack on whites. Finally, in what appears to have been a last attempt to talk the Indians into submission (and perhaps simultaneously to survey their forces), Father Martínez and the secretaries of Chamula, Mitontic, and Chenalhó arranged to meet in Tzajalhemel the morning of June 13. As it happened, Martínez and his escort from Chamula—the secretary-teacher, the secretary's brother, and Martínez's own Indian servant—arrived early for this appointment. Finding only a few Indians at the shrine, they nevertheless went ahead and tried to persuade them to abandon their "rebellion" and go home. The Indians, for their part, are reported to have received these representations respectfully, even asking the priest's blessing before he left. Unfortunately, they were so respectful that they turned over the shrine's new religious objects when he asked for them. With that the die was cast: before Martínez and his companions could return to Chamula, they were overtaken by a body of Indians who, learning what had happened in Tzajalhemel, had pursued them, determined to retrieve their possessions. In the ensuing struggle, Martínez and the ladinos with him were killed. The "Caste War" was on.[78]

Ladino blood having been spilt, panic swept the highlands. In the city, the self-defense companies, certain an Indian attack was imminent, prepared for the siege. In the outlying villages and hamlets, those who had no immediate escape route gathered at a few of the larger hamlets and prepared to fight. Perhaps the Indians saw in these gatherings potential acts of aggression; perhaps, one set of killings having been committed, some among them felt they no longer had anything to lose. In any case, on June 15 and 16, in what were arguably the only Indian-initiated actions of the entire "war," men from the southern end of the vicarate of Chamula attacked and killed the ladinos sheltered in "Natividad," near San Andrés, and "La Merced," near Santa Marta.[79] At about the same time, the people of Chalchiguitán assassinated their schoolteacher and his family and their priest as they fled toward Simojovel, and the Chamulas dispatched five ladino peddlers on the road to San Cristóbal.[80] Even at its height, however, the violence does not appear to have been indiscriminate: eleven cattle-buyers from Chicoasén seized near Tzajalhemel on June 13 were released unharmed a day later, and ten ladinos and their children resident in Chenalhó during the entire "Caste War" emerged unscathed in mid-July.[81] Apparently most of the Indians' rage was directly at those with whom they had old scores to settle or who had in some way threatened them.

Finally, on June 17, Galindo, in what was evidently an attempt to redirect the Indians' energy, led several thousand of them to San Cristóbal to secure the release of Cuzcat. Despite the terror this "siege" seems to have caused San Cristóbal's already edgy citizens, the Indians' behavior was not what might have been expected of an attacking army: not only did they come under a white flag, but they came at dusk, when fighting would be difficult. What Galindo offered in their behalf was a trade: Cuzcat, Checheb, and the others in exchange for himself, his wife, and Trejo as good-faith hostages.[82]

Explaining this apparent capitulation has always called for the greatest ingenuity on the part of those who would see the events of 1869 as a premeditated "caste war": why would Galindo, "general" of a "force" typically described as overwhelmingly superior, have delivered himself voluntarily into the hands of his "enemies"? The answers have ranged from cowardice to stupidity to the belief that the Indians would soon attack to free him.[83] In fact, however, none of the suggested solutions makes as much sense as that he simply thought he had done no wrong; that in acting as an intermediary between the Indians—inflamed by recent tax measures and the unjust imprisonment of a popular leader— and the ladinos—fearful of a race war—he was actually defusing the situation and performing a service to both. Indeed, after the exchange had been consummated, he not only showed no fear of his fellow ladinos but actually "headed for his house as though nothing had happened"![84] San Cristóbal's leaders, however, were not so complaisant: no sooner had the Indians withdrawn than they invalidated the agreement, claiming it had been made under duress, and arrested Galindo, his wife, and the student.[85]

From June 17 to 21, the Indians celebrated Cuzcat's release in Tzajahemel. Expecting reprisals at any moment, however, they left some six hundred of their number camped above the roads leading from San Cristóbal as sentries—sentries whose digging sticks and machetes would be of but little use if a ladino attack did come. Nevertheless, this continued Indian presence played right into the hands of *La Brújula*'s editors, who now wrote that there could "no longer be any doubt that the Indians were sworn enemies of the whites," that their most fervent desire was to "ravish and kill San Cristóbal's tender wives and sisters, to mutilate the corpses of its children." The only solution, they wrote, was a "war to the death between barbarism and civilization," a war in which—and here was the key—Chiapas's ladinos would for the first time in decades recognize their essential unity.[86]

In spite of the passion of this appeal, however, San Cristóbal's situation at first aroused little sympathy in the lowlands. Indeed, as late as June 18 news of Father Martínez's death was carried in the official newspaper under the restrained heading "Scandals."[87] On the morning of June 20, however—more than a month after the crisis had begun, and a week after the first killings—Domínguez suddenly activated the lowland militia and set off to relieve San Cristóbal. What had happened? First, news of the continuing "siege" of San Cristóbal after June 18 does seem to have aroused many in the lowlands, who now feared that the Indians were escaping any ladino control. Second, and perhaps even more important, there had been elections for local office throughout the lowlands on June 11. When the results were announced the evening of June 19, Domínguez's party had been resoundingly defeated, and, since the elections had been widely regarded as a vote of confidence, a pronouncement against the governor was expected momentarily. By mobilizing the forces that would have carried out such a coup, Domínguez neatly sidestepped his own ouster.[88]

From the moment Domínguez and his three hundred heavily-armed troops marched into San Cristóbal in the mid-afternoon of June 21, the Indians' fate was sealed. Within minutes they had attacked those camped north and west of the city—people who in almost a week had taken no hostile action—leaving more than three hundred of them dead by nightfall. Forty-three ladinos also died in this "glorious battle," most of them apparently local men who turned out to watch the sport and got in the way of their own artillery.[89]

After this first engagement, Domínguez and his new conservative allies looked to their own affairs in San Cristóbal. Fear of the Indians now lifted, San Cristóbal tried Galindo and company on the twenty-third, the "defense" attorneys being the very ex-imperialists who had fanned the flames of the "Caste War" during May and early June. Naturally Galindo could not win, and he and Trejo were executed June 26.[90] Domínguez, meanwhile, his government penniless, his expulsion from office delayed only by the "Caste War," occupied himself with composing urgent appeals to local authorities around the state for volunteers and contributions to the cause of "civilization versus barbarism." Within a week, these requests brought him more than two thousand pesos and seven hundred men, more than enough to preserve his government and provide for the coming military campaign.[91]

Finally, on June 30, their ranks swelled to over a thousand men, the ladino forces set out for the definitive attack on Chamula. According to *La Brújula*, they arrived in that pueblo to find the Indians "arrayed in a truly advantageous position atop a hill," a circumstance that forced them to fight "a valiant hand-to-hand battle to gain the higher ground." In spite of these difficulties, however, and in spite of the fact that the Indians

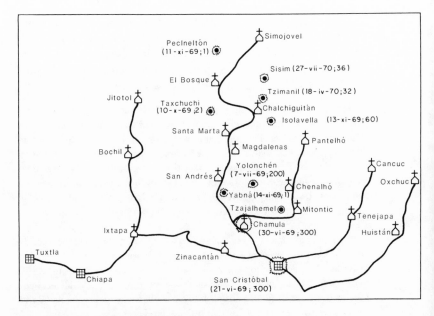

Persecution of the Indian Rebels, 1869–1870 (battle
dates and number of Indians killed in parentheses)

outnumbered them three to one, the government forces somehow prevailed, killing more than three hundred Indians while suffering only
eleven minor injuries of their own![92] Indeed, in light of the very numbers,
a more realistic account of this "battle" is probably that offered by one of
the lowland soldiers present, Pedro José Montesinos:

When we first spied the Chamulas, hundreds of them were scattered in disordered
groups on the hillsides, and before we were within rifle distance all, women and
children as well as men, knelt on their bare knees to beg forgiveness. In spite of the
humble position they took to show submission, however, the government forces
continued to advance, and they, undoubtedly hoping they would be granted the
mercy they begged with tears of sorrow, remained on their knees. At a little less than
200 meters, the soldiers opened fire on their compact masses—and despite the
carnage done to them by the bullets, despite their cries for mercy, continued firing
for some time.

When the government forces finally reached the Chamulas, their thirst for the
blood of that poor, abject race still not slaked, there were suddenly such strident
yells that even knowing nothing of what they said one knew their meaning: with
those shouts they threw themselves against the government forces with an almost
inhuman valor. These poor men, unable to secure the clemency they implored with
tears and prostration, charged with a barbaric bravery.[93]

Following this triumph of "civilization over barbarism," Domínguez repeated a call he had first made several days earlier for the "rebellious
communities to present themselves and surrender. Almost immediately,
what was left of the ayuntamientos of Chamula and Mitontic sent word
through the teacher of Zinacantan that they wished to make peace. Their
suit was accepted on July 4.[94] Meanwhile, on July 3 a squadron of soldiers
had been sent to reconnoiter Tzajalhemel. Although they found the site
deserted, they also found a note, written on official paper, nailed to the
door of the shrine. It was a plea from Cuzcat to Governor Domínguez that
he be forgiven, that he was innocent of any part in a plan to attack ladinos.
Considering that he had been in jail for the half-year before June 17, this
claim is not hard to believe. The soldiers burned the temple and returned
to San Cristóbal.[95]

Ladino leaders now turned to a discussion of what to do next. The
highlanders, having suffered for a year and a half the Indians' boycott of
their churches and businesses, wanted revenge and argued for further
military action. In addition, they proposed that armed garrisons of highland soldiers be stationed in all Indian communities, whether they
had rebelled or not.[96] Clearly, they intended to use the "Caste War" to
strengthen their hold at least on the highlands.

Domínguez, however, chose a course more in keeping with the long-term interests of the lowlands—and himself. First, he placed at the head of each of the pacified communities a native functionary loyal to the state government, enjoining them to prove their loyalty by leading their constituents in the pursuit of the remaining "rebels." Then he ordered the bulk of the state militia—lowlanders unlikely to bow to highland interests—to remain in San Cristóbal to lead this pursuit while he himself returned to Chiapa with the core of professional soldiers to "preserve order" (and thus strengthen his own hand) in the lowlands.[97]

Meanwhile, survivors of the attacks of June 21 and 30 had by this time fled back into the forests north and east of their communities. On July 7, the militia remaining in San Cristóbal had word that one of the "mobs" of these refugees was camped in the hamlet of Yolonchén, near San Andrés. Immediately a force of 360 men was dispatched to deal with it, engaging the Indians—men, women and children—in a fight that left 200 of them dead as against four ladinos.[98] Following this raid, on July 16 an army of 610 infantry, 30 cavalry, and one crew of artillery left San Cristóbal to begin the tour of the Indian townships prescribed by Domínguez. Through July 26, when they returned to the city, they tramped through all the communities as far north as Chalchiguitán—650 ladinos foraging on Indian lands, routing from their homes hundreds of terrified natives who, thus deprived of their livelihoods, were forced to join the refugees from the south in pilfering the stores and butchering the cattle of the abandoned ladino farms that lay in their path. Perversely, the soldiers' descriptions of these ruined farms were then published in La Brújula as further evidence of the destruction being wreaked on the state by the "Indian hordes."[99]

Perhaps most sadly, Indians themselves participated in all these persecutions. Irregular militiamen from Mitontic and Chenalhó took part in the July 16 expedition, and when a second one left San Cristóbal on August 7 it took with it several hundred men from Chamula itself. In their eagerness to prove themselves, these "loyal" Indians were even more ruthless than their ladino masters at hunting down and killing their fellows. Indeed, after mid-September primary responsibility for restoring order was left in their hands, the only direct ladino participants being a squadron of sixty infantry and fourteen cavalry stationed in San Andrés.[100]

Through the fall, there continued to be occasional "contacts" with the "rebels"—from their descriptions, cases in which individual refugees, or at most small family groups, were run down by the soldiers and their native allies and killed. Then, on November 13, the government forces finally caught up with one last camp of exhausted fugitives north of San Andrés. Rather than waste munitions on them, the ladinos sent in 250 Indian lance-bearers, an action that produced the following glowing report from Cresencio Rosas, the expedition's commander: "After an impetuous attack that yielded sixty rebel dead, we retrieved lances, axes, machetes and knives from the field, and took many families prisoner. I send my congratulations to the government and the entire white race for this great triumph of the defenders of humanity against barbarism."[101]

Following this battle, pacification of the central highlands itself was finally judged complete. Some resistance did continue just to the north among bands of highland Indians who had taken advantage of the confusion to flee the haciendas where they had been held as laborers. However, on April 18, 1870, and again on July 27, volunteers from Simojovel attacked the camps of these people, killing thirty-two on the first occasion and thirty-six on the second.[102] With that, the great "Caste War" was finished.

The Myth of the "Caste War," 1871–1981

After 1869, the lowlanders finally had what they sought for decades: effective control of the highland Indians. Although the church resumed its activities in the native communities as soon as they were secured, it never regained the power it had had before the 1860s. Highland conservatives, on the other hand, did recover some authority over the Indians, though nothing like what they had previously enjoyed: in 1872, the state capital was returned to San Cristóbal, and through resumption of their roles as merchants and civil servants the Cristobalenses were able to indebt the Indians, and so dispose of their labor. This was an arrangement apparently acceptable to the lowlanders through the 1870s and 80s. Assured of access to Indian labor, they seemed for the time being to have been willing to leave to highlanders the tasks of organizing and administering that labor at its source.

Meanwhile, there was very little mention of the "Caste War" in ladino society after 1871. When it was introduced, as for instance in Flavio Paniagua's 1876 geography of the state, it was treated as simply one of many interesting facts about the Chamulas and their neighbors, people who were otherwise credited with being very "industrious and hardworking."[103] The repression having been successful, and ladino society itself being prosperous and harmonious for the first time in half a century, no one had any particular interest in reopening the wounds of the 1860s.

Among the Indians, on the other hand, the violence of 1869–70 was not so easily forgotten. Whether they had participated in the "resistance" that preceded it or not, the fighting had affected them all, and all now had to come to grips with it. At least in the larger communities, however, the explanations that have survived have virtually all been anti-Cuzcat—and ultimately anti-Indian. The reasons for this are not hard to find. First, the new leaders imposed on these communities in 1869 continued for several years to use the "Caste War" to justify their rule. In Chamula, for instance, opponents of the ayuntamiento were still in late 1870 being executed on the grounds that they had led, or tried to revive, the "Caste War."[104] Not surprisingly, this had a chilling effect on those who might otherwise have spoken in favor of Cuzcat and Tzajalhemel. Then too, many who had participated in the withdrawals of 1868–69 emigrated from the highlands during the repression and immediately after, some as refugees who never returned, others as forced exiles to Gulf and Pacific coast plantations, and still others as refugees from the too "loyal" ayuntamiento.[105] This removed from the community many who could have passed on a favorable view of the Indians' movement. Unfortunately, those who remained, in order to survive, accepted—and propagated as "ethno-history"—a version of the events of 1868–70 not so different from that of the most conservative of highland ladinos: Cuzcat and his followers became religious fanatics bent on killing ladinos, and the persecution and repression that followed became justified measures of ladino self-defense.[106]

In the late 1880s, after almost twenty years of neglect, San Cristóbal's elite suddenly rediscovered the "Caste War," two books on the subject being published within a few months of each other in 1888–89, and articles and flyers appearing regularly for the next several years.[107] What had happened was that the lowlanders, with the approval of the national government, had begun to talk about moving the state capital, permanently, from San Cristóbal to Tuxtla. The coffee and fruit plantations of Chiapas's southern Pacific coast—up to three hundred miles from San Cristóbal—had begun to boom by this time, and the cattle, cane, and cotton of the central lowlands were also flourishing. There had even begun to be talk of connecting Chiapas to the rest of Mexico by rail. Tuxtla, closer to the center of these developments, was already the state's commercial capital, and the liberals who controlled the state government saw no reason why it should not be the political capital as well.

Against these arguments, all the Cristobalenses could offer were their city's supposedly "aristocratic" traditions and its position at the center of the state's Indian population. The first being a point hardly likely to influence the liberal politicians who would decide between the two cities, they concentrated on the second. What they now claimed was that the peace and prosperity of the highlands, and with them of the entire state, depended on the capital's remaining where it could best "impose respect on the numerous Indian pueblos" of the central plateau. The last time the capital had been removed, they argued, the Indians had taken advantage of its remoteness to stage a rebellion that had threatened the very existence of the state's whites. Who knew what might happen if it were moved again?[108]

With time and the demands of politics, this retelling of the story of the "Caste War" had acquired some interesting new twists. Not wishing to blame the violence on the very liberals they hoped to sway, the highlanders now made Galindo not a liberal from central Mexico but an exiled imperialist who had hoped tc destroy Chiapas's "decent liberal society." Indeed, according to one, he had even had the Indians address him as "monsieur"! (Considering that Flavio Paniagua and Vicente Pineda, the authors of the two books, were themselves ex-imperialists and lifelong opponents of liberalism, this was a particularly cynical distortion.) Second, the Indians' religion—actually a tame, if native, variant of Catholicism—was made as outlandish as possible to emphasize the savagery into which the natives would sink if not closely supervised. Thus the invention of the crucifixion of an Indian boy on Good Friday, 1868, an event not mentioned in even the most virulently racist newspaper stories of 1868–71—stories that otherwise exulted in exaggerating the Indians' cruelty and inhumanity. Finally, the actual battles of the "Caste War" itself were magnified until it seemed that the Indians had actually been on the point of overrunning San Cristóbal and slaughtering its inhabitants. In this new telling, the encampments on the edge of the city between June 17 and 21 became a bloody siege; the "battles" of June 21 and 30 became closely-fought confrontations from which the ladino soldiers had been lucky to escape with their lives; and the persecution of July-November 1869 became a merciless guerrilla war in which Indian fanatics managed to hold off the entire state militia.[109]

But for all the effort that went into this elaborate justification for keeping the capital in San Cristóbal, in 1892 the federal government authorized its transfer to Tuxtla anyway. If the highland revisionists did not accomplish their first purpose, however, they did permanently blacken the reputation of the Indians. Ironically, when the state government decided a few years later to by-pass San Cristóbal and manage the highland work-force itself, it fell back on the conservatives' own argument that the Indians needed to feel a strong, direct authority to remain peaceful. Using this as an excuse, in 1896 the lowlanders removed all the communities north of San Cristóbal from the city's control and placed them under administrators dependent on Tuxtla itself.[110] To further insure the preservation of peace—and the enforcement of labor contracts—lowland troops were stationed in all the major communities and native government, such as it was, was truncated.

This was the situation when Frederick Starr, in 1901, became the first American anthropologist to visit Chiapas. One of the many bits of information he collected to accompany his accounts of the Indians' brutal exploitation at the hands of the state's ladinos was Paniagua's and Pineda's account of the "Caste War," complete with crucifixion.[111] The horror of this story, providing as it did "objective" proof of the Indians' low level of civilization, was by this time an accepted justification of the system of debt and plantation labor to which they were being subjected.

And so it has continued to be through the almost eighty years since. Unfortunately, modern anthropologists, collecting tales of the "Caste War" from native informants, and then looking to the "classic" sources to check their accuracy, have only compounded the problem: essentially, the Indians' stories, products of the post–"Caste War" repression, seem to confirm the racist accounts of the nineteenth-century conservatives. Indeed, by this time many of the Indian stories may be little more than native retellings of those accounts that have filtered back into the communities through the priests, schoolteachers, and others. So seductive has been the "window on the native soul" offered by these stories that scholars, instead of remaining skeptical, have simply repeated them, lending the imprimatur of their science to what may only be a myth.

Lately, still another genre has been added to writings about the "Caste War," that of the romantic radicals who see in the events of 1868–70 a glorious popular revolution—proof positive that the Chamulas and their neighbors have risen violently, en masse, in the past, and could perhaps do so again. That they were supposedly led by a ladino vanguard only enhances the attraction of the story for exponents of this school.[112]

In fact, however, the Indian movement of 1867–69, when it *was* their movement, appears to have been a peaceful one. What they sought was to be left alone to farm their fields, conduct their markets, and worship their saints as they themselves chose. That they could not do these things—that they were finally slaughtered for trying—is not so much evidence of passivity and submissiveness on their part as of the inhumanity of those who regarded them, not as people, but as objects, "resources," to be fought over and controlled.

Notes

Abbreviations

AGCh	Archivo General de Chiapas, Tuxtla Gutiérrez, Chiapas
AHDSC	Archivo Histórico Diocesano de San Cristóbal, San Cristóbal, Chiapas
BFB	Biblioteca "Fray Bartolomé de las Casas," San Cristóbal, Chiapas
CM	Colección Moscoso, San Cristóbal, Chiapas
TC	Tulane Collection, Latin American Library, Tulane University, New Orleans (microfilms of nineteenth-century Chiapas newspapers)

1. Vicente Pineda, *Historia de las sublevaciones indígenas habidas en el estado de Chiapas* (San Cristóbal, 1888); Flavio Paniagua, *Florinda* (San Cristóbal, 1889); Cristóbal Molina, *War of the Castes: Indian Uprisings in Chiapas, 1867–1870* (New Orleans, 1934; English translation of a contemporary memoir). Also see the serialized account of the war published in *La Brújula,* newspaper of the San Cristóbal conservatives (Aug.-Oct. 1869) (TC).

2. See, for example, V. R. Bricker, "Algunas consecuencias religiosas y sociales del ativismo maya en el siglo XIX," *América Indígena* 33 (1973): 327–48, and *The Indian Christ, The Indian King* (Austin, 1981). Also see H. Favre, *Changement et continuité chez les Mayas du Mexique* (Paris, 1971), pp. 269–306; G. H. Gossen, "Translating Cuzcat's War: Understanding Maya Oral Tradition," *Journal of Latin American Lore* 3 (1977): 249–78. Finally, see Carter Wilson's novel, *A Green Tree and a Dry Tree* (New York, 1972).

3. For political aspects of the lowland-highland division, see Manuel Trens, *Historia de Chiapas,* books 3–7 (Mexico City, 1957). Unfortunately, there is no reliable socioeconomic history of nineteenth-century Chiapas as a whole, although some aspects are covered in R. W. Wasserstrom, "White Fathers, Red Souls: Indian-Ladino Relations in Highland Chiapas, 1528–1973," Ph.D. dissertation, Harvard University, 1976.

4. Flavio Paniagua, *Catecismo elemental de historia y estadística de Chiapas* (San Cristóbal, 1876) (CM).

5. CM, *Colección de leyes agrarias y demás disposiciones que se han emitido en relación al ramo de tierras* (San Cristóbal, 1878); AGCh, "Prontuario del inventario del ramo de tierras" (Tuxtla, 1891).

6. The transformation of the lowlands is reflected in the remarkable growth of the region's ladino population between 1819 and 1860 (see table 1). For the highlands, it is easily traced through the entries of the "Prontuario del inventario del ramo de tierras" (AGCh).

7. AHDSC, Enrique Mijangos, párroco of Chamula, to the provisor of the diocese,

May 7, 1855, and "Plan de Chamula," Saturnino Rivas, agrimensor, June 1855. Also see CM, *La Voz del Pueblo*, Dec. 8, 1855, and Feb. 2, 1856. (*La Voz del Pueblo* was the official newspaper of the state government.)

8. AHDSC, Enrique Zepeda, vicario of Chamula, to the Ecclesiastical Government, San Cristóbal, Oct. 27, 1804.

9. CM, *La Voz del Pueblo*, Feb. 2, 1856. There were 637 families of non-Chamulas on the 44 percent of the estate not Chamula. Assuming an even population density on the entire property—actually a conservative assumption, since the Chamula density was undoubtedly higher—this would give approximately 740 families on Chamula's 56 percent.

10. TC, *El Espíritu del Siglo*, Oct. 12, 1862.

11. Chiapas's legislature ratified the national decree of April 28, 1823, which specified many of the duties of the clergy, in 1826. Soon after, measures were adopted for each of the state's own religious sub-divisions, as for instance the "Arancel de cobranzas y mensualidades autorizadas para el vicario de Chamula," promulgated on Aug. 10, 1827 (AHDSC).

12. Wasserstrom, "White Fathers, Red Souls," pp. 142–48.

13. Trens, *Historia de Chiapas*, p. 591, gives complete figures for 1856, one of the few years for which comparisons are possible.

14. Trens, *Historia de Chiapas*, pp. 328–30; AGCh, Decreto del 20 del julio, 1831, Gobierno del Estado de Chiapas.

15. Trens, *Historia de Chiapas*, pp. 441–43. Also, AGCh, baldiaje, Decreto del 9 de junio, 1849; and lands, Decretos del 28 de enero, 1847, 24 de marzo, 1847, and 24 de mayo, 1849.

16. Chamula, with 12,000 inhabitants, would have constituted 31 percent of San Cristóbal's total departmental population of 38,000 in the 1850s. Its share of the head tax of 11,552 pesos paid in the department in 1855 would therefore have been approximately 3,600 pesos—or, at 1.5 reales a day for native labor, something more than 19,200 man-days of labor. See population sources in table 1; in Trens, *Historia de Chiapas*, p. 591; and in CM, *La Voz del Pueblo*, Feb. 2, 1856.

17. 1,460 man-days in personal service, and 15,500 in cash and kind. AHDSC, "Cuadrante de San Juan Chamula" (1855) and "Estados trimestrales de Chamula" (July 14, 1855, and January 14, 1856).

18. In addition to the payments already enumerated, Chamulas were also providing an undetermined amount as stipends for their schoolteacher and secretary. In 1856, these were described as one of the most onerous of the Indians' burdens in *La Voz del Pueblo*, Jan. 19 (CM).

19. Cases involving priests and secretaries were compiled from AHDSC; land cases were compiled from AGCh, "Prontuario del inventario del ramo de tierras."

20. Reflected in AHDSC, "Estados trimestrales de parroquias" (1848–57). This was a kind of report first required of priests in 1848 and discontinued in most of the diocese during the War of Reform in the late 1850s.

21. Wasserstrom, "White Fathers, Red Souls," p. 159.

22. The abolition of serfdom was repealed by the Decreto del 22 de mayo, 1851,

and the controls on agricultural exports established by the Decreto del 8 de noviembre, 1853 (AHCH). For information about the land laws, see Trens, *Historia de Chiapas*, pp. 522–31.

23. Trens, *Historia de Chiapas*, pp. 515–60.

24. For general background of the Reforma, see Luis González, "La Reforma," in Daniel Cosío Villegas et al., *Historia Mínima de México* (Mexico City, 1974), pp. 104–14.

25. González, "La Reforma," pp. 111–14.

26. Trens, *Historia de Chiapas*, pp. 565–83.

27. According to *La Voz del Pueblo*, Feb. 2, 1856 (CM), Mitontic, Chenalhó, and Tenejapa were asked to pay 3,000 pesos to redeem their shares of "Nuevo Edén" in 1855—a total of some 16,000 man-days of labor. Chamula reportedly made a deal for some 5,000 pesos—26,666 man-days—slightly earlier (AHDSC, "Estado de Chamula," 1855). Whether any of these amounts were ever paid is unknown.

28. The case for the Chamulas' helping the conservative insurgents is largely circumstantial. From the start of the War of Reform in Chiapas near Ixtapa in mid-1856, through Ortega's final defeat near Chanal in June 1860, most of the fighting took place across the Indian townships of the central highlands, and the priests of several of these communities were among the conservative sympathizers who fled to Guatemala in 1859 (see Trens, *Historia de Chiapas*, pp. 601–24). There is also some evidence to suggest that Chamulas served in the liberal armies during the same period, although it is uncertain whether the charges that the liberals were using "chamulas" referred to the people of that township or to poor and Indian troops in general (TC, *La Bandera Constitucional* (Tuxtla), Oct. 9, 1858).

29. Trens, *Historia de Chiapas*, pp. 608–09; Flavio Paniagua, *Salvador Guzmán* (San Cristóbal, 1891), p. 107. The drop in religious taxes between 1858 and 1861 was recorded in "Cuentas de parroquias" (AHDSC). At this early date, the decline was undoubtedly due more to the flight of the priests than to the 1857 decree outlawing church collections from the poor—a decree unenforceable in Chiapas until the mid-1860s (AHDSC, Decreto del 11 de abril, 1857, México; Trens, *Historia de Chiapas*, p. 617).

30. CM, Decreto de 21 de noviembre, 1861, Tuxtla ("Recaudación de capitación"); CM, Ley Reglamentaria de la Administración Pública de los Dptos. y Municipios, Chiapa, Jan. 15, 1862. The number of soldiers required of the state is from Trens, *Historia de Chiapas*, pp. 627, 630; of Chamula, from the letter from Manual María Suárez, vicario of Chamula, to the Ecclesiastical Government, July 28, 1862 (AHDSC).

31. AHDSC, Suárez to Ecclesiastical Government, July 28, 1862.

32. AHDSC, Pueblo of Cancuc to the Ecclesiastical Government, April 12, 1863; AHDSC, Juan M. Gutiérrez y Aguilar, párroco of Cancuc, to the Ecclesiastical Government, April 19, 1863.

33. AHDSC, "Cuentes de Chamulas, varios años."

34. Trens, *Historia de Chiapas*, pp. 661–88; M.B.Trens, *El Imperio en Chiapas* (Tuxtla, 1956); CM, "Manuscrito del Sr. Villafuerte" (contemporary diary).

35. Trens, *El Imperio en Chiapas*, pp. 18–27, 33; CM, "Noticias de las personas que . . . prestaron servicios a la facción intervencionista," *El Espíritu del Siglo*, May 21, 1864.

36. Trens, *El Imperio en Chiapas*, pp. 33–43; Trens, *Historia de Chiapas*, pp. 661–65.

37. Trens, *El Imperio en Chiapas*, p. 39; AHDSC, Enrique Mijangos, párroco of Zinacantan, to the Secretary of the Ecclesiástical Government, Oct. 19, 1863.

38. AHDSC, Superior Gobierno Eclesiastico to Prefecto Superior, Gobierno Imperial, Nov. 10, 1863; AHDSC, J. Agustín Velasco, párroco of Tenejapa, to the Ecclesiastical Government, Oct. 12, 1863.

39. AHDSC, "A los habitantes del departamento de San Cristóbal Las Casas" (a flyer), Manuel Arévalo, San Cristóbal, Jan. 26, 1863.

40. AHDSC, Manuel María Suárez, vicario of Chamula, to the Ecclesiastical Government, Sept. 22, 1863.

41. TC, *La Brújula* (San Cristóbal), April 23, May 28, and Sept. 24, 1869.

42. C.C. Cumberland, *Mexico: The Struggle for Modernity* (New York, 1968), pp. 163–66; Trens, *Historia de Chiapas*, p. 675.

43. Trens, *Historia de Chiapas*, pp. 672–80.

44. Ibid., pp. 680–92. Domínguez was elected on Oct. 29, 1867, and took office constitutionally on Dec. 1.

45. CM, "Correspondencia interceptada a los traidores y mandada publicar de orden del c. Governador," *Espíritu del Siglo*, April 9, 1864. *Espíritu del Siglo* also carried lists of "traitors" "con expresión de sus bienes sobre las cuales debe recaer la pena de confiscación" on April 21, May 28, and June 4, 1864.

46. TC, *La Brújula*, April 23 and Sept. 17, 1869; AHDSC, Enrique Mijangos, párroco of Mitontic and Chenalhó, to Manuel Suárez, vicario of Chamula, Sept. 16, 1864; AHDSC, J. Augustín Velasco, párroco of Oxchuc and Huistán, to the Ecclesiastical Government, June 21, 1865.

47. During 1863–64, the government had been able to collect only regular head and property taxes in the departments of Chiapa, Tuxtla, and Pichucalco. With Ortega's defeat in 1864, it also began to extract revenues from the highlands in the form of forced loans, but when the head tax was again enforced in the region in 1869 it was decried as a "new" tax (Trens, *Historia de Chiapas*, pp. 674–75; CM, "Manuscrito del Sr. Villafuerte," pp. 8–9; TC, *La Brújula*, April 23, 1868).

48. Justo Sierra, *Juárez, su obra y su tiempo* (Mexico City 1905), pp. 428–32.

49. Supremo Decreto del 22 de julio, 1867, México (reported in Vicente Pineda, *Chiapas: Translación de los poderes públicos* (San Cristóbal, 1892).

50. Trens, *Historia de Chiapas*, p. 692. (Domínguez took office on Dec. 1, 1867, and ordered the capital moved on Dec. 31.)

51. The escalation of these measures is reflected in the following: AHDSC, Bruno Domínguez, párroco of Zinacantan, to the Ecclesiastical Government, June 4, 1867; AHDSC, Domínguez to the Ecclesiastical Government, Feb. 26, 1868; and AHDSC, Enrique Mijangos, párroco of Mitontic, Chenalhó, and Chalchiguitán, to the

Ecclesiastical Government, May 15, 1868. In his letter of Feb. 26, the priest of Zinacantan wrote: "The ayuntamiento and maestro of this pueblo have just informed me for the second time that the state has decreed, among other things, the complete dissolution of the mayordomos who serve in this holy church, as well as the abolition of the position of alférez, and since without these it will not be possible to preserve organized religion, much less provide for the subsistence of the minister, and since it is possible to see behind this decision the purpose of driving the priest from the town, I ask that I might be removed from here as soon as possible in order that this community might understand how sorely it will feel the absence of a priest."

52. AHDSC, M. Francisco Gordillo, párroco of Oxchuc and Huistán, to the Ecclesiastical Government, Oct. 27 and Nov. 15, 1868; AHDSC, Enrique Mijangos, párroco of Pantelhó, to the Ecclesiastical Government, Feb. 13, 1869. In the last of these letters, Mijangos reported that in Pantelhó "the native justicias rejected me, demanding to know who had sent for me. After calming down a bit, they unanimously confessed that the maestro had instructed them to act as they did."

53. For Zinacantan, Chalchiguitán, Mitontic, and Chenalhó, see note 51; for Oxchuc, Huistán, and Pantelhó, note 52; for Tenejapa, AHDSC, Manuel Suárez, párroco, to the Ecclesiastical Government, Nov. 21, 1868.

54. AHDSC, M. Francisco Gordillo, párroco of Oxchuc and Huistán, to the Ecclesiastical Government, Oct. 27 and Nov. 15, 1868. In the second of these letters, Gordillo wrote: "I am just now returning from a fiesta where the damned Indians acted vilely, refusing even to pay twelve pesos for the service without threats. I wanted to raise the prices for baptisms and marriages to compensate, but saw that if I did they would not baptize anybody."

55. AHDSC, Manuel Suárez, párroco of Tenejapa, to the Ecclesiastical Government, Nov. 21, 1868.

56. R. F. Wasserstrom, personal communication.

57. AHDSC, Anselmo Guillén, párroco of Chamula, to J. Facundo Bonifaz, Secretario of the Ecclesiastical Government, April 8, 1870; "Cuentas de Chamula, varios años" (AHDSC) contains both accounts and notes for 1865–69; TC, El Baluarte (Tuxtla), Oct. 1, 1869.

58. Molina, War of the Castes, p.365. According to Paniagua (Florinda, pp.4–10), the cult was started by Checheb in October 1867 and by the time of Cuzcat's first visit was already flourishing. Pineda (Historia de las sublevaciones pp.71–72), on the other hand, says that Cuzcat and Checheb made a clay idol together in late 1867 and that their intention throughout was to start a lucrative new religion.

59. Molina, War of the Castes, pp. 365–66.

60. AHDSC, Enrique Mijangos, vicario interino, "Estado trimestral de Chamula," July 14, 1855.

61. AHDSC, Mijangos, "Estado trimestral."

62. Molina, War of the Castes, p. 367.

63. Ibid.

64. Ibid.; CM, "Manuscrito del Sr. Villafuerte," p. 8.

65. TC, *La Brújula*, June 11, 1869. CM, "Manuscrito del Sr. Villafuerte," p. 8. According to Villafuerte, San Cristóbal began frantic preparations for an expected Indian attack on May 1, 1868, all able-bodied men being organized into military companies under jefes militares.

66. Molina, *War of the Castes*, p. 367; CM, "Manuscrito del Sr. Villafuerte," p. 8; TC, *La Brújula*, June 11, 1869.

67. Molina, *War of the Castes*, p. 367. The three priests were Manuel Suárez, Bruno Domínguez, and Enrique Mijangos.

68. Ibid., p. 368. Melchor Gómez, a scribe from the ayuntamiento of Chamula, was named mayordomo—an office outlawed in the Indian pueblos by the state government.

69. Ibid.

70. Ibid.

71. Ibid., p. 368–69; TC, *La Brújula*, July 9, 1869.

72. E.g., TC, *La Brújula*, April 23 and May 28, 1869. In answer to the carping of the highlanders, the liberal newspaper of Chiapa, *El Baluarte*, ran a long series during 1868–69 on the political "crimes" of the conservatives during the 1860s: "La lucha contra el llamado 'Imperio Mexicano' en Chiapas."

73. TC, *Espíritu del Siglo*, May 9, 11, and 23, and Dec. 3, 1868.

74. Ibid., March 27, 1869; TC, *La Brújula*, April 30, 1869.

75. TC, *La Brújula*, May 28, 1869; TC, *El Baluarte*, Oct. 1, 1869.

76. Galindo's history and motives are discussed in Molina, *War of the Castes*, p. 360; TC, *La Brújula*, Dec. 17, 1869; and TC, *El Baluarte*, Sept. 22, 1870. San Cristóbal's mood during this period can be detected in *La Brújula*, April 11 and June 11, 1869—indeed, the issue of June 11 was already talking about a "caste war," this several days before the outbreak of violence that supposedly started the "Caste War" of 1869."

77. Paniagua, *Florinda*, pp. 32–34; Pineda, *Historia de las sublevaciones*, pp. 78–79. Galindo's construction of the facts is from his testimony at his trial, "Proceso instruido contra Ignacio Fernández de Galindo, 23 de junio, 1869," reprinted as Note F in Paniagua, *Florinda*.

78. CM, "Manuscrito del Sr. Villafuerte," p. 9; Molina, *War of the Castes*, pp. 372–73. At Galindo's trial, it was reported that he had been present at three killings, to which he replied that he had only gone along to try to restrain the Indians, to prevent killing ("Proceso," in Paniagua, *Florinda*).

79. Molina, *War of the Castes*, p. 375; CM, "Manuscrito del Sr. Villafuerte," p. 9. From other sources, it can be calculated that a total of sixteen ladinos died in these two fights. How many Indians were killed is unknown (see note 81).

80. TC, *La Brújula*, July 25, 1869; Molina, *War of the Castes*, p. 375.

81. TC, *La Baluarte, Alcance #5*, June 22, 1869; CM, "Manuscrito del Sr. Villafuerte," p. 10. Paniagua (*Florinda*, Note C) and Pineda (*Historia de las sublevaciones*, p. 82) later claimed that many more ladino civilians were killed in

"brutal attacks" that lasted through June. Paniagua even provides a list of supposed "victims," although he provides no dates or places of death, or even, in most cases, complete names. From the lists of casualties published in *La Brújula* (July 9 and 25, 1869), however, it appears that 79 ladinos were killed in the entire "Caste War," of whom 47 were combatants, 16 were accounted for individually (see notes 79 and 80), and 16 were apparently killed in the attacks on "Natividad" and "La Merced" in mid-June.

82. Molina, *War of the Castes*, p. 375.

83. Pineda (*Historia de las sublevaciones*, pp. 87–93) argues that Galindo was tricked by the "extreme cleverness" of San Cristóbal's jefe político into turning himself over. Paniagua (*Florinda*, p. 48), on the other hand, has it that he thought the Indians would soon attack to free him—though why he, the supposed military leader, would have turned over the army to Cuzcat if an attack was eventually going to be necessary anyway is never explained. Finally, a lowland commentator, José M. Montesinos—an enemy of Governor Domínguez—claims that Galindo was an agent provocateur of the governor and fully expected the governor to ride to his rescue (*Memorias del Sargento, 1866–1878* (Tuxtla, 1935).

84. TC, *El Baluarte*, July 9, 1869.

85. Ibid.; TC, *La Brújula*, Dec. 17, 1869.

86. Molina, *War of the Castes*, p. 376; TC, *La Brújula*, June 25, 1869. From the internal evidence, it appears that *La Brújula* was often published up to a week earlier than the date it bore, so the number of June 25 may actually have come out any time between June 18 and 25.

87. TC, *El Baluarte*, June 18, 1869. Later it was claimed that Domínguez had begun organizing a force to defend San Cristóbal as early as June 14—and, indeed, among the forces that bargained with Galindo on June 17 were twenty-five troops sent from Chiapa as observers three days earlier. There is no evidence that he intended to take any further action, however (TC, *La Brújula*, June 18, 1869).

88. Montesinos, *Memorias del Sargento*, p. 66; see also the letter from Tuxtla correspondent of *La Brújula*, July 16, 1869 (TC).

89. Molina, *War of the Castes*, p. 377; TC, *La Brújula*, July 2, 1869; TC, *El Baluarte*, July 9, 1869. From contemporary sources, it appears that the Indians actually fled when confronted by the lowland soldiers and that the only ones who fought back were those who were cornered against steep hills with no escape possible. One such group, in its desperation, ran directly toward the lowland cannons, causing the wild firing that accounted for most of the ladino casualties. (Even Pineda [*Historia de las sublevaciones*, p. 101] concedes most of these facts.)

90. TC, *La Brújula*, July 2, 1869.

91. Reported in *La Brújula*, July 9 and 16, 1869 (TC). Domínguez's circular to the officials around the state was dated June 26.

92. TC, *La Brújula*, July 9, 1869.

93. As reported to his nephew, J. M. Montesinos (*Memorias del Sargento*, pp. 61–62).

94. Molina, *War of the Castes*, p. 379; CM, "Manuscrito del Sr. Villafuerte," p. 10.

95. Molina, *War of the Castes*, p. 379.

96. F. Paniagua, "Guerra de castas," *La Brújula*, July 9, 1869 (TC). As evidence of the tone of the discussion, an unsigned editorial in the same number suggested exiling the highland rebels to the Soconusco, where they could become a permanent work-force, and still a third piece, on July 16, 1869, argued that the rebels should be defeated utterly, killed to the last man, as an example to those who remained.

97. TC, *El Baluarte*, July 23, 1869. Some lowland troops were released after July 3, but most were assigned to the highlands indefinitely as of that date. This probably accounts for the "dissatisfaction" noted in *El Baluarte* on July 23.

98. TC, *La Brújula*, Sept. 17, 1869. *La Brújula* of July 16, 1869, says the Indian dead were too numerous to count, and "El Manuscrito del Sr. Villafuerte" (CM, p. 10) says there were no fewer than 300.

99. "Informes del comandante militar," July-December, 1869 (collected in Paniagua, *Florinda*, Note G-J). In a letter to *La Brújula*, published Sept. 24, 1869, Victor Domínguez, owner of one of the ruined farms, described the Indians as "monsters of ingratitude."

100. "Informes," in Paniagua, *Florinda*, Notes I-J; TC, *El Baluarte*, Aug. 13, 1869. On August 24, 1869, a crowd of fugitive Indians from Chamula, San Andrés, and Santiago took their revenge on one settlement of such "loyal" Indians in San Andrés, killing twenty of them and burning their houses (TC, *La Brújula*, Sept. 3, 1869).

101. Rosas to the state government, Nov. 13, 1869 (published in TC, *La Brújula*, Nov. 19, 1869).

102. TC, *La Brújula*, Dec. 24, 1869; "Informes," in Paniagua, *Florinda*, Note K.

103. Flavio Paniagua, *Catecismo elemental de historia y estadística de Chiapas* (San Cristóbal, 1876).

104. Molina (*War of the Castes*, p. 379) reports executions of "rebel leaders" turned over by Chamula's ayuntamiento on July 26, 1869 (five), and October 3, 1869 (three). In addition, the "Manuscrito del Sr. Villafuerte" (CM, p. 11) reports that the presiding officer of Chamula brought the head of one rebel to San Cristóbal on July 10, 1870, and two more on August 4. Ladino forces also intervened directly in the native communities through 1870, attending all the major fiestas, and on July 7 arresting and summarily executing a Chamula scribe who had tried to arouse a protest against the head tax (Molina, *War of the Castes*, p. 383; CM, "Manuscrito del Sr. Villafuerte," p. 11).

105. Many of those who fled during the summer of 1969 settled in San Juan Chamula El Bosque, a settlement north of Chalchihuitán that also became a refuge for emigrés in 1870–71. That groups of "rebels" were also exiled by the government is known from the letter from Agustín Velasco, *párroco* of Chamula, to Dr. Feliciano Lazos, lector of the Ecclesiastical Government, Jan. 15, 1864, in which he inquired about religious jurisdiction over the children of exiles from the state of Veracruz (AHDSC).

106. The first steps of this process can be detected in the "Manifiesto del indígena

c. Domingo Pérez" (TC, *La Brújula*, Nov. 26, 1869), in which Pérez, apparently a Chamula, refers to the "rebels" whom he was then pursuing as "barbarians whose wish it is to eliminate the ladino class and sow their own deprived vices among their fellows." By the 1970s, the surviving stories in Chamula had it that Cuzcat and his followers were entirely to blame for the violence they brought down on the community (see Gossen, "Translating Cuzcat's War"), whereas in Chalchihuitán, for instance, Chamulas in general were blamed (Ulrich Köhler, personal communication). Only in such out-of-the-way villages as Magdalenas did versions of the events survive in which Cuzcat and his followers were depicted as "good" and the persecution of them unjust (Amber Past, "Lo que cuenta una mujer de Magdalenas," in J. Burstein and R. Wasserstrom, *En sus proprias palabras: Cuatro vidas tzotziles* (San Cristóbal, 1979).

107. Pineda, *Historia de las sublevaciones* (1888); Paniagua, *Florinda* (1889). Vicente Pineda also wrote the most important of the subsequent articles, "La traslación de los poderes públicos del estado" (San Cristóbal, 1892), a pamphlet (AGCh).

108. The citation is from Pineda, "La traslación de los poderes," who went on to argue that "the capital must remain where there are the most individuals to govern, direct, repress, educate, civilize, and enlighten." The first two appendices of Paniagua's *Florinda* were about the transfer of the capital to Tuxtla in 1867 and its supposed consequences (Note A) and the cultural and educational advantages of San Cristóbal (Note B).

109. Galindo is identified as an imperialist in Paniagua, *Florinda*, p. 12. The first mention of the supposed crucifixion is in Pineda, *Historia de las sublevaciones* (pp. 76–77), and the exaggerated battles are to be found in Paniagua, *Florinda*, pp. 48–74, and Pineda, *Historia de las sublevaciones*, pp. 94–116.

110. Transfer of the capital: AGCh, Decreto del 11 de agosto, 1892, Tuxtla. Formation of the Partido de Chamula: AGCh, Decreto del 24 de abril, 1896, Tuxtla.

111. Frederick Starr, *In Indian Mexico: A Narrative of Travel and Labor* (Chicago, 1908).

112. Antonio García de León et al., *La violencia en Chamula* (San Cristóbal, 1979); Juan J. Manguén et al., *La Guerra de Castas, 1869–1870* (San Cristóbal, 1979).

William L. Sherman

Some Aspects of Change in
Guatemalan Society, 1470–1620

The state of historical writing on early Guatemala would be dismal indeed if it were not for the fact that, comparatively speaking, quite a respectable amount of research has been published in recent years. The output in just the last decade alone has significantly advanced our knowledge of the subject. Most of the studies have been substantial works, and the quality has rather consistently been high. Although some very good work has come out of Central America, Mexico, and Spain and other European countries, much of the best scholarly production has come from investigators in the United States.[1]

There is an ephemeral quality to any broad history, no matter how carefully formulated. Hardly is the ink dry before two or three doctoral dissertations are conceived, fastening on one generalization or another, demonstrating that this thesis or that is invalid for whatever locale the writer has chosen to examine. If his research merely confirms the findings of the general study he had hoped to challenge, the young historian's work will go unnoticed, but if he states persuasively that he has found an exception to the general rule, then he will be cited often, and his career will prosper. Thus are regional studies born, and many of them have produced useful, and sometimes even surprising, results. The effect has been in certain cases to diminish somewhat the reputation of those who have given us pioneering studies of a broad nature. Still, efforts of scholars like Robert Ricard and François Chevalier, because of the great contributions of their seminal works, retain the high esteem in which they are generally held. But even general works that promise less than Ricard and Chevalier should be encouraged, and the authors should not fear the consequences. Especially for a small region like Guatemala, there is a need to pull together the findings to date, patchy as they are, in order to bring some coherence to the country's history, to develop a framework that facilitates a comprehensive overview. Fortunately, many of the recent publications have dealt with substantial blocks of time with fairly broad themes. Consequently, it now becomes feasible to delineate more precisely some of the prominent periods of history. Such chronological limits are rarely as neat as we would like, but the division of a country's history into units is nevertheless a useful pedagogical device, and it can even be helpful to the beginning historian as a pattern within which various topics can be studied.

The one-hundred-and-fifty-year period being examined falls logically enough into three fifty-year chronological units: 1470–1520, 1520–1570, and 1570–1620. Herewith, some observations on these periods.

1470–1520

The year 1470 is a convenient and appropriate point of demarcation. Toltec-influenced groups invaded the Guatemalan highlands around the year 1250 and gradually extended their influence over neighboring cultures. By 1470, the dominant group, the Quiché, exerted control from their capital at Utatlán over an extensive region in which an estimated one million people lived. The Quiché, however, did not enjoy control comparable to that of the Aztecs of central Mexico, though both seem to have embraced the Toltec traditions of the conquest state. Also powerful in Guatemala were the Cakchiquel, but any chance they had of successfully challenging the Quiché was lost when they quarreled among themselves, owing most probably to population pressures. While the Cakchiquel center remained at Iximché, a splinter group, becoming known as the Zutuhil, settled at Atitlán. The subsequent history of these groups is a familiar one: because of their fighting among themselves they were unable to put together a united resistence to the Spaniards. As in the case of Mexico, some Indian rulers sent embassies with gifts and offers of friendship, only to oppose the intruders later. The Cakchiquels welcomed the Christians and became their allies, but subsequently they rebelled in reaction to oppressive treatment.

Notwithstanding some excellent general sources on native cultures written by the Indians themselves and valuable Spanish histories written during the colonial period,[2] there is still a paucity of the kind of detailed information we need for a reasonably complete history for the half-century preceding the Spanish conquest. It would be exceedingly helpful if we had a better appreciation of the early Guatemalans' daily routines, their labor systems, their various social classes, the specific aspects of their economy, their political organization, and their modes of warfare. We need to know more about family life, the role of women, the status of slaves, the special privileges of the *principales* (leaders) and the system of justice, among other subjects. In short, we need more information about almost all aspects of preconquest society in order to make valid comparisons with other prehispanic cultures and with condtions in the Spanish colonial system.

Robert Carmack, in his *Quichean Civlization*, has made an important contribution through his discussion of the various sources from which early history can be written, and he notes the rich possibilities. There was, unfortunately, no Sahagún in Guatemala, and we still await someone to tie together various loose ends in the way it was done by Wigberto Jiménez Moreno for Mexico. It must be said that the anthropologists have accomplished more toward the goal of such an account than the historians. Carmack, Munro Edmondson, and John Fox, among others in the United States, have examined early Guatemalan cultures from the standpoint of their own disciplines, and historians need to follow their lead, asking their own questions and using their own methodologies.[3] More exchanges of views and techniques among scholars in other fields engaged in Mesoamerican research would unquestionably be productive.

The fact remains, however, that very little of the Indian tradition is mentioned in the surviving Spanish manuscripts that form the bases of research for the historian. Nor is it likely that much significantly new date will come to light, though of course one does not discount that seductive possibility. My own research would be infinitely less interesting if I did not expect to find Gonzalo de Alvarado's account of the conquest at any time now.

We would be able to assess Spanish colonial Indian policy in Guatemala with more perspective if we were more knowledgeable about native society prior to the conquest. For example, it seems apparent that almost all forms of labor requirements imposed by the conquerors were slight variations of Indian customs. It is generally assumed that forced labor conditions under the colonial system were much harsher than they had been before 1524, and no doubt in many respects they were. A basic principle of crown Indian legislation was that the Indians were not to find themselves in worse situations under the Christians than they were under their native systems. It would therefore contribute significantly to our understanding of Guatemalan colonial society and our interpretation of it if we were able to determine more specifically in what ways and to what extent Indians' suffering increased under their new masters.

We need to know more about prehistoric Guatemalan society if we hope to make valid comparisons with other colonial systems. As compared to Guatemalan societies, for instance, what kind of effect did the character of Aztec society have on post-conquest treatment of Indians in central Mexico? Did the religious fervor of the Aztecs, with its human sacrifice and its aggressive policies of conquest war and subsequent imposition of tribute, result in harsher treatment of the Aztecs by the Spaniards than of other native groups? Las Casas wrote that Spanish treatment of Indians was worst in Guatemala and Chiapas. Was that really so and, if so, why? Many other such questions are germane to the study of colonial society and could well have a bearing on future interpretations, provided we learn more about societies prior to the conquest.

1520–70

This middle period is a crucial one for the formation of modern Guatemalan society. Because of the drama of the conquest and the subsequent founding of a Spanish colony with all its complexities and prominent individuals, it is only natural that this period of the so-called "conquest society" has been studied with more care than others. Owing to the rich sources, both in the archival documentation and in colonial chronicles, the subject is compelling.

Aside from the obvious conveniences of denoting these particular chronological limits—dividing the 150-year period into three equal segments—there are some other reasons that prevent its being arbitrary. Even though the conquest of Guatemala did not get under way until 1524, by 1520 the Spanish presence in Mexico had had repercussions farther south. The various implications of European technology and military capabilities had already prompted war leaders and diplomats to ponder courses of action. Moreover, the dread specter of pestilence was soon to appear, with very serious consequences.

As for the terminal date of 1570, it is somewhat arguable but it seems as valid as any other, since no one year indicates a definite break.[4] The first generation of mestizos and creoles was by then in middle age, and the grandchildren of the conquerors were themselves young adults. For the majority of them, Spain was the remote land of their ancestors, and their attitudes toward the land of their birth and its Indians were certainly much different from those of their conquering grandfathers. By 1570, the first decades of violence and disorder had given way to a more settled routine, and the boom-town mentality yielded to acceptance of a more mundane existence. As in Mexico, the church seems to have lost some of its initial enthusiasm after half a century of extraordinarily vigorous missionizing. Beginning about 1570, many Spaniards, apparently disillusioned with the economy, left Guatemala.

Enough is known about this middle period to lend credence to further divisions. The following are proposed as working subdivisions: 1520–1541, years of the conquest and pacification, followed by the domination of the conquistadors and ending with the death of Alvarado; 1542–1548, from the issuance of the New Laws through the creation and tenure of the first *Audiencia de los Confines;* and 1548–1570, years during which the president of the second audiencia, Alonso López de Cerrato, implemented many reforms in favor of the Indians, followed by a time in which Indian legislation was relaxed while the royal bureaucracy implanted its authority more strongly. Herewith some considerations of each subdivision.

1520–41. We have no accounts of the conquest of Guatemala comparable to those of the fall of the Aztecs. The account said to have been written by Gonzalo de Alvarado has not yet been found, though it appears that some of the early chroniclers had access to it. The chroniclers provided outlines of the conquest, and Alvarado's few letters, though in no way comparable to the epistles of Cortés, do provide valuable information. No doubt more will emerge as the various "probanzas de méritos y servicios," along with lawsuits and other documents, are studied with care, but probably nothing of great significance will come to light.

Only rarely has one individual dominated the society of his time and place in the way that Alvarado did in Guatemala for eighteen years.[5] Perhaps no other Spanish conqueror left his personal imprint so clearly on a colony as the conqueror of Guatemala. He was a true *caudillo,* noted for both his ruthlessness and his charm. His bravery and sanguine outlook made him popular with his men, who were all the more his followers because he allowed them the spoils of conquest. The natives were in awe of him, and it was said that his mere presence discouraged Indian revolts. There were some who were not favored by the *adelantado* and were therefore often against him, but during the long years he was master of Guatemala there were no serious challenges to his leadership, even though he was often absent on some other adventure.

It is clear that he was responsible for cruel punishment of native leaders. Many principales were hanged, burned alive, or mutilated. Such treatment of Indian nobles who resisted Spanish domination was common enough during Spain's conquest of the New World, and it must have had an intimidating effect on the native aristocracy. Alvarado, like most of the early captains, also allowed enslavement of many of the conquered people. But if these campaigns and the months immediately following were tragically similar to scenes in other regions, most of the Spanish captains who became the first governors were replaced before long by outside appointees of the crown.

Alvarado's presence as the authority figure in Guatemala certainly had an important influence on events there, but in what way? No doubt most assume that his bluff and cavalier ways (curiously similar to those of Pancho Villa) could only redound to the detriment of peace and stability, yet comparisons of the Alvarado years in Guatemala with contemporary administrations in other colonies might turn up some surprising conclusions. Who knows how the Pizarros and Almagros would have run Central America? Consider the brutality of Pedrarias Dávila in Panama and Miguel Díaz in Colombia. On the other hand, a conquest of Guatemala by Francisco de Montejo would have lent a distinctly milder tone to the settlement, though he might well have faced a Spanish mutiny by trying to prohibit slavery.[6]

Sundry wild and gory scenes of cruelty, chaos, and injustices in New Spain, Peru, Tierra Firme, Chile, La Plata, and other colonies during the 1520s and 1540s make life in early Santiago de Guatemala seem relatively stable.

It must be said to begin with that the native peoples certainly suffered from the time of the conquest until Alvarado's death. Whether, all things considered, they fared worse than the Indians in other colonies is difficult to ascertain, but it may not be excessive to state that people living in Santiago enjoyed at least as much justice and order as those living in other Spanish colonial cities of those years. At least part of the relative calm is attributable to the stabilizing effect of the adelantado, whose prestige and authority allowed no challenge, and although he is often painted in quite sanguinary accents, in a non-combative role he seems to have abstained from policies that were noteworthy for their cruelty.[7]

During many of those years his brother Jorge was acting governor, and he seems to have been a person of intelligence and moderation. Moreover, the men who conquered the land were given *encomiendas* and allowed to exploit the Indians. As they were kept relatively content, they saw little reason to rebel against their leader, and if they became restless or discontent with their lot, they could usually join the governor on one of his various expeditions to Quito, the Pacific, or Mexico or to other regions of Central America. Also favorable to their cause was the moderate stance of the first bishop, Francisco Marroquín. Although the bishop considered himself a protector of the Indians, and attempted to relieve the natives of some of their burdens, the fact is that Marroquín was also sympathetic to the *encomenderos*. In his opinion, the very existence of the Spanish colony would be jeopardized if the conquerors lost their encomiendas or were in other ways deprived of rewards. Consequently, he advocated a policy of gradualism. He was also a close friend of Alvarado and, as something of a statesman, probably gave good counsel to the governor. Again, by way of comparison, consider the clashes in Mexico, not only those between Cortés and his enemies but also between President Nuño de Guzmán and Bishop Zumárraga. Other violent confrontations between conquerors and clergymen in various colonies during these early days also come to mind.

Alvarado's death occurred in 1541, a few days after the murder of Francisco Pizarro. By that time most of the major figures of the American conquests were either dead or neutralized politically. In the absence of such commanding personalities, the militant encomenderos lacked effective leadership. Now it was safer to implement reforms, and in the following year, 1542, the New Laws were issued. The time of the conquerors was about to give way to the time of the lawyers—but not before the encomenderos made their last stand.

1542–48. The New Laws of 1542 created the Audiencia de los Confines, instructing the judges of that body to enforce the reform legislation, but the *oidores* did not convene in Gracias a Dios until 1544, which afforded the encomenderos sufficient lead-time to gird for battle. As it happened, they found judges who were not uncongenial; in fact, the members of the new court did not take very seriously their charge to effect reforms.

The crown determined to establish royal power more effectively by replacing independent governors whose interests were identified all too closely with the encomenderos. Thus Rodrigo de Contreras was replaced as governor of Nicaragua and Francisco de Montejo as governor of Honduras-Higueras and Chiapas. In the case of Contreras, his sons subsequently led a serious rebellion in 1550, whereas Montejo lost his governorship but gained a son-in-law, the president of the new audiencia. President Alonso Maldonado married Catalina de Montejo, after which he engaged openly and illegally in several business enterprises with Montejo. The spectacle of the two most prestigious individuals in Central America behaving in such a manner offered a poor example for the settlers.[8] The oidores were no less indiscreet. They carried on scandalous affairs with women, both Spanish and Indian, had interests in mines in which black slaves were used, abused Indian labor in a variety of ways, and sometimes comported themselves in the most vulgar manner. Those who were charged with implementing laws, especially those relieving the burdens of the natives, were the most visible scofflaws of all. When their performances were reviewed later, Judge Alonso López de Cerrato wrote: "How can Indian slaves be liberated when the oidor himself has two or three hundred slaves? And how can personal service be taken away when the oidor has fifty Indians in his house, carrying water and food and fodder and other things? And how can *tamemes* [bearers] be taken away by an oidor who has eight hundred *tamemes* in the mines, and when even his dogs are carried by tamemes?"[9]

Under the circumstances, encomenderos fared relatively well, because the judges of the audiencia represented limited moral forces. Yet the oidores did perform some commendable acts, and parts of the Indian legislation were temporarily enforced. *Licenciado* Diego de Herrera no doubt inhibited further excesses in Nicaragua when he traveled to that province in 1544 to take the *residencia* of Contreras, and licenciado Juan Rogel visited Chiapas in 1546 and effected a number of changes. He restricted the use of personal service and limited the use of tamemes. In Guatemala itself, the audiencia was more accessible to litigants, and, notwithstanding the avarice and general misbehavior that tarnished that court, its conduct never approached the outrageous character of Mexico's first audiencia. Of course, since most of the encomenderos were relatively content under President Alonso Maldonado, and since the bishop believed in moderation, few were inclined to complain very much in letters to the crown. Had the Indians been writing reports, we might well have a darker picture of these years. As it is, we gain a better appreciation of the first court's mixed performance from the findings of their *juez de residencia* (examining magistrate), Alonso López de Cerrato, president of the second audiencia (1548–55).

The relationship of the Spanish crown to the conquered peoples for the first quarter century of colonization in Guatemala was one of malign neglect. Although Spanish Indian legislation was, under the circumstances, reasonable enough in theory, for a variety of reasons it was not effectively implemented. Application of the laws by royal officials was highly selective and often capricious. Thus, thousands of Indians were illegally enslaved and transported to other regions, where most succumbed within a short time. *Macehuales* engaged in forced labor were fatigued and physically mistreated by Spaniards' *calpisques*, and villagers paid excessive tributes. Family life was disrupted and often ruined when husbands drafted as tamemes left home for weeks or months, and often never returned at all. To make matters worse, women were sometimes required to leave home for days at a time to work for Spaniards. Such separation necessarily caused neglect of their children and husbands, and the women were sometimes overworked and abused sexually.

The family and general social structure of native society was altered significantly by the sexual intrusions of the conquerors. Although not all relationships of this sort were forced, many were, and the result was often clearly damaging to family unity. Without confusing our notions of fidelity and morality with theirs (which were apparently quite different), we can surmise that the presence of mestizo children in an Indian household contributed to the alienation of affections. These offspring, the majority of whom in the early decades were born out of wedlock, became very numerous, and they constituted a new social element.

Native society was further affected by the weakened state of the traditional aristocracy. Many of the principales were killed during the conquest, and others from mistreatment. The surviving members of the Indian elite all too often found themselves deprived of their offices in their villages or, if allowed to retain them, were usually intimidated by the Spaniards, whose creatures they became. Left without effective leadership, the macehuales understood their own officials to be little more than agents of the white men. These and other disruptions of the traditional social order disoriented village life. To complete the social tragedy that overtook the bewildered Guatemalans, waves of pestilence devastated their population.

1548–70. Cerrato was a very controversial man who was detested and bitterly criticized by many, which is the fate of most serious reformers. Because he appears to have been the first judge effectively to enforce important parts of the New Laws, Cerrato's influence was widely felt in the Indies, since his actions encouraged other judges to follow suit.

Cerrato freed Indian slaves (about five thousand of them in the audiencia district), lowered tributes by as much as half, took Indians from delinquent encomenderos, reduced the labor of tamemes, and in other ways ameliorated the conditions of the natives. His personality and character were discussed as much as his controversial policies. The aging president was brusque in his dealings with colonists, frequently intemperate, and sometimes insulting in his remarks to the conquistadors, so jealous of their dignity. He wasted little time in tact, and he showed contempt for most of his fellow Spaniards, including some fellow judges in his own court. Although a man of high integrity, and one of the few judges who died poor, Cerrato did succumb to the common practice of rewarding his various relatives and others close to him. Nepotism was widely practiced by almost all officials with patronage, but Cerrato was particularly vulnerable to criticism because of his harsh judgments of others. However, judging from the laxity of prosecution, the crown seemed little concerned about nepotism.

Probably there was some substance to complaints of Cerrato's style, but the shock to the settlers was that the new president, unlike previous royal officials, could neither be seduced by the customary blandishments nor intimidated by threats. The laws had been ignored with impunity for so many years that Cerrato's abrupt and irreversible applications of the legislation stunned the encomenderos. Some reasoned that each case should be judged on its merits, whereas the president's reforms were sweeping. Colonists feared a collapse of the economy and a subsequent exodus of Spaniards because of a labor shortage. Further complicating the picture was the 1549 law ending the labor requirement for encomienda Indians. However, the emerging *repartimiento* system—under which natives were required to work a number of weeks a year through a village pool for reasonable pay and good treatment—helped alleviate the shortage of workers, and the economy did recover and stabilize.

There are certain ironies in Cerrato's example. Almost sixty years old when he arrived in the colony, and afflicted by kidney stones and other infirmities of age, Cerrato, while still in Santo Domingo, had implored the crown to let him return to Spain to die in peace. Instead, he was to have seven more years of bitter struggle with the encomenderos, with precious few allies. It is probably true that the crown, to ease its conscience, wanted the laws applied if it could be done without unsettling the colonies too much, but, about the time Cerrato began to clamp down, important events were occurring with ominous consequences for the Indians. The Cerro de Potosí was proving to be an extremely rich source of income, requiring native labor. Soon other rich strikes at Guanajuato and Zacatecas augmented the need for forced labor. Although the crown had earlier given Cerrato strong support, by 1552 it seemed indifferent and almost hostile toward him. It is likely that royal concern was more with silver than with the plight of the Indian. After all the abuse he had suffered from the colonists, the president was now deserted by the crown. Even Las Casas, once an ally of Cerrato, now seemed to dwell more on the president's practice of nepotism, for some reason spilling more ink on that score than on the courage and integrity displayed by Cerrato during the reforms. In

1553, Alonso de Zorita, who shared Cerrato's concern for the exploited natives, arrived as an oidor. However, instead of being appointed president in Guatemala to continue the reforms, he was allowed to remain only as oidor before being transferred to Mexico three years later.[10]

How significant were the reforms of Cerrato? Although historians have not always acknowledged their full effect, his actions had very important consequences, not only because they measurably lightened the burden of the Indians but also because of the example he set for other judges. He demonstrated that a disinterested official with courage and integrity could implement unpopular laws, and soon thereafter other oidores followed suit. Some idea of their effectiveness can be gleaned from reviewing the flood of complaints that followed. It is true that later officials were less zealous, which caused some backsliding. But Indian slavery was effectively abolished,[11] many of the abuses of encomenderos were checked, tributes were revised, and labor conditions generally were eased. Of course exploitation of the Indians continued, but less frequently and of less severity. Moreover, some natives became "muy ladino" in matters of litigation, and they were successful to a surprising degree. Still, there was no rush to broaden reforms. Philip II came to the throne in 1556 with a heavy debt, a vast empire, and a very expensive foreign policy, as a result of which he did little to restrict further the use of native labor. The succeeding oidores reflected that apathy toward the social consequences, and their administrations were marred by much of the callous disregard for the welfare of the Guatemalans as those bureaucratic entrepreneurs of the first court. Some, like the criminal President Juan Núñez de Landecho, were worse.

The changes occurring with the second audiencia coincided with other phenomena that had notable effects on the changing society. By 1548, the conquerors' children were grown, many with offspring of their own. This first generation of Hispanicized Guatemalans, both creole and *mestizo*, having experienced formative years radically distinct from those of their parents, held sharply divergent attitudes. What despair these parents—of both races—must have felt in observing their childrens' proclivities! But however dissimilar their demeanor, the conquerors' heirs inevitably formed part of the new social and economic elite. They inherited encomiendas that were already in a state of transition. No longer (after 1549) could they count on free Indian labor to generate profits, nor could they so flagrantly abuse native workers under the repartimiento system. Reduced tributes further contributed to the declining income of most encomiendas, except for the cacao encomenderos, who enjoyed continuing prosperity.

Expanded cacao production also affected demographic patterns because of increased demands for native labor. Workers from Verapaz as well as from various regions of Mexico were sent to cacao plantations. Trade with Mexico, as well as with Panama and Peru, reflected the growing diversity of commerce in the colony. Santiago became the most important settlement between Mexico City and South America.

Much of the change came simply with the passage of time and the inevitable phasing out of the conquest society. Most of the original conquistadors had been born around 1500, and by the 1560s those who were still around had lived long lives for the times. By 1570 very few of them were among the quick.

1570–1620

This third segment is less sharply defined than the one preceding it. It lacks the drama of the conquest and the resulting cultural clash. There is less violence, and fewer of the strong, colorful individuals who figured in earlier Guatemalan society are in evidence. The conqueror-encomendero cliques that dominated affairs in previous decades had lost their overwhelming power. The menacing encomendero demonstrations of years gone by were no longer credible actions because the groups were now greatly outnumbered. Moreover, the crown had dealt decisively and harshly with the principals in the revolts of Gonzalo Pizarro, the Contreras brothers, and the Avila-Cortés conspiracy, as well as others in various provinces. Curiously, no such uprisings of any consequence appeared in Guatemala, even though the encomenderos there were subject to the same laws and conditions, especially under Cerrato. It was alleged that the reforms of Cerrato provoked the Contreras affair in Nicaragua, but there was little overt support for that rebellion in Guatemala.

With the decline of encomendero power, some of the more outrageous examples of violent and exploitative behavior declined. Oddly enough, the conquerors had comparatively few legitimate descendants by late in the century. Doubtless with royal blessing, the entrenched power group consisted of bureaucratic lawyers and treasury officials. In and around Santiago the Indians were less vexed by the new types of masters, although they were commonly victimized by officials in the provincial districts. Earlier *corregidores* and *alcaldes mayores*, often lacking any respectable preparation for such positions, physically mistreated the natives and cheated them as well. Their successors, somewhat smoother around the edges, were nevertheless just as greedy. Indians continued to complain about the plague of *jueces* of this or that, along with other petty bureaucrats, clergymen, and calpisques.

Consequently, although the repartimiento system of labor was certainly preferable to slavery (at least for the Indian), conditions were still deplorable in some respects. Workers were often paid less than they were promised, and sometimes they received no pay at all. Some of them complained of being overworked and physically punished for minor infractions. Despite the many orders against personal service, the practice still existed. The continuing abuses, by the early seventeenth century, resulted in more reform legislation.[12] However, such extreme behavior on the part of the Spanish overseers became more the exception than the rule. There was clearly a decline both in the frequency and the severity of crimes against the Indians. This can be noted generally in the official reports, but especially in the *residencias* of officials. Indian complaints increasingly dealt with such matters as their being required to gather fodder for Spaniards' horses, or to carry firewood, to sweep streets, or to herd sheep or goats. If they were being forced to perform these tasks against their wills, then it was of course unjust; but it was not labor likely to result in their being ill, crippled, mutilated, or dead. Women still remonstrated, understandably, at orders to spin and weave away from home, but conditions were less tragic than they had been decades earlier. Natives could no longer be raped, whipped, disfigured, or killed with impunity.

During the years 1570–1620, the relationship between Spaniard and Indian gradually assumed the outlines it would follow for the remainder of the colonial period. Unfortunately, many vestiges of the colonial patterns prejudicial to the Indians have persisted into the twentieth century.

An examination of the more settled colonial society that emerged in this period has yet to be made with the thoroughness it deserves. Severo Martínez Peláez begins the discussion in his *La patria del criollo*, and one hopes that his conclusions will provoke a response leading to further revelations. André Saint-Lu and Pilar Sanchíz Ochoa have both written on the subject, but not as extensively as the importance of the topic demands.[13] Both are more concerned with creole attitudes than with Indians.

The evolving nature of the colony, and Santiago in particular, into a more civilized society was a natural consequence of changing times. It was the familiar story of a rough frontier settlement being tamed by a number of influences. Early hopes of wealth faded for most of the conquerors. The spoils of conquest were few in terms of readily convertible riches, and not many prospered from the years of the Indian slave trade. Very few did well in mining, and only the most prominent men received highly profitable encomiendas. The dream of returning to Spain rich and famous materialized for only a handful. The realities of the post-conquest situation led most to settle for a modest encomienda or perhaps a minor post in the bureaucracy or a small pension. They could finish out their lives in more or less dignified leisure, but they would not be rich. In the end, this was probably beneficial, because the lack of easy wealth encouraged adventurers to move on, and since they were often trouble-makers, society was spared their mischief.

The bureaucrats, independent professionals, and craftsmen seem to have been just as greedy as the conquerors, but they were, as a rule, less violent. Royal officials and many clergymen arrived, adding a substantial increase to the level of education, and their more refined tastes resulted not only in an improved cultural climate but also in a better measure of justice. As the city of Santiago became more populous, and as the character of the population changed from that of soldiers-of-fortune and vagabonds to that of more settled families and people in business and trade, stability was all the more desirable. This more prosaic environment fostered a community pride that was less inclined to indulge the boorish antics of early years. The presence of more women, children, and clergymen naturally resulted in churches, schools, handsome public buildings, and substantial residences. The economy, already examined with care by Murdo MacLeod,[14] reflected the changing nature of society, which by 1620 was dramatically changed from its first half-century of Spanish colonial life.

With fewer encomiendas to award, the deserving were given land grants, some of which became stock ranches. Agricultural activities also attracted wider interest among the Spaniards. The production of indigo dye, for example, was encouraged by the crown, with the result that profitable dye works brought good revenues to the colony. Production of both sugar and cochineal dye brought modest profits as well. But commerce was still impeded by the difficulty of transportation; even on important routes to ports and mines, roads consisted of rough mule trails, and goods moving to the many small villages went on the backs of tamemes.

Not everyone will agree with the foregoing impressions and conclusions. They are offered as points of departure for discussion, and they will no doubt be modified and refined by others in years ahead. For the moment, they may serve as a working outline.

I should like to suggest here some topics that seem to me to be fruitful as future research projects. Biography, as Charles Gibson noted recently, has been out of fashion for many years among those writing Latin American history.[15] The tendency in recent decades has been to write fairly broad social and economic history, instead of dealing with prominent individuals and dramatic subjects such as the various conquests or piracy, to take two examples. The result has certainly been to give historians a much better appreciation of history, even though these depersonalized works have less appeal for non-specialists. Their influence on more general works of history may even have had a stifling effect, as we have seen a steady decline in the interest in studying history.

In any event, Guatemala's early history offers few figures whose biographies would find a publisher, at least in English. Alvarado has been the subject of three or four in Spanish and one in English, and Marroquín's life and work have been written about by Carmelo Sáenz de Santa María, and both Zorita and Bernal Díaz del Castillo have been the subjects of biographical studies.[16]

Some day perhaps we shall see studies of other important individuals written, in Spanish, at least, because there are some highly interesting characters who played important historical roles—Jorge de Alvarado, licenciado Alonso Maldonado, licenciado Pedro de Quiñones, and Dr. Antonio Mexía, to mention only a few in the early years. There is the added problem of finding enough interesting material on them to justify a full-length book. Perhaps the most satisfactory compromise would be collective biographies, as part of broader studies of certain audiencias. Certainly both the first (Maldonado) court and the second (Cerrato) court deserve detailed examination. Few have investigated the oidores with the care their historical roles demand. Such studies would have interest beyond the borders of Guatemala, especially since almost all judges served in other audiencia districts as well. The social and economic backgrounds of judges, their political connections in Spain, their education, and their socioeconomic predilections in the Indies would all contribute to a clearer picture of the kinds of men who were the administrators of the colonies.

As part of this kind of study, one might include a section on nepotism, regionalism, and possible "old-boy" networks. The closer one looks into family connections, the more it becomes clear that male relatives were usually part of the power structure in all colonies. Since even brothers sometimes used different surnames, it is not always obvious to us that officials and encomenderos, for example, were relations, but it was certainly well known—and no doubt resented—by contemporaries. In the many dangerous situations in which conquistadors found themselves, captains understandably felt more secure in the company of those bound to them by family ties. Most leaders were accompanied by brothers, cousins, sons, sons-in-law, nephews, uncles, or even fathers, as well as childhood friends or other males close to the family. Thus we see that the Alvarados, the Pizarros, the Montejos, and most other conquistadors shared dangers, responsibilities, and rewards with trusted kinsmen. This extended family concept was firmly implanted in the colonies and it remains an important part of the social structure in Latin America generally today.

Favoritism was therefore anticipated, as a captain's relatives were routinely given good encomiendas, lucrative official positions, land grants, and other rewards. Because these familial arrangements had political, social, and economic implications, those who were left out often complained of such flagrant nepotism, but it was very likely accepted grudgingly by most as a fact of life.

Preference was also usually extended to men from the leader's home town or province, the best-known example being the men from the province of Extremadura in western Spain, among whom were found many of the most prominent conquerors of the Spanish Indies. Alvarado and his brothers, and many of his companions, were from that region and they stuck together. When don Pedro was absent from Guatemala (which was about half the time), he felt that his office of governor was safe because his loyal and able brother Jorge managed affairs for him. President Alonso Maldonado strengthened his position by an alliance with the adelantado Francisco de Montejo, to whom he was bound not only through marriage to his daughter but also through their mutual origins in Salamanca. In studying the Pedrarias Dávila–Contreras relationship in Nicaragua, I have found important family ties, in addition to their mutual ties to the city of Segovia.

One could easily find other, similar cases for Guatemala, and with some archival digging the network grows broader and more complicated. Records permitting, it might prove fruitful to look into the extent of an old-boy—or at least an old-school-ties—network, specifically among graduates of the school of law at the University of Salamanca. Such links could very well go a long way to explain part of the reason that so few officials (more often than not lawyers) were punished for their crimes. It might also have a bearing on the fact that many oidores who were clearly guilty of serious infractions were not only reappointed to audiencia positions but frequently given promotions.

Other officials—corregidores, alcaldes mayores, jueces de milpa, and jueces de repartimiento, among others—should also be subjects of more research. Even though many of them, especially during the early decades, had little qualification for the positions, those who came later were better prepared. Naturally one would not expect to find these men with the same levels of background as the oidores, but since they had control over the Indians they are worthy of close examination.

We are fortunate that important chroniclers left detailed historical accounts of Guatemala's history, despite the limitations of these works. Most of them were written by clergymen, and so we have to take into account their particular biases. The Dominicans, because of their extraordinary influence, require special attention by dispassionate researchers. Their documented struggles with the encomenderos, as well as with other men of the church, and their questionable administration of the Indians, reveal considerable detail about the bitter and sometimes violent nature of jurisdictional disputes. Consequently, we should look with a more critical eye at individual Dominicans, as well as at the general policies of the order and their place in the community. Such a study, if done with thoroughness, would almost certainly be controversial; however, it would add important dimensions to our understanding of colonial society.

But if some members of the regular orders were powerful, parish priests were often held in contempt by colonists, and occasionally even physically mistreated.[17] Respect for men of the cloth was not only often lacking to a surprising degree, but outright hostility frequently led to violence. Father Las Casas was fired upon, Bishop Marroquín sustained a slight cut from a sword, and Bishop Valdivieso of Nicaragua was assassinated.[18] Prelates were, however, outspoken, politically active, and rather free in handing out excommunications to persons of high office for slight cause. These and other factors lead one to believe that our understanding of early colonists' religious convictions and their relationships with clergymen is not very accurate. Judging from the immoral behavior of the *vecinos*, they appear not to have been very concerned about their souls, nor is it apparent that the moral suasion of the clergymen had any appreciable effect on the scandalous behavior of the settlers. We infer that oidores and other royal officials led dissolute lives because of the charges in their residencias, and there is no good reason to believe that those below them were any less intemperate and adulterous.

Most of the topics for research published for Mexico would probably be equally valid for Guatemala. Certainly many aspects of the economy need to be researched, along with more work on women, the native aristocracy, and the encomienda.[19]

A final observation here on a general subject that seems to justify special consideration in Guatemalan history, that is, the remarkable survival of distinctive regional dress, diet, languages, rituals, and customs among the various Indian groups. The explanation for this lack of assimilation may not be simple, but one suspects that it is part of the larger question of the Indian's traditional position in Guatemalan society. That historical position, moreover, may well be somewhat different from our usual perception of it.

The historian who strives to be objective faces the same problem that confronted the crown in the sixteenth century: which of the accounts describing the conditions of the colony were reflective of the true picture? In particular, I refer to the conflicting reports and opinions regarding the treatment of the Indians. One might expect that the views of some—the encomenderos being the most obvious—would be self-serving. Yet, of all the individuals giving opinions, one would expect the bishops to have some unanimity of thought. In fact, however, they disagreed rather strongly about many aspects of Spanish-Indian relations. Although the views of Las Casas, which were generally supported by bishops Valdivieso and Pedraza (of Honduras), have tended to prevail among historians outside of Spain and Guatemala, they were often contradicted by such other outstanding men as Marroquín and Motolinia.

Moreover, we must reassess our own perceptions of the Indian in colonial society, which may well be quite different from the view of the Indian himself. If the official policy saw the natives as "miserables," as perpetual minors in the legal sense, and as wards of the state and church, perhaps the natives did not regard themselves in that light. Historians are fond of observing that the conquered people were forbidden to ride horses, carry Spanish arms, and wear Spanish clothes at times. This is a clear case of discrimination, and it may have mattered to Spanish jurists. But did the natives really care? Perhaps being limited to their native dress, restricted to the use of their traditional weapons, and required to travel on foot (as they always had) constituted no great hardships. Is it not likely that such deprivations did little, if anything, to lower their self-esteem? Some caciques, eventually allowed these privileges, were perhaps flattered, and they were no doubt seen as status symbols by Hispanicized natives. But one suspects that most of the Indians were quite content to carry on in the old ways, and, if they could avoid contact with the white man, so much the better.

Notes

1. Among work by American scholars in recent years treating early colonial history of Guatemala the following are noted: Verle L. Annis, *The Architecture of Antigua Guatemala, 1543–1773* (Guatemala City, 1968), bilingual edition; Robert M. Carmack, *Quichean Civilization: The Ethnohistoric, Ethnographic, and Archaeological Sources* (Berkeley, 1973); John W. Fox, *Quiché Conquest. Centralism and Regionalism in Highland Guatemalan State Development* (Albuquerque, 1978); Christopher H. Lutz, *Santiago de Guatemala, 1541–1773; The Socio-Demographic History of a Spanish American Colonial City* (Ann Arbor: University Microfilms International, 1977); Murdo J. MacLeod, *Spanish Central America: A Socioeconomic History, 1520–1720* (Berkeley, 1973); and William L. Sherman, *Forced Native Labor in Sixteenth-Century Central America* (Lincoln, 1979).

2. These works are dealt with in considerable detail by Carmack, *Quichean Civilization.*

3. A good model is Wigberto Jiménez Moreno, "Mesoamerica Before the Toltecs," in John Paddock, ed., *Ancient Oaxaca* (Stanford, 1966), pp. 1–82.

4. MacLeod, *Spanish Central America*, uses a chronological division of 1576.

5. Pedrarias Dávila, however, was master of Panama and Nicaragua for almost as long.

6. At least Montejo claims that he allowed no slavery in Honduras, which is doubtless one of the reasons the settlers there preferred Alvarado. But there were allegations that Montejo had earlier authorized the enslavement and branding of more than 50,000 Indian slaves, who were shipped out of Yucatan. These and other accusations and counter-claims may be seen in documents from the Archivo General de Indias, as follows: Montejo to the Crown, Salamanca, 10 August 1534, Patronato 184, ramo 25; royal cédula, 10 March 1548, Guatemala 393, libro 3; Montejo to the Crown, Gracias a Dios, 15 August 1539, Guatemala 9; Montejo to the Crown, 31 December 1545, Guatemala 9; "Segunda memorial . . ." (n.p., n.d.), Guatemala 965; and Cerrato to the Crown, Santiago, 8 April 1549, Guatemala 9. Regarding Montejo's alleged authorization of 50,000 slaves, see the royal provision of 10 March 1548, Guatemala 393, libro 3, folios 72v.–73 and "Memoria para el ill[mo] senor Bisorrey de la nueva spaña sobre lo tocante a los puntos auisos en la prouança que haçe doña catalina de montejo hija del adelantado don francisco de montejo sobre la governacion de yucatan" (n.p., n.d., probably ca. 1563), Guatemala 965. Part of the text of the latter appears in Sherman, *Forced Native Labor*, p. 381.

7. Although no evidence attaches blame to Alvarado for ordering his lieutenants to behave violently, gratuitous brutality sometimes occurred. See, for example,

accounts of the depredations of Francisco Gil in Chiapas, 1535–36. Cabildo of San Cristóbal de los Llanos, 4 June 1537, to D. Antonio de Mendoza and the Audiencia of Mexico, AGI, Guatemala 110.

8. Bishop Pedraza to the Crown, Trujillo, 1 May 1547, AGI, Guatemala 9.

9. Cerrato to the Crown, Gracias a Dios, 28 September 1548, AGI, Guatemala 9.

10. Zorita is the subject of a book-length manuscript near completion by Ralph H. Vigil.

11. However, the crown authorized the enslavement of the Lacandones in the 1550s because of their "insolence and troublemaking." Audiencia to the Crown, Santiago, 22 August 1559, AGI, Guatemala 386, libro Q-1, folios 229–31. Apparently no Lacandones were enslaved, although there is some dispute. See Sherman, *Forced Native Labor*, pp. 216, 426.

12. See William L. Sherman, "Abusos contra los indios de Guatemala (1602–1605). Relaciones del Obispo," *Cahiers du monde Hispanique et Luso Brésilien. Caravelle.* 11 (1968): 4–28.

13. Severo Martínez Peláez, *La patria del criollo* (Guatemala City, 1973); André Saint-Lu, *Condition coloniale et conscience créole au Guatemala* (Paris, 1970); Pilar Sanchíz Ochoa, *Los hidalgos de Guatemala: Realidad y apariencia en un sistema de valores* (Seville, 1976). In a more restricted sense, the society of the encomenderos is treated in Salvador Rodríguez Becerra, *Encomienda y conquista. Los inicios de la colonización* en Guatemala (Seville, 1977).

14. MacLeod, *Spanish Central America*, and his essay following this one.

15. Charles Gibson, "Writings on Colonial Mexico," *Hispanic American Historical Review* 55 (1975): 287–323.

16. Though neither work is distinguished, the reader is referred to John E. Kelly, *Pedro de Alvarado, Conquistador* (Princeton, 1932), and Adrian Recinos, *Pedro de Alvarado, conquistador de México y Guatemala* (Mexico City, 1952). See also Carmelo Sáenz de Santamaría, *El licenciado don Francisco Marroquín, primer obispo de Guatemala (1499–1563)* (Madrid, 1964); Ralph H. Vigil, "Alonso de Zorita, Crown Oidor in the Indies, 1548–1556," Ph.D. dissertation, University of New Mexico, 1969; Herbert Cerwin, *Bernal Díaz, Historian of the Conquest* (Norman, 1963).

17. See Marcel Bataillon's remarks about the low esteem in which, according to Las Casas, priests were held. Bataillon, "The Clérigo Casas, Colonist and Colonial Reformer," in Juan Friede and Benjamin Keen, eds., *Bartolomé de Las Casas in History. Toward an Understanding of the Man and His Work* (Dekalb, 1971).

18. See Sherman, *Forced Native Labor*, pp. 142–43. See also Sherman, "Encomenderos in Revolt," *Proceedings of the 28th Annual Rocky Mountain Council on Latin American Studies* (Lincoln, 1981).

19. The long-awaited work of Salvador Rodríguez Becerra, *Encomienda y conquista: Los inicios de la colonización en Guatemala*, is disappointing, being based to great extent on the tribute assessment in AGI, Guatemala, 128.

Murdo J. MacLeod

Ethnic Relations and Indian Society in the Province of Guatemala, ca. 1620–ca. 1800

The Spanish colonial province of Guatemala, an area that today would include Guatemala and El Salvador, was and is one of great geographic and climatic diversity. Extremes of altitude and the proximity of the Caribbean and the Pacific have provided a large number of habitats for such a relatively small area. Part of a larger governmental unit called the Audiencia de Guatemala, colonial Guatemala's population contained a majority of ethnic Amerindians and large minorities of African blacks, European whites, and combinations of these three groups, often referred to by people of the time as *castas*. The four populations also varied widely within each group and, in comparison to one another, in their responses and adaptations to the geographic and climatic diversity. The various ethnic populations also acted upon one another biologically, culturally, and economically.

In the period under consideration here, approximately 1620 to 1800, regional and ethnic diversity was further complicated by change and divergence over time. Each population group and region responded to a long series of pressures and stimuli, to periods of slow change and to periods of accelerated social and economic activity.

The historiography of this increasing diversity and divergence is slight, even by Latin American standards. Much of it has been from the "top down," and has moved quickly to the level of large studies of the whole region. The monographic regional work on which such general studies perhaps should have been based has hardly begun.

The five great Central American colonial chroniclers, Antonio de Remesal, Francisco Antonio de Fuentes y Guzmán, Francisco Vásquez, Francisco Ximénez, and Pedro Cortés y Larraz, began this "macro" tradition, and it continued to flourish in the nineteenth and twentieth centuries in the works of Hubert Howe Bancroft, Santiago I. Barberena,

Antonio Batres Jáuregui, Ernesto Chinchilla Aguilar, Francisco de Paula García Peláez, Domingo Juarros, Jorge Lardé y Larín, José Milla, Lorenzo Montúfar, and J. Antonio Villacorta Calderón. All of these chroniclers and historians covered a multitude of topics, but in general their writings were preoccupied with political events and the social, cultural, and economic history of the civil and clerical elites and governments. Even today, some of the best works on the Guatemalan seventeenth and eighteenth centuries are primarily concerned with elite mentality, the emergence of a creole collective consciousness, the artistic products of creole culture, or the economic activities of late colonial elites. The main works of Sidney D. Markman, Severo Martínez Peláez, Manuel Rubio Sánchez, André Saint-Lu, and Ralph Lee Woodward are concerned with ethnohistory and regional cultural change only to a secondary degree.[1]

Regional and ethnic diversity, different responses to and rates of change, and a dominant historiography that has emphasized the whole region and the history of the relatively powerful—together they mean that any attempt such as this to study past Indian society and ethnic relations lacks a substantial data base, is too much of a generalization, and will undergo heavy revision, if not demolition, as the detailed monographic literature grows.

The remainder of this essay will consist of three parts. First to be considered will be some general factors, such as taxation, labor systems, geography, and comparative demography, which affected the Indian colonial populations in Guatemala (and El Salvador) throughout the seventeenth and eighteenth centuries. This synchronic approach will then lead to a brief review of change over time, the historical process or periodication of these two centuries as they affected the Indians. Finally, the essay will review the state of present research and offer some suggestions for the future.

Taxation was the main peacetime coercive device used by the Spanish authorities, and it was especially important in its effects on the Indian population. The main tax levied on the Indians was the tribute, in theory at least a capitation tax paid by heads of families and single adults because of their Indian status. Compared to central Mexico, little is known of the workings of Guatemalan tribute. In Mexico it became standardized, and settled to a recognized, official mix of money and goods, usually paid twice a year to royal officials or, more frequently, to their representatives.[2] In Guatemala the tribute never reached the standardized uniformity found in Mexico. One can only guess at the reasons for this. Perhaps the area's peripherality as far as the crown was concerned meant that less enthusiastic efforts were made to regulate the tribute. Perhaps the lack of silver mines, and the recurring seventeenth- and eighteenth-century crises over currency shortages, meant that more emphasis had to be placed on whatever goods were locally available at the village level. Probably the Guatemalan central authorities, sitting in Santiago and sallying out only intermittently to the more distant parts of the countryside, had neither the will nor the ability to impose royal regulation, at least over this matter.

Thus Guatemalan tribute history, dimly perceived, is a mosaic of local practices, goods, degrees of severity, and multifarious complaints. In areas of intense economic activity, where the means of production and the land had remained in Indian hands, tribute was notoriously exorbitant and destructive. In the cacao-producing areas, for example, it became normal to run two systems of tribute concurrently. One was the official system, more or less supervised by the crown and its collectors, whereby assigned quantities of cacao were paid over. The other, assessed by local *encomenderos* or royal officials, was based on the number of cacao bushes in production. Sometimes these second tributes reached confiscatory levels. The practice was common in the great days of the sixteenth-century cacao boom, and continued in a more or less clandestine fashion throughout the seventeenth century.[3]

In less dynamic areas there are also seventeenth- and eighteenth-century examples of a two-tribute system. First there was a personal tribute, usually twelve reales a year plus some local produce such as maize, beans, hens, and woven clothes. On top of this tax there was the second tribute sometimes referred to as the "tributo real." This was an attempt to take a percentage of any noticeable local speciality.[4]

Like those in Mexico, Guatemalan authorities and tribute collectors used the tribute as a coercive device to push Indians into other activities or attitudes. The introduction of silver as a tribute item forced Indians out of their self-sufficient agriculture and into the market, either to sell their produce in return for cash or to sell their labor for cash wages. There is some evidence that in areas such as Verapaz, where there was no local silver and very little coinage, silver coinage was introduced as a tribute item for the express purpose of driving Indians to the Pacific coast, where the seasonal work would earn the silver coinage needed to pay tribute at home.[5]

The acculturative implications of these examples of tribute manipulations are clear. The introduction of coinage as a tribute item forced Indians to leave home, to work for Spaniards or castes, and to learn the ways of the marketplace. The collection of tribute in items such as wheat and wool obliged Indians to grow, herd, or buy new European crops or animals. Here again, regional variation was enormous, and our knowledge of what went on is blurred when compared to Mexico.[6]

Many other taxes were collected in the Indian villages, some legal and some not. In the provinces distant from Santiago, where Spanish-dominated economic activities were few or absent, and where the great monastic orders governed with slight interference from the center, villages delivered considerable sums to the clergy. In Verapaz and the Cuchumatanes, visiting parish priests regularly collected the *salutación*, a visiting fee.[7] Clergy also drew funds from *cofradías* and *cajas de comunidad*, institutions that some Indians in some places favored as mechanisms of defense or of community cohesiveness. Minor royal officials played the same games in these poorer, more distant, and more Indian regions. There the gains to be made by trading or by investing in cacao, indigo, or cattle were far less than around Santiago or San Salvador. Local *alcaldes mayores*, *corregidores*, and their deputies gouged what surpluses they could, collecting fees or victuals on their *visitas* and other travels and exacting payments for every permit or scrap of paper. There was a fine line to be walked here, although we cannot yet discern where the line was. Some villages in some areas seem to have been reasonably happy to pay these additional imposts if they would buy off official or clerical interferences. Some seventeenth- and eighteenth-century cofradías ran permanent deficits, scrutinized yearly by members of the clergy and by local Indian village officials. One is led to suppose that these cofradías existed, at least in part, to provide bribes or presents to potentially intrusive outsiders. But Indian villages, Indian authorities, cofradías, and cajas de comunidad could be pushed or goaded too far. If the local corregidor or priest refused to be bought off and returned time after time for more, he might well, especially after about 1690, face protests, appeals to the *audiencia* from the Indian community, refusals to pay, or even attacks on his person.[8]

Labor exactions in the seventeenth and eighteenth centuries followed some of the patterns discerned in taxation. Minor exactions were varied and followed regional custom. Many of them were the ones indignant reformers complained about in the sixteenth century. Indian women were used as concubines or as house serfs by local Spaniards, and Spanish farmers and officials forced Indians from nearby villages to perform illegal personal services such as ploughing, planting, weeding, and repairs of houses, streets, or churches, often without compensation.[9] But in general the types of labor exactions fell into two large categories. Around the Spanish cities, in areas where Spanish or casta farms dominated the countryside, and in the zones where Spanish export crops were of importance, that is, in the regions running south and east of Santiago all the way to San Salvador and San Miguel, Indians were employed to a greater degree in Spanish-dominated tasks or in jobs where Spaniards or castas owned or controlled the means of production. Around Santiago, in the so-called valley of Guatemala, Indians were employed as suppliers to the city, bringing in wood, cloth, and groceries as required. The large repartimientos, which survived, indeed flourished, much longer in this region of Guatemala than elsewhere in the province or in Mexico, were heavily employed in city maintenance—street-sweeping, work on public buildings, repairs to bridges, aqueducts, and public fountains—and, at planting, weeding, and harvesting seasons, on the wheat farms that surrounded Santiago for many miles. The valley repartimiento meant that at least once a year Indians had to leave their villages to work in a Spanish city, or at least in a Spanish environment, at Spanish-appointed tasks.[10] Villages near Spanish cattle haciendas and indigo *obrajes* found themselves in similar circumstances. Either by coercive methods such as debt or harassment, or by enticements such as offers of free land away from the restrictive, overtaxed village, indigo obrajes scoured the surrounding countryside and brought in the permanent or seasonal labor they needed.[11] Again the villagers were obliged to leave home, even if the journey were only a mile or two in some cases, and again they found themselves working in a Spanish-supervised environment where the forms of work and the means of production were controlled by Spaniards. Here too the acculturative implications are clear. By 1800, except for a few isolated pockets, areas such as the valley of Guatemala and the plains around San Salvador had ceased being "Indian." They were occupied by a *ladino* peasantry, tied willingly or unwillingly to the cities or to the European farms and indigo obrajes.[12]

The exact nature of the links between these peasants and their places of employment has caused some debate. The labor repartimiento remained important long after its demise in other regions. Recently scholarship has tended to doubt the importance of debt peonage as a device for the recruitment and detention of labor.[13] We do find Guatemalan hacendados and owners of indigo obrajes who, at their deaths, reported that dozens of nearby villagers owed them small sums such as three or five pesos.[14]. This looks suspiciously like a recognized system. But by and large the critics may be correct. Debt peonage does not seem to have been the major way of recruiting peasant labor in the south and east of the province of Guatemala in the seventeenth and eighteenth centuries. What one tends to find is a whole range of regional or individual improvisations. Indians were recruited at church doors with offers of prepayments or with offers to pay their tribute and other taxes.[15] A surprising number of Indians seem to have been happy to leave the villages. The hacienda or obraje was no paradise, but it offered some protection against the depredations of corregidores, petty merchants, parish priests, and Indian alcaldes and regidores. By mid-eighteenth century the population had begun to recover from the conquest and its subsequent population collapse, and signs of land hunger began to appear as villages grew and discovered that nearby vacant land had been taken up by Spaniards or castas.[16] Hacienda or obraje owners were able to attract people from such villages by offering them plots in return for their labor, an offer that many Indian agriculturalists were in no position to refuse. By 1800 many haciendas and obrajes had established permanent, ladinoized labor forces, with several individual peasant families each working a small plot of land containing a straw hut and a plot of maize, beans, and squash, and in return paying rent in the form of a few days of work under the farm owner's or mayordomo's directions.[17]

In the poorer, higher regions north and west of Santiago, all the way to the borders with Chiapas and the Petén, areas less attractive to Spaniards and castas, and much more Indian in composition as a result, labor exactions were of a different type. With few exceptions the powerful encomenderos of the sixteenth century had disappeared. Local Spaniards were more commonly minor officials, friars, small farmers, or petty merchants and muleskinners. These entrepreneurs did not have the capital, expertise, or facilities to mount European enterprises. As a result, they sought to accumulate wealth and utilize the available Indian labor force by living off Indian forms of production. Often the Spanish official or merchant would attempt to intensify or enlarge the Indian cottage industry, but essentially the Indian men and women engaged in these tasks stayed at home and worked at jobs that they had mastered and that Spaniards found too menial or too complicated to perform.

Repartimientos de efectos, whereby Spanish merchants and officials introduced European goods, foodstuffs and clothing to Indian regions, sometimes forcing the local populations to buy them at artificially high prices, did occur in highland Guatemala, but they never became a common system like that in highland Peru.[18] Presumably both Spaniards and Indians were too poor and too short of coinage and liquid capital for such a system to develop. What did take root in the poorer areas of highland Guatemala (and Chiapas) was the *derrama*. This was a method of siphoning off Indian cottage production in spite of the constraints of the situation. It was well established by the middle of the seventeenth century and became widespread in the eighteenth, when the derrama became a dominant feature, practically a system. In a typical situation, a minor local official such as a corregidor would buy up raw cotton or newly-sheared unwashed wool and would then turn it over to Indian villagers, usually women, for washing, carding, spinning, weaving into cloth, and dying, or for any previously specified part of that series of processes. After the work had been performed the official or his agents would take back the finished cotton or wool, paying the Indian spinner or weaver far below the going rate for her work, if he paid her at all. Then the cloth was taken to the city or to market villages for sale at a profit. Complaints about derramas abound, but the practice flourished in the eighteenth century.[19]

Once again, however, there was a line, so far invisible to moderns, but usually recognized by both sides of these transactions. If Indian villages were pushed too far by repeated or excessive derramas, they would, and did on several occasions, protest, riot, destroy the derrama goods, or even attack the exploitive Spaniard and his agents. Many of the small uprisings of the late seventeenth and early eighteenth centuries may be traced back to derramas that Indians believed had gone past tolerable limits.[20]

Another unknown is Indian wage labor. It is obvious that this category grew, both absolutely and relatively, in the mid and late eighteenth centuries. Gangs of laborers are especially noticeable in the cities and in the areas of intensive or plantation agriculture. Wages and conditions seem to have changed little over the two centuries, but apart from such vague generalizations little is known about the lives and work of this important group of people.[21]

Thus our knowledge of the labor connections between the dominant society and the lower classes in the seventeenth and eighteenth centuries is, if anything, murkier than our knowledge of the tax system. Our regional generalizations will be modified when more is known about the local customs, economies, and personalities of the many micro regions in the Guatemalan mosaic. Whole groups, such as wage laborers and petty merchants, are almost unknown and must enter any future, properly-balanced survey of labor conditions.

Much of what we have examined above in the categories of taxation and labor often spilled over into a third set of generalizations, one that for our present purposes has been labeled economic geography.

It is clear that economic activities in any age of slow and difficult communications most affected those who were closest to them in distance. And, of course, different activities have different degrees of work intensity and varying sizes of "catchment" areas for their labor supplies. Furthermore, some areas were more attractive to the powerful in society because they had better soils, easier access to cities, communication routes, mines, or other desirables, or because they were culturally perceived by the elites as having better climates. By and large, for example, all Europeans tended to avoid great extremes of altitude, temperature, or humidity, unless some very attractive feature such as the silver mines of Potosí or the great annual fairs of Portobelo enticed them there.

As noted above, these activities and preferences had an effect on relationships between Indians and non-Indians. In Guatemala, Indian groups near such main towns as Santiago, San Salvador, or San Miguel tended to become "ladinoized" more quickly. By the late seventeenth century, Mixco and Chimaltenango had become villages containing many ladinos.[22] Main ports or royal highways had a similar effect on Indians in villages near them. Villages on the road between Santiago and Sonsonate, and, more rarely, on the thinly-populated roads between Santiago and the tiny ports of the Gulf of Honduras, complained of having to supply Spanish foodstuffs, mules, horses, and hay to officials, clergy, and even ordinary merchants. At other times these Indians were called upon to supply porters, inn servants, hostlers, and postal couriers. Villages back from these main roads sometimes escaped these unwelcome attentions, much to the disgust of their *cabeceras* nearer the road, whose *cabildos* of course believed that these tasks should be spread out to all in the region. Ports, especially the hot, sickly ports of the thinly-occupied Caribbean coast, had larger catchment areas than the roads to them, and made recruitment raids far afield in their attempts to find labor for castles and forts, stevedores, crews for longshore vessels, and workers for everyday town maintenance. Several presidents and audiencias transported Indian villagers from distant areas and resettled them near the Gulf of Honduras landing stages in the hopes that they would provide a handy pool of workers. These schemes were dismal failures, but again one can appreciate the acculturative, or at least the culturally disruptive, aspects of a port and its environs.[23]

Roads, inns, and ports, then, although they did not have an effect upon

Indian society to be compared with that of the larger Spanish towns, nevertheless were economic and geographical features of importance in the study of inter-ethnic relations.

Related to geography and economic geography was Spanish-dominated agriculture, its degree of intensity and its location. In general, Spaniards found the areas to the south and east of Santiago, that is, the Guatemalan Pacific coast and most of present-day El Salvador, more suited to their agricultural enterprises than the colder and more mountainous areas to the north and west. Cacao, cattle ranching, indigo, cochineal, coffee, and bananas, in all their various phases of prosperity and failure, from the years after the conquest to the present, have all been concentrated in the Central American fertile cresent. Verapaz with its German-led coffee industry was an exception, but in general the northwest has suffered the effect of these booms mainly as a source of migrant labor. The direct effect of European agriculture, intensification, and sometimes mechanization has been heaviest to the south and east.

It may be possible to draw up an acculturative continuum as far as these agricultural enterprises are concerned. Of all the ones mentioned in Guatemala, sugar was probably the one with the most effect. Sugar cultivation, after all, has been called "the factory in the field" because of its intensity, mechanization, relatively large capital input, and multiplicity of standardized tasks. For the seventeenth and eighteenth centuries, then, sugar was modern in its methods and aims.

Sugar was never of great importance in seventeenth-century Guatemala, but in the mid-eighteenth century the great monastic orders, especially the Jesuits and the Dominicans, developed some half-dozen large enterprises in Guatemala. These mills were employers of slaves and of paid day laborers, usually ladinos or castas, but at the heaviest seasons of the year they would recruit large armies of Indians for the harvest. Some Indians also became carpenters, operators of rollers, crushers, and boiling vats, and even, rarely, supervisors. Many worked inside the refinery buildings in spite of royal and loyal prohibitions, and helped with the sorters, crushers, and vats, on the purification process, and on bottling and packing.

We know little about the Guatemalan sugar industry, but a cursory examination of Jesuit account books would seem to show that, in scale, organization, and level of mechanization, a few of these mills in the late eighteenth century matched their Mexican counterparts.[24]

Many students of sugar have commented on the pervasiveness of its influences. Indians owned mills, in fact a surprising number in some

areas, but it was a Spanish-, indeed church-dominated industry of Guatemala, and it tended to alter people's lives in its recruitment area.

If sugar was a minor product in Guatemala, then indigo, for most of the
period that concerns us, was the major product of the region. As worked
in the seventeenth and eighteenth centuries it was never as intensive,
capital-hungry, or profitable as sugar, but it did draw many Indians and
other groups into its orbit and had lasting effects.

The making of indigo had nothing arcane, native, or mysterious about
it. If one had some basic capital it was a simple series of processes. A few
skilled men were needed, and in El Salvador they were usually castas or
black slaves. Most of the laborers were semi-skilled cutters or machine
tenders. No meticulous individual care was needed during the growing
period. As a result, standardization, rationalization, and inexpensive
mechanization were all possible in times of expansion, and the indigo
plants, sown broadcast fashion, could be combined with cattle raising in
bad times or if the hacienda/obraje were being used as a hedge against
possible hard times. All this meant that as soon as the export of indigo was
well established and reasonably profitable, Spaniards interested in it had
an inducement to supervise production, to own the land, to introduce
more efficient techniques and economies of scale, and to impose new
notions of agriculture and labor use on the nearby populations.

Indian labor on indigo obrajes was formally forbidden, but growers in
Guatemala and El Salvador had solved this problem by the early seventeenth century. A "fine-bribe" system was so common by 1620 that it
became one of the largest sources of official wealth. Quite early in the
century, Indian and even ladino peons were already living on the indigo
obrajes, and villages close by were tied seasonally to the obrajes by
devices such as debt or land shortage and the need to rent additional land.
As the industry grew and intensified in the mid-eighteenth century, more
and more villagers and even migrant laborers from the highlands were
dragged into its orbit, and people around San Salvador became Spanish-
speaking peasants, living part of the year in villages but tied for the rest of
the year to a Europeanized agriculture with a heavy export-market orientation. By the end of the colonial period the native peoples of the indigo-
growing areas were mostly ladinos.[25]

Other industries were much less acculturative than sugar and indigo.
Cacao, which had put such heavy pressures on some Indians in the
sixteenth century, survived the age of the great *encomenderos* in only a
spotty fashion. It was a peculiar agriculture, with plantation-like groves of
cacao bushes planted under shade trees, but requiring, at least in some

seasons of the year, an intensity and skill in care that was almost like horticulture. This did not attract non-experts, and most Spaniards fell into this category. As a result, Indians were often left in charge of the production process, Spaniards taking over only after the beans had been picked, sorted, and dried. Thus, although pressure and exploitive practices could be severe, acculturation seems to have been relatively slow. We cannot be sure of this because many of the areas that had been of importance to the cacao industry in the sixteenth century became indigo-growing areas in the seventeenth and eighteenth centuries. But in areas where cacao persisted and indigo did not intrude, such as some parts of Suchitepéquez, the pace of acculturation seems to have been slower than in the indigo zones.[26]

Cochineal had a chequered history in Guatemala. The Conde de la Gómera, president of the audiencia from 1611 until 1626, tried to promote it with no real success. Toward the end of the eighteenth and into the nineteenth century the industry did develop, and for a few years it became Guatemala's most important export crop. With the invention of synthetic dyes it fell away again to the level of a local Indian cottage industry, where it has remained to this day.

The making of "domesticated" cochineal dye (there was a "wild" variety too) was a process of great complexity. In Europe beyond the Iberian peninsula it was somewhat of a mystery for centuries. The process required patient, intricate, detailed, individual work and skills that were passed on from parents to children. There was a long apprenticeship, and good workers knew details about climate, soils, the nopal cactus, and the life cycle of the dye-producing insects that fed on the cactus. Suffice it to say that non-Indians found it difficult to break into this system of production or even to supervise it. Few Spaniards attempted to grow cactus and produce cochineal, and many of those who did failed. It was also difficult to spread the planting of cactus to new areas where the plants, insects, and processes had not been known previously. Indians who were experts were brought in, but local Indians could not or would not acquire such a long work-tradition, and the Spaniards, either local hacendados or officials, did not understand the production cycle or system well enough to supervise them.

Eager Spaniards became exasperated at times when they thought of the potentials for profits and general prosperity locked up in this peculiar form of agriculture. Local merchants, or even a president of the Audiencia de Guatemala, the Conde de la Gómera, would exert pressure on Indians to expand their cactus plantings or change their production methods. But these Indians possessed a skill, a knowledge monopoly or "trade secret," that made Spanish attempts to interfere ineffective. Thus cochineal plantations, seldom of great importance in Guatemala during the colonial period anyway, tended to remain in Indian hands, and Spaniards and castas were rarely found in the workplace. They could not even supervise the process of production. Cochineal came to the crown and its agents by way of the tribute. Non-Indians, unable to take over earlier, moved back to the collection, distribution, and marketing of the finished product. Here they had greater success, but even at this commercial end of the business there were problems. Most Indians were small producers and lived in relatively isolated areas—cactus did not need good soils—so that collecting the output was difficult and involved many stops at small regional village markets. Large capitalists preferred not to become involved at this level. Petty merchants, often Indians or castas themselves, traveled the countryside from market to market. In some regions, especially Nicaragua and Chiapas, but perhaps within Guatemala too, these petty traders were scorned by the Indians and had a reputation for swindling and abusing them. They had neither the economic power nor the social prestige to influence Indians in their mode of living.[27]

Cochineal was not entirely exempt from market factors. When demand increased in Europe in the late eighteenth and early nineteenth centuries, and profitability rose sharply, large merchants from Santiago and the capitalists from Europe who were behind them began to take more interest in it. Officials and merchants began to lend money to Indian growers against their future harvests or to force sales on them—a late resurgence of *repartos de efectos* (compulsory purchases) in Guatemala, a province where such a system had never flourished, the sales to be repaid in cochineal. Some Indians nearer to Santiago had become integrated enough into the larger commercial system to be persuaded by higher prices and other inducements to plant more cactus and to restrict other areas on their farms that had been planted to competing crops. But this era when cochineal began to act powerfully as an agent of change on Indian communities was of brief duration in Guatemala. The whole industry was destroyed by the invention of analine dyes in the 1850s.[28]

Even in the greatest days of the cochineal trade, however, in the early nineteenth century, outsiders were never really able to invade or capture the workplace or the means of production or to change radically the techniques, methods, and rhythms of production. Partly as a result of these characteristics, cochineal areas remained more Indian than one would have expected, especially when compared with the indigo zones.

Wheat in Guatemala is a special case. It was too bulky, too quickly spoiled by mold, and too marginally profitable to be transported any distance. So wheat zones were limited to fertile soils near sizeable markets. In the province of Guatemala this meant the valleys near Santiago. Indians in these valleys acculturated quickly, as noted above, but one suspects, without much evidence, that it was the pull of the cities rather than the work characteristics of wheat cultivation that caused the changes. But certainly the labor repartimientos for wheat cultivation in the valley of Guatemala, especially around Pinula, were large in the seventeenth and eighteenth centuries, and the disruptive and other effects of this institution, when combined with wheat cultivation, would provide an interesting topic for further investigation.[29]

Cattle ranching had fairly dramatic effects on Indians in the sixteenth century and sometimes even as late as the early seventeenth century. It introduced some Indians to horseback riding, mule trains, the herding of large horned beasts, and the consumption of a largely meat diet. But after the initial period the effects of cattle ranching may have faded. The work was seldom intensive, and it may be that relatively few Indians were involved. Cattle herders reported in to the hacienda or overseer as rarely as possible and led marginal, isolated lives. In some parts of southeastern Guatemala, San Salvador and San Miguel, cattle herding became the occupation of these "free" yet unfree members of society, the castas. As cowboys, castas contrived to escape from the close supervision and menial tasks of the cities and plantations while at the same time satisfying the official requirement that these "inferior" yet legally free peoples be gainfully and steadily employed. These castas, skilled on horseback and with lances and lassos, out of sight most of the time, worried officials and some of the wealthy, who compared them with the supposedly soft, sedentary Spanish city dwellers. What if these hardy, disaffected castas were to ally with the Indians or with the Dutch and English pirates on the Caribbean shores? Even more sinister, given that many of the castas were of black or mulatto origins, what if they led a slave uprising? If we can believe the volume of complaints from Indian villages, the likelihood of an alliance between casta cowboys, muleskinners, and petty merchants, and Indian villagers, was slight. Casta cowboys "shot up" villages, raided stores, barns, and fields, harassed Indian men and molested Indian women, and were given to long, drunken midnight sprees. Of course there were probably many unknown instances of cooperation between these two groups too. They had a common upper class to avoid, deceive, or confront, after all. Once again we have to confess that we know little beyond official information, complaints to officialdom, and royal policy about the relationships, and the effects of these relationships, between Indians and castas. In the cities we know even less. Castas and Indians joined together and fought each other and Spaniards over guilds and jobs. But when and why we do not know.[30]

All things considered, wheat farming and cattle raising do not seem to have had great or at least greatly visible effects on Indian societies after the shock of the sixteenth century had pased. They were not factories in the fields like sugar, or an early form of monocultural plantations like indigo.

Sheepherding seems to have altered Indian society even less. Indians to the north and west of Santiago quickly adopted the sheep, a smaller and more docile animal than the cow and horse. Wool joined cotton in the sixteenth century as a basic cloth in Indian weaving. We find mention of a few Spaniards around Quetzaltenango and Huehuetenango running huge herds of sheep on large farms, but generally sheepherding in the higher, colder, poorer areas most suited to sheep became an Indian occupation. Spaniards intruded at the latter end of the production process, trading for wool, or appropriating it through taxation or confiscations of various types.[31]

Generally speaking, then, intensive industries in the countryside, especially those that were export-oriented, and where Spaniards had taken over the production process, had heavy acculturative effects on Indian society. Most of these were located in the fertile areas to the south and west of Santiago. Extensive land uses, such as cattle raising or sheepherding, left Indian society relatively undisturbed.

All of the above types of contact and acculturation lead the student to the study of comparative demography. Here again our knowledge is slight, although some recent research results are promising and a general vague outline is beginning to appear.

To be somewhat obvious for a moment, it is clear that where Indian populations had been sparse before the conquest, and where large numbers of Indians disappeared in the century after the conquest, then little "Indian" culture survived, especially if Spaniards or castas moved in in large numbers. Soconusco or the shores of the Gulf of Fonseca would seem to be examples of this type of situation. The opposite end of the demographic continuum would be areas such as the northwest corner of Guatemala or Chiapas, where large numbers of Indians survived the effects of the first century after the conquest, and where Spaniards, for a variety of reasons, did not settle in very large numbers. The core territory of Guatemala saw more complicated situations. Generally speaking, Indians survived until 1620 in relatively large numbers, and Spaniards settled or intruded in a large variety of ways, as noted above. A close study of the types of settlements and forms of intrusions is one way to unravel the puzzle. A closer study of the comparative demography of the various cultural and racial groups involved, by micro region if possible, is another.[32]

Our knowledge of population movements in Central America ranges from fairly good to nonexistent. All of the studies show noticeable to severe drops in population after the Spanish conquest. In some areas revival began in mid-seventeenth century, or perhaps even before. In other areas the decline continued until a belated eighteenth-century revival or until the recognizably Indian population disappeared. We know little about such important matters as family size, fertility rates, or replacement rates. Our ignorance extends to Indians, castas, blacks, and Spaniards. In general the late seventeenth and entire eighteenth centuries seem to be an era of population growth, but such growth varied widely from region to region, and was interrupted or even reversed by frequent local epidemics and rarer but significant pandemics of various types.[33]

Verapaz, a small isolated province, had several good tribute and visita counts but was complicated for much of the period by an open or recently conquered frontier to the Chol-Manché and the Petén. Like parts of Chiapas it was also a source of labor for more prosperous areas, and many of these migrants to the Pacific coast and foothills did not return. After a rapid population decline in the second half of the sixteenth century, a decline that had probably started much earlier, the population reached a nadir somewhere around 1600 with fewer than 1,800 tributaries. When next we hear of Verapaz population, in 1664, the number of tributaries had climbed to 2,105, and thereafter a wavering but noticeable climb continued, much interrupted by famines, epidemics, flight, and seasonal labor migrations. Verapaz did not suffer the fate of Soconusco because it was a highland province for the most part, and because no intense economic activity developed during the colonial period. The exclusiveness of the dominant Dominicans helped, no doubt, and there was no large influx of non-Indians. Noteworthy also is that Verapaz probably reached its lowest population point around 1600, thus fitting more closely to the Mexican rather than the Chiapan or Yucatecan model.[34]

The west of Guatemala, from the heights of the Cuchumatanes mountains through the string of large villages that run from Huehuetenango through Momostenango, Totonicapán, and Quezaltenango to the foothills below Mazatenango and Coatepeque, seems to have followed a pattern similar to that of Verapaz, although our knowledge of the area's demography is very spotty.[35]

The Caribbean coast, not a very large area in the province of Guatemala, quickly lost nearly all of its Indian population in spite of legal and illegal efforts to repopulate it. The growth of the Kekchi population in the area and in Belize is a post-independence phenomenon.[36]

The heartland of Guatemala stretching from Santiago to San Miguel presents many problems. There are few general surveys of the area and only a very few local studies. These studies seem to show slow population growth, especially among the ladino and casta populations, for most of the seventeenth and nearly all of the eighteenth century. The area is large and diverse. It has none of the geographic unity of a Soconusco or a Verapaz. There were areas and periods of intense economic activity, cacao in Izalcos, then indigo in San Salvador and San Miguel. The areas around Santiago and then around the new city of Nueva Guatemala de la Asunción were attracted to a city market. There was large internal migration from village to village and toward the productive coasts. In spite of these movements, in some of the coastal areas of intense activity there was a general population growth but a continuing decline of the group identified as Indian. Indians were gradually becoming ladinos.[37]

The only general study finds that Guatemala had a total population of about 300,000 at contact, a figure this writer finds to be too low. This declined to about 148,000 in 1572, and revived briskly (the central Mexican model, perhaps?) to 195,000 around 1604. Growth continued until around 1750, when the author counts 310,000 Indians. Then there was a decline in the second half of the eighteenth century, a decline this writer questions, at least for many places. The second trough took place about 1779, when the population classified as Indian numbered about 233,000. Thereafter growth resumed until independence.[38]

The few scholars who have studied the subject find growth in all the non-Indian groups throughout the period. These populations probably enjoyed higher fertility rates and lower mortality rates. Acculturation from the Indian community and immigration also added to their numbers. Although there was growth in the seventeenth century, it was stagnation compared to Mexico. No doubt the absence of a great magnet industry such as silver and the general depression that engulfed the area were factors. Growth rates seem to have increased after 1720, and especially after about 1770. There are all kinds of regional variations, exceptions, and changes within this general periodization. Knowledge of colonial Guatemala's black population is especially scanty, almost nonexistent.[39]

What is surely needed is some comparative regional demography in which the population figures, birthrates, deathrates, and family size of each group are compared. This may lead to a better understanding of each region's ethnic interrelationships.

To conclude this segment, there was a drastic population decline in Guatemala after the Spanish conquest, or beginning even before, over 50 percent and as high as 95 percent depending on the precontact figure used. In some areas, because of low replacement rates, epidemics, flight, intensive economic activities, or acculturation this decline continued after 1570–1600 at a slower pace until the group identified as Indian disappeared. In other areas the Indian population bottomed out and began to grow. The critical factors seem to have been the size of the precolumbian population of a region, the extent of Spanish and casta demographic intrusions and economic activities, diseases, and, perhaps, altitude and climate. Some population revivals started earlier or later than others.

So far, our discussion has concentrated on specific factors—taxation, labor, industries and economic geography, and comparative demography—as they influenced ethnic relations and Indian society. But unless seen in a historical context, as part of a process of change over time, these factors remain synchronic and unvarying in their effects, hardly real-life situations. Let us now turn to an attempt to periodize our era. What were the various phases in the socioeconomic history of the province of Guatemala between 1620 and 1800?

The third decade of the seventeenth century found Guatemala and its governing elites facing a series of intractable problems. The cacao industry was in decline, a victim of overcultivation, labor shortages, and the rivalry of Caracas and Guayaquil. Attempts to revive the cacao trade or to find substitutes for it—such as the Conde de la Gómera's promotion of cochineal—had all failed. Not only export trades had fallen away. The Indian population had declined constantly since the conquest, leaving vast tracts of land vacant and uncultivated. Indian supplies to the cities grew smaller and more expensive. At first the vacant lands had been occupied by herds of semi-feral cattle, but these herds too went through a seemingly ineluctable Malthusian cycle of their own, and by the 1620s meat was no longer as plentiful and cheap as it once had been.[40] The result for a while was an attempt by the Spanish authorities to force Indian villages, especially those near the cities, to produce more staples such as maize, beans, wheat, hay, and textiles. The infamous *jueces de milpas*, local officials who were supposed to inspect Indian farms, were one device, but were ineffective. The crown abolished the post repeatedly, claiming that these inspectors were little more than another layer of parasites and exploiters. Some of them, the crown claimed, never visited the villages under their charge, but simply collected fees.[41]

Spaniards had taken up farms and cattle ranges in the countryside since the earliest days of the conquest. Each subsequent earthquake, plague, or other disaster sent others fleeing from the city. Around Santiago some entrepreneurs had profited by supplying wheat and other European crops to the city consumers. Nevertheless, until the hard times of the seventeenth century most Spaniards preferred to think of themselves as city dwellers. Now, with prices rising, with food supplies falling, and with no solid export industry, not even indigo yet, to bring prosperity, the countryside began to appear more attractive. Nor was there any real obstacle any more to Spanish occupation of land. Much of it had been left vacant by the shrinking Indian villages and the declining herds of cattle. Royal authorities, anxious to put the land to work and to build up the food supplies, readily granted land to applicants. Thus, during the seventeenth-century depression in Guatemala, Spaniards took to the countryside in considerable numbers, some to grow indigo for the export market, especially around Guazacapán and San Salvador, others to self-sufficient small farms, poor but inexpensive refuges from hard times.[42]

The general lessening of intensive agriculture and the Spanish flight to the countryside had some important effects on Indian communities. Those that were near the areas the Spaniards and castas took up as farms felt considerable pressure. Many were induced to leave their villages to settle on the new Spanish estates. Some did so willingly to escape village obligations and exactions. Those who remained in the villages were called repeatedly to agricultural repartimientos or labor drafts, and ended up working several weeks per year on Spanish farms or in the Spanish cities. Other villages found themselves tied by a series of obligations or needs to nearby indigo obrajes or haciendas. In short, in the areas where Spaniards settled in fair numbers the types of pressures on Indian villages may have changed, but it is unlikely that they lessened much.[43]

The decline in economic activity, however, did lead to some significant changes in Indian villages far from Spanish settlement. These areas had been exploited by the encomienda when it was a powerful institution.

They had also provided migrant labor to the cacao industry. Now distant villages in the Cuchumatanes, in Verapaz, and even in Quezaltenango were neglected and had little to fear except the attentions of the local corregidor or parish priest, two types of problems that had been there since the conquest anyway. These relatively neglected villages were able to reconstitute fairly autonomous cultures during the seventeenth century. Some of the old cacique class had disappeared; others had drifted off into ladino society; many probably became part of a hereditary class of office holders in the new Indian cabildos in the villages, these cabildos having been imposed to lessen the power of that very cacique class and to make the villages conform more to the recognized Spanish model. Two other Spanish institutions were imposed on the Indian village and in some seventeenth-century villages were adopted with such enthusiasm that Spanish authorities became suspicious and tried to control them. These two institutions were the cofradía, or religious sodality, and the caja de comunidad, or community chest. We know far too little about the real workings and functions of these institutions. In some villages they were used by parish priests or petty officials as means of extracting capital from Indians, and some of these villages resisted paying money to the cofradías and cajas, fled to escape holding office in them, or absconded with funds. Many villages, however, responded enthusiastically to the cofradía and caja, used them to create community solidarity, and found them a screen behind which ceremonies and fiestas could be conducted without too much Spanish interference. In these villages the cofradías were brokers, paying off potentially intrusive and disruptive forces in return for the right to establish a somewhat autonomous religious and cultural life. Of course these reconstructed Indian villages, even with the help of cofradías and other brokerage arrangements, survived only because pressure had slackened. An influx of Spaniards or an intensive industry would have destroyed their hard-won autonomy quite quickly.[44]

The years between the late 1680s and the 1720s are a puzzle. The indigo trade finally blossomed in response to a rise in demand in Jamaica and northwestern Europe. Yet the period was also one of great difficulties. A new currency crisis, pandemics, and harvest failures, the difficulties caused by the War of The Spanish Succession, all slowed recovery.

The renewed economic activity meant new intrusions on the Indian communities. To the ones in the south and east this was nothing new, but the new pressures on the villages of the north and west, such as more vigorous tax collection, derramas, and "trading" by officials, clergy, and merchants, plus heavier labor recruitment for the indigo obrajes, caused a rash of local riots and revolts in these years, culminating in a large rebellion in Chiapas in 1712.[45]

By the 1730s the crisis had passed. The more distant villages persisted in their "Indianness," but had to accommodate to far more intrusion than in the seventeenth century. Villages near Santiago and the other cities, or ones used extensively in obraje work, rapidly became more ladino. The non-Indian population grew and occupied much of the best land. Most Indian populations were now growing also and suffered increasingly from land hunger, which put them at the mercy of haciendas and obrajes.

The seventeenth and eighteenth centuries seem to be in direct contrast to one another in Guatemala. The seventeenth century was an era of extensive land utilization with a few highly commercial enclaves, low labor utilization, small local markets with little market pull, and low capital investment. The eighteenth century, after a period of difficulties, was one of rising land values as population grew. A growing export sector led to heavier investment in plants and ports and an intensified use of land and labor. Indian villages in the remoter areas flourished more in bad times for the Spanish economy, and vice versa.

Where should scholars interested in colonial Guatemala direct their attentions? The field is almost limitless. One should begin by establishing the geographical context and by putting the people into it. Historical geography and demography are both in their infancy as far as this region is concerned, but enormous quantities of documents are available. Historical geography has much to tell us about soils and changes in soils, about changes in ground cover during these centuries of Spanish rule, about the effect of new animals, extensive livestock raising, and agricultural methods on soils and vegetation, about the interaction between climate and altitude and the new society that emerged after the conquest. Using the pioneering works of Denevan, Johannessen, and Veblen as springboards, the historical geographer can be among the first to pursue such topics in colonial Guatemala.[46]

Much more work is needed on Guatemalan demography. Local studies of Indians and Spaniards, such as those of Lutz and Lovell, may save us from polemics over the size of the population collapse and what such a collapse means about Spanish imperialism or morals. Other demographic questions that are fairly well known in Mexico but have been ignored in Guatemala include mestizaje, the slave trade and slave numbers, interregional migration, movement between rural areas and cities, and differences in morbidity and mortality between highlands and lowlands, all subjects for research that have been examined in the Mexican case. Tribute records, parish records of births, confirmations, marriages, and deaths, and secular and ecclesiastical visita records are quite abundant in the archives of Guatemala and Spain and await the student pioneer.[47]

The history of food supply and diet is a bridge between some of the above questions and cultural history. What were the connections between such factors as famines, dearths, crop failures, new European crop introductions such as wheat or pigs, local plagues, locusts, and economic dislocation, and the gradual changes in diet, especially Indian diet, after the conquest? And how much was diet a function of deterministic necessities, how much a question of cultural preferences and dictates? Many historians of colonial Guatemala know of anecdotes and brief documentary references to such matters as the prestige of wheat when compared to lowly maize—one the staple of the European conquerors, the other the staple of the conquered.[48]

Population, mortality, food supply, and diet lead us next to the source of most food. How was the land used, abused, divided up, and held? Studies of land use would quickly lead scholars to a consideration of the effect of Central America's great colonial commercial crops such as cacao, sugar, indigo, cochineal, and tobacco. Although the general histories of these boom crops are quite well known, the internal and social histories of the merchants, growers, middlemen, and laborers involved in them are not.[49] Land tenure is another vast unknown in colonial Guatemala. Hacienda studies, so much in vogue in Mexico, have attracted few students of colonial Guatemala.[50]

Much of the preceding has been concerned with the interaction between people and the environment and what grows from that tension. What of the influences of men and women on one another, either singly or in groups or classes? The effect of Spanish activity and settlement, in its fine grain, is hardly known. What, for example, became of Chorti society in the seventeenth and eighteenth centuries? Here was a particular group, tribe, or nation with its own distinguishable language and culture. And in much modified form this group remains unique today. Feldman has assembled a catalog of the documents on the Chorti in the Guatemalan national archives, and such a case study would be of immense value.[51] Similar studies of distinct Indian groups are possible where Indians and documents survived in numbers.

In the same vein, we know little of the effect of the New World of Indian Guatemala on Spanish society. Lutz, Markman, and others have pointed the way, but so far the whole world of the city, the hacienda, the convent, and the monastery in colonial Guatemala awaits curious scholars.[52]

Notable when one studies colonial Guatemala is the concentration of research in certain epochs. The beginning and end of the colonial period draw the attention of scholars, the middle does not. So, once more, let us appeal for some work and interest in the neglected and unknown seventeenth century. (The gap in Mexico is relatively just as bad.) In general we have a sizeable corpus of modern writing on the conquest and on the period running up to the 1620s. But the "real" or classic seventeenth century running from that decade to the late 1680s is known only in its roughest outlines. Even more neglected has been the complicated period between 1690 and 1730. A period of wars, disasters, revolts, and shortages, at the same time, paradoxically, it saw Guatemala and indeed all of Central America emerging from its commercial isolation, renewing old ties with Mexico and Peru, and establishing new ones with Jamaica, Cuba, and the northern European world beyond. The paradoxical nature of these years, with their different effects on Indian, casta, and Spanish societies, requires a sophisticated explanation. The period up to 1770 has hardly suffered from over-examination either. The effects of population and economic growth on the various groups in Guatemala at this time would be an interesting and important topic.

In short, research on colonial Guatemala has hardly begun, and the more advanced research on Mexican colonial history can provide many helpful directions for future study.

Notes

1. The best and most up-to-date bibliography is Sidney David Markman, *Colonial Central America: A Bibliography* (Tempe, Arizona, 1977). See also Murdo J. Mac-Leod, "Colonial Latin America: Central America," in Charles C. Griffin, ed., *Latin America, A Guide to the Historical Literature*. (Austin, 1971), pp. 228–36. Among the most important works on the emergence of a creole consciousness in the local elites are Severo Martínez Peláez, *La patria del criollo* (Guatemala City, 1971), and André Saint-Lu, *Condition colonial et conscience créole au Guatemala* (Paris, 1970).

2. The leading study of the Mexican tribute system is José Miranda, *El tributo indígena en la Nueva España durante el siglo XVI* (Mexico City, 1952). Large detailed tribute lists from Mexico include Archivo General de la Nación, *El libro de las tasaciones de pueblos en la Nueva España, Siglo XVI* (Mexico City, 1952). No Guatemalan publication can match this, although pieces of Archivo General de Indias (AGI), Guatemala 128, have been published.

3. References to the various kinds of double tribute system are numerous. See, for

example, AGI, Guatemala 10, Audiencia to the Crown, 1584, ff. 2-5v., and various letters by Bishop Juan Ramírez to the Crown in AGI, Guatemala 156. (See the article by William Sherman, "Abusos contra los indios de Guatemala (1602–1605). Relaciones del Obispo," *Cahiers du Monde Hispanique et Luso-Brésilien, Caravelle* 11 [1968]; 4–28, for an analysis of these letters.) See also Antonio Batres Jáuregui, *La América Central ante la historia*, 3 vols. (Guatemala City, 1920), I, 397–98.

4. See the article by Sherman, above.

5. For example, Biblioteca del Real Palacio (Madrid), Miscelanea de Ayala, XXXV (1664).

6. On Mexican standardization of the tribute, see Miranda, *El tributo*, pp. 15, 35, 125, 204–207.

7. Such taxes were especially heavy in Verapaz, western Guatemala, and Chiapas. See the following typical documents from the Archivo Nacional de Centroamérica (ANC) in Guatemala: ANC, A1. 23, legajo 4590, f. 100v. (1692); ANC, A1. 24, legajo 10205, expediente 1561, f. 26 (1655). An eighteenth-century chronicler's comments can be found in Francisco Ximénez, *Historia de la provincia de San Vicente de Chiapa y Guatemala de la orden de predicadores*, 3 vols. (Guatemala City, 1929–31), I, 345; III, 255–57.

8. See Severo Martínez Peláez's article on Indian riots and revolts in Congreso Centroamericano de Historia Demográfica, Económica y Social, Germán Romero Vargas et al., contribs., *Ensayos de historia centroamericana*. (San José, Costa Rica, 1974).

9. The archives are full of documents describing such practices. E.g., ANC, A1. 24, legajo 1566, f. 233 (1681); ANC, A1. 24, 10208, 1564, f. 115 (1672). See also José Joaquín Pardo, *Efemérides para escribir la historia de la . . . ciudad de Santiago de . . . Guatemala* (Guatemala City, 1944), p. 140.

10. We do not yet know why the valley repartimientos survived so long, but they certainly did. See Silvio Zavala, *Contribución a la historia de las instituciones coloniales en Guatemala* (Guatemala City, 1953), pp. 103–108. See also Pardo, *Efemérides*, pp. 72, 136.

11. See my *Spanish Central America, A Socioeconomic History, 1520–1720* (Berkeley, 1973), pp. 187–89, 307–8, 313.

12. See my "Forms and Types of Work and the Acculturation of the Colonial Indian of Mesoamerica: Some Preliminary Observations" in Elsa Cecilia Frost et al., eds., *El trabajo y los trabajadores en la historia de México* (Mexico City, 1979), pp. 79–91.

13. See, for example, the article by Arnold J. Bauer, "Rural Workers in Spanish America: Problems of Peonage and Oppression," *Hispanic American Historical Review* 59 (1979): 34–63. See also the forum on this subject in the same volume, pp. 478–89.

14. E.g., ANC, A1. 43, 41513, 4817, ff. 181v.-189, 197v.-205 (1598); ANC, A1.43, 41553, 4827 (1604). There are many later examples.

15. E.g., ANC, A1. 23, legajo 1520, f. 71 (1672); ANC, A1. 1, 23, 2 (1687). The practice was far less common in the eighteenth century.

16. Quarrels between Indian villages over land, and between villages and Spanish landowners, increase noticeably in the eighteenth century. See ANC, Tierras for verification. The same seems to be true in Honduras and Costa Rica.

17. See MacLeod, *Spanish Central America*, pp. 225–27, 297.

18. E.g., ANC, A1. 24, 10211, 1567, f. 113 (1676); ANC, A3. 12, 40167 (1696).

19. E.g., ANC, A1. 14-16, 31664, 4064 (1641); ANC, A1. 24, 51202, 5919 (1677). In the late seventeenth century derramas still caused outrage among some Spanish officials and clergy. By the mid-eighteenth century the practice was common and accepted.

20. See the article by Martínez Peláez cited above. See also ANC, A1. 24, 10224, 1580, f. 292 (1713); ANC, A1. 24, 10226, 1582, f. 32 (1717).

21. Not much is known about these groups in Mexico either. Hector Humberto Samayoa Guevara, in his *Los gremios de artesanos en la ciudad de Guatemala* (Guatemala City, 1962), touches on some of these matters but is, of course, more concerned with guilds of artisans. See also the treatment of the various social classes in Francisco de Solano Pérez-Lila, "Tierra, comercio y sociedad (un análisis de la estructura social agraria centroamericana durante el siglo XVIII)," *Revista de Indias* 31 (1971): 311–65.

22. On this and on late seventeenth-century repartimientos in the valley, see Pilar Hernández Aparicio, "Problemas socioeconómicos en el Valle de Guatemala: 1670–1680," *Revista de Indias* 37 (1977): 585–637, and the comments on the cultural composition of the countryside in the Solano Pérez-Lila article cited above.

23. Manuel Rubio Sánchez has specialized in the study of ports and trades. His most recent work of this kind is his *Historia del puerto de Trujillo*, 3 vols. (Tegucigalpa, 1975), which mentions many of the matters touched on here. See also Pedro Pérez Valenzuela, *Santo Tomás de Castilla: Apuntes para la historia de las colonizaciones en la costa atlántica* (Guatemala City, 1956).

24. Carmelo Sáenz de Santa María "La vida económica de los Jesuitas en Santiago de Guatemala," *Revista de Indias* 37 (1977): 543–84; Solano Pérez-Lila, "Tierra, comercio y sociedad." There are several Jesuit account books in the ANC, for example ANC, A1. 11-15, 48954, 5801 (1651), entitled "Cuentas de las haciendas." The wealth and power of these factories in the countryside provoked the jealousy of local laymen. See Francisco Antonio de Fuentes y Guzmán, *Recordación Florida*, 3 vols. (Guatemala City, 1932–33), I, 224.

25. See my chapter on indigo in *Spanish Central America*, pp. 176–203. See also Manuel Rubio Sánchez, *Historia del añil o xiquilite en Centroamérica*, 2 vols. (San Salvador, 1976, 1978).

26. MacLeod, *Spanish Central America*, pp. 235–52.

27. The information on cochineal is a composite of the following sources. José Antonio Alzate y Ramírez, *Memoria sobre la naturaleza, cultibo [sic] y beneficio de la grana* (Mexico City, 1777). Copies of this book can be found in The Newberry Library, Chicago, and in the Biblioteca del Real Palacio, Madrid. AGI, Guatemala 13 and 14, contain accounts of Guatemalan cochineal. See also Barbro Dahlgren de

Jordan's prologue to her edited book, *La grana cochinilla* (Mexico City, 1963), pp. 15–16. For the larger Spanish side of the trade in late colonial Mexico, see Brian R. Hamnet, *Politics and Trade in Southern Mexico, 1750–1821* (Cambridge, 1971).

28. Manuel Rubio Sánchez, *Comercio terrestre de y entre las provincias de Centroamérica* (Guatemala City, 1973).

29. Meanwhile, see Hernández Aparicio, "Problemas socioeconómicos."

30. On these and related topics, see Magnus Mörner, "La política de segregación y el mestizaje en la Audiencia de Guatemala," *Revista de Indias* 24 (1964): 137–51.

31. MacLeod, *Spanish Central America*, pp. 130, 216.

32. For example, Jorge Luján Muñoz, "Fundación de villas de ladinos en Guatemala en el último tercio del siglo XVIII," *Revista de Indias* 36 (1976): 51–81; Christopher H. Lutz, "Population History of the Parish of San Miguel Dueñas, c. 1530–1770." (Mimeo. Paper delivered at the Symposium on Highland Guatemalan Historical Demography, Albany, New York, October 11–13, 1979.)

33. See Christopher H. Lutz, "Santiago de Guatemala, 1541–1773: The Socio-demographic History of a Spanish-American Colonial City" (Ph.D. dissertation, University of Wisconsin-Madison, 1976), appendix 4, for a list of eighteenth-century epidemics. See also MacLeod, *Spanish Central America*, pp. 98–100.

34. MacLeod, *Spanish Central America*, p. 93; Michel Bertrand, "Estudio demográfico de la región de Rabinal y del Chixoy en Guatemala," *Mesoamérica* 1 (1980): 232–49.

35. See T. T. Veblen, "Native Population Decline in Totonicapán, Guatemala," *Annals of the Association of American Geographers* 67 (1977); 486–99; W. George Lovell, "Collapse and Recovery: A Demographic Profile of the Cuchumatán Highlands of Guatemala (1520–1821)" (Mimeo. Paper delivered at the Symposium on Highland Guatemalan Historical Demography, Albany, New York, October 11–13, 1979).

36. Complaints that the Caribbean coast had been emptied and must be restocked are frequent. See the letters to the crown from President Alonso Criado de Castilla, and several other expedientes on this subject, all in AGI, Guatemala 129. See also Rubio Sánchez, *Trujillo*, I, 120.

37. See the previously cited work of Luján Muñoz, "Fundación de villas de ladinos." See also the same author's "Indios, ladinos y aculturación en San Miguel Petapa (Guatemala) en el siglo XVIII," *Estudios sobre política indigenista española en América* (Valladolid, 1975), I, 331–46.

38. Francisco de Solano Pérez-Lila, *Los mayas del siglo XVIII: Pervivencia y transformación de la sociedad indígena guatemalteca durante la administración borbónica.* (Madrid, 1974).

39. See the aforementioned works by Luján Muñoz, Lutz, and Solano Pérez-Lila on this subject.

40. MacLeod, *Spanish Central America*, pp. 211–16.

41. There is a huge pile of paper in AGI Guatemala 131 (1651) on the jueces de milpas.

42. MacLeod, *Spanish Central America*, pp. 216–24.

43. Ibid., pp. 226, 229–30.

44. Ibid., pp. 229, 326–28.

45. See the aforementioned article by Martínez Peláez on Indian revolts. The major source for the Tzeltal Revolt is AGI Guatemala, legajos 293–296. Repartimientos also intensified in these years. See, for example, ANC, A3.12, 3984, 223 (1703); ANC, A1. 24, 10226, 1582, f. 32 (1717).

46. William M. Denevan, *The Upland Pine Forest of Nicaragua: A Study in Cultural Plant Geography*. (Berkeley, 1961); Carl L. Johannessen, *Savannas of Interior Honduras*. (Berkeley, 1963); Thomas T. Veblen, "The Ecological, Cultural, and Historical Bases of Forest Preservation in Totonicapán, Guatemala," (Ph.D. dissertation, University of California, Berkeley, 1975).

47. For a discussion of one of these problems see Mörner, "La política de segregación." Work on the other topics mentioned is just beginning.

48. For comparative purposes, see the article by Sherburne F. Cook and Woodrow Borah, "Indian Food Production and Consumption in Central Mexico before and after the Conquest (1500–1650)," in their *Essays in Population History*, vol. 3 (Berkeley, 1979), pp. 129–76. Thomas Gage and others noticed enormous changes and local variations in Guatemalan Indian diet, but none of this information has been studied systematically.

49. For the time being, Rubio Sánchez, *El añil*, provides information. On cacao see J. F. Bergman, "Cacao and Its Production in Central America," *Tijdschrift voor economische en sociale Geografie* 48 (1957): 43–49.

50. Costa Rica is even better served. See for example the numerous essays by Carlos Meléndez Ch. on land and land tenure.

51. Lawrence F. Feldman, *A Survey of Chorti Manuscript Resources in Central America*. (Columbia, Mo., mimeo., 1978).

52. See Lutz, "Santiago de Guatemala." On Spanish colonial architecture and the society that created it, see Sidney David Markman, *Colonial Architecture of Antigua Guatemala*. (Philadelphia, 1966).

Robert M. Carmack

Spanish-Indian Relations in Highland Guatemala, 1800–1944

Introduction

I intend to discuss ethnohistorical studies of the highland Guatemalan Indians from 1800 to 1944 A.D. Robert Wasserstrom has recently shown that the post-1944 revolutionary period in Guatemala, as it relates to the Indians, can also be treated ethnohistorically.[1] But a proper understanding of Indian culture for that period requires heavy reliance on ethnographic studies, and also continues to be steeped in political controversy. Therefore, I limit my summary to the pre-revolutionary years.

I admit that the time period and subject selected for review—highland Guatemalan Indian cultures between 1800 and 1944—have received scant ethnohistoric attention. Unquestionably, prehispanic, colonial, and post-1944 periods are much better known. This limitation, however, can work to our advantage. It directs our attention to the need for more studies of that time period, while at the same time it forces us to make better use of the information already available. The situation also tends to promote greater integration of the disciplines, especially history and anthropology. At least, I feel this has been true in my own case, as I have turned to historians and other social scientists more than usual when anthropological studies are relatively abundant. Finally, the situation has freed me to use more of my own research, including unpublished manuscripts, than might otherwise be appropriate.

In my analysis, I begin with a review of general studies dealing either with highland Guatemala or with Mesoamerica as a whole for the period under discussion. I have selected only those studies that pay substantive attention to the Indians or to relations between the Indians and ladinos. In the second section of the essay I examine ethnohistoric studies of specific highland Guatemalan Indian institutions. Little research of this kind has been carried out to date. In the third section I review historical and ethnohistorical studies of particular communities or regions in highland Guatemala. Only a handful of detailed case studies of this type exist for the highlands of Guatemala, including my own ethnohistorical account of Momostenango reviewed in this section. In the final section I offer a few tentative conclusions about Indian culture in highland Guatemala during the 1800–1944 years, and point to some possible similarities to and differences with other Indian cultures of Mesoamerica.

General Studies

In this section I review *general* treatments of the highland Guatemalan Indians for the 1800–1944 period. Historical accounts are numerous, but very few of them pay much attention to the Indians. Studies by anthropologists usually focus on the Indians but are limited in detail and numbers. For convenience of discussion, I divide these more general studies into two categories, Acculturation and Marxist. Acculturation studies have generally not been Marxist in orientation, but, as will become evident, there is considerable overlap between the two.

Acculturation

The "zero-point" of anthropological generalization about the Maya Indians for the period under discussion is Oliver La Farge's sequence of highland Maya cultures.[2] La Farge attempted to reconstruct the sequence of culture change among the highland Mayas largely on the basis of his own studies of the Cuchumatanes area. By his own admission, not much ethnohistorical research went into the formulation, and much of it was largely "guesswork."

La Farge's main thesis was that between 1800 and 1880 a new Indian culture solidified and took hold, not based on prehispanic but on submerged, syncretised patterns deriving from a rather unsatisfactory fusion of Spanish and native cultures during the colonial period. This new cultural transformation began during a transitional phase, 1720 to 1800, as Spanish control relaxed, and flowered during the early Republican years when the government was tied up with wars and other problems. He cites testimony from J. L. Stephens to the effect that there were "great areas of territory within which the authority of the central government was only vaguely felt," and that the Catholic priests were few in number and not energetically involved in the Indians' affairs.[3] La Farge illustrates the nature of the new culture by describing calendric survivals, which everywhere lost elements of the aboriginal system; they had the "tinctures of Catholicism and Spanish culture." The new culture was aliterate, since native literacy was lost with the disappearance of Spanish rule. Without literacy, there was a loss of some esoteric native patterns, especially those associated with rituals that depended on written texts for their survival.

La Farge called this new culture "Recent Indian," and argued that it had persisted in many places down to his time (ca. 1940). Serious modification of Recent Indian culture, however, began with the land and labor reforms of Justo Rufino Barrios just before 1880, and was also affected by *ladino* penetration into formerly undisturbed Indian territory. Machine-age culture of the twentieth century further accelerated the changes, though overall the process "is much gentler than the Conquest."

La Farge has been widely followed by anthropologists on the "culture history" of the highland Mayas and even Mesoamerica as a whole.[4] In particular, Ralph Beals has argued for the validity of La Farge's sequence and has refined it in his various essays on Mesoamerican acculturation. Beals stresses the importance of cultural contact (acculturation) for understanding changing native cultures in Mesoamerica.[5]

Beals accepts La Farge's thesis that the latter part of the colonial period was a time when the natives were left relatively isolated, in which state they synthesized more integrated cultural forms from Spanish and indigenous sources. He then argues for a more dynamic culture phase than that reconstructed by La Farge, the period from 1800 to the reforms of the latter part of the century (called First Republican Indian period by Beals). This was a time when the Indians participated in the independence movement—mainly they struggled for freedom from local creoles—and experienced increasing pressures from governments more exploitative than the Spaniards had been. As a result, the Indians were involved in repeated uprisings, and some of their communities became strongly "mestizoized."

The reforms, beginning in 1857 in Mexico and 1871 in Guatemala (called the Second Republican Period by Beals), did much to erode the Indian communities as their communal lands were sub-divided and their able-bodied men forced to labor on plantations. Nevertheless, communities in more isolated areas with strong civil-religious hierarchies were able to maintain traditional culture. That is, there was "resistance to acculturative influences," and in the case of Guatemala traditional Indian culture persisted without major alteration all the way to the revolutionary period (1944). Revolutionary developments in both Guatemala and

Mexico led to destruction of the Indian cultures of the past as a "Modern Indian Period" was initiated.

Richard N. Adams accepts the La Farge thesis that nineteenth-century isolation allowed the Indians of Guatemala to consolidate their culture after having accepted many Spanish colonial patterns. The culture that developed was characterized by a relativity view, according to which the culture of ladinos (or of other Indian communities) was seen as appropriate for that group but not for Indians. This culture was egalitarian, everyone participating in an "age hierarchy" in which social mobility was disallowed because within the community real differences could not be admitted. Indian ideas of cultural relativity rather than barriers created by ladino-Indian caste relations have been the basic cause of cultural persistence among the Indians.

Adams calls attention to the dramatic cultural differences between the eastern and western highlands of Guatemala, and notes that it goes back to at least the end of the colonial period. He explains the difference on ethnic grounds: the Mayas, who have been fiercely resistant to assimilation, were relatively absent in the east; more Spaniards and ladinos moved into the east to exploit the two to three annual maize harvests possible there. In places like the east, where ladinos gained political control, "latinization" has been extensive.

More general latinizing forces began to operate toward the end of the nineteenth century in the west, too, as Indians migrated to the coast, first to work on cattle ranches, next on coffee plantations, and finally on banana plantations. Political and religious forces were also at work on the Indians, such as reintroduction of the *intendente* system (of appointed mayors) by Jorge Ubico, the gradual adoption of education and welfare programs, and the coming of Protestant religions (and later Catholic Action). A continuum of latinized Indian cultures resulted from the "transculturation" process: Traditional Indians, Indians little affected by these changes; Modified Indians, acculturated Indians near ladino centers but still identified as Indians; Latinized Indians, most of the eastern Indians who form barrios of ladino communities; and New Ladinos, lower classes in ladino centers that retain some Indian cultural traits. Adams recognizes that different communities and regions of Guatemala have entered these transculturation phases at different times. But, generally, western highland Indians were primarily Traditional until 1870. Many of them were transformed by the forces mentioned above into Modified Indians between 1870 and 1944. Since then, many western

Indian communities have been placed on the path to becoming Latinized Indians and New Ladinos. Nevertheless, he predicts that in seventy-five to a hundred years there may still be Modified Indians around.[6]

In the study summarized above, Adams interprets changes in Indian culture as a latinization process; in a later study the same process is studied in terms of "nationalization." Nationalization in Middle America, he says, has involved the Indian communities as autonomous competitors of the state: "Indian nationalization is a sub-process within the whole whereby new cultures are formed through the elimination of Indian communities."

Middle American nationalization begins with independence, and is seen by Adams as a continuous process to the present; it reached maturity in Mexico by 1940, whereas Guatemala and the rest of Central America only now are "entering the period of Nationhood." The drive to nationalization during the nineteenth century oscillated with Conservative and Liberal policies, and these differentially affected the Indians. Conservative policy was laissez-faire, giving more autonomy to the Indians; it was personalistic and church-allied. Liberal policy was Social Darwinist, seeking to assimilate the Indians through secular, egalitarian, commercial programs. Guatemala was early Liberal (1828–1838), followed by a long Conservative period, especially under Rafael Carrera, only to experience powerful Liberalization again after 1870. The early twentieth century saw a relaxation of Liberal policy and the implementation of practices reminiscent of Conservative goals. The Carrera Conservatives reintroduced the Laws of the Indies, along with Indian *gobernadores* (mayors) and caste structure. Barrios and the Liberals brought to the Indians loss of their communal lands, weakening of the church, forced labor, obligatory education, and pressure for latinization.

Adams mentions Indian rebellions as a problem for nationalization, noting that revolts were dealt with ruthlessly in most cases. Caste wars in Yucatan and Chiapas at mid-nineteenth century took on a "civil war" character, and similar though more limited wars occurred in Guatemala (he cites the Ixtahuacán and Ixcoy uprisings of 1839 and 1898). Adams generally fails to note the correlattion between such "wars" and coercive Liberal policies toward the Indians, except for the following remark in connection with the San Juan Ixcoy uprising: "In this region the pressure of Liberal policies evidently was not entirely appreciated."[7]

Brief mention should be made of two anthropological summaries of Middle American culture and history, by Eric Wolf and Mary Helms.

Wolf stresses the continuation of the Indian community during the period under discussion in a form similar to its seventeenth-century development. It was a closed corporate peasant community protecting agricultural lands by leveling wealth and holding to traditional cultural patterns. The post-independence Indian community was made possible in part by the continuation of the hacienda, which absorbed excess Indian labor; the two were in "perpetual if hostile symbiosis." Independence only strengthened the haciendas and, in making the Indians more subject to creole and ladino exploitation, caused them to "withdraw further into their communal shells." Late in the nineteenth century, industrial forces began to shift power away from the rural zones, but the Indians largely remained in their closed communities. Only revolution and the entry of mestizos into power positions would later significantly alter the cultural condition of the Middle American Indians.[8]

Helms has little to say about the Indians during the nineteenth century, focusing instead on the *caudillo* struggles that characterized politics of the period. Indians sometimes fought under rural caudillos, but this is seen by Helms as an individual, latinizing phenomenon. Collectively, the Indians remained in their traditional villages, widely separated from creole elites; ladinos (mestizos) were relatively few in number in Guatemala compared to Mexico. Coffee and banana plantations in Guatemala after 1860 forced the Indians out of their communities and into broader participation in the economy; forced labor and anti-communal land ownership laws were needed to push the Indians onto the plantations. These attempts to open up the closed Indian communities were only partially successful, however, and the traditional Indian community survived into modern times in varying degrees of corporateness and native cultural pattern. The process is generally seen by Helms in terms of Adams's latinization, the Indians gradually taking on the ladino language, dress, beliefs, and open community.[9]

Marxist

Most Marxist studies of Guatemala begin with the revolution of 1944, but a few examine the socioeconomic position of the Indians in the past. The brief summary to follow treats only those studies that seem most relevant to the topic under discussion. More orthodox Western histories of Guatemala and Central America invariably have little to say about the Indians and, therefore, are not dealt with here despite their importance for other topics (for a summary of these sources, see Ralph Lee Woodward, Jr.'s general survey.[10]) Marxist historical writings on Guatemala have limitations, but generally they stress the importance of the Indians; hence, their special place in the discussion to follow.

Luis Cardoza y Aragón, in his stimulating critique of Guatemalan culture, is an early example of the Marxist view of nineteenth-century social history. He reminds us that independence and the idea of a nation came from the creoles and mestizos, not the Indians. The Indian was "an outcast in his country"; far from being the essential nationalist element that he should be, at that time he was thought to be nothing other than an "animal force."[11]

Carrera, the mestizo who manipulated the creole aristocracy, also manipulated the Indians. They provided him with military support, and he became the "king of the Indians."[12] But the Indians' support for Carrera was blind, and worked against their interests as he led the new republic back to a "theocratic feudalism," this time subject to Protestant England rather than Catholic Spain.

Barrios and the Liberals created a capitalist revolution for the bourgeois landlord class. In the process, the Indians were made slaves again, forced to labor for capitalists. Many Indian communities were broken through destruction of their communal lands, and the destitute Indians were "exploited iniquitously."[13] Subsequent Liberal leaders turned highly reactionary, handed over the country to the Yankees, and were unable to achieve major development. Despite the "liberal" reforms, from secularization of the church to universal education, the Indians were more exploited than ever before.

Carlos Guzmán Böckler and Jean-Loup Herbert devote little attention to the nineteenth century in their remarkably polemical book on Guatemala. They note the loss of Spanish economic protection, beginning well before independence, and the "feudal regression" that resulted. The situation allowed the Indians "to reconquer a certain social identity and solidarity" and to clearly define their relations of class antagonism with the ladinos. The new autonomy even gave the Indians hopes of gaining political independence, and uprisings like the one led by Atanasio Tzul were motivated by that goal.

The years following independence, especially during Carrera's rule, saw the firm implantation of British economic monopoly in Guatemala. Attempts to colonize the northeast lowlands with European settlers, ignoring the large Indian population present in Guatemala, reveal "the typical colonial mental structure." This same mentality continued under the Barrios Liberals. Coffee and banana production required large land holdings, leading to expropriation of Indian lands "as had not been seen since the colony." Pushed into "refuge" zones of subsistence, the Indians were forced to work on the plantations. The Liberal revolution "did not signify a step from feudalism to capitalism, but the intensification of capitalism in its colonial form."

The first half of the twentieth century was a continuation of processes from the previous century. The Indians were converted into laborers, "more or less proletarianized." The ladinos, of course, were the capitalists who exploited their labor.[14]

Rodolfo Stavenhagen, in his study of ethnic and class relations in Chiapas and highland Guatemala, argues for the need to study the Indian communities in terms of their relations with regional, national, and international powers. His examination of changes in those relations through time includes a brief nineteenth-century social history.[15]

Before independence, relations between the Spaniards and Indians had been colonial, the Indians serving as ethnic reserves providing serfs and forced laborers for the ruling aristocracy. Incipient class relations existed, but were subordinate to colonial ones. Independence brought no essential change in the Indians' conditions, as traditional patterns of inferiority maintained colonial relations despite changes in the laws. The second half of the nineteenth century, however, saw an expansion of capitalist economic forces, and relations between the Indians and ladinos "were transformed into class relationships."[16] The change consisted of Indians' beginning to dispose of their land and labor on the market, a process associated with "extension of commercial farming; penetration of ladinos into communities inhabited by Indian ethnic groups; appropriation of land by ladinos; formation of great haciendas and the Indians' wage labor on these properties."[17]

Stavenhagen refers to late-nineteenth-century developments as "internal colonialism," for the Indians lost their land, were forced to labor, and became subject to external economic and political powers. Under these conditions the Indian communities inevitably break down, though aspects of ethnicity and corporateness may hang on for a while.

Severo Martínez Peláez's masterful essay on colonial Guatemala includes a brief discussion of post-independence developments. He starts with the thesis, dealt with at length in his book, that colonial Indians formed a "servile class," a proletariat subject to the dominant creole hacendado class (the Indians made up about 65 percent of the population at the beginning of the nineteenth century). The fact that some 50 percent of the Guatemalan population today is Indian demonstrates, says Martínez, that the same colonial class structure has persisted to our day.

Independence and subsequent reforms changed nothing essential, since the creoles and middle-level ladinos who were responsible for those movements did so precisely in order to co-opt colonial structure for their own benefit. The federation wars during the first years after independence were a reflection of class conflicts between creole aristocrats and middle-level ladinos. Liberal rulers representing the ladinos favored the cities and acted against the interests of Indians. Creoles, especially under Carrera rule, removed tributes from the Indians but only to impose forced labor; "the 30-year creole dictatorship, in few words, was a colonial development without a metropolis."[18]

The reforms beginning in 1871 broke down the old colonial forms of exploitation, but only to replace them with new ones. The ladino landed class that took power, after achieving economic success from indigo and then coffee production, used the reforms to acquire more and larger latifundias than ever before, and greater numbers of Indian laborers. Liberal ladinos merged with the creole class, thus preserving the fundamental features of colonial structure. A major consequence of the reforms for the Indians was the breakdown of their community structure through the loss of communal lands, the development of minifundias, the suppression of local Indian elites, the loss of municipal leadership to migrant ladinos, and the displacement of inhabitants to plantations for seasonal or longer periods of time.[19]

Liberal dictators of the twentieth century intensified the neo-colonial relations created by the reforms. Ubico's vagrancy law, for example, with its "libreto de jornaleros," (laborer's passbook), brought forced labor to its perfection after four hundred years of previous existence.

Since Martínez's classic study, many Marxist analyses of Guatemala have appeared. One of the best and most historically oriented is Susanne Jonas's analysis of Guatemalan dependency. She uses mainly secondary sources, but her interpretations of those sources often provide new viewpoints.

Jonas sees Guatemala as capitalistically underdeveloped by the end of the colonial period, stratified into a discontented creole aristocracy, a weak merchant class, and a proletarianized, poor lower class. Initiatives for independence came from the creoles, aided by petty-bourgeois ladinos. The Indians played a role too, since their uprisings—in Cobán, Sololá, Chiquimula, Sacapulas, and Totonicapán—caused the elites to fear popular revolution unless they took matters in hand. "The revolt in Totonicapán (by Atanasio Tzul) may well have been the final evidence of the danger of revolution."[20] Independence left colonial structures intact, only changing the identity of the ruling class (from Spanish to creole).

Both the Liberals and Conservatives were creole bourgeoisie, "and neither showed the slightest concern for the Indians."[21] Under the Liberals, Indians were forced into unwanted schools, made to abandon native dress, levied a head tax, and sent to work on construction projects. Indian support for Carrera in the overthrow of the Liberals, therefore, is understandable. Only after Carrera came to power, in fact, were secession revolts in the Indians' provinces of Quezaltenango, Totonicapán, and Sololá put down. Carrera relaxed many of the Liberal programs, but overall his long dictatorship, in developmental terms, was not strikingly different. The main social development during this time was the emergence of an important ladino plantation class, based first on indigo, then cochineal, and later sugar, cotton, and coffee; the main political development was economic dependency on England.

Shifts in foreign capitalist economies promoted the ladino plantation class, and they gained power in the revolution of 1871 (with Martínez, Jonas sees the ladinos challenging, then joining, the creole elite). In order to provide land and labor for the coffee plantations, Liberals dispossessed the Indians of their lands (only 7.3 percent of the population owned land in 1926), shattered their villages, and instituted forced labor (through debt peonage). The powerful apparatus of a government patterned after the colonial system—with forced labor, *jefes políticos, alcaldes,* and so forth—enforced the new structure: "Liberalism subjected the Indians to the institutionalized violence of a police state."

Despite modernizing programs, as in health and education, and the reduction of church power and property, the situation of the Indians worsened under Liberal rule. Finally, with Estrada Cabrera and Ubico "the apparatus of repression was perfected."[22]

Institutional Studies

It cannot be said, in reality, that a scholarly tradition yet exists for the reconstruction of nineteenth-century Guatemalan Indian social institutions. Most of the studies summarized below were based largely on early twentieth-century ethnographic sources. Some of them represent hypotheses projected to the past century (e.g., the market studies of Carol Smith); others come closer to being general histories than institutional studies (e.g., Chester Jones's economic analysis). Nevertheless, they point to directions for future research of great potential in highland Guatemala ethnohistory.[23]

Production

Paul McDowell points out that little has been written on the effects of the Liberal reforms on the Indian communities, despite the fact that they "suffered heavily as a consequence." He is referring to late-nineteenth-century reforms, but the statement applies with even more force to the preceding years of that century. The most important changes, according to McDowell, were brought about by land and labor laws. They led to fragmentation of Indian landholdings, accumulations of lands by a few, and increased differentiation of wealth. Associated with these changes were the invasion of Indian comunities by ladinos and the transformation of community organization. Unfortunately, McDowell's study of Indian land and labor during the Liberal period is still in progress, and the results are not yet available.[24]

The most important work on Indian land and labor during the nineteenth century and the first third of the twentieth remains that by Chester L. Jones. Jones documents the continuation of forced labor from the colonial into the Republican period, new legislation against slavery notwithstanding. Even the development of indigo production failed to alter the situation, for "mandamientos [forced labor] and the wage contract could be adapted to the new needs." Although forced labor continued at first under the Barrios regime, the heavy need for labor on coffee plantations led to wage contracts with indebtedness, contracts that gradually received the backing of the Liberals. Indians either contracted directly with the plantations for two or three years as indentured workers or were endebted by hiring-agents to work in groups for a month or two. The entire political apparatus of the state was at the disposal of the plantation owners to enforce the contracts and, if necessary, "to hunt down and bring back the fugitives who leave the plantations without paying off in work what they have received in money."

Debt peonage continued to characterize Indian labor in the twentieth century. Minor changes were introduced by the government, such as establishing agricultural judges, standardizing punishments for contract failures meted out by jefes políticos, and suppressing the use of municipal officials as hiring-agents. By the 1930s, available Indian labor for the expanding coffee plantations was inadequate, so a vagrancy law was instituted. The law was directed specifically to the Indians, "laborers who neither have contracted their services in the fincas, nor cultivate with their personal work, at least three manzanas of coffee, sugar cane or tobacco in some zone; three manzanas of corn with two crops per year in a hot zone, four manzanas of corn in a cold zone, or four manzanas of wheat, potatoes, vegetables or other product in any zone." Labor cards had to be carried by Indians at all times to prove their non-vagrancy status, and this held for Indian merchants as well (though not at first). The law received the full legal backing of the government and had the desired effect as far as plantations were concerned. A later modification dropped the obligatory labor requirement from 150 to 100 days for Indians farming not less than 1 and 5/16 manzanas of land.[25]

Jones argues that lack of funds was not a problem for the Indians in the nineteenth century, and not even in the twentieth: "In Guatemala the problem is . . . to find which lands the state owns, to make them accessible, and to induce the Indians to exploit them."[26] Colonization programs, however, always sought European immigrants, and internal colonization of the early twentieth century was not pushed for the Indians so that a large "floating labor supply" could be maintained. The land tenure situation in the 1930s was typical of the past: Indians cultivated small plots of land owned communally, publicly (idle lands used by Indians), or "nominally" privately. For this reason, and because of large private landholdings, only 7.3 percent of the population owned land in 1926.

Jones's discussion of the Indians' subsistence agriculture is little more than a brief summary of McBryde's ethnographic notes from the 1930s on Sololá. Corn was the staple crop, planted by slash-and-burn techniques. Agricultural rites involving copal were carried out early in the growing season. Some cash crops, especially vegetables, were grown near the lake using irrigation methods.[27]

Alain Dessaint has summarized the effect through time of foreign agricultural methods, especially the hacienda and plantation, on Guatemalan Indians. Closely following Jones, he notes that the sequence of forced labor parallels La Farge's cultural periods: encomienda labor, corresponding to the conquest period, forced labor to the colonial period, debt-bondage and vagrancy laws to the Recent Indian period, and finally, the abolishment of forced labor in 1945 to a modern period.

Citing mostly ethnographic studies from the first half of the twentieth century, Dessaint lists five main effects of these agricultural systems: (1) They have dispersed the Indian population, mainly in the form of migrations from highland communities to coastal haciendas and plantations. Some communities have drained off significant surplus population in this way; the Nebaj region is said to have lost some six thousand laborers between 1894 and 1930. Social marginals have also left through this means. (2) They have helped break down traditional cultural practices in the Indian communities. The sources suggest decreases in *milpa* farming, traditional crafts, community service, and ceremony. Yet, in contradictory fashion, in some cases earnings from plantation work have been Guatemala's "melting pot," transforming Indians into Adams's "Modified Indian" as native practices are abandoned, usually without receiving European substitutes. Indian workers on the banana plantations were generally transformed into "rural proletariats," with a virtual total loss of Indian culture. (4) They have led to the demise of communal landholdings, and disproportionate acquisition of lands by the wealthy; in some highland areas, plantation owners have large landholdings to ensure a labor supply from the local population. (5) They have disrupted family unity, as abandonment, divorce, promiscuity, and elopement become common.

Dessaint concludes that plantation and hacienda labor introduced cultural brokers into the Indian communities while also removing many Indians through out-migration who later adopted new cultural patterns. By removing the Indian from his traditional community, the plantation can instill in him new "drives." Thus, change occurs within the Indian communities, but it is more "compelling" and extensive on the plantations.[28]

Exchange

Manning Nash claims that the nineteenth century was a time of "slow but massive economic and social changes," producing "a sectored economy, with the Indians at the bottom of the economic heap, unprovided with means to enter the narrow entrepreneurial sector of the export economy."[29] Following La Farge, he argues that the Indian was only marginally involved in colonial economy, but during the "second republican period" became subject to great economic pressures. In the Liberals' march toward nationalism, he was seen as anachronistic, and efforts were made to destroy his culture and take away his lands.

On the basis of "fragmentary" information, Nash suggests that the highland Indians fell into a regional, "solar" market system scarcely tied to the national export-oriented economy. Characteristics of the Indian market system persist to the present, allowing their description. They are "only partially integrated by a single set of prices," goods are labor- rather than capital-intensive, and goods specialization has a corporate community basis.

In coastal areas, nineteenth-century pressures either transformed Indians into wage laborers or integrated them through "adjunct export" markets. The Indians produced non-processed goods that were exchanged with ladinos from the outside in markets controlled by ladinos. Community specialization and rotating schedules were absent. This kind of market is associated with the loss of traditional Indian community and culture and, potentially, with large-scale nativistic uprisings.

Carol Smith's aforementioned studies on western Guatemalan markets contain many suggestive ideas about that institution during the nineteenth century and earlier. Although her ideas generally derive from theoretical projection rather than ethnohistoric research on the past, they deserve careful consideration. Her central thesis, perhaps, is that relations with the marketing system are primary determinants of ethnicity, wealth, and occupation in the western area, and that these relations essentially developed with the coming of coffee plantations.

Smith believes the Period I colonial market system persisted into the Republican period, the market, in fact, largely replacing tributes as a source of economic exploitation of the Indians by ruling elites. Markets were mainly located in administrative towns where food and other goods produced by Indian peasants were exchanged for European goods produced or traded in by ladinos. Exchanges in town usually took place in conjunction with the "fiesta cycle." Smith calls this system "the simple two-level 'solar' model."[30]

At some unspecified time, "not too far into the post-colonial period," trade *between* communities was developed by Indians. This probably developed out of the fiesta cycle, "for in the course of each community's celebration a fair was held, at which time producer-specialists from other communities brought in goods to exchange for products of other areas."[31] It is suggested that communities poor in agricultural possibilities developed trading specialization and became "rural bulking centers" oriented to "annual fair trade." Thus, two market types (solar and fair cycle) developed, involving different ethnic groups, exchange goods, and social structures.

Smith's Period II (late nineteenth and early twentieth centuries) witnessed a dramatic change as ladino townspeople shifted their interests away from local markets to international trade associated with coffee production. Indians specialized in inter-community fair trade moved to fill the void left by the ladinos, converting the ladino-controlled solar system to an Indian institution and linking it with the fair cycle in place. In addition, Indian peasants lacking sufficient lands (due to over-population and Liberal land policies) took over most of the ladino craft specialities, and also entered into trading. The resulting regional market-ing system was a "network" rather than a "hierarchy" because of the primarily rural base of the Indian traders and their relatively weak politi-cal authority. Meanwhile, ladino market towns become "dendritic," small centers being linked directly with them so that plantation-related goods could be bulked and shipped to national export centers. "The effect of this system was to concentrate economic and political power in the center of the region (near Quezaltenango), and even more around Guatemala City." Thus, the highland market system discovered by twentieth-century ethnographers showed a "clear separation of rural peasant and urban ladino economic systems."[32]

The Indian market system also revealed a clear separation between the central area (Totonicapán, Quezaltenango, Sololá, Chimaltenango, southern Quiché) and the peasant periphery (northern Quiché, northern Huehuetenango, southern San Marcos). Compared to those on the pe-riphery, the central Indians have less land but are more specialized in non-agricultural occupations, more urban, ethnically more stable, and more wealthy. The differences, according to Smith, are primarily a conse-quence of the central area's being closer to the southern coastal plantation zone and developing its market system to exploit that geographic fact. Smith also notes that the central area always had—even in prehispanic times—more commercialized economic patterns than the periphery, and this "preconditioning" facilitated the developments connected with cof-fee production.

Smith's reconstruction of specific economic developments in Toton-icapán, the highlands' market core, should be mentioned. Totonicapán was highly specialized in marketing activities in Period II times: "The merchants, really petty traders at that time, distributed Totonicapán's specialized products by visiting the few large marketplaces located in administrative centers throughout the region." With coffee production came the need to provision workers and coastal towns. Administrative control was relaxed over conveniently located and commercially oriented places like Totonicapán, and commerce there expanded. Although wage laborers may at first have come from Totonicapán, their places of origin soon shifted to peripheral zones. In the core, agriculture was widely abandoned, wage labor replaced family labor, and society divided into merchant-capitalist and proletariat classes. The rapid commercial growth experienced by Totonicapán had the same causes, Smith says, that led to European development one hundred years before. Totonicapán finally peaked by 1921, after which the system's dependency on internationally-controlled coffee production inevitably led to its decline.[33]

Political

According to Nash, "The political structure of corporate continuity was laid down in essence by the Spanish rules for the 'Indian Republic,' but the defensive, hostile posture of the corporate community toward the larger national society was an outgrowth of the economic facts of the nineteenth century, coupled with the ideology of elimination of the Indian, his cultures, and his local social organizations." The essential feature of that political structure was a civil-religious hierarchy that allowed the communities to exist as virtual autonomous units within the state. This structure was as basic to the Indians as kinship was to the African tribes. It related each family to the community, it gave ranked prestige according to service, it was the means for carrying out public activities (e.g., law and order, physical upkeep, ritual to the saints), it established boundaries between the Indians and ladinos, and it provided brokers for mediating with outside powers. The civil-religious hierarchy was also a powerful leveling institution, for large expenditures associated with office kept the families roughly equivalent from generation to generation.

Nash describes the functioning of the hierarchy "in simplified form" as

a series of offices, some nominally religious and others nominally secular. These offices are ranked as to prestige and social honor. A man as representative of a family enters on the lowest rung of the hierarchy, and for the rest of his adult life alternates between posts on the civil ladder and posts on the religious ladder. Between offices, he gets longer and shorter 'rest' periods. On completion of one of the top posts, he retires from community service and becomes an elder or a principal. The offices are unpaid, and, in fact, require outlays of cash and food by those holding them. In Indian parlance they are literally cargos, burdens. And to the community they are servicios, services necessary to daily life. Typically, as one ascends the ladder of ranked offices, the costs increase, the time devoted to the office approaches full time, and the prestige increases.

Nash's reconstruction of the form and function of civil-religious hierarchy was based almost wholly on ethnographic research from the early twentieth century. He believed its boundary-maintaining and internal homogenizing functions were even stronger in the nineteenth century. It helped provide the Indians with "passive, defensive resistence" so effective during the nineteenth century that violent rebellion was uncommon.[34]

Richard N. Adams summarized the pre-1944 political condition in Guatemalan Indian communities as part of his analysis of changes brought by the revolutionary government. With Nash, he stresses the primary significance of the political hierarchy in these communities, noting that "so long as these systems remain unchanged, the culture as a whole presents a strong front against change."[35] Nevertheless, he also argues for the importance of higher line authority pressing down on the local civil-religious hierarchy after 1870. It consisted of the national dictator, departmental jefes políticos, and ladino alcaldes or, in the time of Ubico, intendentes. Of great importance too, were lines running from military generals to local commanders, and from plantation administrators to local officials.

The force for change that these outside hierarchies represented was greater than scholars had realized, according to Adams. Even before 1944, in five out of eight communities reviewed by Adams political control was transferred from the Indians to local ladinos, and in another the civil-religious hierarchy broke down despite the absence of ladinos.

Roland Ebel has examined "the traditional political structure" of Guatemalan Indian communities. He argues that, in general, "traditional" structure persisted until 1944. Nevertheless, the appointment of intendentes in 1935 blocked exclusive naming of civil-religious officials by elders in one case cited, and eliminated the hierarchy altogether in another. A process of political change, then, began before the revolution, though the major changes occurred after 1944. The general steps by which the civil-religious hierarchy breaks down, according to Ebel, are: (1) separation of civil from religious offices; (2) weakening of elders' power; (3) introduction of new powers, especially political parties; and (4) domination of Indian decision-making by ladinos.[36]

Paul McDowell argues that significant changes in the civil-religious hierarchy of Indian communities occurred as a result of the Barrios reforms and again under pressures from Ubico. The early changes came mainly from the abolition of communal lands, which eventually led (through land loss to ladinos, bilateral inheritance, et cetera) to wealth differences in the communities. Civil-religious service, formerly supported by cofradía lands, "now shifted to the wealthier, so that they sustained the entire cost." The intendente system introduced by Ubico "modified the political and religious organization considerably in many native communities." Nevertheless, the major changes did not come until after 1944, when viable economic alternatives to service became available, as well as "some ideological form of rationalization."[37]

Political conflict has been largely ignored by students of Indian ethnohistory. We have only the study of the Atanasio Tzul revolt by Daniel Contreras and my own account of rebellions in Momostenango associated with independence and later with the Barrios reforms. Since I will summarize my Momostenango findings in the next section, only Contreras's paper will be dealt with here.

Contreras reconstructs the political structure of Totonicapán at the beginning of the nineteenth century: cabildo controlled by Indian elders occupying alcalde and regidor positions; confradías and parcialidades — the latter being described as "survivals of the primitive tribes that were joined together to congregate the Indians" — integrated with the cabildo; Indian gobernador and caciques used by Spanish officials to carry out goals of the colony; alcalde mayor, the creole representative of the crown, backed by provincial militias and neighboring militias if necessary.

The leaders of the rebellion came from the Indian elders — Tzul himself had been alcalde, and his associate, Aguilar, a cofradía head. They were illiterate, partially acculturated peasants; for example, Tzul had adopted Spanish-style dress. Their seizure of power in 1820, based on the claim that they had obtained "papers" from Guatemala announcing the end of tribute payments, was broadly supported by the Indian masses. The local creoles, ladinos, and Spanish officials opposed them, of course, but so did some cabildo officials and the Indian gobernador (and the caciques?). The rebels attempted to set up an Indian kingdom in which Tzul was crowned king, using the crown of Saint Joseph; his wife was given the crown of Saint Cecilia. Aguilar was made president, the chief executive officer. Elders from surrounding provincial towns were recruited as loyal chiefs, and local provincial guard-soldiers were organized.

According to Contreras the limited world view of the rebels and the social divisions between the Indian communities made the formation of a true native state impossible. Tzul reigned for only twenty-nine days before being easily subdued by the alcalde mayor and his Quezaltenango reinforcements. A few minor skirmishes took place between the rebels and the Spanish soldiers, but Tzul, Aguilar, and the other leaders were quickly taken prisoners. Contreras's sources do not reveal what eventually happened to them, though he speculates that they were later freed in the aftermath of independence.

Contreras places the Tzul revolt in the context of the political movements leading to national independence, though its causes, leadership, scope, and results were very different from contemporary "creole style." It was a "manifestation of the spirit of freedom" by a dominated people "who had never lost their aspiration for freedom." Contreras correctly describes the Spaniards' belief that the Indians were seditious and rebellious and could be controlled only by the terror of force. He documents the almost continous Indian uprisings preceding the Tzul affair, such as the attack on the alcalde mayor over the Mactzul lands in 1813, as well as post-independence revolts such as the one at Ixtahuacán in 1839. In many of these the Indians of Totonicapán were involved, providing "the directing hand." Ostensibly most of the revolts were brought on by the tribute issue, but other issues were just as basic, Contreras observes, especially racial discimination, political tutelege, and the threat of cultural extermination.

Contreras's essay is an excellent model for the type of political studies that might be made relative to nineteenth- and early-twentieth-century Guatemalan Indians. His analysis reveals the sure hand of the historian who knows the period in which he works. He is concerned to place the events in their native institutional context as well as within the broader national picture. He is sensitive and sympathetic, moreover, to Indian problems and goals, a rare quality even today among students of Guatemala.[38]

Juridical

Jorge Skinner-Klee has published the texts of legislative laws dealing with Indians in Guatemala from independence to 1945. He gives no commentary or discussion of native institutions, since that would "pertain to the field of the historian and the ethnologist."[39] His study, therefore, does not fall under our topic, though it remains a useful reference work.

The only other historical study of Indian legal institutions is J. Hernández Sifontes's *Realidad jurídica del indígena guatemalteco*. The avowed purpose of the book is to examine the nature of Indian legal institutions and how they articulated with national juridical forms. He includes a brief ethnographic account of Santa Catarina Ixtahuacán legal practices in the 1960s, but because it was based on only four days of residence in the community its value is extremely limited. His summary of Indian legislation for the "national" period is more useful than Skinner-Klee's texts, since it contains some material on social conditions either provoking or resulting from legislation. He also includes quasi-legal authoritative decisions that along with legislation were binding on the Indians.

The main juridical events involving Indians in the years preceding independence (1800–1821) as summarized by Hernández Sifontes are as follows: the crown orders corregidores to cease "repartimientos de Indios" (1803); Cobán Indians revolt against their alcalde mayor (1803); the giving of rations by Indians (to priests) is prohibited (1808); Indians are found to be working for the church without salary, according to Real Consulado (1810); Indians are to cease paying tributes (1811); revolts take place against the Spaniards in San Martín Chuchumatán, the alcalde mayor in Totonicapán, and the gobernador in Santa Catarina Ixtahuacán (1812); the Atanasio Tzul uprising takes place in Totonicapán (1820).

The following juridical events are from independence to 1900: the federal constitution eliminates slavery and tributes but obligates the Indians to abandon their native languages and dress (1824); the government establishes an Indian interpreter, gobernadores, and special ministry to hear requests; an uprising occurs in Santa Catarina Ixtahuacán to oppose taxes imposed by the "Estado de los Altos" (1839); the old colonial law that Indians are not to pay legal costs is mandated (1845); uprisings take place in many Indian towns, including Verapaz, Sololá, Santa Catarina Ixtahuacán, Sajcabaja, Chichicastenango, Cozal (1846); the republic declares the Laws of the Indies in force, including forced labor, and a protector of Indians is named (1851); Indians of San Pedro Sacatepéquez are declared ladinos (1876); it is mandated that communal properties be made private, cofradías suspended, and laborers supplied to plantations (1877); indebtedness is made legal, giving ladinos the right to force Indians to work on plantations (1879); a congress is convoked on how best to civilize the Indians (1892); by decree Indians are allowed to escape military service by paying fifteen pesos to the state or by learning to read and abandoning native dress (1894); an uprising takes place in San Juan Ixcoy against ladinos there (1898).

Finally, Hernández Sifontes's twentieth-century juridical events up to the 1944 revolution may be abridged as follows: an Indian messiah of Totonicapán is executed (1905); a massacre of visitors to Volcán Santa María occurs because of destruction of Indian altars (1917); it is decreed that *alcaldes primeros* (mayors) and *síndicos primeros* (deputy mayors) must be ladinos, and entire cabildos must be half Indian and half ladino (1927); obligatory public labor for two weeks each year is established (1933); indebted labor is banned, but a vagrancy law is established (1934); one hundred days of labor are required of Indian farmers; Indians are exempted from presenting health certificates upon marrying (1935); a massacre of ladinos by Indians takes place at Patzicia, incited by pro-Ubico forces (1944); the revolutionary constitution eliminates forced labor or any other discrimination against Indians and makes their "economic, social and cultural improvement" mandatory (1945).

Hernández Sifontes concludes that the Indians have their own "common law," inextricably bound to their culture, but that this fact has never been taken into account within ladino-dominated Guatemalan law: "I set out a working hypothesis that our legislation was foreign to the cultural context of the Indian, the majority population of Guatemala. . . . I succeeded in establishing, much to my sorrow, that my original proposition was correct." Unfortunately, his book does not succeed in reconstructing what that legal system might have been like.[40]

Calendric

This institutional topic will be discussed more as an illustration of the lack of ethnohistoric treatment than as a summary of useful results. Despite the relatively good historical information on the native calendar in highland Guatemala, almost all students have used the sources either to reconstruct the prehispanic calendar or to describe it synchronically. Thompson, for example, in his monumental study of the Maya calendar, cites most of the nineteenth- and early twentieth-century sources, but only to reconstruct prehispanic calendric patterns.[41] No attempt is made to show changes in the calendar through time, though such a procedure would seem to be a logical starting point, as La Farge pointed out long ago. (See the introduction above).

Otto Stoll and Daniel Brinton both cited a description of the native calendar practiced at Santa Catarina Ixtahuacán in the 1850s, but rather than interpret it historically they assumed it represents a "not materially differed" preservation from the prehispanic past. Stoll draws on his observation of swarming insects around Antigua to suggest a March 22 starting date for the Cakchiquel solar calendar. Brinton informs us that "the natives of Guatemala of aboriginal blood continue to reckon by this ancient calendar, and regulate it by certain recurrent festivals and rites which have little to do with the Christianity to which they are ostensibly adherents."[42]

La Farge's comparison of the Jacaltec calendar with other Maya calendars manifests some sensitivity to historical changes. He notes the loss of month names, year counts, and writing from the aboriginal system, despite the "really remarkable survival of the old ceremonial." He notes apparent changes through time—no dates are specified—of such features as Jacaltec yearbearers taking on Quiché word forms and days slipping "a peg," and "in modern times, and probably in ancient times as well, day-names lost their meaning and then received new ones by folk-etymology." He further remarks on the potential confusion introduced by ladinos who misspelled native terms and dated events incorrectly by not counting "by nights" as the Indians do. Nevertheless, La Farge concludes that "these shamans, many of them for generations having had no writing, have maintained their count of days unbroken and without error since the time of the conquest."[43]

Suzanne Miles and Manning Nash have analyzed the differing survival of native calendric components in highland Guatemala. They found a pronounced geographic break between calendar systems that retained both solar and 260-day counts and those that retained only the 260-day count. Despite the potential for tracing out the historical changes related to the two types of calendar systems, neither author attempts to draw such conclusions from their data. Barbara Tedlock has also pointed to serious factual errors in their accounts, such as the existence of combined solar and 260-day systems well within the region where supposedly only the 260-day count was found.[44]

The range of calendric variation discussed by Miles in the ethnographic sources is impressive. Components found in varying degrees of completeness include the calendar round (52-day "year"), "month" (of 20 days), yearbearers, solar year (365 days), 260-day count, and 20-day count. The 20-day count would appear to have the greatest survival capacity, followed by the 260-day and solar counts (the latter can lose its 18 internal divisions). The yearbearer and sacred round components have the least survival capacity.

Miles found two different sets of yearbearers present in the highlands, the Ik, Quej, E, and Noj set characterizing all but the Chuj and Jacaltec groups. Surprisingly, she also found that all the 260-day calendars were in sequence, any given day in all the calendars corresponding to the same Gregorian date. Miles argued that the two types of calendar systems and the synchronous 260-day calendars are survivals from the prehispanic past, though no historical evidence is presented to demonstrate changes in them through time.

Nash is content to correlate Miles's two calendric types with two different social structures. Those Indian communities with both solar and 260-day counts have calendric priests who form part of a civil-religious hierarchy, whereas in those with only the 260-day count, calendric shamans are tied to clients through loose networks. Nash provides a functionalist explanation for this correlation: "The role of calendar expert and the kind of calendar retention go along together because the differences in role and social structure call for a different kind of knowledge and performance based upon different elements of the calender."[45]

Nash concludes that "the problem of Mesoamerican survivals or retentions is ultimately to be explained through a series of historical events." Like almost every other student of the native calendar, however, he seems uninterested in the research that would be required to elucidate those events.

Religion

Historically-oriented studies of highland Guatemalan Indian religion have not yet been made. Nineteenth-century accounts by students like Otto Stoll, Daniel G. Brinton, and José Milla refer exclusively to prehispanic religious beliefs and practices. More recent accounts, including E. M. Mendelson's impressive summary of Mesoamerican myth and ritual, contain only synchronic projections into the past. Even Mary P. Holleran's superb reconstruction of church and state relations in Guatemalan history suffers from this defect. The brief review to follow is meant to illustrate the kind of studies available and to show their generally ahistorical bias.[46]

Chester Jones reserves his discussion of Indian religion for the section on "present-day social life," and bases it exclusively on ethnographic sources such as Tax, La Farge, and Goubaud Carrera. He notes the non-Christian character of many practices, "some indicating preconquest origin." The Indians seem to have incorporated Christian elements into their religious system, though "many features of religious life which do not have community character are distinctly pagan." Jones argues that native religion was "driven under cover" during certain (unspecified) periods, when shamans kept it alive. The early part of the twentieth century, however, was a time of relaxation by the church, and non-Christian practices became more prominent than in the past.[47]

Mary Holleran directs her detailed analysis of the church in Guatemala to the highest official levels of church and state. If it were not for brief descriptions of Indian religion during the early colonial period and in the twentieth century, one would hardly know from her book that the Indians were part of the Guatemalan church. Her extensive coverage of the nineteenth century contains only four brief references to the Indians: early in the first Liberal period the clergy opposed educating the Indians for fear they would become disobedient; the Indians opposed Gálvez, in part because of his church reforms, and became supporters of the rebel Carrera; Carrera returned the Palencia hacienda to the Dominicans in order to placate the Indians in Sacatepéquez, over whom they had influence; the Los Altos Indians demanded the return of the archbishop and Franciscan priests expelled by the Barrios regime.

Holleran argues that in her time "the manner of celebrating the numerous fiestas had not changed from that of past centuries," and that this was true for both ladino towns and Indian villages. The religion that has come down to the Indians was derived from "old Mayan beliefs," to which Christian elements were added. It was close to the "hills and plains" where the Indian spends his life, but far from the formal workings of the orthodox church. Holleran believed the gap between the native and Christian religions was created by the Indian's practical bent ("He has no idea of abstraction"), his inability to speak or understand Spanish, and the small number of Catholic priests (the number of priests had remained static since 1872, when there were 119 of them).[48]

Mention may be made of two other religious studies that are suggestive of historical developments without actually providing ethnohistorical analysis. One is Sol Tax's examination of Guatemalan Indian religion or "world view." The Indians, he claims, have retained a "primitive" world view, characterized by "animism": physical forces and objects have life, deformed persons are magical, females are dangerous, people cause sickness by merely looking at others, plants and animals change their nature according to the phases of the moon, persons and animals are transformed one into the other, phantom spirits walk the earth, the soul leaves a person for hours or even days. What is strange, says Tax, is that, in contrast with their "primitive" world vision, the Indians have "civilized" social relations: they are commercial, impersonal, practical, individual, secular. Tax explains the Indian's "civilized" social relations as largely an inheritance from the advanced society of the prehispanic past. Since world view is not functionally determined by social relations, the Indians' "primitive" view could also be inherited from the prehispanic past.

Western ideas did not transform the Indians' world view through the years because there were few Catholic priests and the Indians were isolated from the Ladinos.[49]

The other study is by Michael Mendelson, who implies that a "cyclic view of life" derived from the prehispanic period has persisted to recent times in the highlands of Guatemala. This view has undergone complex transformations, and Mendelson rejects the "romantic" idea of any pure survival. Varying degrees of "decomposition" are possible, such as the traditional view becoming "folklore" rather than "living myth." The basic features of this ancient cyclic view of life consist of the belief that natural forces are owned by spirits, both good and bad, male and female, one and many; shamans are servants of the owners, with whom they maintain reciprocal ties; men must serve the owners through their servants in order to prevent catastrophe and world destruction. Man's destiny is "to get through one's allotted time, to escape the spirits when they are angry, and to play one's part in the upkeep of the world." This view is found in Christo-pagan form at Santiago Atitlán and other places in highland Guatemala.[50]

Case Studies

Many ethnographic reports on the Indian cultures of highland Guatemala include brief historical accounts of the events leading to the modern period, but these provide little new substantive information. Examples of such works would be Rubén Reina's important ethnographic studies of Chinautla, which contain only sketchy historical information, and David Brintnall's recent analysis of social change in Aguacatan, which reconstructs "traditional" social life mainly on the basis of ethnographic projections into the past.[51] These same historical limitations characterize most Guatemalan Indian community studies, such as the works by Redfield, Tax, Mendelson, Hinshaw, and Nash. Although hypothetical statements about the past derived from ethnographic sources are not without merit, in an important sense they are the antithesis of the ethnohistorical research under review here. Only detailed case studies based on documentary sources can provide the empirical detail needed to revise and expand the more general reconstructions summarized in the two previous sections.

Detailed Cases

Few studies have been made of specific cases in highland Guatemala that give emphasis to documentary research on the Indian cultures for the period under discussion. The most important of these are Douglas Madigan's account of Santiago Atitlán from prehispanic times to the present, Roland Ebel's study of political modernization in San Juan Ostuncalco, Ricardo Falla's investigation of religious conversion in San Antonio Ilotenango, Arden King's reconstruction of sociocultural changes in Verapaz, and my own studies of the central Quiché area and of Santiago Momostenango.[52] It would be valuable to review the methods and findings of each one of these case studies, but space limitations oblige me to confine my review to the Momostenango case, which, perhaps, gives the most extensive account of the period being discussed.

Momostenango

I have attempted to reconstruct the social history of the Quiché-speaking community of Santiago Momostenango from prehispanic to modern times. I have given much attention to the nineteenth and early twentieth centuries in this study, for which purposes I have used documents from the Guatemalan national archives, municipal records, papers in the hands of individuals resident in the community, published materials, and informants' memory of the past. It is my thesis that the Indians have fiercely resisted destruction of their resources and culture through time, have struggled with intelligence and, when necessary, with force against outside forces. I reconstruct changing material conditions through time in order to examine their influence on the traditional cultural system. Political conflict is also recorded in detail, for it expresses, I believe, the dialectical relationship operating between material and cultural conditions.

The last years of colonial life in Momostenango were politically volatile. Land was already in short supply; population was growing rapidly, and by the nineteenth century was approaching prehispanic levels; large numbers of ladinos and creoles had taken up residence in the community, as many as three hundred persons; and many Indians were engaged in the production, transportation, and selling of wool, as well as in weaving it into fabrics. These "woolers" provided leadership for a chronic rebellion against outside interference in community affairs. The Indians objected to encroachment onto their lands by creole hacendados, the implanting of creole and ladino municipal officials to rule over the indigenous cabildo, the secularization of the church, including the withdrawal of the Franciscan priests, and the restoration of tribute payments after their having been removed. The rebel leaders, and they were supported by almost the entire native population, sought nothing less than independence from creole and ladino rule. They supported the Spanish king, but were willing to shift allegiance to Atanasio Tzul for the few days he was able to stay in power. At the time national independence was proclaimed, Momostecos were in uncontrollable revolt, and subsequently gave their loyalty to the Mexican emperor rather than to the Central American leaders.

The Liberal government established during the first two decades after independence was never able to gain the allegiance of the Momostecan Indians. They opposed attempts to hold open elections, fighting pitched battles with government forces over the issue. Eventually, the Liberals made concessions, and the Indians organized town government according to their own manner and independent of the ladinos. This situation was ratified by Carrera, who became a paternalistic symbol for the Indians much as the Spanish crown had been. Resident creoles, however, remained loyal to the Liberals, and were able to enhance their power locally during the interlude when Carrera was out of office. This generated intense hostility between the two ethnic groups, resulting in a near "caste war."

Encouraged by Carrera, who was fighting in the west in order to overthrow the Liberals again, Momostecan Indians terrified the local ladinos. On Concepción of 1849, they massed in town with the avowed purpose of exterminating all the ladinos. The rebels were led by local caciques, who assumed the office of captain; the rest of the organization consisted of the gobernador and "uniformed rounds of soldiers dressed in red, with arms and munitions." They rushed from the cofradía houses shouting, "Kill [the ladinos] . . . we have orders from our General to finish off the ladinos here . . . make crosses on them with the tips [of your knives]." The ladinos defended themselves with all the weapons they could muster, and, apparently because the Indians lacked firearms, no one was killed during the rioting.

Carrera was finally able to co-opt the rebellious Momostecan Indians with a mixture of threats and paternalism. He pardoned them of their excesses—for example, rebels who had accidentally killed two mailmen were not prosecuted—and allowed them to set up their own political structure. But any disobedience was met with the threat of troops, to which was added paternalistic entreaties: let it "not be said in the other towns of the Republic that Momostenango is bad and does not know the law." In general, during the Carrera years the Momostecan Indians were allowed to conduct social life according to traditional patterns, and they were always able to appeal directly to the president himself should local ladino oppression become too great.

The Barrios reforms were disastrous for the Momostecan Indians, and they reacted violently against them. Local ladinos were placed in all the important authority positions, and exercised a firmer and more efficient political control than had existed prior to then in the community. A virulent racism characterized their attitude toward the Indians. The Church lost power, mainly through the transfer of birth and death registration to civil hands. The Indians were especially displeased with the tampering with the cemetary by the civil authorities, since it was the sacred home of their ancestors. But by far the most objectionable features of the Liberal's program were land and labor policies.

Momostecan Indians lost their best agricultural lands under Liberal rule, forty-six caballerías of rich, flat lands in Buenabaj, and several hundred caballerías of piedmont lands at El Palmar and Samala. In addition, they received unfavorable decisions in boundary disputes with neighboring Santa María Chiquimula and San Francisco El Alto. With population doubling during the century, land shortage reached crisis proportions. Several hundred Momostecans migrated to other townships during this time, to such places as Malacatán, San Pedro Jocopilas, Chiche, and the Cuchumantanes. Forced labor on coastal plantations also hit Momostecans hard. Local officials could not keep up with the demand, which reached more than five hundred men each year for the community. This was an especially onerous obligation for the Momostecans because land losses forced thousands of them into commercial and artisan work, thus placing additional demands on their time.

Hostility against the Barrios government in Momostenango broke into full-scale guerrilla warfare in 1876. The spark that lit the fire was the government's rigid stance relative to boundary claims with neighboring communities. When troops were sent against the Momostecans, the rebels, led by their canton chiefs, opened fire on the troops and retreated to the mountains. Ladino officials were pinned down in town as the rebels secured all roads into and out of the community. By 1877 the rebels had joined forces with a Conservative revolutionary movement to topple the Liberal government. The regional leader of the movement was Julián Rubio, a creole rancher living on the outskirts of Momostenango. Rubio had married into a prominent Momostecan Indian family, and through his father-in-law was able to recruit the rebel chiefs into his army. He supplied the rebels with weapons and trained them in the wild canyon country north of San Bartolo Aguas Calientes. Rubio led his Momostecan army in an attack on the Quiché military base in September of 1877. They were badly defeated, and many Momostecans were killed. As punishment for this act, Barrios authorized the Sija militia to burn houses and crops in all rebel zones of Momostenango and many families suspected of aiding the rebels were forced to resettle in town. Captured rebel soldiers were imprisoned, and some were executed.

Barrios appears to have changed tactics somewhat as a result of his Momostenango experience, for after the revolt of 1877 he began to treat the Indians there with a "forceful paternalism" reminiscent of earlier Conservative ways. He ordered the resettled families returned to their homes, and hinted that "these poor naturals" should be treated with more understanding. Later, he compromised on the disputed boundaries with the neighboring communities, and peace once again settled over Momostenango.

The final fifty years of Liberal rule in Momostenango were a time of intense political and economic repression for the Indians. Local ladinos established close personal links with national dictators and used these to establish an authoritarian system of government within the community. Forced labor not only supplied the plantations—and from one to two thousand Indian laborers migrated to the coasts each year from Momostenango during those years—but also the local ladinos, whose lands were acquired through grants from the dictators. The military organization was even more exploitative, the entire Indian population becoming involved in almost constant militia and active duty service. Combining capitalist agriculture and rigid military authority, the ladino elites controlled a virtual fascist state. They undertook massive public works based on the forced labor of the Indian masses, constructing the impressive buildings whose monumentality even today surprises the visitor to Momostenango. A rough estimate from our sources of the labor required of the Indians in those days suggests that it surpassed 336,000 man days per year, some 16 percent of their total available work days (calculated on a six-day week). This obligation was especially heavy to bear for Momostecans, since six to eight thousand persons were being added to the population each year, average landholdings had dropped to less than a half hectare per family, and over 70 percent of the men were engaged in weaving or the selling of woolen products as a supplement to farming.

The exploitation of those years was perhaps greater than any since the Spanish conquest. The ladinos ruled by an elaborate mix of terror and paternalism. Recalcitrant Indians could be forced to work in disagreeable places, could be thrown in jail, where they were literally made to split stones, or, for more serious offenders, could be secretly shot by legally armed ladino soldiers. But the system would not have functioned as well as it did without the highly paternalistic ties established between ladino leaders and the Indian masses. Native religion, for example, was not only tolerated but fostered. Ladinos helped "rationalize" the Quiché religion by overseeing the development of a hierarchy of native priests (chuch-kajaw) assigned to different levels in the cantons, the town center, and the military bases. Elders were respected, as were many other traditional social groups; for instance, the Vico caciques were allowed to form an equestrian military squadron, a direct throwback to colonial times when the caciques were the only Indians allowed to possess horses. The military organization, in fact, appears to have been the single most important institution for binding the Indians to the ladinos in patron-client relationships. Momostecan Indians were fierce soldiers, and took pride in their claim to have killed the Salvadoran president, Tomás Regaldo, in the war of 1906. They were proud, too, to serve as the honor guards of several Liberal presidents. Furthermore, many Indians gained officer status, achieving at one time over one hundred lieutenant, better than twenty captain, and six colonel positions. The most powerful ladino in Momostenango during the Estrada Cabrera reign so favored the Indians with promotions that he became known nationally as "that Indian general." Although the ladino officers retained dominant control, the military establishment was the only sector in which some Indians had higher status than some ladinos.

The possibility of open revolt by the Indians was very limited during those years, especially in the Ubico period. Only when changes at the national level eroded local ladino derivative power could the Indians contemplate freeing themselves of their oppressors. The best opportunity came with the fall of Estrada Cabrera in 1920. Local ladino rulers acted quickly to change their allegiance to the Unionist cause, threatening to continue their stranglehold over the community under a new banner. When the departmental commander, Salvador Alarcón, held out against the Unionist forces, Momostecan Indians seized the opportunity to revolt against the ladinos and support Alarcón. An Indian militia officer named

Manuel Chanchabac took command of the rebels and led them in an attack on a Unionist delegation sent from Quezaltenango to take control of the town. Six Unionist men were killed, three of them hacked to death by Indians in one of the cantons where they had gone to hide. The local ladinos quickly regrouped, assumed control of the militia, captured fourteen of the rebels, including Chanchabac, and summarily executed them. This event is still politically sensitive in Momostenango, and no one seems to have captured its significance: "In the political game being played, the indigenous leaders must have realized that if they supported the Unionists the Ladinos would continue to rule over them with little change. If, however, they were to support Estrada Cabrera, and win, the Ladinos would be traitors, and the Indians would replace them as the government's leaders in Momostenango."

Momostecan Indians strongly supported Ponce at the time the Revolution of 1944 occurred, and several of them were killed defending him. But the October revolution destroyed the militia as an effective force in Momostenango, and it radically altered the exploitative structure of that community.[53]

Conclusions

It will be useful to summarize briefly what has been reviewed above. Acculturation studies, it was found, stress the development of syncretized Spanish-native culture during the last years of the colonial period and the first half of the Republican period. Native patterns persisted, and closed corporate communities remained strong. Nineteenth-century liberalism opened up the native communities and latinized their culture, processes that were rapidly accelerated with the onset of twentiety-century revolutions.

Marxist students stress the proletariate condition of the Indians vis à vis the creoles, its roots in colonial society, and its persistence into Republican times. Late-nineteenth-century and early-twentieth-century developments are said to be more of the same, as ladinos joined with creoles to form an expanded bourgeois class.

Examination of studies of nineteenth-century native institutions reveals that very little research has been done on this topic. Most research has focused either on prehispanic or present-day native cultures, projecting reconstructions forward in the one case and backward in the other. It was suggested that institutional studies could provide a fruitful area for future research, and we should not be surprised if such research radically alters our general ideas about native culture in the nineteenth and twentieth centuries.

The case studies reviewed above introduce new questions and perspectives into the topic under discussion. Political violence is highlighted, more than in the general studies. Cultural changes internal to the native communities, not made sufficiently clear in the more general works, are revealed. Examples would be varying modes of relations between ladino and Indian authority structures, demographic dynamics, and the emergence of new, commercially-linked native leadership. The case study does, on the other hand, tend to support the general studies in ascribing a major influence on native culture to late-nineteenth-century Liberal policies. Especially does it support the thesis that repressive land and labor practices brought dramatic cultural changes to the communities.

A few critical comments relative to the studies reviewed here should be added, in part to help chart the future course of our research. We may begin with a criticism often made of acculturation studies similar to the ones reviewed here: too much emphasis given to aboriginal cultural patterns and not enough attention to cultural development (or change). Syncretistic cultures are largely taken as given, and the particular processes and cultural patterns involved in their formation ignored. The study of calendrics, where such a reconstruction of processes of change is so feasible, illustrates well the deficiency. It is my belief, too, that conflict has been too much neglected in anthropological studies. Even Marxist studies tend to be uncomfortably "functionalist," that is, Indians and ladinos are seen as being in reciprocal patron-client relationships, and the problem is even more acute for the acculturation studies. The case studies suggest that culture change has been closely tied to major conflicts between the Indians and outside political and economic agents, but this can be demonstrated only if adequate attention is given to conflict.

Marxist students would seem to illustrate the oft-cited Marxist unwillingness to come to grips with the reality of the peasant condition. This prevents them in the Guatemalan case, and elsewhere, from examining the social role of native communities or native cultural patterns. Stavenhagen is a partial exception to this criticism, though even his sensitive study would have benefited from more careful consideration of the native cultures involved in the process of class formation.

Criticism of institutional studies is premature since such studies as yet do not exist. Nevertheless, that we have no serious reconstruction of nineteenth-century native religion, economics, politics, law, or literacy is a sad commentary on the level of Guatemalan ethnohistory. Further, the studies we do have are largely interpolations from synchronic studies of earlier or later cultures, or hypothetical projections based on theoretical models of what must have existed in the past. Although it makes good sense to start our study of, say, markets with an examination of how they have been found ethnographically in the twentieth century, that surely is only a first step. Empirical, historical research on markets will be a difficult topic, but until it is undertaken our reconstructions of past marketing patterns must be viewed with extreme skepticism. I suggest that we will find more and better data on these institutional topics than might be supposed, and that this research will give our history-making a more interesting, anthropological charcter.

The case studies represent, I suggest, our finest ethnohistorical research on the topic under discussion. This is not to say, of course, that they do not have their flaws. For example, my study of the central Quiché native cultures barely taps the wealth of documents that would be available for such a study. Falla only hypothesizes about what conditions were like in Ilotenango during the Liberal period, and the other case studies suggest that his reconstruction is probably incorrect on this point. Ebel's admirable study was based almost wholly on municipal papers, leaving aside the profoundly important documents in the Archivo de Centroamérica. His account is overly formal also, and does little to penetrate the traditional native political culture. King is never clear about the main objectives of his study, and his regional focus remains vague and incomplete throughout. Furthermore, the Indians seem somewhat marginal to the Germans and other powers in his study, at least as far as the reconstruction of their culture is concerned. Madigan's problem orientation—the persistence of an Indian tradition—is too imprecise, and his attempts to explain it rather eclectic and deductive. Since my own study of Momostenango, presented above in detail, has not even been published yet, further comments on it would be quite meaningless.

I close with a few remarks comparing highland Guatemalan ethnohistory for the period under discussion with similar research elsewhere in Mesoamerica. These remarks must be highly impressionistic for now, though a serious, detailed comparison would cast much light on our Guatemalan studies, I believe. I have not attempted to arrange the following comments in order of generality or significance.

Oscar Lewis's Tepoztlán study is possibly the best single social anthropology done in a Mesoameican context. We do not have for highland

Guatemala a study that equals it in terms of effectively integrating ethnographic and ethnohistorical data. His study has a surprisingly strong historical component, a fact often overlooked because of Lewis's ethnographic fame.

We also have no equal to Charles Gibson's Aztec case study, though of course it provides no post-colonial coverage. His ethnic and cultural focus and his control of documentary sources are features worthy of emulation in the Guatemalan field. I readily admit that I have consciously followed his model in my study of Momostenango.

Sudies of the caste war in Yucatan represent, I believe, a more developed institutional study than any so far carried out for nineteenth-century highland Guatemala. In part, this reflects the fact that several good researchers have focused on the problem. Caste war research has especially benefited from its integration with available data on changing economic patterns in Yucatan.

We have a literature for highland Guatemala equivalent to the Mexican revolutionary studies, but it lacks the depth, objectivity, and dramatic quality of the Mexican case. This is an area where continuing conditions of political conflict in Guatemala should stimulate much research in the future. Such events as the Patzicia and Panzos massacres rapidly become mythologized, and we desperately need on-going ethnohistorical studies of them.

Ethnohistorical research on nineteenth-century highland Guatemala might well be more advanced than what is now available for such Mexican areas as Chiapas, Oaxaca, Michoacán, and the northwest coast. But this is more the result of limited research in the Mexican areas than adequate coverage of highland Guatemala. Substantive comparisons between these areas are still premature, in my opinion, because of the poverty of work done so far.

Finally, I want to call attention to Fernando Cámara Barbachano's reconstruction of Maya culture process.[54] I believe it is the general sequence that best fits the highland Guatemalan data and that better stresses significant factors for change than other available schemes. Cámara argues, for example, that a single phase characterizes the Maya area from about 1711 to 1870. In this phase, the prior, native-dominated sociocultural equilibrium was broken and a long period of cultural fragmentation and instability existed. He associates the phase with large-scale native uprisings, messianic in character, that challenged the destruction of the old structure. These dynamic movements were linked to the mestizaje process, as well as to civil and religious reforms and capitalistic developments. The great increase in mestizos and creoles during this period brought intense demands on the Indians, and this played a major role in the unsettled conditions of the times.

Although the studies of highland Guatemalan Indians reviewed above do not necessarily support Cámara on all his points, my own case study does. The analysis of interrelations between economic (capitalistic), social (mestizaje), and political (nativistic movements) factors would seem to provide a reasonable focus for our ethnohistorical studies. To these I would add the cultural interests of acculturation-oriented anthropologists.

Notes

1. Robert Wasserstrom, "Revolution in Guatemala: Peasants and Politics under the Arbenz Government," *Comparative Studies in Society and History* 17 (1975): 443–78.

2. Oliver La Farge, "Maya Ethnoloy: The Sequence of Cultures," *The Maya and their Neighbors* (New York, 1940), pp. 281–91.

3. John Lloyd Stephens, *Incidents of Travel in Central America, Chiapas, and Yucatan,* 2 vols. (New York, 1841).

4. E.g., Sol Tax, "World View and Social Relations in Guatemala," *American Anthropologist* 43 (1941): 27–42.

5. See, for example, his "History of Acculturation in Mexico," in *Homenaje al Doctor Alfonso Caso* (Mexico City, 1951); "Notes on Acculturation," in Sol Tax, ed., *Heritage of Conquest: The Ethnology of Middle America* (Glencoe, Ill., 1952); "Acculturation," in Manning Nash, ed., *Social Anthropology,* vol. 6 of *Handbook of Middle American Indians,* (Austin, 1967).

6. Richard N. Adams, *Encuesta sobre la cultura de los ladinos en Guatemala* (Guatemala City, 1956).

7. Richard N. Adams, "Nationalization," in *Social Anthropology,* vol. 6 of *Handbook of Middle American Indians* (Austin, 1967). Quotations are from pp. 488, 479, 480.

8. Eric R. Wolf, *Sons of the Shaking Earth* (Chicago, 1959), pp. 230, 246.

9. Mary W. Helms, *Middle America. A Culture History of Heartland and Frontiers.* (Englewood Cliffs, N.J., 1975), especially pp. 219–32, 288–92.

10. Ralph Lee Woodward, Jr., *Central America. A Nation Divided* (New York, 1976).

11. Luis Cardoza y Aragón, *Guatemala, las lineas de su mano* (Mexico City, 1955), pp. 324–25.

12. Ibid., pp. 340–41.

13. Ibid., p. 355.

14. Carlos Guzmán Böckler and Jean-Loup Herbert, *Guatemala: Una interpretación histórico-social* (Mexico City, 1970), pp. 71–73.

15. Rodolfo Stavenhagen, *Social Classes in Agrarian Societies* (Garden City, N.J., 1975), pp. 170–74, 199–204. See also his "Clases, colonialismo y aculturación. Ensayo sobre un sistema de relaciones interétnicas en Mesoamérica (La región maya de los altos de Chiapas y Guatemala)," in *Ensayos sobre las clases sociales en México* (Mexico City, 1969).

16. Stavenhagen, *Social Classes,* p. 204.

17. Ibid., p. 203.

18. Severo Martínez Peláez, *la patria del criollo* (Guatemala City, 1971), pp. 566, 575–76.

19. Ibid., p. 579.

20. Susanne Jonas, "Guatemala: Land of Eternal Struggle," in Ronald H. Chilcote and Joel C. Edelstein, eds., *Latin America: The Struggle with Dependency and Beyond* (New York, 1974), pp. 118–19.

21. Ibid., p. 121.

22. Ibid., pp. 137–38.

23. Carol A. Smith's works include, "The Domestic Marketing System in Western Guatemala: An Economic, Locational, and Cultural Analysis" (Stanford University, Ph.D. dissertation, 1972), and "Beyond Dependency Theory: National and Regional Patterns of Underdevelopment in Guatemala," *American Ethnologist* 5 (1978). Chester L. Jones's book is *Guatemala: Past and Present.* (Minneapolis, 1940).

24. But meanwhile see his two manuscripts, "The Effects of the Liberal Reforms upon the Corporate Structures of Guatemalan Indian Communities," and "Change and Continuity in Local Political and Religious Organization: The Case of Five Mayan Communities in Guatemala" (paper read at the meeting of the Canadian Ethnology Society, Halifax, Nova Scotia, 1977).

25. Jones, *Guatemala,* quotes from pp. 148, 155, 163. The discussion paraphrased here runs between pp. 147 and 176.

26. Ibid., pp. 172–76.

27. Ibid., pp. 312–13.

28. Alain T. Dessaint, "Effects of the Hacienda and Plantation Systems on Guatemala's Indians," *América Indígena* 22 (1962): 323–54, and especially pp. 333, 340–41.

29. Manning Nash, "The Impact of Mid-Nineteenth Century Economic Change upon the Indians of Middle America," in Magnus Mörner, ed., *Race and Class in Latin America* (New York, 1970), p. 183.

30. Carol A. Smith, "La evolucion de los sistemas del mercadero en el occidente de Guatemala," *Estudios Sociales* 10 (1973); pp. 38–71.

31. Smith, "Domestic Marketing System," p. 21.

32. Smith, "La evolución de los sistemas del mercadero," pp. 27–28.

33. Smith, "Beyond Dependency Theory," contains these general arguments.

34. Nash, "Impact," pp. 176, 177. See also his "Cultural Persistence and Social Structure: The Mesoamerican Calendar Survivals," *Southwestern Journal of Anthropology* 13 (1957): 149–55.

35. Richard N. Adams, in Margaret A. L. Harrison and Robert Wauchope, eds., *Political Changes in Guatemalan Indian Communities. Community Culture and National Change* (New Orleans, 1971), p. 48.

36. Roland H. Ebel, "Political Change in Guatemalan Indian Communities," *Journal of Inter-American Studies* 6 (1964); 91–104, especially 94, 96, 98.

37. McDowell, "Change and Continuity," pp. 4, 17.

38. Daniel Contreras, *Una rebelión indígena en el partido de Totonicapán en 1820: El indio y la independencia* (Guatemala City, 1951), pp. 26, 47. Other revolts are mentioned in footnotes on pp. 29 and 65.

39. Jorge Skinner-Klee, *Legislación indigenista de Guatemala.* (Mexico City, 1954), p. 16.

40. J. Hernández Sifontes, *Realidad jurídica del indígena guatemalteco* (Guatemala City, 1965). Quotations are from pp. 16 and 391.

41. J. Eric S. Thompson, *Maya Hieroglyphic Writing* (Norman, Oklahoma, 1960).

42. Otto Stoll, *Die Ethnologie der Indianerstämme von Guatemala* (Leyden, 1889), p. 60; Daniel Brinton, *The Native Calendar of Central America and Mexico* (Philadelphia, 1893), pp. 271–72.

43. Oliver LaFarge, *The Year Bearer's People*, with D. Byers (New Orleans, 1938), pp. 166, 171, 176.

44. Suzanne W. Miles, "An Analysis of Modern Middle American Calendars: A Study in Conservation," in Sol Tax, ed., *Acculturation in the Americas* (Chicago, 1952); Nash, "Cultural Persistence"; Barbara Tedlock, "Quiché Maya Divination; a Theory of Practise" (SUNY Albany, Ph.D. dissertation, 1978).

45. Nash, "Cultural Persistence," p. 155.

46. References are to Stoll, *Die Ethnologie*; Daniel G. Brinton, *The Names of the Gods in the Kiche Myths, Central America* (Philadelphia, 1881); José Milla, *Historia de la América Central*, 2 vols. (Guatemala City, 1937); E. M. Mendelson, "Ritual and Mythology," in *Social Anthropology*, vol. 6 of *Handbook of Middle American Indians* (Austin, 1967); and Mary P. Holleran, *Church and State in Guatemala* (New York, 1949).

47. Jones, *Guatemala*, pp. 320–25.

48. Holleran, *Church and State*, pp. 95, 123–24, 129, 171–72, 236.

49. Tax, "World View."

50. Mendelson, "Ritual and Mythology," pp. 411–14.

51. Rubén E. Reina, *The Law of the Saints: A Pokomam Pueblo and its Community Culture* (New York, 1966), and the same author's "Chinautla. A Guatemalan Indian Community," in Margaret A. L. Harrison and Robert Wauchope, eds., *Community Culture and National Change* (New Orleans, 1971). The other reference is to David E. Brintnall's *Revolt against the Dead: The Modernization of a Mayan Community in Highland Guatemala* (New York, 1979).

52. The works mentioned are Douglas G. Madigan, "Santiago Atitlán, Guatemala: A Socioeconomic and Demographic History," (University of Pittsburgh, Ph.D. dissertation, 1976); Roland Ebel, in Margaret A. L. Harrison and Robert Wauchope,

eds., *Political Modernization in Three Guatemalan Indian Communities* (New Orleans, 1971); Ricardo Falla's two works, "Actitud de los indígenas de Guatemala en la época de la independencia, 1800–1850," *Estudios Centroamericanos* 27 (1971): 701–18, and *Quiché Rebelde: Estudio de un movimiento de conversión religiosa, rebelde a las creencias tradicionales, en San Antonio Ilotenango, Quiché (1948–1970).* (Guatemala City, 1978); Arden R. King, *Coban and the Verapaz: History and Cultural Process in Northern Guatemala* (New Orleans, 1974); and Robert Carmack's four works, *Historia Social de los Quichés* (Guatemala City, 1979), *La evolución del Reino Quiché* (Guatemala City, 1979), *The Quiché-Mayas of Utatlán* (Norman, Oklahoma, 1981), and "Ethnohistoric Study of a Quiché-Maya Community" (descriptive title, (ms., n.d.a.).

53. See the work noted above, and also Carmack, "Barrios y los indígenas, el caso de Santiago Momostenango," *Estudios Sociales* 6 (1972); 52–73, and Carmack, "Motines indígenas en Momostenango en tiempo de la Independencia de Guatemala," *Estudios Sociales* 9 (1973): 49–66.

54. Fernando Cámara Barbachano, "El mestísaje en México" *Revista de Indias* 24 (1964).

Glossary

Adelantado. Governor of a frontier province; leader of a military or exploring expedition.

Alcalde. Highest ranking member of a cabildo (town council).

Alcalde mayor. Spanish official in charge of a district.

Alcaldía. District governed by an alcalde mayor.

Alférez. Honorary member of a town council; also an officer in the Spanish militia.

Arroba. Measure, 25 lbs.

Audiencia. Court or governing body of a region; by extension, the region itself.

Ayuntamiento. Town council or cabildo.

Batab. In Yucatán, the ruler or governor of an Indian town.

Caballería. Unit of land, about 105 acres.

Cabecera. Head village, usually with several hamlets under its jurisdiction.

Cabildo. Town council or ayuntamiento.

Cabildo eclesiástico. Cathedral chapter; the dean and other functionaries of a cathedral.

Cacique. Indian governor or nobleman of the highest rank.

Cacicazgo. Hereditary domain of a cacique.

Caja de comunidad. Community fund from which taxes or religious fees were often collected.

Calpisque. Indian tax collector or agent.

Caluac. In pre-conquest Yucatán, the governor of an important administrative center.

Cargo. Religious office in Indian communities, particularly in Chiapas and Guatemala.

Casta. Person of lowly birth and mixed ancestry; mestizo or mulatto of lower classes.

Caudillo. Political boss or strongman.

Cédula. Royal decree.

Chinampa. Aquatic or floating garden.

Clérigo. Secular priest or cleric.

Cofradía. Religious society or brotherhood responsible for celebrating certain festivals.

Corregidor. Official in charge of certain Indian districts.

Cura. Parish priest.

Curato. Parish administered by a secular priest.

Derecho. Church tax or fee, usually quasi-legal in nature.

Derrama. In colonial Guatemala and Chiapas, a system of forced production involving Indian communities.

Doctrina. A temporary parish administered by missionary orders.

Doctrinero. Missionary in charge of a doctrina.

Ejido. Common land assigned to Indian communities.

Encomendero. Holder of an encomienda grant.

Encomienda. Grant of Indian labor or tribute.

Entrada. Expedition for the purpose of conquest or reprisal against unpacified Indians.

Fanega. Unit of measure, 116 lbs.

Finca. Farm; in Chiapas, also a cattle ranch.

Finquero. Farmer; in Chiapas, also a cattle rancher.

Fiscal. Royal prosecutor.

Halach uinic. In pre-conquest and early colonial Yucatan, a regional lord or ruler.

Jefe político. District administrator.

Juez de milpa. Spanish official charged with supervising Indian agriculture.

Juez de repartimiento. Spanish official charged with assigning Indian labor drafts.

Justicia. Official in a cabildo.

Ladino. In Chiapas and Guatemala, any non-Indian.

Macehual. Indian commonor.

Mayordomo. Overseer on farm or ranch; also *cofradía* official.

Mestizo. Person of mixed ancestry.

Milpa. Native farm plot.

Natural (n.). Native (Indian).

Obraje. Dye works; any workshop.

Oidor. Judge of royal court (audiencia).

Real patronato. Royal prerogative to govern in temporal affairs and to appoint church officials in the New World.

Regidor. Town counselor.

Repartimiento. A system of Indian labor drafts.

Repartimiento de mercancías. A system of compulsory purchases which native communities repaid by producing specified commodities.

Terrenos baldíos. Unoccupied lands belonging to the crown or (later) state governments.

Vecino. Legal resident of a community.

Visita. Official inspection tour; also an outlying village within the jurisdiction of another community.

Bibliography

Archives

Guatemala City. Archivo General de Guatemala.

New Orleans, Louisiana. Tulane Collection. Latin American Library, Tulane University.

San Cristóbal, Chiapas, Mexico. Archivo Histórico Diocesano de San Cristóbal.

San Cristóbal, Chiapas, Mexico. Biblioteca Fray Bartolomé de Las Casas.

San Cristóbal, Chiapas, Mexico. Colección Moscoso.

Seville, Spain. Archivo General de Indias.

Tuxtla Gutiérrez, Chiapas, Mexico. Archivo General de Chiapas.

Tuxtla Gutiérrez, Chiapas, Mexico. Archivo Histórico del Estado (succeeded by Archivo General de Chiapas).

Unpublished Papers

Carmack, Robert M. "Ethnohistoric Study of a Quiché-Maya Community." Ms., n.d.

Feldman, Lawrence H. "Belize and its Neighbors: Spanish Colonial Records of the Audiencia of Guatemala, a Preliminary Report." Ms., 1981.

Feldman, Lawrence H. "A Survey of Chorti Manuscript Resources in Central America." Mimeo. Columbia: University of Missouri, Museum of Anthropology, 1978.

Freidlander, Judith. "The Secularization of the Civil-Religious Hierarchy: An Example from Post-Revolutionary Mexico." Ms., 1978.

Gosner, Kevin. "The Tzeltal Revolt of 1712: A Brief Overview." Paper presented at the XLIII International Congress of Americanists, Vancouver, British Columbia, 1979.

———. "Uman Parish: Open, Corporate Communities in Eighteenth-Century Yucatan." Paper presented at the Association of American Geographers, Philadelphia, 1979.

Hellmuth, Nicholas. "Some Notes on the Ytza, Quejache, Verapaz Chol, and Toquegua Maya." Mimeo. New Haven, 1971.

Jones, Grant D., and Robert R. Kautz. "Archaeology and Ethnohistory on a Spanish Colonial Frontier: The Macal-Tipu Project in Western Belize." Paper presented at the XVII Mesa Redonda de la Sociedad Mexicana de Antropología, San Cristóbal de las Casas, Chiapas, 1981.

————. "Native Elites on the Colonial Frontiers of Yucatan: A Model for Continuing Research." Ms. 80th Annual Meeting of the Mexican Anthropological Association, Los Angeles, 1981.

Lovell, W. George. "Collapse and Recovery: A Demographic Profile of the Cuchamatán Highlands of Guatemala (1520–1821)." Paper delivered at the Symposium on Highland Guatemalan Historical Demography, Albany, New York, October 11–13, 1979.

Lutz, Christopher H. "Population History of the Parish of San Miguel Dueñas, c. 1530–1770." Paper delivered at the Symposium on Highland Guatemalan Historical Demography, Albany, New York, October 11–13, 1979.

McDowell, Paul. "Change and Continuity in Local Political and Religious Organization: The Case of Five Mayan Communities in Guatemala." Paper read at the meeting of the Canadian Ethnology Society, Halifax, Nova Scotia, 1977.

————. "The Effects of the Liberal Reforms upon the Corporate Structures of Guatemalan Indian Communities." Ms., n.d.

Morris, Michael. "Ethno-Linguistic Systems in the Southern Maya Area." M.A. thesis, University of Pennysylvania, 1973.

Robinson, David J. "Indian Migration in Eighteenth-Century Yucatan." Paper presented at the XLIII International Congress of Americanists, Vancouver, British Columbia, 1979.

————, and Carolyn G. McGovern. "Population Change in the Yucatan, 1700–1820." Paper presented at the Association of American Geographers, Philadelphia, 1979.

Varese, Stéfano. "El Estado y lo múltiple." Ms., 1978.

Wasserstrom, Robert. "Life and Society in Colonial Chiapas, 1528–1790." Paper presented at the XLIII International Congress of Americanists, Vancouver, British Columbia, 1979.

————. "Religious Service in Zinacantan, 1793–1975." Ms., 1978.

Published Sources

Adams, R. E. W., ed. The Origins of Maya Civilization. Albuquerque: University of New Mexico Press, 1977.

————, W. E. Brown, Jr., and T. Patrick Culbert. "Radar Mapping, Archaeology, and Ancient Maya Land Use." Science 213 (1981): 1457–63.

Adams, Richard N. Encuesta sobre la cultura de los ladinos en Guatemala. Publication No. 2. Guatemala City: Seminario de Integración Social Guatemalteca, 1956.

Aguirre Beltrán, Gonzalo. *Regiones de refugio*. Mexico City: Instituto Nacional Indigenista, 1967.

Altman, Ida, and James Lockhart, eds. *Provinces of Early Mexico*. Los Angeles: University of California at Los Angeles, Latin American Center Publications, 1976.

Alzate y Ramírez, José Antonio. *Memoria sobre la naturaleza, cultibo y beneficio de la grana*. Mexico City: 1777.

Andrews, Anthony P. "Historical Archaeology in Yucatán: A Preliminary Framework." *Historical Archaeology* 15 (1981): 1–18.

———. "Salt-Making, Merchants and Markets: The Role of a Critical Resource in the Development of Maya Civilization." Ph.D. dissertation, University of New Mexico, 1980.

Andrews, E. W., IV, and Anthony P. Andrews. *A Preliminary Study of the Ruins of Xcaret, Quintana Roo, Mexico*. Middle American Research Institute Publication No. 40. New Orleans: Tulane University, 1975.

Annis, Verle L. *The Architecture of Antigua Guatemala, 1543–1773*. Guatemala City: Universidad de San Carlos, 1968.

Ashmore, Wendy, ed. *Lowland Maya Settlement Patterns*. Albuquerque: University of New Mexico Press, 1981.

Bancroft, Hubert Howe. *History of Central America*. 3 vols. San Francisco: The History Company, 1882–1887.

Barón Castro, Rodolfo. *La población de El Salvador*. Madrid: Consejo Superior de Investigaciones Científicas, Instituto Gonzalo Fernández de Oviedo, 1942.

Batres Jáuregui, Antonio. *La América Central ante la historia*. 3 vols. Guatemala City: Tipografía Sánchez y De Guise, 1920.

Bauer, Arnold J. "Rural Workers in Spanish America: Problems of Peonage and Oppression." *Hispanic American Historical Review* 59 (1979): 34–63.

Benavides, Antonio C., and Antonio P. Andrews. *Ecab: Poblado y provincia del siglo XVI en Yucatán*. Mexico City: Instituto Nacional de Antropología e Historia, Cuadernos de los Centros Regionales, Sureste, 1979.

Bergman, John F. "Cacao and Its Production in Central America." *Tijdschrift voor economische en sociale Geografie* 48 (1957): 43–49.

Bertrand, Michel. "Estudio demográfico de la región de Rabinal y de Chixoy en Guatemala." *Mesoamérica* 1 (1980): 232–49.

Blanton, Richard E. *Monte Albán, Settlement Patterns at the Ancient Zapotec Capital*. New York: Academic Press, 1978.

Bolland, O. Nigel. *The Formation of a Colonial Society: Belize, from Conquest to Crown Colony*. Baltimore: Johns Hopkins University Press, 1977.

Bricker, Victoria R. "Algunas consecuencias religiosas y sociales del nativismo maya en el siglo XIX." *América Indígena* 33 (1973): 327–48.

———. *The Indian Christ, the Indian King*. Austin: University of Texas Press, 1981.

Brintnall, Douglas E. Revolt against the Dead. The Modernization of a Mayan Community in Highland Guatemala. New York: Gordon and Breach, 1979.

Brinton, Daniel G. The Names of the Gods in the Kiche Myths, Central America. Philadelphia: McCalla and Stavely, 1881.

———. "The Native Calendar of Central America and Mexico." Proceedings of the American Philosophical Society 31 (1893): 25–314.

Bunting, Ethel-Jane W. "From Cahabon to Bacalar in 1677." Maya Society Quarterly 1 (1932): 112–19.

Burstein, John, et al. En sus propias palabras: Cuatro vidas tzotziles. San Cristóbal: Editorial "Fray Bartolomé de las Casas," 1979.

Cáceres López, Carlos. Historia general del estado de Chiapas. Mexico City: The Author, 1958.

Calnek, Edward E. "Highland Chiapas before the Spanish Conquest." Ph.D. dissertation, University of Chicago, 1962.

Cámara Barbachano, Fernando. "El mestisaje en México." Revista de Indias 24 (1964): 27–85.

Cancian, Frank. Economics and Prestige in a Maya Community. Stanford: Stanford University Press, 1965.

Cardoza y Aragón, Luis. Guatemala, las lineas de su mano. Mexico City, Fondo de Cultura Económica, 1955.

Carmack, Robert M. "Barrios y los indígenas: El caso de Santiago Momostenango." Estudios Sociales 6 (1972): 52–73.

———. La evolución del Reino Quiché. Guatemala City: Editorial Piedra Santa, 1979.

———. Historia social de los Quichés. Publication No. 38. Guatemala City: Seminario de Integración Social Guatemalteca, 1979.

———. "Motines indígenas en Momostenango en tiempo de la independencia de Guatemala." Estudios Sociales 9 (1973): 49–66.

———. The Quiche-Mayas of Utatlan. Norman: University of Oklahoma Press, 1981.

———. Quichean Civilization: The Ethnohistoric, Ethnographic, and Archaeological Sources. Berkeley: University of California Press, 1973.

Cerwin, Herbert. Bernal Díaz, Historian of the Conquest. Norman: University of Oklahoma Press, 1963.

Chamberlain, Robert S. The Conquest and Colonization of Yucatan, 1517–1550. Publication No. 509. Washington, D.C.: Carnegie Institution, 1948.

Chase, Arlen F. "Topoxte and Tayasal: Ethnohistory in Archaeology." American Antiquity 41 (1976): 154–67.

Chilcote, Ronald H., and Joel C. Edelstein, eds. Latin America: The Struggle with Dependency and Beyond. New York: John Wiley and Sons, 1974.

Cline, Howard F. "The Henequen Episode in Yucatan." Inter-American Economic Affairs 2 (1948): 30–51.

———. "The Sugar Episode in Yucatan, 1825–1850." *Inter-American Economic Affairs* 1 (1948): 79–100.

Coe, Michael D. "A Model of Ancient Community Structure in the Maya Lowlands." *Southwestern Journal of Anthropology* 21 (1965): 97–114.

Collier, George. *Fields of the Tzotzil*. Austin: University of Texas Press, 1975.

Contreras R., J. Daniel. *Una rebelión indígena en el partido de Totonicapán en 1820: El indio y la independencia*. Guatemala City: Imprenta Universitaria, 1951.

Contributions to American Anthropology and History 6. Publication No. 523. Washington, D.C.: Carnegie Institution, 1952.

Contributions to American Anthropology and History 11. Publication No. 596. Washington, D.C.: Carnegie Institution, 1952.

Cook, Sherburne F., and Woodrow Borah. *Essays in Population History: Mexico and the Caribbean*. 3 vols. Berkeley: University of California Press, 1971, 1974, 1979.

Cooperation in Research. Publication No. 501. Washington, D.C.: Carnegie Institution, 1938.

Cortés, Hernán. *Cartas de relación*. 9th edition. Mexico City: Editorial Porrúa, 1976.

Cortés y Larraz, Pedro. *Descripción geográfico-moral de la diócesis de Goathemala*. 2 vols. Guatemala City: Sociedad de Geografía e Historia, Biblioteca "Goathemala," 1958.

Cosío Villegas, Daniel, et al. *Historia mínima de México*. Mexico City: El Colegio de México, 1974.

Coulborn, Rushton, ed. *Feudalism in History*. Princeton: Princeton University Press, 1956.

Culbert, T. Patrick, ed. *The Classic Maya Collapse*. Albuquerque: University of New Mexico Press, 1973.

Cumberland, Charles C. *Mexico: The Struggle for Modernity*. New York: Oxford University Press, 1968.

Dahlgren de Jordan, Barbro. *La grana cochinilla*. Mexico City: Nueva Biblioteca Mexicana de Obras Históricas I, 1963.

Deevy, E. S., et al. "Maya Urbanism: Impact on a Tropical Karst Environment." *Science* 206 (1979): 298–306.

Denevan, William M. *The Upland Pine Forest of Nicaragua: A Study in Cultural Plant Geography*. Publications in Geography Vol. 12, No. 4. Berkeley: University of California Press, 1961.

Dessaint, Alain T. "Effects of the Hacienda and Plantation Systems on Guatemala's Indians." *América Indígena* 22 (1962): 323–54.

Ebel, Roland H. "Political Change in Guatemalan Indian Communities." *Journal of Inter-American Studies* 6 (1964): 91–104.

Escalona Ramos, Alberto. "Algunas construcciones de tipo colonial en Quintana Roo." *Anales del Instituto de Investigaciones Estéticas* 3 (1943): 17–40.

———. "Algunas ruinas prehispánicas en Quintana Roo." *Boletín de la Sociedad*

Mexicana de Geografía y Estadística 61 (1946): 513–628.

Estudios sobre política indigenista española en América, vol. 1. Valladolid: Seminario de Historia de América, Universidad de Valladolid, 1975.

Falla, Ricardo. "Actitud de los indígenas de Guatemala en la época de la independencia, 1800–1850." Estudios Centroamericanos 278 (1971): 701–18.

———. Quiché rebelde. Estudio de un movimiento de conversión religiosa, rebelde a las creencias tradicionales, en San Antonio Ilotenango, Quiché (1948–1970). Guatemala: Editorial Universitaria, 1978.

Farriss, Nancy M. Colonial Maya Society: The Collective Purchase of Survival (forthcoming).

———. Crown and Clergy in Colonial Mexico. London: Athlone Press, 1968.

———. "Nucleation vs. Dispersal: The Dynamics of Population Movement in Colonial Yucatan." Hispanic American Historical Review 58 (1978): 187–216.

———. "Propiedades territoriales en Yucatán en la época colonial." Historia Mexicana 30 (1980): 153–208.

Favre, Henri. Changement et continuité chez les Mayas du Mexique. Paris: Anthropos, 1971.

Fernández de Oviedo y Valdez, Gonzalo. Historia general y natural de las Indias, vol. 4. Biblioteca de Autores Españoles, Tomo CXX. Madrid: Ediciones Atlas, 1959.

Flannery, Kent V., ed. Maya Subsistence. New York: Academic Press, 1982.

Foster, George M. Culture and Conquest: America's Spanish Heritage. New York: Wenner Gren/Viking Fund, 1961.

Fox, John W. Quiché Conquest. Centralism and Regionalism in Highland Guatemalan State Development. Albuquerque: University of New Mexico Press, 1978.

Frank, André Gunder. Capitalism and Underdevelopment in Latin America. 2nd ed., New York: Monthly Review Press, 1969.

Freidel, David A. "Culture Areas and Interaction Spheres." American Antiquity 44 (1979): 36–56.

———. "Late Postclassic Settlement Patterns on Cozumel Island." Ph.D. dissertation, Harvard University, 1976.

Friede, Juan, and Benjamin Keen, eds. Bartolomé de Las Casas in History. Toward an Understanding of the Man and His Work. DeKalb: Northern Illinois University Press, 1971.

Friedlander, Judith. Being Indian in Hueyapan. New York: St. Martin's Press, 1976.

Frost, Elsa Cecilia, et al., eds. El trabajo y los trabajadores en la historia de México. Mexico City: El Colegio de México, 1979.

Fuentes y Guzmán, Francisco Antonio de, Recordación Florida. 3 vols. Guatemala City: Sociedad de Geografía e Historia, Biblioteca "Goathemala," 1932–33.

Gage, Thomas. The English-American. Guatemala City: El Patio, 1946.

García Bernal, Manuela Cristina. La sociedad de Yucatán, 1700–1750. Seville: Escuela de Estudios Hispano-Americanos, 1972.

————. "La visita de Fray Luis de Cifuentes, obispo de Yucatán." *Anuario de Estudios Americanos* 29 (1972) 229–60.

García Bernal, Manuela Cristina. *Yucatán: Población y encomienda bajo los Austrias*. Seville: Escuela de Estudios Hispano-Americanos, 1978.

García de León, Antonio, et al., eds. *La Violencia en Chamula*. San Cristóbal: Universidad Autónoma de Chiapas, 1979.

García Peláez, Francisco de Paula. *Memorias para la historia del antiguo reino de Guatemala*. 3 vols. 2d. ed. Guatemala City: Tipografía Nacional, 1943–44.

Gerhard, Peter. *The Southeast Frontier of New Spain*. Princeton: Princeton University Press, 1979.

Gibson, Charles. "The Aztec Aristocracy in Colonial Mexico." *Comparative Studies in Society and History* 2 (1959–60): 169–96.

————. *The Aztecs under Spanish Rule*. Stanford: Stanford University Press, 1964.

————. "Writings on Colonial Mexico." *Hispanic American Historical Review* 55 (1975): 287–323.

González Navarro, Moisés. *Raza y tierra*. Mexico City: Colegio de México, 1972.

Gosner, Kevin. "Soldiers of the Virgin: An Ethnohistorical Analysis of the Tzeltal Revolt of 1712 in Highland Chiapas." Ph.D. dissertation, University of Pennsylvania, 1984.

Gossen, Gary H. "Translating Cuzcat's War: Understanding Maya Oral Tradition." *Journal of Latin American Lore* 3 (1977): 249–78.

Greenleaf, Richard E. *Zumárraga and the Mexican Inquisition, 1536–1543*. Washington, D.C.: Academy of American Franciscan History, 1962.

Griffin, Charles C., ed. *Latin America, A Guide to the Historical Literature*. Conference on Latin American History, Publ. No. 4. Austin: University of Texas Press, 1971.

Guzmán Böckler, Carlos, and Jean Louis Herbert. *Guatemala: Una interpretación histórico-social*. Mexico City: Siglo Veintiuno, 1970.

Hammond, Norman., ed. *Mesoamerican Archaeology: New Approaches*. London: Duckworth Ltd., 1974.

————, ed. *Social Process in Maya Prehistory: Studies in Memory of Sir Eric Thompson*. London: Academic Press, 1977.

————, and Gordon R. Willey, eds. *Maya Archaeology and Ethnohistory*. Austin and London: University of Texas Press, 1979.

Hamnet, Brian R. *Politics and Trade in Southern Mexico, 1750–1821*. Cambridge: Cambridge University Press, 1971.

Handbook of Middle American Indians, vols. 2, 3, and 6. Austin: University of Texas Press, 1965–1967.

Harrison, Margaret A. L., and Robert Wauchope, eds. *Community Culture and National Change*. Middle American Research Institute Publication 24. New Orleans: Tulane University, 1971.

————, eds. *Nativism and Syncretism*. Middle American Research Institute Publication 19. New Orleans: Tulane University, 1960.

Harrison, P.D., and B.L. Turner, II, eds. *Pre-Hispanic Maya Agriculture.* Albuquerque: University of New Mexico Press, 1978.

Hellmuth, Nicholas M. "Progreso y notas sobre la investigación etnohistórica de las tierras bajas mayas de los siglos XVI a XIX." *América Indígena* 32 (1972): 179–244.

Helms, Mary W. *Middle America. A Culture History of Heartland and Frontiers.* Englewood Cliffs: Prentice-Hall, 1975.

Hernández Aparicio, Pilar. "Problemas socioeconómicos en el Valle de Guatemala: 1670–1680." *Revista de Indias* 37 (1977): 585–637.

Hernández Sifontes, J. *Realidad jurídica del indígena guatemalteco.* Guatemala City: Ministerio de Educación, 1965.

Hidalgo, P. Manuel. *Libro en que se trata de la lengua tzotzil* . . . . Paris: Bibliothèque Nationale, Départment des Manuscrits, Ms. Mexicain 412, R27.747, 1735.

Holleran, Mary P. *Church and State in Guatemala.* New York: Columbia University Press, 1949.

Homenaje al Doctor Alfonso Caso. Mexico City: Nuevo Mundo, 1951.

Hunt, Marta Espejo-Ponce. "Colonial Yucatan: Town and Region in the Seventeenth Century." Ph.D. dissertation, University of California at Los Angeles, 1974.

Isbell, William H., and K.J. Schrieber. "Was Huari a State?" *American Antiquity* 43 (1978): 372–89.

Johannessen, Carl L. *Savannas of Interior Honduras.* Berkeley and Los Angeles: University of California Press, 1963.

Jones, Charles L. *Guatemala: Past and Present.* Minneapolis: University of Minnesota Press, 1940.

Jones, Grant D. "Southern Lowland Maya Political Organization: A Model of Change from Protohistoric through Colonial Times." Actes de XLIIIᵉ Congrès International des Américanistes, *Congrès de Centenaire, Paris, 2–9 Septembre 1976* 8 (1979): 83–94.

———, ed. *Anthropology and History in Yucatan.* Austin and London: University of Texas Press, 1977.

———, Don S. Rice, and Prudence M. Rice. "The Location of Tayasal: A Reconsideration in Light of Peten Maya Ethnohistory and Archaeology." *American Antiquity* 46 (1981): 530–47.

Kelly, John E. *Pedro de Alvarado, Conquistador.* Princeton: Princeton University Press, 1932.

King, Arden R. *Coban and the Verapaz: History and Cultural Process in Northern Guatemala.* Middle American Research Institute Publication No. 37. New Orleans: Tulane University, 1974.

Lafarge, Oliver, and D. Byers. *The Year Bearer's People.* Middle American Research Institute Publication No. 3. New Orleans: Tulane University, 1938.

Lange, Frederick. "Una reevaluación de la población del norte de Yucatán en el tiempo del contacto español, 1528." *América Indígena* 31 (1971): 117–39.

López de Cogolludo, Diego. *Historia de Yucatán*. Mexico City: Editorial Academia Literaria, 1957 (facsimile of 1688 edition).

López Sánchez, Hermilio. *Apuntes históricos de San Cristóbal de las Casas, Chiapas, México*. Mexico City: The Author, 1960.

Lothrop, S. K. *Tulum: An Archaeological Study of the East Coast of Yucatan*. Publication No. 335. Washington, D.C.: Carnegie Institution, 1924.

Luján Muñoz, Jorge. "Fundación de villas de ladinos en Guatemala en el último tercio del siglo XVIII." *Revista de Indias* 36 (1976): 51–81.

Lutz, Christopher H. "Santiago de Guatemala, 1541–1773: The Sociodemographic History of a Spanish-American Colonial City." Ph.D. dissertation, University of Wisconsin, Madison, 1976.

MacLeod, Murdo J. *Spanish Central America. A Socioeconomic History, 1520–1720*. Berkeley and Los Angeles: University of California Press, 1973.

McQuown, Norman A., and Julian Pitt-Rivers, eds. *Ensayos de antropología en la zona central de Chiapas*. Mexico City: Instituto Nacional Indigenista, 1970.

Madigan, Douglas G. "Santiago Atitlán, Guatemala: A Socioeconomic and Demographic History." Ph.D. dissertation, University of Pittsburgh, 1976.

Manguén, Juan J., et al., eds. *La Guerra de Castas, 1869–1870*. San Cristóbal: Talleres de Editorial Fray Bartolomé de las Casas, 1979.

Markman, Sidney David. *Colonial Architecture of Antigua Guatemala*. Philadelphia: American Philosophical Society, 1966.

—— *Colonial Central America: A Bibliography*. Tempe: Arizona State University, Center for Latin American Studies, 1977.

Martínez Peláez, Severo. *La patria del criollo*. Guatemala City: Editorial Universitario, 1971.

Maurer, Eugenio. "Les Tseltales, des paiens superficeillement christianisés ou des indiens fondamentalement chrétiens." Thèse pour le Doctorat en 3ème Cycle, Ecole des Hautes Etudes en Sciences Sociales, Paris, 1978.

The Maya and Their Neighbors. New York: D. Appleton-Century Co., 1940.

Milla, José. *Historia de la América Central*. 2 vols. Guatemala City: Tipografía Nacional, 1937.

Mintz, Sidney W., and Richard Price. *An Anthropological Approach to the Afro-American Past: A Caribbean Perspective*. Philadelphia: Institute for the Study of Human Issues, 1976.

Miranda, José. *El tributo indígena en la Nueva España durante el siglo XVI*. Mexico City: Fondo de Cultura Económica, El Colegio de México, 1952.

Molina, Cristóbal. *War of the Castes: Indian Uprisings in Chiapas, 1867–1870*. Middle American Series, Pamphlet 8, Publication 5. New Orleans: Tulane University, 1934.

Molina Solís, Juan Francisco. *Historia de Yucatán durante la dominación española*. 4 vols. Mérida: Imprenta de la Lotería del Estado, 1904–1912.

Montesinos, José María. *Memorias del Sargento, 1866–1878*. Tuxtla Gutiérrez: Imprenta del Gobierno del Estado, 1935.

Mörner, Magnus. "La política de segregación y el mestizaje en la Audiencia de Guatemala." *Revista de Indias* 24 (1964): 137–51.

———, ed. *Race and Class in Latin America.* New York: Columbia University Press, 1970.

Nash, Manning. "Cultural Persistence and Social Structure: The Mesoamerican Calendar Survivals." *Southwestern Journal of Anthropology* 13 (1957): 149–55.

Nutini, Hugo, et al. *Essays on Mexican Kinship.* Pittsburgh: University of Pittsburgh Press, 1976.

Orozco y Jiménez, Francisco. *Colección de documentos inéditos relativos a la iglesia de Chiapas.* 2 vols. San Cristóbal: Imprenta de la Sociedad Católica, 1905, 1911.

Othón de Mendizaba, Miguel, et al., eds. *Ensayos sobre las clases en México.* Mexico City: Editorial Nuestro Tiempo, 1969.

Paddock, John, ed. *Ancient Oaxaca.* Stanford: Stanford University Press, 1966.

Pagden, A. R., trans. and ed. *Hernan Cortes: Letters from Mexico.* New York: Orion/Grossman, 1971.

Paniagua, Flavio. *Catecismo elemental de historia y estadística de Chiapas.* San Cristóbal: Tipografía del Porvenir, 1876.

———. *Florinda.* San Cristóbal: 1889.

———. *Salvador Guzmán.* San Cristóbal: 1891.

Pardo, José Joaquín. *Efemérides para escribir la historia de la . . . ciudad de Santiago de . . . Guatemala.* Guatemala City: Tipografía nacional, 1944.

Paso y Troncoso, Francisco del, ed. *Epistolario de Nueva España.* 16 vols. Mexico City: Antigua Librería Robredo de José Porrúa e Hijos, 1940.

———, ed. *Papeles de Nueva España.* 7 vols. Madrid: Establecimiento Tipográfico "Sucesores de Rivadeneyra," 1905–1910.

Patch, Robert W. "A Colonial Regime: Maya and Spaniard in Yucatan." Ph.D. dissertation, Princeton University, 1979.

———. "La formación de estancias y haciendas en Yucatán durante la colonia." *Boletín de la Escuela de Ciencias Antropológicas de la Universidad de Yucatán* 19 (1976): 21–61.

Peel, J. D. Y. *Aladura: A Religious Movement among the Yoruba.* London: Oxford University Press for the International African Institute, 1968.

Pendergast, David M. "The Church in the Jungle; The ROM's First Season at Lamanai." *Rotunda* 8 (1975): 32–40.

———. "Lamanai, Belize: Summary of Excavation Results, 1974–1980." *Journal of Field Archaeology* 8 (1981): 29–53.

———. "Royal Ontario Museum Excavation: Finds at Lamanai, Belize," *Archaeology* 30 (1977): 139–41.

Pérez Valenzuela, Pedro. *Santo Tomás de Castilla: Apuntes para la historia de las colonizaciones en la costa atlántica.* Guatemala City: Tipografía Nacional, 1956.

Pineda, Vicente. *Chiapas: Traslación de los poderes públicos del estado.* San

Cristóbal: Imprenta de los Chiapanecos Libres en la Frontera, 1892.

——. *Historia de las sublevaciones indígenas habidas en el estado de Chiapas.* San Cristóbal: Tipografía del Gobierno, 1888.

Pollock, H. E., et al. *Mayapan, Yucatan, Mexico.* Publication No. 619. Washington, D.C.: Carnegie Institution, 1962.

Pozas, Ricardo. *Chamula, un pueblo indio de los altos de Chiapas.* Mexico City: Instituto Nacional Indigenista, 1957.

——. *Los indios en las clases sociales de México.* Mexico City: Siglo Veintiuno, 1971.

Rathje, William L. "The Origin and Development of Lowland Classic Maya Civilization." *American Antiquity* 36 (1971): 275–85.

Recinos, Adrián. *Pedro de Alvarado, conquistador de México y Guatemala.* Mexico City: Fondo de Cultura Económica, 1952.

Reina, Rubén E. *The Law of the Saints. A Pokomam Pueblo and Its Community Culture.* New York: Bobbs-Merrill, 1966.

——. "A Peninsula That May Have Been an Island: Tayasal, Petén, Guatemala." *Expeditions* 9 (1966): 16–29.

Relaciones histórico-geográficas de América Central, vol. 3. Madrid: Colección de Libros y Documentos Referentes a la Historia de América, 1908.

Remesal, Antonio de. *Historia general de las indias occidentales, y particular de la gobernación de Chiapa y Guatemala.* Guatemala City: Biblioteca de la Sociedad de Geografía e Historia, 1932.

Ricketson, O. G., and E. B. Ricketson. *Uaxactun, Guatemala, Group E, 1926–1931.* Publication No. 477. Washington, D.C.: Carnegie Institution, 1937.

Rodríguez Becerra, Salvador. *Encomienda y conquista. Los inicios de la colonización en Guatemala.* Seville: Universidad de Sevilla, 1977.

Romero Vargas, Germán, et al., contribs., *Ensayos de historia centroamericana.* San José, Costa Rica: Centro de Estudios Democráticos de América Latina (CEDAL), 1974.

Rostow, Walt W. *The Stages of Economic Growth.* Cambridge: Cambridge University Press, 1960.

Roys, Ralph L. *Indian Background of Colonial Yucatan.* Publication No. 548. Washington, D.C.: Carnegie Institution, 1943.

——. *The Political Geography of the Yucatan Maya.* Publication No. 613. Washington, D.C.: Carnegie Institution, 1957.

——. *The Title of Ebtun.* Publication No. 505. Washington, D.C.: Carnegie Institution, 1939.

——, ed. *The Book of Chilam Balam of Chumayel.* Norman: University of Oklahoma Press, 1967.

——, ed. *Ritual of the Bacabs.* Norman: University of Oklahoma Press, 1965.

——, France V. Scholes, and Eleanor B. Adams, "Census and Inspection of the Town of Pencuyut." *Ethnohistory* 6 (1959): 195–225.

Rubio Mañé, J. Ignacio. "Las jurisdicciones de Yucatán. La creación de la plaza de teniente de rey de Campeche." *Boletín del Archivo de la Nación* (Mexico City), New Series No. 7 (1966): 549–631.

———. *Los Sanjuanistas de Yucatán.* Mexico City: Archivo General de la Nación, 1971.

Rubio Sánchez, Manuel. *Comercio terrestre de y entre las provincias de Centroamérica.* Guatemala City: Ministerio de Educación Pública, 1973.

———. *Historia del añil o xiquilite en Centroamérica.* 2 vols. San Salvador: Ministerio de Educación, 1976, 1978.

———. *Historia del puerto de Trujillo.* 3 vols. Tegucigalpa: Banco Central de Honduras, 1975.

Rus, Jan, and Robert Wasserstrom. "Civil-Religious Hierarchies in Central Chiapas: A Critical Perspective." *American Ethnologist* 7 (1980): 466–78.

Sabloff, Jeffrey A., and C. C. Lamberg-Karlovsky, eds. *Ancient Civilization and Trade.* Albuquerque: University of New Mexico Press, 1975.

———, and W. L. Rathje, eds. *Changing Pre-Columbian Commercial Systems: The 1972–1973 Seasons at Cozumel, Mexico.* Monographs of the Peabody Museum No. 3. Cambridge: Harvard University, Peabody Museum, 1975.

Sáenz de Santamaría, Carmelo. *El licenciado don Francisco Marroquín, primer obispo de Guatemala (1499–1563).* Madrid: Ediciones Cultura Hispánica, 1964.

———. "La vida económica de los Jesuitas en Santiago de Guatemala." *Revista de Indias* 37 (1977): 543–84.

Saint-Lu, André. *Condition colonial et conscience créole en Guatemala.* Publications de la Faculté des Lettres et Sciences Humaines de Poitiers 8. Paris: Presses Universitaires de France, 1970.

Samayoa Guevara, Héctor Humberto. *Los gremios de artesanos en la ciudad de Guatemala.* Guatemala City: Editorial Universitaria, 1962.

Sanchíz Ochoa, Pilar. *Los hidalgos de Guatemala: Realidad y apariencia en un sistema de valores.* Seville: Universidad de Sevilla, 1976.

Sanders, William T. "Cultural Ecology of the Maya Lowlands, Part 1." *Estudios de Cultura Maya* 2 (1962): 79–121.

———. "Cultural Ecology of the Maya Lowlands, Part 2." *Estudios de Cultura Maya* 3 (1963): 203–41.

———. *Prehistoric Ceramics and Settlement Patterns in Quintana Roo, Mexico.* Publication No. 606. Washington, D.C.: Carnegie Institution, 1960.

———, and B. J. Price. *Mesoamerica: The Evolution of a Civilization.* New York: Random House, 1968.

Scholes, France V., and Eleanor B. Adams. *Don Diego de Quijada, Alcalde Mayor de Yucatán, 1561–1565.* 2 vols. Mexico City: Antigua Librería Robredo de José Porrúa e Hijos, 1938.

———, and Ralph L. Roys. *The Maya Chontal Indians of Acalan-Tixchel: A Contribution to the History and Ethnography of the Yucatan Peninsula.* Publication No. 560. Washington, D.C.: Carnegie Institution, 1948.

Seimens, Alfred H., and D. E. Puleston. "Ridged Fields and Associated Features in Southern Campeche." *American Antiquity* 37 (1972): 228–39.

Semo, Enrique. *Historia del capitalismo en México*. Mexico City: Editorial Era, 1973.

Sherman, William. L. "Abusos contra los indios de Guatemala (1602–1605). Relaciones del Obispo." *Cahiers du Monde Hispanique et Luso-Brésilien, Caravelle* 11 (1968): 4–28.

———. "Encomenderos in Revolt." *Proceedings of the 28th Annual Rocky Mountain Council on Latin American Studies*. Lincoln: University of Nebraska Press, 1981.

———. *Forced Native Labor in Sixteenth-Century Central America*. Lincoln: University of Nebraska Press, 1979.

Sierra, Justo. *Juárez, su obra y su tiempo*. Mexico City: Editorial Porrúa, 1974. (originally published in 1905).

Simpson, Lesley B., trans. and ed. *Cortés: The Life of the Conqueror by His Secretary Francisco López de Gómara*. Berkeley and Los Angeles: University of California Press, 1966.

Skinner-Klee, Jorge. *Legislación indigenista de Guatemala*. Mexico City: Instituto Indigenista Interamericano, 1954.

Smith, Carol A. "Beyond Dependency Theory: National and Regional Patterns of Underdevelopment in Guatemala." *American Ethnologist* 5 (1978): 574–617.

———. "La evolución de los sistemas del mercadero en el occidente de Guatemala." *Estudios Sociales* 10 (1973): 38–71.

———. "The Domestic Marketing System in Western Guatemala: An Economic, Locational, and Cultural Analysis." Ph.D. dissertation, Stanford University, 1972.

Solano y Pérez-Lila, Francisco de. "La población indígena de Yucatán durante la primera mitad del siglo 17." *Anuario de Estudios Americanos* 28 (1971): 165–200.

———. *Los Mayas del siglo XVIII: Pervivencia y transformación de la sociedad indígena guatemalteca durante la administración borbónica*. Madrid: Ediciones Cultura Hispánica, 1974.

———. "Tierra, comercio y sociedad (un análisis de la estructura social agraria centroamericana durante el siglo XVIII)." *Revista de Indias* 31 (1971): 311–65.

Spalding, Karen. "Indian Rural Society in Colonial Peru." Ph.D. dissertation, University of California, Berkeley, 1967.

———. "Kurakas and Commerce: A Chapter in the Evolution of Andean Civilization." *Hispanic American Historical Review* 53 (1973): 581–99.

———. "Social Climbers: Changing Patterns of Mobility among the Indians of Colonial Peru." *Hispanic American Historical Review* 50 (1970): 645–64.

Stark, Barbara, and B. Voorhies, eds. *Prehistoric Coastal Adaptations*. New York: Academic Press, 1978.

Starr, Frederick. *In Indian Mexico: A Narrative of Travel and Labor*. Chicago: Forbes and Co., 1908.

Stavenhagen, Rodolfo. Las clases sociales en las sociedades agrarias. Mexico City: Siglo Veintiuno, 1969.

———. Social Classes in Agrarian Societies. Garden City: Anchor Books, 1969.

Stephens, John Lloyd. Incidents of Travel in Central America, Chiapas, and Yucatan. 2 vols. New York: Harper, 1841.

Stoll, Otto. Die Ethnologie der Indianerstämme von Guatemala. Leyden: P. W. M. Trap, 1889.

Tax, Sol. "World View and Social Relations in Guatemala." American Anthropologist 43 (1941): 27–42.

———, ed. Acculturation in the Americas. Selected Papers of the 29th International Congress of Americanists. Chicago: University of Chicago Press, 1952.

———, ed. Heritage of Conquest: The Ethnology of Middle America. Glencoe; Free Press, 1952.

Taylor, William B. "Landed Society in New Spain." Hispanic American Historical Review 54 (1974): 387–413.

———. Landlord and Peasant in Colonial Oaxaca. Stanford: Stanford University Press, 1972.

Tedlock, B. "Quiche Maya Divination: A Theory of Practice." Ph.D. dissertation, State University of New York at Albany, 1978.

Thompson, J.Eric S. Maya Hieroglyphic Writing. Norman: University of Oklahoma Press, 1960.

———. Maya History and Religion. Norman: University of Oklahoma Press, 1970.

———. The Maya of Belize: Historical Chapters since Columbus. Belize: Benex Press, 1972.

———. The Rise and Fall of Maya Civilization. Norman: University of Oklahoma Press, 1966.

———. Thomas Gage's Travels in the New World. Norman: University of Oklahoma Press, 1958.

Thompson, Philip. "Tekanto in the Eighteenth Century." Ph.D. dissertation, Tulane University, 1978.

Torre Villar, Ernesto de la. "Algunos aspectos de las cofradías y la propiedad territorial en Michoacán." Jahrbuch für Geschichte von Staat, Wirtschaft und Gesellschaft Lateinamerikas 4 (1967): 410–39.

Tozzer, Alfred M. Landa's Relación de las Cosas de Yucatán, a Translation. Papers of the Peabody Museum No. 18. Cambridge: Harvard University Press, 1941.

Trens, Manuel B. Historia de Chiapas. Mexico City: Talleres Gráficos de la Nación, 1942 (2nd. ed., 1957).

———. El Imperio en Chiapas, 1863–64. Tuxtla Gutiérrez: Imprenta del Gobierno del Estado, 1956.

Turner, B. L., II. "Prehistoric Intensive Agriculture in the Mayan Lowlands." Science 185 (1974): 118–24.

Vázquez, Francisco. Crónica de la provincia del Santísimo Nombre de Jesús de

Guatemala. 4 vols. Guatemala: Sociedad de Geografía e Historia, Biblioteca "Goathemala," 1937–1944.

Veblen, Thorstein T. "The Ecological, Cultural, and Historical Bases of Forest Preservation in Totonicapán, Guatemala." Ph.D. dissertation, University of California, Berkeley, 1975.

———. "Native Population Decline in Totonicapán, Guatemala." *Annals of the Association of American Geographers* 67 (1977): 486–99.

Vigil, Ralph H. "Alonso de Zorita, Crown Oidor in the Indies, 1548–1556." Ph.D. dissertation, University of New Mexico, 1969.

Villagutierre Soto-Mayor, Juan de. *Historia de la conquista de la provincia de el Itzá, reducción y progresos de la de el Lacandón.* vol. 9. Guatemala: Tipografía nacional, 1933 (orig. 1701).

Vogt, Evon Z. *Los Zinacantecos.* Mexico City: Instituto Nacional Indigenista, 1966.

———, and R. M. Leventhal, eds., *Prehistoric Settlement Patterns: Retrospect and Prospect.* Albuquerque: University of New Mexico Press, in press.

Wagner, Henry R., trans. and ed. *The Discovery of New Spain in 1518 by Juan de Grijalva.* Pasadena: The Cortes Society Val Triez Press, 1942.

Wallerstein, Immanuel. "The Rise and Fall of the World Capitalist System." *Comparative Studies in Society and History* 19 (1974): 387–415.

Wasserstrom, Robert. "El desarrollo de la economía regional en Chiapas." *Problemas del Desarrollo* 76 (1976): 83–104.

———. "Land and Labour in Central Chiapas: A Regional Analysis." *Development and Change* 8 (1977): 441–64.

———. "Population Growth and Economic Development in Chiapas, 1524–1975." *Human Ecology* 6 (1978): 127–43.

———. "Revolution in Guatemala: Peasants and Politics under the Arbenz Government." *Comparative Studies in Society and History* 17 (1975): 443–78.

———. "White Fathers and Red Souls: Indian-Ladino Relations in Highland Chiapas, 1528–1973." Ph.D. dissertation, Harvard University, 1977.

Wauchope, Robert. *Modern Maya Houses: A Study of Their Archaeological Significance.* Publication No. 502. Washington, D.C.: Carnegie Institution, 1938.

Willey, Gordon R. "Mesoamerican Art and Iconography." In *The Iconography of Middle American Sculpture.* New York: Metropolitan Museum of Art, 1973.

———. "Towards an Holistic View of Ancient Maya Civilization." *Man* 15 (1980): 249–66.

———, William R. Bullard, Jr., John B. Glass, and James C. Gifford. *Prehistoric Maya Settlements in the Belize Valley.* Papers of the Peabody Museum. Publications of Archaeology and Ethnography Vol. 54. Cambridge: Harvard University, 1965.

Wilson, Carter. *A Green Tree and a Dry Tree.* New York: Macmillan, 1972.

Wolf, Eric R. "Closed Corporate Peasant Communities in Meso-America and Central Java." *Southwestern Journal of Anthropology* 13 (1957); 1–18.

———. *Sons of the Shaking Earth.* Chicago: University of Chicago Press, 1959.

Woodward, Ralph Lee, Jr. *Central America. A Nation Divided.* New York: Oxford University Press, 1976.

———. *Class Privilege and Economic Development. The Consulado de Comercio of Guatemala, 1793–1871.* Chapel Hill: University of North Carolina Press, 1966.

Worsley, Peter. *The Trumpet Shall Sound.* London: McGibbon and Kee, 1957.

Wright, Henry T., and G. A. Johnson. "Population, Exchange and Early State Formation in Southwestern Iran." *American Anthropologist* 77 (1975): 267–89.

Ximénez, Francisco. *Historia de la provincia de San Vicente de Chiapa y Guatemala de la orden de predicadores.* 3 vols. Guatemala City: Sociedad de Geografía e Historia, Biblioteca "Goathemala," 1929–31.

Zavala, Silvio. *Contribución a la historia de las instituciones coloniales en Guatemala.* Guatemala City: Tipografía Nacional, 1944.

The Contributors

Robert M. Carmack is Professor of Social Anthropology and Ethnohistory in the Department of Anthropology, State University of New York, Albany.

Nancy M. Farriss is Professor of History at the University of Pennsylvania.

David A. Freidel is Associate Professor of Anthropology at Southern Methodist University.

Grant D. Jones is Professor of Anthropology at Hamilton College.

Murdo J. MacLeod is Professor of History at the University of Arizona.

Jan Rus is a doctoral candidate in anthropology at Harvard University.

William L. Sherman is Professor of History at the University of Nebraska–Lincoln.

Robert Wasserstrom is a research scientist at the Center for Social Sciences, Columbia University, and a special adviser to the Inter-American Foundation, Rosslyn, Virginia.

Index